AFRIKAANS ART SONG LITERATURE

AFRIKAANS ART SONG LITERATURE

A Translation and Pronunciation Guide

CHRISTIAN BESTER
AND BRONWEN FORBAY

OXFORD
UNIVERSITY PRESS

Oxford University Press is a department of the University of Oxford.
It furthers the University's objective of excellence in research, scholarship,
and education by publishing worldwide. Oxford is a registered trade mark of
Oxford University Press in the UK and certain other countries.

Published in the United States of America by Oxford University Press
198 Madison Avenue, New York, NY 10016, United States of America.

© Oxford University Press 2025

All rights reserved. No part of this publication may be reproduced, stored in a retrieval system, transmitted, used for text and data mining, or used for training artificial intelligence, in any form or by any means, without the prior permission in writing of Oxford University Press, or as expressly permitted by law, by license or under terms agreed with the appropriate reprographics rights organization. Inquiries concerning reproduction outside the scope of the above should be sent to the Rights Department, Oxford University Press, at the address above.

You must not circulate this work in any other form
and you must impose this same condition on any acquirer.

Library of Congress Cataloging-in-Publication Data

ISBN 9780197660829 (pbk.)
ISBN 9780197660812 (hbk.)

DOI: 10.1093/oso/9780197660812.001.0001

Paperback printed by Integrated Books International, United States of America
Hardback printed by Bridgeport National Bindery, Inc., United States of America

The manufacturer's authorised representative in the EU for product safety is Oxford University Press España S.A. of El Parque Empresarial San Fernando de Henares, Avenida de Castilla, 2 – 28830 Madrid (www.oup.es/en or product.safety@oup.com).
OUP España S.A. also acts as importer into Spain of products
made by the manufacturer.

For our beloved mothers,
Isabel Bester (née Miller) and
Priscilla Forbay (née Parker)

CONTENTS

PREFACE   xvii

ACKNOWLEDGMENTS   xix

NOTES ON TRANSLATION AND METHODOLOGIES   xxi

PRONUNCIATION GUIDE   xxiii

INTRODUCTION   **1**

AFRIKAANS ART SONGS   **7**

HENNIE AUCAMP (1934–2014)   9
"The Wind Drones like a Ghoera: A Bushmen Myth Song Cycle"
[*Die Wind dreun soos 'n Ghoera: 'n Boesmanmite-sangsiklus*]   9

1. The Sun [*Die Son*]   9
2. The Stars [*Die Sterre*]   10
3. The Moon [*Die Maan*]   10
4. The Sun and the Moon [*Die Son en die Maan*]   11
5. The Milky Way [*Die Melkweg*]   11
6. The Clouds [*Die Wolke*]   12
7. The Wind [*Die Wind*]   13
8. Cradle Song [*Wieglied*]   13

BOERNEEF (1897–1967) Pseudonym of Izak Wilhelmus van der Merwe   15
"On the Concertina: Nine Songs for Medium Voice and Piano" [*Op die
Flottina: Nege Liedere vir Middelstem en Klavier*]   15

1. How Quiet It Becomes When the South-Easterly Wind Wanes [*Hoe stil
   kan dit word as Sedoos gaan lê*]   15
2. Young Poplar Bark, Smooth and Cool [*Jong Pappelierbas glad en koel*]   16
3. Old Damon Shepherds His Little Flock of Lambs Roundabout [*Ou
   Damon loop sy Lammertroppie om*]   16
4. It's Whipping Around like the Flick of a Wrist [*Dis omdraaislaan soos
   Handomkeer*]   17
5. Old Nincompoop on Stilts [*Ou Poegenpol op Pale*]   18
6. Who's Batty and Who Has Lost It [*Wies getik en wiesit kwyt*]   18
7. Somewhere in the Karoo, I Have a Shelter [*Êrens in die Kro het ek 'n Skerm*]   19

CONTENTS

8.	The Hillock Behind Acorn's Pen [*Agter Akkerskraalsekop*]	20
9.	From Reed Marsh's Wasteland All the Way to Pleading Spring [*Van Rietvleisemoorsand tot by Soetbasfontein*]	20
"Seven Ditsy Songs" [*Sewe Boerneef Liedjies/Sewe lawwe Liedjies*]		21
1.	Blow on the Pumpkin Stalk [*Blaas op die Pampoenstingel*]	21
2.	Little Piedeplooi [*Klein Piedeplooi*]	22
3.	The Mountain-Goose Feather [*Die Berggansveer*]	22
4.	Why Is the Devil Afraid of the Grindstone [*Waarom is die Duiwel vir die Slypsteen bang*]	23
5.	The Evening-Flower Is a White Flower [*Aandblom is 'n Witblom*]	24
6.	My Speckled, Cross-Feathered Hen [*My Koekiesveerhen jou Verkereveer*]	24
7.	Up There High Against the Ridge [*Doer bo teen die Rant*]	25

Stand-Alone Poetry   **25**

Rendezvous [*Krymekaar*]   25

From Kirstenbosch Yonder to Namaqualand [*Van Kirstenbosch tot in Namakwaland*]   27

JAN FRANCOIS ELIAS CELLIERS (1865–1940) aka Jan F. E. Celliers   29

From "Six Afrikaans Art Songs" [*Ses Afrikaanse Kunsliedere*]   29

3.	A Crown of Thorns [*'n Doringkroon*]	29
4.	The Waves [*Die Branders*]	29

Stand-Alone Poetry   **30**

Cupid's Confetti [*Amors Konfetti*]   30

The Ox-Wagon [*Die Ossewa*]   31

The Seeking Mother [*Die soekende Moeder*]   32

The Little Country Breeze [*Die Veldwindjie*]   33

That's All [*Dis al*]   34

DOLL DE VILLIERS (1920–2016)   35

Where the Night in Breathless Stillness [*Waar die Nag in ademlose Stilte*]   35

IZAK LOUIS DE VILLIERS (1936–2009) aka I. L. de Villiers   37

Balance Sheet [*Balansstaat*]   37

PIERRE DE VILLIERS PIENAAR (1904–1978) aka P. de Villiers Pienaar   39

The Evening-Flower [*Die Aandblom*]   39

PHILIP DE VOS (b. 1939)   42

"Oh My Goodness! An Insect—Silly Verses for Naughty Children, Song Cycle" [*O togga! 'n Gogga—Lawwe Versies vir stout Kinders, Sangsiklus*]   42

1.	Pluck the Strings, Blow (on) the Flute [*Pluk die Snare, blaas die Fluit*]	42
2.	Come with Me to Toorberg [*Kom saam met my na Toorberg*]	42
3.	Whirlwind [*Warrelwind*]	43
4.	The Tumbleweed Is a Rolling Stone [*Rolbos is 'n Tolbos*]	43
5.	Take a Small Piece of (the) Sun [*Neem 'n stukkie Son*]	44
6.	If You Come to Visit Me [*As jy by my kom kuier*]	44
7.	You Remain Little [*Jy bly klein*]	45
8.	The Mantis and the Spider [*Hotnotsgot en Spinnekop*]	45
9.	Gosh, Dang It! [*Gomverdorie, Poetoepap*]	46
10.	Petronella, Cockroach [*Petronella, Kokkerot*]	47
11.	Grandma's Lay-Away Hen [*Ouma het 'n Weglêhoender*]	47
12.	The Sharks in the Sea [*Die Haaie in die See*]	48
13.	Oh Golly Gosh [*O gits en gaats*]	48
14.	I Arrived Here [*Ek kom hier aan*]	49
15.	Devil's Children Give Me the Heebie-Jeebies [*Satanskinders laat my gril*]	49
16.	Twelve Little Sardines in a Can [*Twaalf Sardientjies in 'n Blik*]	50
17.	The Cat's Cheek [*Die Kat se Kies*]	51
18.	Little Turtle Dove [*Tortelduifie*]	51
19.	Up in the Attic [*Bo in die Solder*]	52
20.	If You Find Yourself Malingering [*Kry jy papelellekoors*]	52
21.	Piet Fourie [*Piet Fourie*]	53
22.	What Is the Difference? [*Wat is die verskil?*]	53
23.	Consternation [*Konsternasie*]	54
24.	Susanna Viljee [*Susanna Viljee*]	55

BEN DREYER (n.d.) — 57

Little Bushveld House [*Bosveld Huisie*] — 57

IZAK DAVID DU PLESSIS (1900–1981) aka I. D. du Plessis — 58

From "Four Melancholy Songs" [*Vier weemoedige Liedjies*] — 58

3.	In the Stillness of My Garden [*In die stilte van my Tuin*]	58
4.	Cold Is the Wind [*Koud is die Wind*]	59

"Queer Love" [*Vreemde Liefde*] — 59

1.	If I Have to Reveal This Queer Love of Mine [*As ek my vreemde Liefde bloot moes lê*]	59
2.	I Surrendered to You [*Ek het my aan jou oorgegee*]	60
3.	The Heart of Dawn [*Die Hart van die Daeraad*]	61
4.	Coward with a Wife and Child [*Swakkeling met Vrou en Kind*]	62
5.	I Know That in the Calm Togetherness [*Ek weet dat in die kalme Samesyn*]	63

x   CONTENTS

6.	No, Rather Death [*Nee, liewer die Dood*]	64
7.	At Dusk [*Met Skemering*]	64
8.	Oh Queer Love [*O vreemde Liefde*]	65

Stand-Alone Poetry — **66**

If My Heart Now Wants to Sing [*As my Hart nou wil sing*]	66
A Prayer [*'n Gebed*]	67
We Said Farewell [*Ons het mekaar gegroet*]	68
Tranquility and Quietness [*Rus en Stilte*]	69
Snow on the Mountains [*Sneeu op die Berge*]	70

MORNAY ANDRÉ DU PLESSIS (1909–1941) — 71

Love's Grief [*Liefdeswee*]	71

ERLANK EITEMAL (1901–1984) — 73

A Time to Dream [*Droomtyd*]	73

GIDEON FAGAN (1904–1980) — 75

The Little Dove [*Die Duifie*]	75

HENRY ALLAN FAGAN (1889–1963) aka H. A. Fagan — 76

Like the Murmuring Breeze [*Soos die Windjie wat suis*]	76

BURGER GERICKE (1916–1989) aka B. Gericke — 77

The Abundant Heathlands [*Heideweelde*]	77

THEODORE WALTER JANDRELL (1888–1968) aka Theo W. Jandrell — 78

Homeward [*Huistoe*]	78
Come Home, Beloved! [*Kom huistoe, Liefste!*]	79
Beside Still Waters [*Langs stille Waters*]	81
Until the Morning Glows [*Tot die Oggend-gloor*]	83
The Weary Pilgrim [*Vermoeide Pelgrim*]	84

INGRID JONKER (1933–1965) — 85

"Five Songs on Texts" by Ingrid Jonker, Song Cycle [*Vyf Liedere op Tekste van Ingrid Jonker, Sangsiklus*]		85
1.	Song of the Rag Doll [*Lied van die Lappop*]	85
2.	The Wind's Little Song [*Windliedjie*]	86
3.	Puberty [*Puberteit*]	87
4.	I Had Thought [*Ek het gedink*]	87
5.	Rude Awakening [*Ontnugtering*]	88

Stand-Alone Poetry	**89**
Bitter Berry Daybreak [*Bitterbessie Dagbreek*]	89
The Child [*Die Kind*]	90

ALBERTUS DANIËL KEET (1888–1972) aka A. D. Keet	**93**
Adoration [*Adoratio*]	93
When in the Evening [*As saans*]	93
It Is Late in the Night [*Dit is laat in die Nag*]	94
I Love (the Color) Blue [*Ek hou van blou*]	95
Mr. Sandman [*Klaas Vakie*]	96
A Song of the Sea [*'n Lied van die See*]	97
Mother [*Moeder*]	98

BESSIE KOTZÉ (NÉE BADENHORST) (n.d.)	**100**
The Freckled Maiden [*Sproetenooi*]	100

CHRIS LAMPRECHT (b. 1927)	**101**
Homage to the Northwest [*Aan die Noordweste*]	101
1. The Old Camel Thorn Tree [*Die ou Kameeldoringboom*]	101
2. The Fiscal of the Great River [*Die Grootrivier se Voël*]	102
3. Rain (Is Pouring) on the Veld [*Reën op die Veld*]	102
4. Namaqualand's Little Flowers [*Namakwaland se Blommetjies*]	103
5. Loeries Fountain [*Loeriesfontein*]	103

CHRISTIAN FREDERICK LOUIS LEIPOLDT (1880–1947)	
aka C. Louis Leipoldt	104
"Four Loitering Ditties (Carousel Songs)" [*Vier Slampamperliedjies*]	104
1. The Curly-Haired Lad [*Krulkop-klonkie*]	104
2. Secretary-Bird [*Sekretarisvoël*]	105
3. On My Old Ramkie Guitar [*Op my ou Ramkietjie*]	106
4. Good-for-Nothing and Sod-Off [*Boggom en Voertsek*]	107

Stand-Alone Poetry	**108**
The Sea Is Wild [*Die See is wild*]	108
The Little Star [*Die Sterretjie*]	109
Dingaan, the Zulu [*Dingaan, die Zoeloe*]	110
Claim of the Spark [*Eis van die Vonk*]	111
I Sing of the Wind [*Ek sing van die Wind*]	112
Whistle, Swift, Sing and Whistle [*Fluit, Windswael, sing en fluit*]	113
Give Me a Wedding Ring [*Gee vir my 'n Trouring*]	114
In a Hole Beneath the Sickle Bush [*In 'n Gat daar onder die Sukkeldoring*]	115

Japie [*Japie*]	117
The Choice from the Best [*Keur van die Beste*]	118
Trek, Trek Along the Meandering Road! [*Klim op, klim op met die Slingerpad!*]	119
African Corn Lilies You Tremble and Shiver [*Klossies, jul bewe en bibber*]	120
Come Dance with Me! [*Kom dans met my!*]	120
The Whining Little Cricket in the Attic [*Kriekie, jy wat op die Solder sanik*]	122
A Little Springtime Song [*Lenteliedjie*]	122
A New Song to a Familiar Tune ['*n Nuwe Liedjie op 'n ou Deuntjie (Siembamba)*]	124
The Month of October [*Oktobermaand*]	126
Sing, Little Finch, Sing! [*Sing, Vinkie, sing!*]	128
Sing to Me Again [*Sing weer vir my*]	129
Like a Bubbling Finch Freeing Its Heart [*Soos 'n borrelende Vink sy Hart verlos*]	130
Tirelli, Lirelli, La [*Toeral, loeral, la*]	131
A Weeping Song ['*n Treurlied*]	132
The Garden Rose Among the Tulips [*Tuinroos tussen die Tulpe*]	133
From the Lotus Land Where the Lilies Grow, Song of Mali, the Slave [*Van die Lotosland waar die Lelies groei*]	134
Show Me the Place [*Wys my die Plek*]	135

WILLIAM EWART GLADSTONE LOUW (1913–1980) aka W. E. G. Louw | 138

From "Four Melancholy Little Songs" [*Vier weemoedige Liedjies*]	138
1. Kestrel [*Vaalvalk*]	138
2. First Day of Winter [*Eerste Winterdag*]	139

Stand-Alone Poetry | 139

In Front of the Window [*Voor die Venster*]	139

DANIËL FRANÇOIS MALHERBE (1881–1969) aka D. F. Malherbe | 141

Evening Gaze [*Aandblik*]	141
The Rosebud [*Die Roosknoppie*]	142
Youth of My People [*Jeug van my Volk*]	143

EUGÈNE MARAIS (1871–1936) | 144

"Of Love and Forsakenness" [*Van Liefde en verlatenheid*]	144
1. The Sorceress [*Die Towenares*]	144
2. The Desert Lark [*Die Woestyn-lewerkie*]	145
3. Winter Night [*Winternag*]	146
4. Heart of the Dawn [*Hart-van-die-Dagbreek*]	147
5. Deep River [*Diep Rivier*]	147

CONTENTS xiii

Stand-Alone Poetry **148**
Grim Reaper [*Skoppensboer*] 148
Stay, Sweetie, Stay! [*Staan, Poppie, staan!*] 150

FRANCOIS MARAIS (n.d.) 152
The Star from the East [*Die Ster uit die Ooste*] 152

DIRK MOSTERT (1897–1982) 153
Love Songs [*Amoreuse Liedeken*] 153
There's a Time [*Daar's 'n Tyd*] 154
A Message of the Exiled [*Die Balling se Boodskap*] 155
Slumber, Beloved [*Sluimer, Beminde*] 157

S. J. M. OSBORNE (n.d.) 159
The Karoo Plain [*Die Karoovlakte*] 159
Bushshrike [*Kokkewiet*] 160
Boulder by the Sea [*Rots by die See*] 161

PETER JOHN PHILANDER (1921–2006) aka Piet Philander or
P. J. Philander 162
Eclipse [*Sonsverduistering*] 162

HILDA POSTMA (1895–1993) 164
To Stella [*Aan Stella*] 164

TOTIUS (1877–1953) Pseudonym of Jacob Daniël du Toit 165
The Gardener [*Die Howenier*] 165

JAN REINDER LEONARD VAN BRUGGEN (1895–1948)
aka J. R. L. van Bruggen 168
Outside the Breeze Rustles Softly [*Buite suis die sagte Windjie*] 168
Give Me [*Gee my*] 169
Homesickness/Nostalgia [*Heimwee*] 170
Spring Song [*Lentelied*] 171
My Soul Is Sick with Longing [*My Siel is siek van Heimwee*] 172
Lullaby [*Slaapdeuntjie*] 173

CHRISTIAN MAURITS VAN DEN HEEVER (1902–1957)
aka C. M. van den Heever 175
Autumn Evening [*Herfsaand*] 175

STEVEN VAN VENE (n.d.)   177
A Lullaby [*Slaapliedjie*]   177

NICOLAAS PETRUS VAN WYK LOUW (1906–1970)
aka N. P. van Wyk Louw   178
"Four Seasonal Prayers in the Boland" [*Vier Gebede by Jaargetye in die Boland*]   178

   1. Early Autumn [*Vroegherfs*]   178
   2. Out of This Light-filled Autumn [*Uit hierdie ligte Herfs*]   179
   3. Winter [*Winter*]   180
   4. First Snow [*Eerste Sneeu*]   181

Stand-Alone Poetry   **182**
The Little Chisel [*Die Beiteltjie*]   182
The Love Within me [*Die Liefde in my*]   183
Boundaries [*Grense*]   184
Come Tonight in My Dreams [*Kom vannag in my Drome*]   185
Command [*Opdrag*]   187
Panic-stricken Angst [*Paniese Angs*]   188
Daybreak [*Rooidag*]   189

ANDRIES GERHARDUS VISSER (1879–1929) aka A. G. Visser   190
"Noah's Ark" [*Noag se Ark*]   190

   1. The Elephant [*Die Olifant*]   190
   2. The Rhinoceros [*Die Renoster*]   191
   3. The Hump-Backed Camel [*Die Dromedaris*]   191
   4. The Hippopotamus [*Die Seekoei*]   192
   5. The Giraffe [*Die Kameelperd*]   193
   6. And-So-Forth [*Ensovoorts*]   193

Stand-Alone Poetry   **194**
The Dark Stream [*Die Donker Stroom*]   194
The Little Bells of Paarl [*Die Pêrel se Klokkies*]   195
The Rose [*Die Roos*]   196
The Roses of Remembrance [*Die Rose van Herinnering*]   196
The Black Oxen [*Die swarte Osse*]   198
The Gardener [Die *Tuinman*]   199
The Road Is My Dwelling [*Die Wapad is my Woning*]   200
A Thousand-and-One [*Duisend-en-een*]   203
The Birth of Spring [*Geboorte van die Lente*]   203
Little Ground Fellow, My Shadow [*Grondmannetjie my Skaduwee*]   204

CONTENTS xv

Puppy Love [*Kalwerliefde*] 206
Little Ray of Sunshine [*Klein Sonneskyn*] 208
Country, Nation, and Language [*Land, Volk en Taal*] 209
Song of the Miracle Tree (Sycamore-Fig Tree) [*Lied van die Wonderboom*] 211
Man and Wife [*Man en Vrou*] 212
With a Little Basket of Roses [*Met 'n Mandjie Rose*] 213
Afternoon Nap [*Middagslapie*] 214
Now or Never [*Nimmer of nou*] 215
Because Death [*Omdat die Dood*] 216
The Distant Princess [*Prinses van verre*] 217
A Love Letter [*Salut d'Amour*] 219
(Pretty) Susie [*Sannie*] 220
Dedication [*Toewyding*] 221
From the Forlorn Marsh [*Van Verlore-vlei*] 222
A Light Shines Ahead on the Wagon Trail [*Voor in die Wapad brand 'n Lig*] 224
Question and Answer [*Vraag en Antwoord*] 228
If I Were a Singer [*Was ek 'n Sanger*] 229

CORNELIUS FRANCOIS VISSER (1882–1965) aka C. F. Visser 231
I Love the Morning [*Ek hou van die Môre*] 231
Come Dance Klaradyn [*Kom dans Klaradyn*] 232
Oh, (Beloved) Farmstead [*O, Boereplaas*] 233

THEO WASSENAAR (1892–1982) 235
Sea Sonnet [*See-Sonnet*] 235

C. H. WEICH (1892–1973) 237
"Song Cycle for Soprano and Piano" [*Sangsiklus vir Sopraan en Klavier*] 237
    1.   I Barely Know You [*Ek ken jou skaars*] 237
    2.   I Know You Now [*Ek ken jou nou*] 238
    3.   Why? [*Waarom?*] 238

ANONYMOUS 240
A Lullaby [*Sluimerlied*] 240

BIBLICAL TEXTS 241
Nehemia 241
If I Have to Perish, Beloved [*As ek moet sterwe, liefste*] 241

PSALMS 242
From "Four Songs of Doubt and Faith" [*Vier Liedere van Twyfel en Geloof*] 242

xvi   CONTENTS

In the Lord I Take Refuge [*Ek skuil by die Here (Psalm XI)*]   242
You Forgave My Debt [*U het my Skuld vergewe (Psalm XXXII)*]   243

BIBLIOGRAPHY   247

APPENDICES   251

Appendix A: Musical Anthologies   251
Appendix B: Resources for Obtaining Musical Scores   253
Appendix C: Sound Recordings: A Discography   255
Appendix D: Resources for Obtaining Information on Afrikaans Art Songs, Song
          Cycles, Composers, Performers, and Lyric Diction in English   261
Appendix E: Afrikaans Language, Culture, and History Institutions   263
Appendix F: Research Projects in Progress   265
Appendix G: Afrikaans Lyric Diction Summary   267
Appendix H: Glossary   275

INDEX OF FIRST LINES AND TITLES   279

INDEX OF COMPOSERS AND THEIR WORKS   283

INDEX OF COMPOSERS AND SONGS BY VOICE CATEGORY   293

GENERAL INDEX   311

PREFACE

Afrikaans Art Song Literature: A Translation and Pronunciation Guide introduces those not familiar with the language to the fascinating and rich body of Afrikaans art song literature. The poetry included in this collection is representative of the most beloved and well-known Afrikaans poems set by prominent Afrikaans composers from both the twentieth and twenty-first centuries.

Each poem is accompanied by approachable original English translations, International Phonetic Alphabet (IPA) lyric diction transcriptions, a list of composers who have set the poem to music, as well as the intended voice type when indicated by the composer and/or recommended by the authors to provide a starting point for further exploration. Choral settings are also listed where applicable. While this guide does not include the sheet music referenced, resources for obtaining musical scores are mentioned. Since musical settings vary by degree of difficulty, the authors have made recommendations for repertoire appropriateness from undergraduate through professional levels, providing opportunities for singers at varying stages of development. There is something for everyone! Detailed footnotes offer insight to enhance knowledge of the unique geography, flora and fauna, culture, and people of southern Africa for a more comprehensive understanding of South Africa's multiculturalism and unusual biodiversity. An overview of the history of the Afrikaans language and the origins of the Afrikaans art song genre provides context to galvanize the reader into a deeper appreciation for the Afrikaans language, literature, and art song literature. The authors have also included a thorough discussion of Afrikaans pronunciation rules to equip the singer with the necessary tools to pronounce and sing the text with greater precision and accuracy. Since there is a pressing need for the international singing community to perform diverse, inclusive repertoire and expand the art song canon, we are delighted to contribute to the discipline with this publication.

While Afrikaans has a complex and contentious history due to the legacy of apartheid, it continues to be recognized as one of South Africa's eleven official languages in the twenty-first century, often serving as a bridge for collaboration among diverse communities. This was true during the struggle for liberation as well. Through hard-won experiences, South Africans have learned that our diversity is our strength. It is this reconciliatory spirit of our homeland, this philosophy of *ubuntu*—namely *Umuntu, ngumuntu, ngabantu*, which when translated from isiZulu into English means 'A person is a person by, with, and through other people'—that has motivated us to perform, publish, and encourage accessibility of this little-known yet beautiful genre to singers and teachers around the world.

ACKNOWLEDGMENTS

The authors want to express their heartfelt thanks and appreciation to Professor Ernst Kotzé, Applied Language Studies Professor Emeritus at the Nelson Mandela University in Gqeberha, formerly Port Elizabeth, South Africa, for generously serving as Special Editor and for sharing his unpublished Afrikaans-Japanese dictionary with us. This invaluable resource served as the cornerstone for our phonetics work, as many published Afrikaans dictionaries do not contain IPA. We want to thank the following individuals and institutions for graciously giving us permission to reproduce their work: *Die Afrikaanse Volksang-en Volkspelebeweging*; *Federasie van Afrikaanse Kultuurvereniginge* (FAK); Chris Lamprecht; Philip de Vos; Hendrik Hofmeyr; Ellen Botha; Ilse Keet; Johan de Villiers; Selina Bojosi (Van Schaik Publishers); and Rahiem Whisgary (DALRO). Sincere thanks to Santie De Jongh (Stellenbosch University); Retha Badenhorst (North-West University); and especially to Tarien Lombard (NB Publishers) and Isobel Rycroft (University of Pretoria) for going above and beyond to assist us from afar; Patricia Puckett Sasser, Director of the Maxwell Music Library, for providing research support in the United States and for building an Afrikaans Art Song Literature Collection at Furman University; Max Loppert (former Chief Classical Music Critic of the *Financial Times*) for his steadfast support, encouragement, and advice; and the National Association of Teachers of Singing (NATS) *Journal of Singing* former editor Richard Sjoerdsma, for publishing our two articles and granting permission for us to reuse some of the material in this publication. Financial support was provided by the College of Arts and Sciences, Oklahoma State University; and the Furman Humanities Center, Furman University.

NOTES ON TRANSLATION AND METHODOLOGIES

IPA Methodology

Although vowels and pronunciation can vary by region, the authors' approach was to IPA the selected texts in a manner best suited to support singing and lyric diction. In consultation with Professor Ernst Kotzé, Applied Language Studies Professor Emeritus at the Nelson Mandela University, comparable terms commonly used by linguists have been included to aid further comprehension.

Translation Methodology

While the authors realize that some translation anomalies may be subjective in nature, every effort has been made to provide an accurate literal translation where appropriate. In instances when translations were ambiguous, a literary translation capturing the spirit of the Afrikaans language and possible meaning intended in the phrase has been offered. The authors have made a conscious decision to respect IDEA (Inclusion, Diversity, Equity, and Anti-Racism) principles in this guidebook. As a result, some pejorative original words in titles and within the poems have been substituted with words communicating the spirit of the text while adhering to the rhyming scheme.

Fach (Voice Category) Assignments Methodology

The authors cross-referenced all anthologies mentioned in the Musical Anthologies resources (Appendix A) with personal score and recording collections, the South African Music Encyclopedia (SAME), worldcat.org, available composers' *ouvre* lists, YouTube.com, and Google.com, in hopes of consolidating and providing information that is complete and accurate, given the limitations of what is available. The terms medium/high voice, and so on, have intentionally been assigned to foster inclusivity. Where composers and the SAME have mentioned specific voice types, the word "preferably" has been used.

Sound Recordings: Evolving Discography Methodology

The authors cross-referenced singing recordings in a similar manner to the methodology outlined above by consulting personal and library recording collections, online resources such as worldcat.org, YouTube, Apple Music, Google.com, and by contacting living composers. Despite the limitations of what is available, we are excited to include resources for both singing and some pronunciation recordings in this evolving discography.

PRONUNCIATION GUIDE

Basic Characteristics of Afrikaans Vowels

1. Afrikaans has five pure vowel sounds: *a*, *e*, *i*, *o*, and *u*.
2. It is recommended that vowel sounds be bright, clear, and precise for lyric diction.
3. [ə] can be long or short in duration and can occur in both stressed and unstressed positions.[1]
4. "While mixed vowels (rounded front vowels) are present, they are also phonemes that distinguish the meanings of words."[2] Note that "the rounded front vowels [y], [œ], and the rare [ø], are separate phonemes, and that diphthongs such as [əu], [əj] (with rounded counterpart [œj]), etc., also act as phonemes.... Examples: The [ə] occurs virtually without limit in all syllable positions. [œ] only occurs in a limited number of words of foreign origin. Example: *ultimatum* [œlti'matœm]. This vowel does not occur in final syllables, and is only found infrequently in initial syllables, such as *ultra* ['œltrɑ]."[3]
5. Diacritical marks include the following four accents:
   a. Acute on *í, ó, ú, á, é, ý*: the accented syllable is stressed.[4]
      Example: *dít* ['dət] (this)
      Acute *é* changes the meaning in rare cases:
      Example: *dié* ['di] (this/that) vs. *die* [di] (the)
   b. Grave on *è, ò*: the vowel is stressed, open, and short in duration.[5]
      Examples: *dè* ['dɛ] (there), *nòg* ['nɔx]
   c. Circumflex on *ê, î, ô, û*: the syllable is stressed, and the vowel is long in duration.
      Example: *sê* ['sɛ:]
   d. Diaeresis on *ë, ï, ä, ö, ü*: indicates the start of a new syllable clarifying that it is not part of a diphthong.[6] No vowel modification occurs, unlike German.
      When *ë* is final in monosyllabic and polysyllabic words, a regular schwa [ə] is used:
      Example: *oë* ['u:ə]
      When *ë* is followed by a consonant, only the unstressed, off-glide schwa [ᵊ] is used:
      Examples: *hoëveld* ['ɦuᵊfæᵊlt]; *teëstander* ['teᵊstandər]

---

[1] See Appendix G.

[2] Ernst Kotzé, email message to the authors, October 19, 2023.

[3] Daan Wissing, "The Rounded and Unrounded Mid-Central Vowels /ə/ and /œ/." *Taalportaal* (May 2020) (accessed January 11, 2024), https://taalportaal.org/taalportaal/topic/pid/topic-14613250407051826.

[4] See Appendix G.

[5] Ibid.

[6] Ibid.

xxiv PRONUNCIATION GUIDE

6. Diphthongization through the off glide [ᵊ] occurs between stressed and unstressed *e* and *o* vowels and the consonants that follow them. Example: *weerloos* [ˈveᵊrlʊᵊs]

Afrikaans Word Stress Tips

1. While some prefixes, suffixes, adverbs, and prepositions are stressed, many are unstressed. Stress varies depending on context, that is, whether words "function as separable or inseparable prefixes"[7] or if "stressed suffixes occur in words containing feminine endings."[8]

2. Stems of most words are emphasized.

3. In most words of Germanic origin, stress is often on the first syllable. Exceptions include compound words containing secondary stress where "the first syllable of the second element of the compound bears a secondary stress" and "suffixes (some foreign, but mostly indigenous)[9] and prefixes which, when added to words, cause the stress to shift" to a different syllable.[10]

4. It is important to note that in words of foreign origin and borrowed words, stress can shift to various syllables.

WORD STRESS MARKS

[:]	Lengthens the preceding vowel	*dans* [daːns]
[ˈ]	Indicates primary stress	*boomstam* [ˈbʊᵊmstam]; *oseaan* [ʊᵊsiˈaːn]
[ˌ]	Indicates secondary stress	*grondmannetjie* [ˈxrɔntˌmaniki]

FRONTING VOWELS (also known as Forward/Bright Vowels)[11]

[i]	thief	*iets* [its]; *die* [di]; *diep* [dip]
[iː]	German as in *ihn*, see	*dier* [diːr]; *miershoop* [ˈmiːrsɦuᵊp]
[e]	chaos	*gelede* [xəˈleᵊdə]; *speel* [speᵊl]; *veer* [feᵊr]
[ɛ]	German as in *denn*	*letter* [ˈlɛtər]; *met* [mɛt]; *bed* [bɛt]
[ɛː]	there	*lê* [lɛː]; *sê* [sɛː]
[æ]	cat, carry	*geld* [xæᵊlt]; *reg* [ræx]; *perde* [ˈpærdə]
[æː]	similar to [æ] just longer	*wêreld* [ˈvæːrəlt]; *ver* [fæːr]
[a]	German [a] as in *kann*	*vars* [fars]; *tak* [tak]; *graf* [xraf]
[aː]	Similar to [a] just longer	*blare* [ˈblaːrə]; *pa* [paː]; *daar* [daːr]

BACKING VOWELS (Also known as Dark/Back Vowels)[12]

[ɔ]	bought, call	*rokkie* [ˈrɔki]; *bok* [bɔk]; *aandson* [ˈaːntsɔn]
[ɔː]	cause, law (Neutral American)	*môre* [ˈmɔːrə]; *nôi* [nɔːj]
[u]	blue, move	*groetnis* [ˈxrutnəs]; *moet* [mut]; *genoeg* [xəˈnux]

---

[7] Bruce C. Donaldson, *A Grammar of Afrikaans* (Berlin: Mouton de Gruyter, 1993), 28.

[8] Ibid, 27.

[9] Ibid.

[10] Ibid, 28.

[11] Ernst Kotzé, Microsoft Teams meeting with the authors, October 23, 2023.

[12] Ibid.

[u:]	[u] just longer	*roer* [ru:r]; *koekeloer* [kukə'lu:r]
[ʊᵊ]	look + schwa off glide	*boosaardig* [bʊᵊs'a:rdəx]; *skoon* [skʊᵊn]

OFF GLIDES

[ᵊ]	*boom* [bʊᵊm]; *keer* [keᵊr]
[ꞕ]	*wîe* ['və:ꞕə]; *brûe* ['brœ:ꞕə] (rare)
[ⁱ]	*katjie* ['ka ⁱki]
[ᵃ]	*melk* [mæᵃlk]

MIXED VOWELS (also known as Rounded Front Vowels)[13]

[ø]	French as in *bleu*	*kleur* [kljø̞ᵊr]; *geskeur* [xə'skjø̞ᵊr][14]
[œ]	French as in *coeur*	*hulle* ['ꞕœlə]; *hul* [ꞕœl]
[œ:]	[œ] just longer	*brûe* ['brœ:ꞕə] (rare)
[y]	French as in *plus*	*minuut* [mə'nyt]
[y:]	German as in *früh, Hügel*	*muur* [my:r]

CENTRAL VOWELS

[ə]	German [ə] as in *fernen, Geliebte*	*gespeel* [xə'speᵊl]; *magtig* ['maxtəx]; *se* [sə]

DIPHTHONGS

[əj]	*my* [məj]; *meisie* ['məjsi]
[œu]	*koud* [kœut]; *jou* [jœu]
[œy]	*uit* [œyt]; *besluit* [bə'slœyt]
[aj]	*baie* ['bajə]
[a:j]	*waai* [va:j]
[o:j]	*mooi* [mo:j]; *nôi* [no:j]
[jø̞ᵊ]	*kleur* [kljø̞ᵊr]; *geur* [xjø̞ᵊr]
[iu]	*leeu* [liu]; *Nieu-Seeland* [niu'seᵊlant]
[ui]	*koei* [kui]

DIMINUTIVES

[a ⁱ]	*katjie* ['ka ⁱki]
[a: ⁱ]	*maatjie* ['ma: ⁱki]
[o ⁱ]	*pootjie* ['po ⁱki]
[ɔ ⁱ]	*potjie* ['pɔ ⁱki]
[ə ⁱ]	*pitjie* ['pə ⁱki]
[ɛ]	*prentjie* ['prɛɲki]

---

[13] Ernst Kotzé, email message to the authors, October 19, 2023.

[14] Ernst Kotzé, Microsoft Teams meeting with the authors, October 23, 2023. Prof. Kotzé: "most linguists would transcribe these words as [klø:r] and [xə'skø̞ᵊr] with the [j] glide slipping in automatically between [l] and [ø:] and [k] and [ø], respectively." The authors have included the [j] for clarification for lyric diction.

xxvi   PRONUNCIATION GUIDE

[ɔ]   *hondjie* ['hɔɲki]

[œy]   *fluitjie* ['flœyki]

[œ]   *muntjie* ['mœɲki]

[ø]   *deuntjie* ['djøɲki]

[u]   *soentjie* ['suɲki]

[ə]   *kindjie* ['kəɲki]

Basic Characteristics of Afrikaans Consonants

1. Pronounced generally in the same manner as their English counterparts. Some are gentler and less aspirated.
2. Like the English, *d*, *t*, *n*, and *r*, require an alveolar point of contact.
3. Dental articulation is required for the voiced lateral *l* unlike English, which uses an alveolar point of contact.
4. Little to no aspiration is required for the consonants *p*, *t*, and *k*.
5. Double consonants should be pronounced as a single consonant in lyric diction.
6. *sp* and *st* spellings are pronounced [st] and [sp] in all positions, *never* [ʃt] and [ʃp] like German.
7. While *r* tends to be strongly trilled in spoken diction, it is recommended that it be less energetically rolled when singing to promote *legato*. *R*'s may be rolled energetically, however, to emphasize the meaning of a particular word.

BILABIAL CONSONANTS

| [b] | blow, back | *berg* [bærx]; *bring* [brəŋ] |
| [p] | peace, power | *pa* [pa:]; *Japie* ['ja:pi] |

LABIODENTAL CONSONANTS

| [f] | flower, fair | *familie* [fa'mili]; *veld* [fæᵃlt] |
| [v] | vail, divine | *bewolk* [bə'vɔlk]; *wat* [vat] |

ALVEOLAR CONSONANTS

[d]	dear, dive	*dag* [dax]; *honde* ['hɔndə]
[t]	time, treat	*tak* [tak]; *teken* ['teᵊkən]
[n]	new, hand	*bont* [bɔnt]; *ander* ['andər]
[r]	like Italian rolled *r*	*roos* [rʊᵊs]; *kierie* ['kiri]

DENTAL CONSONANTS

[l]	lift, leap	*liefie* ['lifi]; *lag* [lax]
[s]	so, space	*ses* [sɛs]; *son* [sɔn]; *sebra* ['seᵊbra]
[z]	leaves, birds	*Zulu* ['zulu];[15] *cadenza* [ka'dɛnza]

---

[15] [z] is only found in loan words, such as Zulu.

PRONUNCIATION GUIDE xxvii

FRICATIVES AND AFFRICATES

[ʃ]	shift, washing	*chef* [ʃɛf]; *chic* [ʃik]
[tʃ]	chips, batch	*tjek* [tʃɛk]; *Chile* ['tʃili]
[ç]	German [ç] as in *nicht*	*gieter* ['çitər]; *geel* [çeᵊl]
[x]	German [x] as in *nacht*	*gister* ['xɪstər]; *berg* [bærx]

VELAR CONSONANTS

[g]	give, gloom	*berge* ['bærgə]; *gholf* [gɔlf]
[k]	care, can	*knie* [kni]; *klein* [kləjn]
[ŋ]	sing, being	*sing* [sɪŋ]; *lank* [laŋk]

PREPALATAL CONSONANTS

[ɲ]	French/Italian [ɲ] as in *gnocchi*	*prentjie* ['prɛɲki]; *hondjie* ['fiɔɲki]
[dʒ]	job, judge	*jellie* ['dʒeli]

GLIDES

[j]	yes, yard	*ja* [ja:]; *jy* [jəj]
[w]	quite, sweet	*kwaad* [kwa:t]; *swaar* [swa:r]

Only occur in *dw, kw, sw* and *tw* spellings
(and *ghwarrabos*)

GLOTTAL CONSONANTS

[ɦ]   humble, happy
      Less aspirated than English with reduced breath energy that forms part of
      and flows into the vowel that follows it.
      Examples: *hier* [ɦi:r]; *huil* [ɦœyl]

[ʔ]   While glottals are widely used in spoken Afrikaans, it is recommended that singers
      utilize breath lifts before words beginning with vowels in lyric diction.
      Examples: *is* [ɪs]; *elke* ['æᵃlkə]

Recommended Afrikaans Dictionary: Du Plessis, Madaleine (Chief Editor), *Afrikaans-Engels/ English-Afrikaans Woordeboek · Dictionary*. Cape Town: Pharos Dictionaries, 2010. (ISBN 186 890 0444).

INTRODUCTION

It is generally understood that the Afrikaans language is a product of the cultural and linguistic explosion that took place in southern Africa due to colonization by the Dutch and the British, who expanded their territories into what is now called South Africa from Cape Town during the period from 1652 onward. Considered one of the youngest Germanic languages, Afrikaans has encountered several diverse influences in its over three-hundred-year tenure on the African continent. Linguistically rooted in various regional seventeenth-century Dutch dialects conveyed by colonists and seafarers to the Cape, Afrikaans' numerous multicultural influences included languages from the Indonesian archipelago, including Malay, Ceylon-Portuguese-Creole[1] brought over by enslaved people (or indentured servants) from the late seventeenth century onward,[2] French transported by Huguenots who began arriving at the Cape in 1688,[3] German by immigrants who arrived throughout the eighteenth century,[4] as well as the language of the Indigenous Khoikhoin.[5] However, new research also suggests an "oceanic hypothesis" linking the origins of Afrikaans to the evolution of languages of the East Indies, which were influenced by Dutch from 1596 onward.[6]

Considered inferior to Dutch and English, the appearance of written Afrikaans was somewhat delayed, despite the language being spoken at the Cape prior to it becoming a British colony. The first acknowledged Afrikaans book in the Roman alphabet, *Zamenspraak tusschen Klaas Waarzegger en Jan Twyfelaar* (Conversation between Klaas Soothsayer and Jan Sceptic) by Louis Henri Meurant (1812–1893), only became available in 1861.

Despite its complex history as a divisive language of oppression and its association with apartheid[7] (racial segregation), which officially ended when South Africa became a democracy in 1994, Afrikaans continues to be recognized as one of South Africa's twelve official languages in the twenty-first century. South African Sign Language was added on October 16, 2023. South Africa's population is approximately sixty million, with nearly seven million people speaking

---

[1] C. de Ruyter and E. F. Kotzé, "Oor Austro-Nederlands en die Oorsprong van Afrikaans," *Literator*, accessed January 12, 2024, 139–140, https://doi.org/10.4102/lit.v23i3.347.

[2] T. J. Haarhof, *Afrikaans, Its Origins and Development: Lectures Delivered Before the University of Oxford on the 19th and 20th February 1936* (Oxford: Clarendon Press, 1936), 24. Although Haarhof mentions the term "Malay-Portuguese," this is an oversimplification, as the ethnic group he is referring to includes people from countries in both South and Southeast Asia, as well as some coastal countries in East Africa.

[3] John Christoffel Kannemeyer, *A History of Afrikaans Literature: Die Beiteltjie* [The little chisel] (Pietermaritzburg: Shuter and Shooter, 1993), 1.

[4] Ibid.

[5] Haarhof, *Afrikaans, Its Origins and Development*, 25. While the term Haarhof uses to refer to this ethnic group is considered highly derogatory, the current politically correct term is Khoikhoin or Khoikhoi, which means 'men of men' or 'real people.'

[6] de Ruyter and Kotzé, "Oor Austro-Nederlands en die Oorsprong van Afrikaans," 156–157.

[7] A legal system imposed by the South African government from 1948 to the early 1990s institutionalizing racial segregation and discrimination that impacted all areas of daily life. Its goal was to maintain white minority rule while restricting and controlling non-white (predominantly Black) South Africans through legal and political means.

Afrikaans Art Song Literature. Christian Bester and Bronwen Forbay, Oxford University Press. © Oxford University Press 2025. DOI: 10.1093/oso/9780197660812.003.0001

Afrikaans as a second language after isiZulu and isiXhosa. A noteworthy unanticipated result of the creation of Afrikaans and its dissemination in schools as a mandatory second language was that Afrikaans ultimately served as a bridge for collaboration and reconciliation among diverse communities during the anti-apartheid movement, as well as in the post-apartheid nation-building era. But the scope of Afrikaans's diversity is even more widespread and inclusive, as Ernst Kotzé's article, "The Spelling of Afrikaans," explains:

> Present-day Afrikaans is spoken and written chiefly in South Africa and Namibia, but also by mother-tongue speakers in the global diaspora, which include, numerically from approximately highest to lowest, English-speaking countries such as the United Kingdom and Ireland, Australia, New Zealand, the United States and Canada, but also in the Netherlands and Belgium (and other countries in Europe), Botswana, Zambia, Zimbabwe (and other countries in Africa), and countries in Southeast Asia and South America. Therefore, if one were to combine all users, including second-language speakers and the global diaspora, "the total users in all countries is (approximately) 17 674 200."[8]

Afrikaans art song literature provides a unique opportunity to explore South Africa's rich cultural heritage, breathtaking scenic landscapes, love of nature, and appreciation for *all* citizens of the rainbow nation and beyond. Why not diversify your language skills by learning repertoire in one of the world's youngest Germanic languages? It might be fun!

The Development of the Afrikaans Language

The First Afrikaans Language Movement (1875–1900) produced a simplified colloquial, everyday language with literary works emphasizing subjects pertaining to folklore, fantasy stories, rural Afrikaner life, and experiences encountered on the Great Trek.[9] Eminent writers of this generation included Jan Lion Cachet (1838–1912), S. J. du Toit (1847–1911), C. P. Hoogenhout (1843–1922), and G. R. von Wielligh (1859–1932).

The Second Afrikaans Language Movement (1900–1930) significantly elevated the status of the Afrikaans language as poets grew more attentive to capturing the emotions and culture of the Afrikaner people, depicting the unique South African landscape, and illustrating the struggle against British imperialism. As a result of their efforts, Afrikaans became an official South African language in 1925. Significant poets of this period included Eugène N. Marais (1871–1936), Jan F. Celliers (1865–1940), J. D. du Toit, pseudonym "Totius" (1877–1953), and C. Louis Leipoldt (1880–1947). Marais's highly respected poem "Winternag" (Winter night;

---

[8] Ernst Kotzé, "The Spelling of Afrikaans," in *Handbook of Germanic Writing Systems*, ed. D. Meletis, M. Evertz-Rittich, and R. Treiman (Berlin: Mouton De Gruyter: 2024), 2.

[9] A journey of Afrikaners known as "Voortrekkers," translated as 'forerunners' or 'pioneers,' who migrated through the interior of the country from the mid-1830s onward in hopes of creating their own independent communities, due to dissatisfaction with British colonization and conflicts with Indigenous ethnic groups at the Cape. The term "Afrikaner" was originally associated with urban-based descendants of the Dutch, German, and French Huguenots who settled at the Cape, while the term "Boers," translated as 'farmers,' referred to rural settlers. The "Boers" later became part of the Afrikaner ethnic group during the Great Trek.

1905) is considered "the first successful example of the depiction of nature in Afrikaans: the sound patterns, the imagery and diction charged with deep feeling and the taut construction of the whole made for its striking impact."[10] Thereafter, other thematic offshoots soon developed. Gustav S. Preller (1875–1943) wrote adventure stories and biographies of Afrikaner leaders in a "lyrical celebration of the Afrikaner's heroic past" in a flourishing of romantic fiction.[11] D. F. Malherbe (1881–1969) expanded the genre further "through the use of idealized and usually heroic figures in Biblical antiquity or national history."[12] Didacticism and satire thrived in the pens of Willem Postma (1874–1920), who wrote under the pseudonym "Dr. O'Kulis," and C. J. Langenhoven (1873–1932), who is credited with being the "first successful exponent in Afrikaans" of this tradition.[13] Langenhoven's poem "Die Stem van Suid-Afrika" (The call of South Africa), depicting the vastness and diversity of the South African landscape while reaffirming his patriotism, was set to music by M. L. de Villiers (1885–1977) and became the national anthem.[14] This song forms a vital part of the multilingual, inclusive new national anthem in post-1994 democratic South Africa, which includes five of South Africa's official languages.

In contrast, the Third Afrikaans Language Movement, which writers referred to as the *Dertigers* (Writers of the 1930s), actively distanced themselves from the limited colonial themes cultivated by previous generations. The *Dertigers* primarily dealt with a "confessional tradition" and the exploration of "every aspect of human life."[15] Later works addressing image and form within nature poetry were magnified and improved upon by poets including W. E. G. Louw (1913–1980), highly regarded for his sophisticated and impressionistic nature poetry, his elder brother N. P. van Wyk Louw (1906–1970), and Elisabeth Eybers (1915–2007). Realist authors who rose to prominence after the 1930s infused poetry with regional dialects and anecdotes of people from various ethnic, social, and economic backgrounds in miniaturist poetic dialogues such as those by I. W. van der Merwe (1897–1967), pseudonym "Boerneef" (Farmer cousin/ Farmer-nephew). Boerneef's poetry achieved a special musicality "by means of wordplay and an incantatory repetition of sounds," an important feature that appealed to many art song composers.[16]

The Development of the *Afrikaans Kunslied* (Art Song)

The *Afrikaans Kunslied* was heralded by the publishing of well-crafted original Afrikaans poetry in 1905 by the Second Afrikaans Language Movement poets. This momentous event was significant for composer Jan Gysbert Hugo Bosman (1882–1967), who assumed the stage name Vere di Ravelli when he embarked on a European performing career as a concert pianist in 1902. After returning to South Africa, Bosman composed a collection of *Drie Liederen*

---

[10] Kannemeyer, *A History of Afrikaans Literature*, 22.
[11] Ibid., 18.
[12] Ibid.
[13] Ibid., 19.
[14] Ibid., 19–20.
[15] Ibid., 35.
[16] Ibid., 59.

(Three Art Songs), which included "Winternag" (Winter Night), composed in 1908, based on Eugène N. Marais's famous poem of the same name. Bosman was inspired by Indigenous folk music in his search for a unique South African art song identity. Anchored in various eclectic Western classical compositional styles, early art song composers did not merely imitate and borrow musical ideas, as late nineteenth-century folk song musicians at the Cape had done. While they initially and occasionally made use of European folk song tunes in instrumental works, their goal was to create a unique and sophisticated individual South African sound and genre, like that of other nationalistic composers such as Grieg, Dvořák, Janáček, Bartók, and Kodály. While early Afrikaans art song composers first utilized poetry translated into Afrikaans from texts by Goethe, Heine, Eichendorff, Rückert, Burns, Victor Hugo, and others, the Second Afrikaans Language Movement generated an interest in Afrikaans art songs being set to original Afrikaans poetry. This turning point enabled composers inspired by the natural rhythm and melody inherent in the Afrikaans language to make extensive use of word painting regardless of their preferred compositional style. It is this characteristic, as well as the title of the genre *Kunslied* (art song), that demonstrates the substantial influence of the German Romantic *Lied*. This genre was highly revered by Afrikaans art song composers. In general, early Afrikaans folk songs made use of concertina or harmonium accompaniment, while art songs were predominantly scored for solo voice with piano accompaniment.[17] Later, numerous art songs originally scored for voice and piano were arranged for voice and orchestra, while others were composed for voice and chamber orchestra or string quartet. Although the limited amount of well-crafted original Afrikaans poetry available at the time delayed the *Afrikaanse Kunsliedbeweging* (Afrikaans Art Song Movement), it officially took off about ten years after the Second Afrikaans Language Movement began.[18] Early composers of the art song who made significant contributions to the cultural development of the Afrikaner people included Stephen H. Eyssen (1890–1981), a teacher, composer, and baritone, based in the Cape, who was well known for his song "Segelied" (Victory Song), also known by the alternate title "Hoop" (Hope), written in the style of the Dutch and Flemish *Lied*.[19] Charles Nel (1890–1983), from Bosman's hometown of Piketberg, wrote his first composition on "Dis al" (That's All) to poetry by Celliers in 1914.[20] This poem has been set by more than eight other composers from South Africa, Flanders/Belgium, and Holland.[21] Composers writing in the 1920s include M. L. De Villiers (1885–1977), composer of the first South African national anthem, known as "Die Stem van Suid-Afrika" (The Call of South Africa), and an avid supporter of Schubert, Schumann, and Brahms as role models for composers of the Afrikaans art song.[22] Other prominent composers

---

[17] Jan Bouws, *Die Afrikaanse Volkslied* [The Afrikaans folk song] (Johannesburg: Voortrekkerpers Bpk. [FAK], 1957), 12.

[18] Jan Bouws, "Sestig Jaar Afrikaanse Kunslied 1908–1968 deur Jan Bouws [Sixty years of Afrikaans art song 1908–1968 by Jan Bouws]," *Tydskrif vir Geesteswetenskappe* [Journal for humanities] 9, no. 1 (Pretoria: Sud-Afrikaanse Akademie vir Wetenskap en Kuns [South African Academy for Arts and Culture], March 1969), 73.

[19] Ibid.

[20] Ibid.

[21] Ibid.

[22] Jan Bouws, *Suid-Afrikaanse Komponiste van Vandag en Gister* [South African composers of today and yesterday] (Kaapstad [Cape Town]: A. A. Balkema, 1957), 36.

were the brothers Johannes (1898–1920) and Gideon Fagan (1904–1980) and Petrus Johannes Lemmer (1896–1979), well known for his popular art song "Kokkewiet."[23] Scored for high voice, preferably soprano, this song has been likened to Grieg's scoring of Ibsen's *Peer Gynt* for its descriptive musical depiction of nature's awakening at sunrise.[24]

S. Le Roux Marais (1896–1979) whose output includes more than one hundred art songs, is regarded as one of the most influential pioneering composers of the Afrikaans *Kunslied*. Highly respected during his lifetime, Marais is esteemed as the first South African composer to significantly raise the status of Afrikaans as a musical language by composing genuinely heartfelt, attractive art songs which demonstrated the language's suitability for beautiful, artistic singing. Marais and Chris Lamprecht's (b. 1927) works are tonal, popular, and suitable for performers from undergraduate through professional levels. Distinguished English-speaking Afrikaans art song composers from the 1920s onward whose works are also appropriate for singers from undergraduate through professional levels include Horace Barton (1872–1951), Sydney Richfield (1882–1967), Johannes Joubert (1894–1958) aka Hayden Thomas Matthews, Eva Harvey (1900–1976), Heinz Hirschland (1901–1960), and John Kilburn Pescod (1898–1985). Other important Afrikaans art song composers recommended for advanced undergraduate and graduate students, professional performers, and teachers include P. J. Lemmer (1896–1989), Rosa Nepgen (1909–2000), Arnold van Wyk (1916–1983), Hubert du Plessis (1922–2011), Stefans Grové (1922–2014), P. J. de Villiers (1924–2015), Peter Klatzow (1945–2021), Hendrik Hofmeyr (b. 1957), and Niel van der Watt (b. 1962). These composers' works encompass a wide variety of genres. They are increasingly more challenging but are highly effective in performance.

The *Suid-Afrikaanse Akademie vir Wetenskap en Kuns* (South African Academy for Arts and Sciences), established in 1909, was founded to "protect the interests" of the Afrikaans language, of which a "corollary ... [was] standardizing Afrikaans spelling rules."[25] This resulted in Afrikaans' written form remaining closer to Dutch, rather than to the various other varieties that developed, which included Arabic-influenced written Afrikaans used by people of Malay descent. Most Afrikaans dictionaries do not typically include the International Phonetic Alphabet (IPA), a fact which inspired the authors to undertake this exciting task. Having completed extensive research for their respective doctoral dissertations published in 2011 and 2014, and two National Association of Teachers of Singing (NATS) *Journal of Singing* articles on Afrikaans art songs (2022), the authors have thoroughly reviewed, researched, and compared several documents, while corresponding with various esteemed colleagues in both English and Afrikaans to provide interested readers with the most comprehensive information available in this guidebook.

Excitingly, numerous Afrikaans art song literature composers' works have been published and are available in various editions of the *FAK*[26] *Sangbundels* (FAK Songbooks), which are

---

[23] Bouws, "Sestig Jaar Afrikaanse Kunslied," 74.

[24] Bouws, *Woord en Wys van die Afrikaanse Lied* [Word and melody of the Afrikaans song], (Kaapstad [Cape Town]: Haum, 1961), 20.

[25] Ernst Kotzé, Microsoft Teams meeting with the authors, October 23, 2023.

[26] *Federasie van Afrikaanse Kultuurvereniginge* (Federation of Afrikaans Cultural Associations).

excellent sources for obtaining Afrikaans art songs, folk songs, and choral repertoire. In addition, Afrikaans art songs can be found in publications commissioned by the South African Music Rights Organization, known by its acronym SAMRO, and the Dramatic, Artistic, and Literary Rights Organization, known by its acronym DALRO. For this edition, poems central to the Afrikaans art song canon were selected, as well as poems found in the following art song anthologies: *Liefdeswee:'n Keur van Afrikaanse Kunsliedere* (Love's woes: A compilation of Afrikaans art songs), compiled by Anna Bender and published by DALRO; *FAK—Kunsliedbundel* (FAK—Art song album); *So Sing die Hart* (So sings the heart), compiled by Anna Bender; and *Sing sag menig' lied ... 'n Versameling van toonsettings van die verse van A. G. Visser* (Sing softly many a song: A collection of settings of the verses of A. G. Visser), also compiled by Anna Bender, and published by DALRO.

AFRIKAANS ART SONGS

HENNIE AUCAMP
(1934–2014)

The Wind Drones like a Ghoera: A Bushmen Myth Song Cycle[1]
Die Wind dreun soos 'n Ghoera:[2] *'n Boesmanmite*[3]-*sangsiklus*
[di vənt drjø³n sʊ³s ə ˈxura ə ˈbusmanˌmitə ˈsaŋˌsikləs]
Music: Niel van der Watt (b. 1962)

The Sun
1. *Die Son*
[di sɔn]

From the dawn of time, the Light Man
Die ligman van die voortyd
[di ˈləxman fan di ˈfʊ³rtəjt]

Would not share his light with anyone,
Wou sy lig met niemand deel nie,
[vœu səj ləx mɛt ˈnimant de³l ni]

He carried the sphere of light
Hy dra die ligbol
[ɦəj dra: di ˈləxbɔl]

In his armpit, so that no one could steal it
In sy oksel, dat niemand dit kan steel nie
[ən səj ˈɔksəl dat ˈnimant dət kan ste³l ni]

But one day he slept too soundly
Maar op 'n dag slaap hy te diep
[ma:r ɔp ə dax sla:p ɦəj tə dip]

And a young man grabbed the light
En 'n jong man gryp die lig
[ɛn ə jɔŋ man xrəjp di ləx]

It burned his fingers like an ember of coal
Dit brand sy vingers soos 'n kool
[dət brant səj ˈfəŋərs sʊ³s ə kʊ³l]

And he flung it into the sky.
En hy smyt dit in die lug.
[ɛn ɦəj sməjt dət ən di lœx]

And that coal we call the sun
En daardie kool noem ons son
[ɛn ˈda:rdi kʊ³l num ɔns sɔn]

That shines over us all
Wat oor ons almal skyn
[vat ʊ³r ɔns ˈalmal skəjn]

---

[1] Permission granted by Protea Boekhuis.
[2] A traditional South African bow-like instrument used by the Indigenous Khoikhoin people.
[3] This ethnic group is no longer known by this term, as it is considered derogatory. The current politically correct terms Khoikhoin/Khoikhoi/Khoi refer to the First Nation/Indigenous peoples of southern Africa. Historically, the Khoikhoin were skilled hunter-gatherers and livestock herders. Their language is known for its distinctive clicks.

Afrikaans Art Song Literature. Christian Bester and Bronwen Forbay, Oxford University Press. © Oxford University Press 2025.
DOI: 10.1093/oso/9780197660812.003.0002

10 AFRIKAANS ART SONG LITERATURE

And brings light and life to the earth
En lig en lewe bring op aarde
[ɛn ləx ɛn 'leᵊvə brəŋ ɔp 'a:rdə]

Until he disappears at night.
Totdat hy saans verdwyn.
['tɔdat ɦəj sa:ns fər'dwəjn]

The Stars
2. *Die Sterre*
[di 'stærə]

The sun sleeps under a blanket,
Die son slaap onder 'n kombers,
[di sɔn sla:p 'ɔndər ə kɔm'bærs]

We call these tiny holes stars
Die gaaitjies noem ons sterre
[di 'xa:jkis num ɔns 'stærə]

So old, so old as the universe—with a
hundred-thousand tiny holes
So oud so oud soos die heelal, met
honderdduisend gaaitjies
[sʊᵊ œut sʊᵊ œut sʊᵊs di 'ɦeᵊlal mɛt
'ɦɔndərt̩dœysənt 'xa:jkis]

That can be large or small —
Wat groot kan wees of klein —
[vat xrʊᵊt kan veᵊs ɔf kləjn]

Like (the) Evening Star, Morning Star,
Seven Sisters
Soos aandster, dagster, Sewe Susters
[sʊᵊs 'a:ntstær 'daxstær 'seᵊvə 'sœstərs]

Through which the sunlight streams.
Waardeur die sonlig val.
['va:rdjøᵊr di 'sɔnləx fal]

That shine in the dark.
Wat in die donker skyn.
[vat ən di 'dɔŋkər skəjn]

The Moon
3. *Die Maan*
[di ma:n]

Kaggen cast his shoe
Kaggen het sy skoen gegooi
['kaxən ɦɛt səj skun xə'xo:j]

High into the firmament;
Hoog in die hemeltrans;
[ɦʊᵊx ən di 'ɦeᵊməltrans]

That gingerly, gingerly walks,
Wat versigtig, versigtig,
[vat fər'səxtəx fər'səxtəx]

From cloud to cloud at night.
Van wolk tot wolk loop saans.
[fan vɔlk tɔt vɔlk lʊᵊp sa:ns]

It is now called the moon,
Dit heet die maan nou,
[dət ɦeᵊt di ma:n nœu]

The Sun and the Moon
4. *Die Son en die Maan*
[di sɔn ɛn di ma:n]

The Sun is full and round —
Die son is vol en rond —
[di sɔn əs fɔl ɛn rɔnt]

And healthy throughout the year,
En deur die jaar gesond,
[ɛn djø⁸r di ja:r xə'sɔnt]

The Moon is pale and ailing
Die maan is bleek en sieklik
[di ma:n əs ble⁸k ɛn 'siklək]

And is only round sometimes.
En is net somtyds rond.
[ɛn əs nɛt 'sɔmtəjts rɔnt]

The Sun is bitterly envious
Die son is bitterlik jaloers
[di sɔn əs 'bətərlək ja'lu:rs]

And scoops out the full moon
En hol die volmaan uit
[ɛn fɔl di 'fɔlma:n œyt]

Until only a sliver remains —
Tot later net 'n ietsie oorbly —
[tɔt 'la:tər nɛt ə 'itsi 'ʊ⁸rbləj]

A silver flat-bottomed boat.
'n Silver platboom skuit.
[ə 'səlvər 'platbʊ⁸m skœyt]

With an anxious voice the Moon pleads;
Die maan pleit met 'n benoude stem;
[di ma:n pləjt mɛt ə bə'nœudə stɛm]

"Please let one rib remain!"
"Ag laat een ribstuk bly!"
[ax la:t e⁸n 'rəpstœk bləj]

The Sun replies "yes" and what happens?
Die son sê "ja" en wat gebeur?
[di sɔn sɛ: ja: ɛn vat xə'bjø⁸r]

The Moon begins to grow, anew.
Die maan begin opnuut gedy.
[di ma:n bə'xən ɔp'ny:t xə'dəj]

The Milky Way
5. *Die Melkweg*
[di 'mæ⁸lkvæx]

A woman waits by the fireside at twilight
'n Vrou wag by die skemervuur
[ə frœu vax bəj di 'ske⁸mərfy:r]

But the hunters fail to return.
Maar die jagters kom nie terug.
[ma:r di 'jaxtərs kɔm ni tə'rœx]

It is too dark to walk —
Dit is vir loop te donker —
[dət əs fər lu⁸p tə 'dɔnkər]

There are no stars in the sky.
Geen sterre in die lug.
[çe⁸n 'stærə ən di lœx]

The woman devises a clever plan,
Die vrou maak toe 'n slim plan,
[di frœu ma:k tu ə sləm plan]

She grabs a handful of ash
Sy gryp 'n hand vol as
[səj xrəjp ə ɦant fɔl as]

And throws it into the sky
En gooi dit in die lug op
[ɛn xo:j dət ən di lœx ɔp]

That was so dark before.
Wat eers so donker was.
[vat eᵊrs sʊᵊ 'dɔŋkər vas]

Now a nebulous streak lies across the sky
'n Newelstreep lê oor die lug
[ə 'neᵊvəlstreᵊp lɛ: ʊᵊr di lœx]

That leads the hunters to the fire.
Wat die jagters vuur toe lei.
[vat di 'jaxtərs fy:r tu ləj]

Thus originated the Milky Way,
So het die melkweg dan ontstaan,
[sʊᵊ ɦet di 'mæᵊlkvæx dan ɔnt'sta:n]

And there it remained.
En so het dit gebly.
[ɛn sʊᵊ ɦet dət xə'bləj]

Together with the ash (that is) blown away
Saam met die as het weg gewaai
[sa:m mɛt di as ɦet væ xə'va:jᴬ]

(There are also) sparks of yellow and red
Ook vonke geel en rooi
[ʊᵊk 'fɔŋkə çeᵊl ɛn ro:j]

And they became the bigger stars —
En hulle word die groter sterre —
[ɛn 'ɦœlə vɔrt di 'xrʊᵊtər 'stærə]

Scattered across heaven's expanse.
Oor die hemelveld gestrooi.
[ʊᵊr di 'ɦeᵊməlfæᵊlt xə'stro:j]

The Clouds
6. *Die Wolke*
[di 'vɔlkə]

When someone dies
As iemand sterf
[as 'imant stærf]

His hair becomes the bulging clouds
Dan word sy hare die bollings van die wolke
[dan vɔrt səj 'ɦa:rə di 'bɔləŋs fan di 'vɔlkə]

And bird feathers after their death
En vere van gevogeltes word
[ɛn 'feᵊrə fan xə'fʊᵊxəltəs vɔrt]

Also become clouds
Na hul dood ook volke
[na ɦœl dʊᵊt ʊᵊk 'vɔlkə]

But these clouds do not bring rain
Maar reën bring hierdie wolke nie
[ma:r reᵊn brəŋ 'ɦi:rdi 'vɔlkə ni]

The dead have toppled over.
Die dooies het gekantel.
[di 'do:jəs ɦet xə'kantəl]

---

[4] See Appendix G, Assimilation and Amalgamation of Consonants.

The Big bird comes and blows them away —
Die Grootvoël kom en waai hul weg —
[di ˈxrʊᵊtfʊᵊl kɔm ɛn vaːj fiœl væx]

Enveloped in his cloak.
Gewikkel in sy mantel.
[xəˈvəkəl ən səj ˈmantəl]

The Wind
7. *Die Wind*
[di vənt]

The Windbird from the dim and hazy past
Die Windvoël het reeds van die voortyd
[di ˈvəntfʊᵊl fiɛt reᵊts fan di ˈfʊᵊrtəjt]

The Windbird is a gray flash
Die Windvoël is 'n vaalflits
[di ˈvəntfʊᵊl əs ə ˈfaːlfləts]

Hid himself in caves
Homself in spelonke versteek
[fiɔmˈsæᵊlf ən spəˈlɔŋkə fərˈsteᵊk]

The Windbird is the wind
Want die Windvoël is eintlik die wind
[vant di ˈvəntfʊᵊl əs ˈəjntlək di vənt]

It's he who makes the blue-sky tremble
Dis hy wat die blou lug laat sidder
[dəs fiəj vat di blœu lœx laːt ˈsədər]

Never mock the Windbird
Moet nooit met die Windvoël spot nie
[mut noːjt mɛt di ˈvəntfʊᵊl spɔt ni]

And breaks branches like gathered twigs.
En takke soos sprokkelhoud breek.
[ɛn ˈtakə sʊᵊs ˈsprɔkəlfiœut breᵊk]

And rather keep his name a secret.
En hou maar sy naam toegebind.
[ɛn fiœu maːr səj naːm ˈtuxəˌbənt]

Cradle Song
8. *Wieglied*
[ˈvixlit]

When the time comes for a person to die
Kom daar 'n mens te sterwe
[kɔm daːr ə mɛns tə ˈstærvə]

Soothe the dead with the Moon.
Die Maan die dooie lawe.
[di maːn di ˈdoːjə ˈlaːvə]

And he is buried in a shallow grave,
En word hy vlak begrawe
[ɛn vɔrt fiəj flak bəˈxraːvə]

And when the Moon once more becomes a crescent,
En word die maan weer half,
[ɛn vɔrt di maːn veᵊr fialf]

The weeping Heavens will
Sal van Bo met trane
[sal fan bʊᵊ mɛt ˈtraːnə]

She scoops up this man and
Kom skep sy hierdie mens
[kɔm skɛp səj ˈfiiːrdi mɛns]

Cradles him in her arms
En wieg hom in haar arms
[ɛn vix ɦɔm ən ɦaːr ˈarəms]

Up to his most blissful desires.
Tot aan sy mooiste wens.
[tɔt aːn səj ˈmoːjstə vɛns]

BOERNEEF

(1897–1967)
Pseudonym of Izak Wilhelmus van der Merwe

On the Concertina: Nine Songs for Medium Voice and Piano[1]
Op die Flottina: Nege Liedere vir Middelstem en Klavier
[ɔp die flɔˈtina ˈneᵊxə ˈlidərə fər ˈmədəlstɛm ɛn klaˈfiːr]
Music: Rosa Nepgen (1909–2001)

How Quiet It Becomes When the South-Easterly Wind Wanes
1. *Hoe stil kan dit word as Sedoos gaan lê*
[ɦu stəl kan dət vɔrt as sɛˈdʊᵊs xaːn lɛː]

How quiet it becomes when the south-
easterly wind wanes
Hoe stil kan dit word as Sedoos gaan lê
[ɦu stəl kan dət vɔrt as sɛˈdʊᵊs xaːn lɛː]

Who can proclaim it more sweetly than the
turtle dove
Wie kan dit mooier assie tortel sê
[vi kan dət ˈmoːjər ˈasi ˈtɔrtəl sɛː]

Who more touchingly than the
motionless trees
Wie roerender assie bladstil bome
[vi ˈruːrəndər ˈasi ˈblatstəl ˈbʊᵊmə]

Than the lopsided trees tousled along
the dam
Assie skewe verwaaide damwalbome
[ˈasi ˈskeᵊvə fərˈvaːjdə ˈdamvalˌbʊᵊmə]

In the quiet early morning hours when the
south-easterly wind wanes
Innie stil vroemôre as Sedoos gaan lê
[ˈəni stəl frʊᵊˈmɔːrə as sɛˈdʊᵊs xaːn lɛː]

How (can one) mercifully find peace in
a heart
Hoe om 'n stilte in die hart te vind genadig
[ɦu ɔm ə ˈstəltə ən di ɦart tə fənt xəˈnaːdəx]

Just as when the south-easterly wind wanes
Soos wanneer Sedoos gaan lê
[sʊᵊs ˈvaneᵊr sɛˈdʊᵊs xaːn lɛː]

---

[1] Permission granted by NB Publishers.

Afrikaans Art Song Literature. Christian Bester and Bronwen Forbay, Oxford University Press. © Oxford University Press 2025.
DOI: 10.1093/oso/9780197660812.003.0003

Young Poplar Bark, Smooth and Cool
2. *Jong Pappelierbas[2] glad en koel*
[jɔŋ papə'li:rbas xlat ɛn kul]

Young poplar bark, smooth and cool
Jong pappelierbas glad en koel
[jɔŋ papə'li:rbas xlat ɛn kul]

For the cheek of a lonely child
Virrie wang van 'n eensaam kind
['fəri vaŋ fan ə 'eᵊnsa:m kənt]

Old poplar bark, jagged as a grater
Ou pappelierbas rasperskurf
[œu papə'li:rbas 'raspərskœrf]

From years of gripping like iron in the ground
Van jare se ysterklou innie grond
[fan 'ja:rə sə 'əjstərklœu 'əni xrɔnt]

Straight in the path of the northerly wind
Reg innie pad vannie norewind
[ræx 'əni pat 'fani 'nuᵊrəvənt]

Chafing place for Ebden with the tick-like tail
Skuurplek vir Ebden[3] meddie bosluistert
['sky:rplæk fər 'ɛbdən 'mɛdi 'bɔslœystært]

Crisp in the evenings against the northerly wind
Kroeserig saans tenie norewind
['krusərəx sa:ns 'teᵊni 'nuᵊrəvənt]

Poplar bark consoles horse and child
Pappelierbastroos vir perd en kind
[papə'li:rbastruᵊs fər pært ɛn kənt]

Old Damon Shepherds His Little Flock of Lambs Roundabout
3. *Ou Damon[4] loop sy Lammertroppie om*
[œu 'da:mɔn luᵊp səj 'lamər̩trɔpi ɔm]

Old Damon shepherds his little flock of lambs roundabout
Ou Damon loop sy lammertroppie om
[œu 'da:mɔn luᵊp səj 'lamər̩trɔpi ɔm]

My dear wooly ewe lamb
Lammerooi moflam[5] my ding
['lamər o:j 'mɔflam məj dəŋ]

Why must the wind howl so mournfully?
Hoekom moedie wind so triestag sing?
['ɦukɔm 'mudi vənt suᵊ 'tristax səŋ]

He plays so sorrowfully on the calabash
Hy speel so droewag oppie kalbas
[ɦəj speᵊl suᵊ 'druvəx 'ɔpi kal'bas]

---

[2] Poplar trees (*Populus Simonii*) are usually spelled *Populier* in Afrikaans. They are often planted along boundaries as a windbreaker due to their fast-growing nature.
[3] Likely a horse's name.
[4] The name Damon often occurs in pastoral poetry as an unsophisticated, rustic figure in works by Ovid and Virgil, among others.
[5] A merino sheep.

Why is the rain not coming?
Waar bly die reent?
[va:r bləj di 're^ənt]

Where is the grass?
Waar is die gras?
[va:r əs di xras]

Old Damon knows his wooly lamb like his
own child
Ou Damon ken 'n moflam soos sy kind
[œu 'da:mɔn kɛn ə 'mɔflam sʊ^əs səj kənt]

Wooly lamb my dear lambkin
Moflam my ding my lammerooi
['mɔflam məj dəŋ məj 'lamər o:j]

Last year the Karoo was so beautiful
Verlede jaar wassie Kro[6] so mooi
[fər'le^ədə ja:r 'vasi kro: sʊ^ə mo:j]

Why must the wind howl so mournfully?
Hoekom moedie wind so triestag sing?
['ɦukɔm 'mudi vənt sʊ^ə 'tristəx səŋ]

Cry with such a dreary wail inside the
brown calabash
So treurig huil innie bruin kalbas
[sʊ^ə 'trjø^ərəx ɦœyl 'əni brœyn kal'bas]

But just perhaps my dear wooly lamb
Maar dalk ai tog moflam my lam
[ma:r dalk aj tɔx 'mɔflam məj lam]

He will bring rain and abundant grass
Bring hy die reent en volop gras
[brəŋ ɦəj di re^ənt ɛn 'fɔlɔp xras]

It's Whipping Around like the Flick of a Wrist
4. *Dis omdraaislaan soos Handomkeer*
[dəs 'ɔmdra:j sla:n sʊ^əs 'ɦant̩ɔmke^ər]

It's whipping around like the flick of a wrist
Dis omdraaislaan soos handomkeer
[dəs 'ɔmdra:jsla:n sʊ^əs 'ɦant̩ɔmke^ər]

Constantly begging exhausts my wrists
Pal bakstaan maak my polste tam
[pal 'bakste^ən ma:k məj 'pɔlstə tam]

Tickle-tickle with the fawn-colored feather
Kieliekielie meddie koekiesveer
['kilikili 'mɛdi 'kukisfe^ər]

Sneeze three times for the gentleman
Driekeer nies virrie jentel man
['drike^ər nis 'fəri 'dʒɛntəl man]

Grab it well, steady before he goes
Mooi vat steddie weg is hy
[mo:j fat 'stɛdi væx əs ɦəj]

The evening star hesitantly wants to
speak to me
Die aandster wil-wil praat met my
[di 'a:ntstær vəlvəl pra:t mɛt məj]

---

[6] The Karoo is a semi-arid desert lacking in surface water. It encompasses the Eastern, Western, and Northern Cape Provinces. Its name is derived from the Khoi word for 'land of thirst.' Covering approximately one-third of the total area of South Africa, the Karoo's unique vegetation includes assorted succulents and low scrub bushes.

Old Nincompoop on Stilts
5. *Ou Poegenpol op Pale*
[œu 'puxənpɔl ɔ'pa:lə[7]]

Old Nincompoop on stilts performs such long strides
Ou Poegenpol[8] op pale gee sukke-sukke hale
[œu 'puxənpɔl ɔ'pa:lə çeᵊ 'sœkə 'sœkə 'ɦa:lə]

Throw it down, throw it down far away
Gooiplat-gooiplat die verte in
['xo:jplat 'xo:jplat di 'færtə ən]

But where to, then?
Maar waar dan heen?
[ma:r va:r dan ɦeᵊn]

Why over there?
Hoekom daarheen?
['ɦukɔm 'da:rɦeᵊn]

Must go somewhere, perhaps nowhere
Moet êrens heen dalk nêrens heen
[mut 'æ:rəns ɦeᵊn dalk 'næ:rəns ɦeᵊn]

Must hurry somewhere, perhaps nowhere
Moet haastig êrens-nêrens heen
[mut 'ɦa:stəx 'æ:rəns 'næ:rəns ɦeᵊn]

More and more full steam over there
Aloe volstomer daarheen
['alu 'fɔlˌstʊᵊmər 'da:rɦeᵊn]

That's why Nincompoop on stilts
Daarom gee Poegenpol op pale
['da:rɔm çeᵊ 'puxənpɔl ɔ'pa:lə]

Performs (with) only such long strides
Net sukke-sukke hale
[nɛt 'sœkə 'sœkə 'ɦa:lə]

Who's Batty and Who Has Lost It
6. *Wies getik en wiesit kwyt*
[vis xə'tək ɛn 'visət kwəjt]

Who's batty and who has lost it
Wies getik en wiesit kwyt
[vis xə'tək ɛn 'visət kwəjt]

The world is full of trouble
Die wêreld is vol moeilikgeid
[di 'væ:rəlt əs fɔl 'muiləkxəjt]

Life beats me black and blue, and everyone treats me like a dog
Die lewe slat my blou en bont en ammal maak my hond
[di 'leᵊvə slat məj blœu ɛn bɔnt ɛn 'amal ma:k məj ɦɔnt]

---

[7] See Appendix G, Assimilation and Amalgamation of Consonants.
[8] The poet's folkloristic distortion of the name *Poggenpol* is deliberate and should be maintained in lyric diction.

How many tall trees stand between here
and Rome
Hoevil hoë bome staan tussen hier en Rome
['ɦufəl 'ɦu:ə 'bʊᵊmə sta:n 'tœsən ɦi:r ɛn
'rʊᵊmə]

And why are the trees tall
En hoekom is die bome hoog
[ɛn 'ɦukɔm əs di 'bʊᵊmə ɦʊᵊx]

My luck has dried up, life beats me
black and blue
*My geluk het opgedroog die lewe slat my blou
en bond*
[məj xə'lœk ɦɛt 'ɔpxəˌdrʊᵊx di 'leᵊvə slat məj
blœu ɛn bɔnt]

And everyone treats me like a dog
En ammal maak my hond
[ɛn 'amal ma:k məj ɦɔnt]

It's Saturday evening and very late
Dis Sadragaand en baie laat
[dəs 'sa:drax a:nt ɛn 'bajə la:t]

Somewhere in the Karoo, I Have a Shelter
7. *Êrens in die Kro[9] het ek 'n Skerm[10]*
['æ:rəns ən di kro: ɦɛt ɛk ə 'skærəm]

Somewhere in the Karoo, I have a shelter
Êrens in die Kro het ek 'n skerm
['æ:rəns ən di kro: ɦɛt ɛk ə 'skærəm]

And Karoo food for an indefinite time
En krokos[11] vir 'n ombepaalde tyd
[ɛn 'kro:kɔs fər ə 'ɔmbəˌpa:ldə[12] təjt]

The field lies unutterably quiet and vast
Die veld[13] lê onuitspreeklik stil en wyd
[di fæᵊlt le: ɔnœyt'spreᵊklək stəl en vəjt]

And I have plenty of food and plenty of time
and Pranas-landscapes
*En ek het volop kos en volop tyd en
pranaslandskappe[14]*
[ɛn ɛk ɦɛt 'fɔlɔp kɔs ɛn 'fɔlɔp təjt ɛn
'pranasˌlantskapə]

And Pranas-color all around my shelter.
En pranaskleur rondom my skerm.
[ɛn 'pranaskljøᵊr 'rɔntɔm məj 'skærəm]

Somewhere in the Karoo
Êrens in die Kro
['æ:rəns ən di kro:]

---

[9] See note 6.

[10] A "skerm" is a simple, crude, temporary sleeping-shelter of the nomadic Khoikhoin people. Typically constructed of thorny branches and brushwood, it can also consist of stones, earth, reeds, or animal hides.

[11] The staples of Karoo food include lamb, ostrich, and a plant-based diet.

[12] See Appendix G, Assimilation and Amalgamation of Consonants.

[13] A vast African prairie which may be used in various ways, including agriculture or uncultivated countryside.

[14] The term "pranas," often used by Boerneef, refers to the painter Pranas Domšaitis (1880–1965) and his style.

The Hillock Behind Acorn's Pen
8. *Agter Akkerskraalsekop*[15]
['axtər 'akərskra:lsəkɔp]

Hans Saal's flock of lambs graze on the hillock behind Acorn's Pen
Agter Akkerskraalsekop staan Hans Saal se lammertrop
['axtər 'akərskra:lsəkɔp sta:n ɦans sa:l sə 'lamərtrɔp]

The merino ewe baas for her lamb
Mofooi baskreun vir haar lam
['mɔf o:j 'baskrjøᵊn fər ɦa:r lam]

The darkness is cold and damp
Die donkerte is koud en klam
[di 'dɔŋkərtə əs kœut ɛn klam]

It's a child's nursery rhyme
Dis 'n rympie van 'n kind
[dəs ə 'rəjmpi fan ə kənt]

A child from (the) Ceres-Karoo who lies crying in his little crib
'n Seressekaro[16] se kind wat in sy bedjie lê en huil
[ə 'seᵊrəsəka‚ro: sə kənt vat ən səj 'bɛ:ki lɛ: ɛn ɦœyl]

Over lambs freezing in the wind
Oor lammers koud kry in die wind
[uᵊr 'lamərs kœut krəj ən di vənt]

From Reed Marsh's Wasteland All the Way to Pleading Spring
9. *Van Rietvleisemoorsand tot by Soebatsfontein*
[fan 'ritfləj sə 'muᵊrsant tɔt bəj 'subatsfɔn‚təjn]

From Reed Marsh's Wasteland all the way to Pleading Spring
Van Rietvleisemoorsand tot by Soebatsfontein
[fan 'ritfləj sə 'muᵊrsant tɔt bəj 'subatsfɔn‚təjn]

How dry and how far will it be
Hoe droog sallit wees en hoe ver sallit syn
[ɦu druᵊx 'salət veᵊs en ɦu fæ:r 'salət səjn]

How long does a lean year last?
Hoe lank is 'n maer jaar?
[ɦu laŋk əs ə 'ma:r ja:r]

A wagon road how arid
'n Trekpad hoe dor
[ə 'trækpat ɦiu dɔr]

The dust storm blows far and wide and follows his own will
Die stofwind loop wyd en hy loop soos hy wil
[di 'stɔfvənt luᵊp vəjt ɛn ɦəj luᵊp suᵊs ɦəj vəl]

Have you yet a claim for the late afternoon
Het jy al 'n aanspraak virrie latenstyd
[ɦɛt jəj al ə 'a:nspra:k 'fəri 'la:tənstəjt]

---

[15] This word in the original poem is highly derogatory. While the authors are aware that the word *koeraalboom*, translated as 'coral tree,' is sometimes used as a substitute in present-day South Africa, we have chosen to use the word *Akkers*, translated as 'acorn,' to maintain the rhyming scheme.

[16] The Ceres-Karoo Port, also known as Karoo-Poort R355, is one of the earliest routes used by settlers connecting Cape Town to the arid Karoo region via the verdant Ceres valley.

(A) Skin blanket can warm (you) in the wintertime
Velkombers kan warmmaak innie winter tyd
[ˈfæᵊlkɔmˌbærs kan ˈvarəmaːk ˈəni ˈvəntər təjt]

From Reed Marsh's Wasteland till the end of the race
Van Rietvleisemoorsand toddie end vannie reis
[fan ˈritvləjsəˌmʊᵊrsant ˈtɔdi ɛnt ˈfani rəjs]

Spring has passed and the world has turned gray
Die lente is dood ennie wêreld is grys
[di ˈlɛntə əs dʊᵊt ˈɛni ˈvæːrəlt əs xrəjs]

Where do you get a claim for the dusk
Waar kry jy 'n aanspraak virrie skemertyd
[vaːr krəj jəj ə ˈaːnspraːk ˈfəri ˈskeᵊmərtəjt]

That can warm the heart in the late afternoon
Wat die hart kan warmmaak innie latenstyd
[vat di fiart kan ˈwarəmaːk ˈəni ˈlaːtənstəjt]

The dust storm advances far and wide
Die stofwind loop wyd
[di ˈstɔfvənt lʊᵊp vəjt]

The succulent is tiny
'n Koesnaatjie[17] is klein
[ə kusˈnaːjki əs kləjn]

From Reed Marsh's Wasteland all the way to Pleading Spring
Van Rietvleisemoorsand tot by Soebatsfontein
[fan ˈritfləj sə ˈmʊᵊrsant tɔt bəj ˈsubatsfɔnˌtəjn]

Seven Ditsy Songs[18]
Sewe Boerneef Liedjies/Sewe lawwe Liedjies
[ˈseᵊvə ˈburneᵊf ˈlikis/ ˈseᵊvə ˈlavə ˈlikis]
Music: P. J. de Villiers (1924–2015)

Blow on the Pumpkin Stalk
1. *Blaas op die Pampoenstingel*
[blaːs ɔp di pamˈpunˌstəŋəl]

Blow on the pumpkin stalk
Blaas op die pampoenstingel
[blaːs ɔp di pamˈpunˌstəŋəl]

Make your own music,
Maak jou eie musiek,
[maːk jœu ˈəjə muˈsik]

Puff up your cheeks
Pomp jou kieste op
[pɔmp jœu ˈkistə ɔp]

Blow (as if you were playing) bass music
Blaas basmusiek
[blaːs ˈbasmusik]

---

[17] This tiny succulent (*Crassula columnaris*) is indigenous to South Africa and Namibia. It has a short rigidly upright stem hidden by 8–10 tightly packed leaves that form a tapering, columnar body.
[18] Permission granted by NB Publishers.

A chest-booming song in the bamboo reeds
'n Dreunborslied in die bamboesriet
[ə 'drjø°n‿bɔrslit ən di bam'busrit]

Where waxbills listen with cocked heads
Waar rooibekkies[19] skewekop luister
[va:r 'ro:j‿bɛkis 'ske°vəkɔp 'lœystər]

Little Piedeplooi
2. *Klein Piedeplooi*
[kləjn 'pidəplo:j]

Little Piedeplooi, Little Piedeplooi
Klein Piedeplooi, Klein Piedeplooi
[kləjn 'pidəplo:j kləjn 'pidəplo:j]

Ask the devil why he comes to tickle you.
Vra die josie hoekom hy by jou kom kriewel.
[fra: di 'jʊ°si 'ɦukɔm ɦəj bəj jœu kɔm 'krivəl]

Catch the flea, catch the flea
Vangie flooi vangie flooi
['faŋi flo:j 'faŋi flo:j]

Little Piedeplooi, Little Piedeplooi
Klein Piedeplooi, Klein Piedeplooi
[kləjn 'pidəplo:j kləjn 'pidəplo:j]

In your nice warm bed
In jou lekker warm kooi
[ən jœu 'lækər 'varəm ko:j]

Show him you're his boss.
Wys hom jys sy doekom.
[vəjs ɦɔm jəj səj[20] 'dukɔm]

Look for the scoundrel, seek him out
Soek die tata soekom
[suk di 'tata 'sukɔm]

The Mountain-Goose Feather
3. *Die Berggansveer*[21]
[di 'bærxa:nsfe°r]
Music also by: Hubert du Plessis (1922–2011), titled *"Die Berggans,"*
"Ten Boerneef Songs for Tenor, op. 38, no. 3"
Rosa Nepgen (1909–2001), (*Sewe Boerneef Liedjies/Sewe lawwe Liedjies, no. 2*)
['se°və 'burne°f 'likis/ 'se°və 'lavə 'likis]

The mountain-goose dropped a feather
Die berggans het 'n veer laat val
[di 'bærxa:ns ɦɛt ə fe°r la:t fal]

From the highest crag at Wuppertal
Van die hoogste krans by Woeperdal[22]
[fan di 'ɦʊ°xstə krans bəj'vupərtal]

---

[19] This is most likely the common waxbill (*Estrilda Astrild*), a gray-brown bird indigenous to South Africa.
[20] See Appendix G, Assimilation and Amalgamation of Consonants.
[21] The "Berggans" most likely refers to the Cape shelduck (*Tadorna cana*) which is indigenous to southern Africa. It belongs to the *Anatidae* family, a group of small- to large-sized monogamous water birds that includes swans, geese, and ducks. This term can also refer to the Egyptian goose (*Alopochen aegyptiaca*) which the ancient Egyptians considered sacred. These mountain-geese, commonly found along the Nile Valley and in sub-Saharan Africa, have distinctive dark chocolate-brown-colored eye patches.
[22] "Woeperdal" is a small town on the west coast of the Western Cape Province.

My heart yearns (for you) more and more
My hart staan tuit al meer en meer
[məj ɦart sta:n tœyt al meᵊr ɛn meᵊr]

I am sending you this mountain-goose
feather
Ek stuur vir jou die berggansveer
[ɛk sty:r fər jœu di ˈbærxa:nsfeᵊr]

With this I want to tell you
Mits dese wil ek vir wil jou sê
[məts ˈdeᵊsə vəl ɛk fər jœu sɛ:]

How deep my love for you lies.
Hoe diep my liefde vir jou lê.
[ɦu dip məj ˈlifdə fər jœu lɛ:]

Why Is the Devil Afraid of the Grindstone
4. *Waarom is die Duiwel vir die Slypsteen bang*
['va:rɔm əs di ˈdœyvəl fər di ˈsləjpsteᵊn baŋ]

Why is the devil afraid of the grindstone
Waarom is die duiwel vir die slypsteen bang
['va:rɔm əs di ˈdœyvəl fər di ˈsləjpsteᵊn baŋ]

And not for the pitch-black spitting snake,
En nie vir die pikswart verspoegslang,
[ɛn ni fər di ˈpəkswart ˈfæ:rspuxslaŋ]

Ask your father, ask your mother, my
young master
Vra vir jou pa, vra vir jou ma, my basie
[fra: vər jœu pa: fra: vər jœu ma: məj ˈba:si]

Why is he afraid of the big knapsack?
Hoekom skrik hy vir 'n knapsak groot?
[ˈɦukɔm skrək ɦəj fər ə ˈknapsak xrʊᵊt]

As if a jute bag of salt would really cause
his death
Is 'n mudsak sout konsuis sy dood
[əs ə ˈmutsak sœut kɔnˈsœys səj dʊᵊt]

Ask your mother, ask your father, my
young master
Vra vir jou ma, vra vir jou pa, my basie
[fra: vər jœu ma: fra: vər jœu pa: məj ˈba:si]

Father says we'll discuss this at bedtime,
Pa sê dis praatjies vir die vaak,
[pa: sɛ: dəs ˈpraˈkis fər di fa:k]

Mother does not want to hear anything
more about the horned mandrake.
*Ma wil niks meer hoor van die
horingsmandraak.*[23]
[ma: vəl nəks meᵊr ɦʊᵊr fan di
ˈɦʊᵊrəŋsmandra:k]

---

[23] A "horingsmandraak" is a plant used in witchcraft.

The Evening-Flower Is a White Flower
5. *Aandblom*[24] *is 'n Witblom*
['a:ntblɔm əs ə 'vətblɔm]

(The) evening-flower is a white flower
Aandblom is 'n witblom
['a:ntblɔm əs ə 'vətblɔm]

(The) evening-flower is my scarlet poem
Aandblom is my bloedrooi vers
['a:ntblɔm əs məj 'blutro:j færs]

(The) darling flower is my sweetheart
Hartblom is my meisie
['ɦartblɔm əs məj 'məjsi]

She and I at the courting candle
Ek en sy by die opsitkers
[ɛk ɛn səj bəj di 'ɔpsətkærs]

Little flower don't forget me
Blommetjie vergeet my niet
['blɔmiki fər'xeᵊt məj nit]

Little flower think of me
Blommetjie gedink aan my
['blɔmiki xə'dəŋk a:n məj]

My Speckled, Cross-Feathered Hen
6. *My Koekiesveerhen jou Verkereveer*
[məj 'kukis͵feᵊrɦɛn jœu fər'keᵊrəfeᵊr]

My speckled, cross-feathered hen
My koekiesveerhen jou verkereveer
[məj 'kukis͵feᵊrɦɛn jœu fər'keᵊrəfeᵊr]

When will my (sweetheart's) ghost come back again?
Wanneer kom my ghantang[25] *weer?*
['vaneᵊr kɔm məj 'xaŋtaŋ veᵊr]

I wait here for him by the water trench
Hier wag ek vir hom by die watervoor
[ɦi:r vax ɛk fər ɦɔm bəj di 'va:terfʊᵊr]

Let it be again as it was before.
Laat dit weer wees soos die vorige keer.
[la: dət[26] veᵊr weᵊs sʊᵊs di 'fʊᵊrəxə keᵊr]

---

[24] The evening-flower (*Geophyte*) is a species of *Hesperanthus, Gladiolus, Freesia*, and *Iridacae*. It has soft hairy leaves and petals that range in color from dark purple, nearly black, to an occasional pale yellow. Found in various regions of the Western Cape Province, these flowers are very fragrant at nighttime. Their scent resembles cinnamon.

[25] This word does not exist in Afrikaans but means 'haunted' when translated from Indonesian to English.

[26] See Appendix G, Assimilation and Amalgamation of Consonants.

Up There High Against the Ridge
7. *Doer bo teen die Rant*
[dur bʊᵊ teᵊn di rant]
Music also by: Hubert du Plessis (1922–2011),
"Ten Boerneef Songs for Tenor, op. 38, no. 1"
Rosa Nepgen (1909–2001), *(Sewe Boerneef Liedjies/Sewe lawwe*
Liedjies, no. 7) [ˈseᵊvə ˈburneᵊf ˈlikis/ ˈseᵊvə ˈlavə ˈlikis]

Up there high against the ridge
Doer bo teen die rant
[dur bʊᵊ teᵊn di rant]

A shrub stands planted
Staan 'n bos geplant
[sta:n ə bɔs xəˈplant]

It's a Cederberg shrub
Dis 'n Sederbergse bos
[dəs ə ˈseᵊdərˌbærxsə bɔs]

It's a miraculous little shrub
Dis 'n wonderbossie-bos
[dəs ə ˈvɔndərˌbɔsi bɔs]

Break off a piece of it and steep it (in water)
with herbs
Laat trek van die ding met kruie geming
[la:t træ:k fan di dəŋ mɛt ˈkrœjə xəˈməŋ]

For the sitting and longing that old
age brings
Vir die sit en verlang wat die ouderdom bring
[fər di sət ɛn fərˈlaŋ vat di ˈœudərdɔm brəŋ]

Stand-Alone Poetry

Rendezvous[27]
Krymekaar[28] [ˈkrəjməˌka:r]
Music: Stewart Hylton-Edwards (1924–1987)

We search for one other at (the) Rendezvous
Ons soek mekaar by Krymekaar
[ɔns suk məˈka:r bəj ˈkrəjməˌka:r]

---

[27] Permission granted by NB Publishers.
[28] This term refers to a love nest.

But all that arrived, is you, the African daisy says
Maar al wat kom, is jy, die gousblom²⁹ sê
[ma:r al vat kɔm əs jəj di ˈxœusblɔm sɛ:]

You'll be here now-now and the yellow-milk-bush believes
Jy's nou-nou³⁰ hier en die melkbos³¹ meen
[jəjs nœunœu ɦi:r ɛn di ˈmæᵃlkbɔs meᵃn]

You were over there yesterday.
Jy was gister dáár.
[jəj vas ˈxəstər ˈda:r]

We search for one another at Rendezvous
Ons soek mekaar by Krymekaar
[ɔns suk məˈka:r bəj ˈkrəjməˌka:r]

But are you searching for me, too?
Maar soek jy ook na my?
[ma:r suk jəj ʊᵃk na məj]

The daisy now turns the other way
Die gousblom kyk nou annerpad
[di ˈxœusblɔm kəjk nœu ˈanərpat]

And the yellow-milk-bush says "yes, who knows where?"
En die melkbos sê: "ja, wie weet waar?"
[ɛn di ˈmæᵃlkbɔs sɛ: ja: vi veᵃt wa:r]

I search and wait at Rendezvous
Ek soek en wag by Krymekaar
[ɛk suk ɛn vax bəj ˈkrəjməˌka:r]

Where the African daisy is now just dust
Waar gousblom is nou net sand
[va:r ˈxœusblɔm əs nœu nɛt sant]

The quiver tree has no advice
Die kokerboom³² weet glad geen raad
[di ˈkʊᵃkərbʊᵃm veᵃt xlat çeᵃn ra:t]

And the yellow-milk-bush says: "if only we knew where?"
En die melkbos sê: "wis ons maar waar?"
[ɛn di ˈmæᵃlkbɔs sɛ: vəs ɔns ma:r va:r]

In vain I wait at Rendezvous
Verniet wag ek by Krymekaar
[fərˈnit vax ɛk bəj ˈkrəjməˌka:r]

Because only you arrive
Want al wat kom is jy
[vant al vat kɔm əs jəj]

The daisy is scorched to sand
Die gousblom is tot sand verbrand
[di ˈxœusblɔm əs tɔt sant fərˈbrant]

And the yellow-milk-bush says: "still here, still there."
En die melkbos sê: "nog, hier, nog daar."
[ɛn di ˈmæᵃlkbɔs sɛ: nɔx ɦi:r nɔx da:r]

---

[29] The African daisy *(Gazania Krebsiana)* is indigenous to southern Africa. It flourishes on arid stony slopes.

[30] A colloquial phrase relating to an unspecified time period which will elapse before the given task is completed. It is somewhat nebulous as it can mean anything from five minutes, to next week, beyond, or never.

[31] The yellow milk bush *(Euphorbia mauritanica)* is a succulent shrub with bright yellow flowers.

[32] The quiver tree *(Aloidendron dichotomum*, also known as the *Aloe dichotoma)* is one of the scarcest aloe trees that flourishes in the arid regions of northwestern southern Africa. Its bark appears golden, while its trunk has distinctive white pillar-like stems crowned with pale green leaves.

From Kirstenbosch Yonder to Namaqualand[33]
Van Kirstenbosch[34] tot in Namakwaland[35]
[fan ˈkərstənbɔs tɔt ən naˈmakwalant]
Music: Lourens Faul (b. 1931)

From Kirstenbosch yonder to Namaqualand
Van Kirstenbosch tot in Namakwaland
[fan ˈkərstənbɔs tɔt ən naˈmakwalant]

Neverending rows of spots and patches
form a multicolored tapestry
Kolkol bont lappe ritse-ritse kleur
[ˈkɔlkɔl bɔnt ˈlapə ˈrətsə ˈrətsə kljøˀr]

Spring lays bare her glory
Lê die voorjaar in sy glorie oop
[le: di ˈfuˀrja:r ən səj ˈxluˀri ʋˀp]

From Kirstenbosch yonder to Namaqualand
Van Kirstenbosch tot in Namakwaland
[fan ˈkərstənbɔs tɔt ən naˈmakwalant]

The high ledges of Tierberg are adorned
with proteas
Hoog bo-op Tierberg[36] hang proteas[37] uit
[ɦuˀx ˈbuˀɔp ˈti:rbærx ɦaŋ ˈpruˀtias œyt]

Mountain roses crouch against the
Skurwerand
*Skaamrosies[38] koes-koes teen die
Skurwerand[39]*
[ˈska:m̩ˌrʋˀsis ˈkuskus teˀn di ˈskœrvərant]

Far as the eye can see the glowing vygies
are aflame
Die vygiewêreld[40] gloei en brand
[di ˈfəjxiˌʋæ:rəltxlui ɛn brant]

From Kirstenbosch to way yonder, deep
within Namaqualand
*Van Kirstenbosch tot doer in ver
Namakwaland*
[fan ˈkərstənbɔs tɔt du:r ən fæ:r
naˈmakwalant]

Are you intoxicated and dumbstruck at
seeing such beauty
Is jy bedwelmd gekyk raak jy dalk sonder taal
[əs jəj bəˈdwæˀlmt xəˈkəjk ra:k jəj dalk
ˈsɔndər ta:l]

---

[33] Permission granted by NB Publishers.

[34] Kirstenbosch, established in 1913, is one of nine National Botanical Gardens in South Africa. Situated on the eastern slopes of Table Mountain in Cape Town, this world-famous garden is 528 hectares (1,300 acres) in size and showcases over 7,000 plant species indigenous to southern Africa.

[35] Namaqualand, derived from the Khoi word for 'Khoi people's land,' is a predominantly arid region in the Northern Cape Province of South Africa. It overflows with exquisite wildflowers during the rainy spring season.

[36] Situated close to Vanrhynsdorp in the Northern Cape Province, this area is renowned for its fynbos. It also produces one of South Africa's world-famous export products, Rooibos tea (*Aspalathus linearis*).

[37] The protea (*Proteaceae*) is South Africa's national flower. A fynbos shrub found mostly in southern Africa, it has a distinctive chalice-shaped flower head and ranges in color from cream to bright red.

[38] Mountain roses (*Protea nana*) are green when young, red during maturation, and brown when fully matured. The direct translation of the word *skam* or *skaam* means 'shy' or 'bashful,' possibly referring to the downward tilting posture of the flower.

[39] This may allude to "Skurwerand" hill in the Eastern Cape Province.

[40] Vygies (*Aizoaceae*) are succulent plants mainly found in the Western and Northern Cape Provinces. Their flowers are bright and colorful, ranging from yellow and orange to pink, mauve, white, and purple.

Listen carefully to the sounds across spring's
colorful carpet
Luister hoe klink oor hierdie lentekleurigheid
['lœystər ɦu kləŋk ʊᵊr 'ɦiːrdi 'lɛntə͜
kljøᵊrəxɦəjt]

The happy golden notes of the wine cup
Die bly benjienienote van die kelkiewyn[41]
[di bləj 'bɛnjini͜nʊᵊtə fan di 'kæᵃlkivəjn]

From Kirstenbosch yonder to Namaqualand
Van Kirstenbosch tot in Namakwaland
[fan 'kərstənbɔs tɔt ən na'makwalant]

Spring lays bare her glory
Lê die voorjaar in sy glorie oop
[lɛː di 'fʊᵊrjaːr ən səj 'xlʊᵊri ʊᵊp]

---

[41] Wine cups (*Geissorhiza radians*) are goblet-shaped flowers found in the Western Cape. Highly endangered, they
consist of deep purple flowers with a red center.

JAN FRANCOIS ELIAS CELLIERS
(1865–1940)
aka Jan F. E. Celliers

From "Six Afrikaans Art Songs"
Ses Afrikaanse Kunsliedere
[sɛs afriˈka:nsəˈkœnsˌlidərə]
Music: M. L. de Villiers (1885–1977)

A Crown of Thorns
3. *'n Doringkroon*
[ə ˈdʊᵊrəŋkrʊᵊn])

The work that will grow as God wills
Die werk wat sal groei soos die Meester syn
[di værk vat sal xrui sʊᵊs di ˈmeᵊstər səjn]

Will have to carry ingratitude
Sal ondank moet dra
[sal ˈɔndaŋk mut dra:]

And misjudgment's pain:
En miskenning se pyn:
[ɛn məsˈkɛnəŋ sə pəjn]

The only reward for the biggest sacrifice is,
Vir die grootste werk is die enigste loon,
[fər di ˈxrʊᵊtstə værk əs di ˈeᵊnəxstə lʊᵊn]

A crown of thorns.
'n Doringkroon.
[ə ˈdʊᵊrəŋkrʊᵊn]

The Waves
4. *Die Branders*
[di ˈbrandərs]
Music also by: Blanche Gerstman (1910–1973)

Dance, wild sea!
Dans, wilde see!
[da:ns ˈvəldə seᵊ]

My soul dances along
My siel dans mee
[məj sil da:ns meᵊ]

Afrikaans Art Song Literature. Christian Bester and Bronwen Forbay, Oxford University Press. © Oxford University Press 2025.
DOI: 10.1093/oso/9780197660812.003.0004

And laughs with you when the waves fling the splendor
En lag met jou lag by die opgooiprag
[ɛn lax mɛt jœu lax bəj di 'ɔpxo:jprax]

Of your veil twirling in the breeze,
Van jou sluierswaai in die wind se waai,
[fan jœu 'slœyərswa:j ən di vənt sə va:j]

And dives with you splashing into the frothy fluff,
En duik met jou plons in die skuimedons,
[ɛn dœyk mɛt jœu plɔns ən di 'skœymədɔns]

Floating together on the graceful surge of your majesty,
Swewe saam op die swier van jou deining fier,
['swe°və sa:m ɔp di swi:r fan jœu 'dəjnəŋ fi:r]

Rushing urgently, overwhelmingly in its direction,
Oorromp'lend van gang in aanstormdrang,
[ʊ°'rɔmplənt fan xaŋ ən 'a:nˌstɔrəmdraŋ]

Until there, until there I don't know where —
Tot dáár, tot dáár ek weet nie waar —
[tɔ 'da:r¹ tɔ 'da:r ɛk ve°t ni va:r]

Where beauty forever in heavenly radiance
Waar skoonheid vir ewig in hemelse glans
[va:r 'skʊ°nɦəjt fər 'e°vəx ən 'ɦe°məlsə xlans]

Dances in rhythm to its own ecstasy.
Op ritme van eie ekstase dans.
[ɔp 'rətmə fan 'əjə ɛk'sta:sə da:ns]

Stand-Alone Poetry

Cupid's Confetti
Amors Konfetti
['a:mɔrs kɔn'fɛti]
Music: Doris Beyers (n.d.), "Cupid's Confetti and Five Other Songs" (*Amors Konfetti en vyf ander Liedere, no. 1*) ['a:mɔrs kɔn'fɛti ɛn fəjf 'andər 'lidərə]
S. le Roux Marais (1896–1979), "Four Afrikaans Song Snippets" (*Vier Afrikaanse Sangstukkies, no. 4*) [fi:r afri'ka:nse 'saŋˌstœkis]

The birdies kiss and tweet uproariously in spring's budding leaves,
Die voëltjies vry en skaterlag in voorjaarsblaartjies,
[di 'fʊ°lkis frəj ɛn 'ska:tərlax ən 'fʊ°rja:rsˌbla:rkis]

Young and delicate,
Jong en teer,
[jɔŋ ɛn te°r]

And shake the blossoms (of) roses and white, beloved,
En skud die bloeisels rose en wit, geliefde,
[ɛn skœt di 'bluisəls 'rʊ°sə ɛn vət xə'lifdə]

Upon your hair
Op jou hare neer
[ɔp jœu 'ɦa:rə ne°r]

It's time for our wedding day,
Dis tyd vir onse huw'liksdag,
[dəs təjt fər 'ɔnsə 'ɦyvləksdax]

---

[1] See Appendix G, Assimilation and Amalgamation of Consonants.

It's Cupid who invites you to the wedding.
Dis Amor wat ten bruilof nooi.
[dəs ˈaːmɔr vat tɛn ˈbrœylɔf noːj]

Beloved, come! It's indeed time,
Geliefde, kom! Dis tyd voorwaar,
[xəˈlifdə kɔm dəs təjt fʊ°rˈvaːr]

When Cupid is already sprinkling (the) confetti.
As Amor reeds konfetti strooi.
[as ˈaːmɔr re°ts kɔnˈfɛti stroːj]

The Ox-Wagon
Die Ossewa
[di ˈɔsəvaː]
Music: A. H. Ashworth (1895–1959)
S. C. de Villiers (1895–1929)
John Pescod (1898–1985)
J. P. J. Wierts (1866–1944)

The oxen plod forward on the dusty (trail)
Die osse stap aan deur die stowwe,
[di ˈɔsə stap aːn djø°r di ˈstɔvə]

Patient, docile, submissive;
Geduldig, gedienstig, gedwee;
[xəˈdœldəx xəˈdinstəx xəˈdwe°]

The yokes, pressing (down) on their shoulders,
Die jukke, al drukkend hul skowwe,
[di ˈjœkə al ˈdrœkənt ɦœl ˈskɔvə]

They carry it ungrudgingly and contentedly.
Hul dra dit getroos en tevree.
[ɦœl draː dət xəˈtrʊ°s ɛn təˈfre°]

And quietly, shifting and pushing,
En stille, al stuiwend en stampend,
[ɛn ˈstələ al ˈstœyvənt ɛn ˈstampənt]

The wagon follows slowly,
Kom stadig die wa agterna,
[kɔm ˈstaːdəx di vaː ˌaxtərˈnaː]

The indistinct red dust, all hazy,
Die dowwe rooi stowwe, al dampend,
[di ˈdɔvə roːj ˈstɔvə al ˈdampənt]

Tossed aside, carried by the breeze.
Tersij op die windje gedra.
[tərˈsəj ɔp di ˈvəɲki xəˈdraː]

The afternoon sun burns their heads,
Die middag-son brand op die koppe,
[di ˈmədaxsɔn brant ɔp di ˈkɔpə]

Hunched over in their powerful labor,
Gebuk in hul beurende krag,
[xəˈbœk ən ɦœl ˈbjø°rəndə krax]

They (oxen) swing from side to side in their strops
Hul swaai heen en weer in die stroppe
[ɦœl ˈswaːj ɦe°n ɛn ve°r ən di ˈstrɔpə]

And far (still) is the trek of the day.
En ver is die tog van die dag.
[ɛn fæːr əs di tɔx fan di dax]

It creaks through the broken pieces;
Dit kraak deur die brekende brokke;
[dət kra:k djøᵊr di 'breᵊkəndə 'brɔkə]

The uphill paths are far and heavy;
Die opdraans is ver en is swaar;
[di 'ɔpdra:ns əs fæ:r ɛn əs swa:r]

It creaks in their cracking knuckles,
Dit knars in die knakkende knokke,
[dət knars ən di 'knakəndə 'knɔkə]

But they pull, and they bring the load there.
Maar hul beur, en die vrag bring hul daar.
[ma:r ɦœl bjøᵊr ɛn di frax brəŋ ɦœl da:r]

So, mute till the hour of their passing,
So, stom tot die stond van hul sterwe,
[sʊᵃ stɔm tɔt di stɔnt fan ɦœl 'stæ:rvə]

Each one remains a hero of the deed ...
Bly ieder 'n held van die daad ...
[bləj 'idər ə ɦæat fan di da:t]

Their bones, after (their) labor and roaming,
Hul bene, na swoeë en swerwe,
[ɦœl 'beᵊnə na 'swu:ə ɛn 'swærvə]

Lay far and wide, deserted across the fields ...
Lê ver op die velde² verlaat ...
[lɛ: fæ:r ɔp di 'fæᵃldə fər'la:t]

The Seeking Mother
Die soekende Moeder
[di 'sukəndə 'mudər]
Music: Johannes J. Fagan (1898–1920)

A mother wanders aimlessly among tiny tombs:
'n Moeder dwaal onder graffies rond:
[ə 'mudər dwa:l 'ɔndər 'xrafis rɔnt]

Her little child has been lying here for so many years,
Hier lê haar kindjie al soveel jaar,
[ɦi:r lɛ: ɦa:r 'kəɲki al 'sʊᵃfeᵃl ja:r]

Here in Irene's churchyard cemetery,
Hier in Irene's³ kerkhofgrond,
[ɦi:r ən aə'ri:nis 'kærkɦɔfxrɔnt]

But she doesn't know where, she doesn't know where.
En sy weet nie waar, sy weet nie waar.
[ɛn səj veᵃt ni va:r səj veᵃt ni va:r]

Beloved mother, do dry your tears:
Moedertjie, droog jou trane tog:
['mudərki drʊᵃx jœu 'tra:nə tɔx]

What more can the tiny tomb reveal to you?
Waarom die graffie jou nog te wys?
['va:rɔm di 'xrafi jœu nɔx tə vəjs]

---

² An expansive African prairie, field, or pasture, comprising a wide variety of vegetation which may be used in various ways, including agriculture or uncultivated countryside.

³ "Irene," sometimes spelled *Irini*, refers to a quaint town on the eastern outskirts of Centurion, a suburb of the Gauteng Province. The name is derived from the Greek word for peace, εἰρήνη.

Mother you still seek the dead among
the living
Moeder jy soek die dode nog
['mudər jəj suk di 'dʊᵊdə nɔx]

Where life has already risen from death!
Waar reeds uit die dode die lewe verrys!
[va:r reᵊts œyt di 'dʊᵊdə di 'leᵊvə fə'rəjs]

The Little Country Breeze
Die Veldwindjie
[di 'fæaltˌvəɲki]
Music: Bosman di Ravelli (1882–1967), "Three Songs"
(Drie Liederen, no. 3) [dri 'lidərən]

Oh, listen to the hymn
O, hoor die gesang
[ʊᵊ ɦʊᵊr di xə'saŋ]

Of the ages as it drifts.
Van die eeue op hul gang.
[fan di 'iuə ɔp ɦœl xaŋ]

Over the escarpment's ledge,
Oor die rande se hang,
[ʊᵊr di 'randə sə ɦaŋ]

It arrives floating,
Kom dit geswewe,
[kɔm dət xə'sweᵊvə]

Over the field far and gray,
Oor die veld⁴ vér en vaal,
[ʊᵊr di fæᵊlt 'fæ:r ɛn fa:l]

On the meandering breeze,
Op die windjie wat dwaal,
[ɔp di 'vəɲki vat dwa:l]

Purposeless, indefinable, sighing through
every nook and cranny.
Onbestem, onbepaal, suggies deurwewe.
['ɔmbəˌstɛm⁵ 'ɔmbəˌpa:l 'sœxis djøᵊr've ᵊvə]

Without guidance, untamed,
Sonder stuur, sonder toom,
['sɔndər sty:r 'sɔndər tʊᵊm]

Slowly, languidly …
Middaglou, middagloom …
['mədaxlœu 'mədaxlʊᵊm]

Like a specter from a dream;
Soos die skim van 'n droom;
[sʊᵊs di skəm fan ə drʊᵊm]

Death takes the living.
Sterwe nog lewe.
['stærvə nɔx 'leᵊvə]

---

⁴ See note 2.
⁵ See Appendix G, Assimilation and Amalgamation of Consonants.

That's All

Dis al

[dəs al]

Music: A. H. Ashworth (1895–1959)

Jan Bouws (1902–1978), "Eleven Afrikaans Songs" (*Elf Afrikaanse Liedere, no. 3*)

[æᵊlf afriˈkaːns ˈlidərə]

Daniel Clement (1902–1980), "South Africa Onwards" (*Suid-Afrika vorentoe, no. 13*)

[sœyt ˈaːfrika ˈfʊᵊrəntu]

Stefans Grové (1922–2014), "Three Songs" (*Drie Liedere, no. 1*) [dri ˈlidərə]

Johannes Joubert (1894–1958)

O. A. Lewald (1905–1988), "Six Songs to Words by Jan F. E. Cilliers, no. 3"

Ernst Lowenherz (1874–1958), *Op. 42*

S. le Roux Marais (1896–1979), "The Rose and Other Afrikaans Songs" (*Die Roos en ander Afrikaanse Liedere, no. 2*) [di rʊᵊs en ˈandər afriˈkaːnsə ˈlidərə]

Rudolf Mengelberg (1892–1959), "Nine South African Songs, no. 6"

Charles Nel (1890–1983), "Three Afrikaans Songs" (*Drie Afrikaanse Liedere, no.2*)

[dri afriˈkaːnsə ˈlidərə]

Rosa Nepgen (1909–2001)

It's the fair, it's the blue:
Dis die blond, dis die blou:
[dəs di blɔnt dəs di blœu]

It's the field, it's the air;
Dis die veld,[6] dis die lug;
[dəs di fæᵊlt dəs di lœx]

And a lonesome bird in flight circles above —
En 'n voël draai bowe in eensame vlug —
[ɛn ə ˈfuːəl draːj ˈbʊᵊvə ən ˈeᵊnsaːmə flœx]

That's all, that's all.
Dis al, dis al.
[dəs al dəs al]

It's an exile come across the ocean,
Dis 'n balling gekom oor die oseaan,
[dəs ə ˈbaləŋ xəˈkɔm ʊᵊr di ʊᵊsiˈaːn]

It's a grave in the grass
Dis 'n graf in die gras,
[dəs ə xraf ən di xras]

It's a falling tear —
Dis 'n vallende traan —
[dəs ə ˈfaləndə traːn]

That's all, that's all.
Dis al, dis al.
[dəs al dəs al]

---

[6] See note 2.

DOLL DE VILLIERS
(1920–2016)

Where the Night in Breathless Stillness[1]
Waar die Nag in ademlose Stilte
[va:r di nax ən ˈa:dəmˌlʊᵊsə ˈstəltə]
Music: Dirkie de Villiers (1920–1993)

Where the night in breathless stillness
Waar die nag in ademlose stilte
[va:r di nax ən ˈa:dəmˌlʊᵊsə ˈstəltə]

Hangs above the small inn,
Oor die kleine herberg hang,
[ʊᵊr di ˈkləjnə ˈɦærbærx ɦaŋ]

A star's purest beams are
Word 'n ster se skoonste strale
[vɔrt ə stær sə skʊᵊnstə ˈstra:lə]

Captured in a tiny manger.
In 'n krippie vasgevang.
[ən ə ˈkrəpi ˈfasxəˌfaŋ]

It's the love of a Father
Dis die liefde van 'n Vader
[dəs di ˈlifdə fan ə ˈfa:dər]

That shines on his countenance:
Wat daar blink op sy gelaat:
[vat da:r bləŋk ɔp səj xəˈla:t]

Holy Child, born for us,
Heil'ge Kind, vir ons gebore,
[ˈɦəjlxə kənt fər ɔns xəˈbʊᵊrə]

The result of God's grace.
Vrug van Goddelik' beraad.
[frœx fan ˈxɔdələk bəˈra:t]

Divine Child (lying) so humbly in the manger,
Heil'ge Kindjie in die krip so needrig,
[ˈɦəjlxə ˈkəŋki ən di krəp sʊᵊ ˈneᵊdrəx]

Shepherds beheld You first.
Herders het Jou eerst' aanskou.
[ˈɦærdərs ɦɛt jœu eᵊrst a:nˈskœu]

Throughout the ages humanity
Alle eeue sal die mensdom
[ˈalə ˈiuə sal di ˈmɛnsdɔm]

Will remember You as a Child on Christmas Eve.
Kersnag Jou as Kind onthou.
[ˈkærsnax jœu as kənt ɔntˈɦœu]

Let also in my heart
Laat ook in my hart
[la:t ʊᵊk ən məj ɦart]

---

[1] Permission granted by Johan Marthinus de Villiers.

Afrikaans Art Song Literature. Christian Bester and Bronwen Forbay, Oxford University Press. © Oxford University Press 2025.
DOI: 10.1093/oso/9780197660812.003.0005

The miracle (of your birth) to dawn anew
every day,
Die wonder elke dag opnuut weer daag,
[di ˈvɔndər ˈæᵃlkə dax ɔpˈnyːt veᵊr daːx]

So that I with thanksgiving and joy
Sodat ek met dank en vreugde
[ˈsʊᵊdat ɛk mɛt daŋk ɛn ˈfrjøᵊxdə]

Delight that Heavenly Child.
Daardie Hemelskind behaag.
[ˈdaːrdi ˈɦieᵊməlskənt bəˈɦaːx]

IZAK LOUIS DE VILLIERS

(1936–2009)
aka I. L. de Villiers

Balance Sheet[1]
Balansstaat
[baˈlaːnstaːt]
Music: P. J. de Villiers (1924–2015), "Four Songs of Doubt and Faith"
(*Vier Liedere van Twyfel en Geloof, no. 3*) [fiːr ˈlidərə fanˈtwəjfəl ɛn xəˈlʊᵊf]

Oh, Lord, I thank You for Your patience with me.
O, Heer, ek dank U vir U groot geduld met my.
[ʊᵊ ɦeᵊr ɛk daŋk y fər y xrʊᵊt xəˈdœlt mɛt məj]

I am so heavily indebted to You.
Ek is so in die skuld by U.
[ɛk əs sʊᵊ ən di skœlt bəj y]

My bank statement remains in the red.
My bankstaat bly in die rooi getik.
[məj ˈbaŋkstaːt bləj ən di roːj xəˈtək]

Zeroes keep being added before the comma —
Nulle kom voor die komma by —
[ˈnœlə kɔm fʊᵊr di ˈkɔma bəj]

It is difficult for me to stomach (that) sometimes.
Ek sluk soms swaar daaraan.
[ɛk slœk sɔms swaːr ˈdaːraːn]

I offer so little and yet ask for even more credit
Ek bied so min en vra al meer krediet
[ɛk bit sʊᵊ mən ɛn fraː al meᵊr krəˈdit]

And I receive it, God knows how!
En kry dit, God weet hoe!
[ɛn krəj dət xɔt veᵊt ɦu]

Sometimes I am afraid You will summon me
Ek is soms bang U roep my in
[ɛk əs sɔms baŋ y rup məj ən]

To repay everything
Om alles te betaal
[ɔm ˈaləs tə bəˈtaːl]

And remove me from the at risk (side of Your) scale
En haal my uit U waagskaal uit
[ɛn ɦaːl məj œyt y ˈvaːxskaːl œyt]

---

[1] Permission granted by NB Publishers.

Afrikaans Art Song Literature. Christian Bester and Bronwen Forbay, Oxford University Press. © Oxford University Press 2025.
DOI: 10.1093/oso/9780197660812.003.0006

As too great of a liability:
As 'n té groot risiko:
[as ə 'tə xrʊᵊt 'risiku]

A skeptic that believes.
'n Twyfelaar wat glo.
[ə 'twəjfəla:r vat xlʊᵊ]

PIERRE DE VILLIERS PIENAAR

(1904–1978)
aka P. de Villiers Pienaar

The Evening-Flower[1]
Die Aandblom[2]
[di ˈaːntblɔm]
Music: Arthur Ellis (b. 1931)

Look at how the dusk colors the hillside,
Kyk hoe die aandson die bulte kleur,
[kəjk ɦu di ˈaːntsɔn di ˈbœltə kljøᵊr]

Lift your head right now,
Lig nou jou kop omhoog,
[ləx nœu jœu kɔp ɔmˈɦʊᵊx]

You have wept enough during the day,
Oordag het jy genoeg getreur,
[ˈʊᵊrdax ɦet jəj xəˈnu xəˈtrjøᵊr]

You have suffered enough grief.
Genoeg verdriet gedoog.
[xəˈnux fərˈdrit xəˈdʊᵊx]

The moon peers over the hillside
Die maan agter die bulte loer
[di maːn ˈaxtər di ˈbœltə luːr]

And anoints the pale tiny leaves,
En salf die blaartjies blank,
[ɛn salf di ˈblaːrkis blaŋk]

The calyces stir softly in gratitude,
Wat dankbaar saggies die kelkies roer,
[vat ˈdaŋkbaːr ˈsaxis di ˈkæᵊlkis ruːr]

On fragile and lanky stems.
Op steeltjie teer en slank.
[ɔp ˈsteᵊlki teᵊr ɛn slaŋk]

Away with grief,
Weg met droefheid,
[væx mɛt ˈdruffɦəjt]

Weep no more,
Treur nie meer nie,
[trjøᵊr ni meᵊr ni]

---

[1] Permission granted by the Federasie van Afrikaanse Kultuurvereniginge (FAK).

[2] The evening-flower (*Geophyte*) is a species of *Hesperanthus*, *Gladiolus*, *Freesia*, and *Iridacae*. It has soft hairy leaves and petals that range in color from dark purple, nearly black, to an occasional pale yellow. Found in various regions of the Western Cape Province, these flowers are very fragrant at nighttime. Their scent resembles cinnamon.

Afrikaans Art Song Literature. Christian Bester and Bronwen Forbay, Oxford University Press. © Oxford University Press 2025.
DOI: 10.1093/oso/9780197660812.003.0007

Happy (is) the field and valley,
Vrolik veld³ en vlei,
['frʊᵊlək fæᵊlt ɛn fləj]

The warm sunbeam scorches no more,
Warm sonstraal skroei nie weer nie,
['varəm 'sɔnstra:l skrui ni veᵊr ni]

Come dance, come dance,
Kom dans, kom dans,
[kɔm da:ns kɔm da:ns]

And be merry.
En wees bly.
[ɛn veᵊs bləj]

Dance evening-flower, your
sweetheart waits.
Dans, aandblom, jou liefste wag.
[da:ns 'a:ntblɔm jœu 'lifstə vax]

So long for you,
Al solank op jou,
[al 'sʊᵊlaŋk ɔp jœu]

Bring a pearl for your calyx,
Bring 'n pêrel vir jou kelkie,
[brəŋ ə 'pæ:rəl fər jœu 'kæᵊlki]

Of the purest dew.
Van die reinste dou.
[fan di 'rəjnstə dœu]

The evening-flower listens to the
alluring voice,
Die aandblom luister na die lokstem,
[di 'a:ntblɔm 'lœystər na di 'lɔkstɛm]

Spreads her petals open,
Sprei haar blomrok oop,
[sprəj ɦa:r 'blɔmrɔk ʊᵊp]

Waltzes seductively over the (couch) grass,
Wals aanloklik oor die kweek,
[vals a:n'lɔklək ʊᵊr di kweᵊk]

Christened with moonlight's love.
Word met maanstraalliefd' gedoop.
[vɔrt mɛt 'ma:nstra:lift xə'dʊᵊp]

The moon disappears behind the hillside,
Die maan agter die bult verdwyn,
[di ma:n 'axtər di bœlt fər'dwəjn]

Her Cupid's arrow disappears.
Verdwyn haar liefdeskig.
[fər'dwəjn ɦa:r 'lifdəskəx]

The sun laughs mischievously,
Die son lag skelm,
[di sɔn lax 'skæᵊləm]

He will shine again,
Hy gaan weer skyn,
[ɦəj xa:n veᵊr skəjn]

She folds and closes her little leaves tightly.
Sy vou haar blaartjies dig.
[səj fœu ɦa:r 'bla:rkis dəx]

Away with grief, weep no more,
Weg met droefheid, treur nie meer nie,
[væx mɛt 'druffiəjt trjø°r ni meᵊr ni]

Happy field and valley,
Vrolik veld en vlei,
['frʊᵊlək fæᵊlt ɛn fləj]

---

³ An expansive African prairie, field, or pasture, comprising a wide variety of vegetation which may be used in various ways, including agriculture or uncultivated countryside.

The warm sunbeam scorches no more,
Warm sonstraal skroei nie weer nie,
['varəm 'sɔnstra:l skrui ni veᵊr ni]

Come dance and be merry.
Kom dans, en wees bly.
[kɔm da:ns ɛn veᵊs bləj]

Dance evening-flower, your sweetheart waits
Dans aandblom, jou liefste wag
[da:ns 'a:ntblɔm jœu 'lifstə vax]

So long for you,
Al solank op jou,
[al 'sʊᵊlaŋk ɔp jœu]

Bring a pearl for your calyx,
Bring 'n pêrel vir jou kelkie,
[brəŋ ə 'pæ:rəl fər jœu 'kæᵊlki]

Of the purest dew.
Van die reinste dou.
[fan di 'rəjnstə dœu]

PHILIP DE VOS
(b. 1939)

Oh My Goodness! An Insect—Silly Verses for Naughty Children, Song Cycle[1]
O togga! 'n Gogga—Lawwe Versies vir stout Kinders, Sangsiklus
[ʊᵊ ˈtɔxa ə ˈxɔxa ˈlavə ˈfæːrsis fər stœut ˈkəndərs saŋ ˈsəkləs]
Music: Albie Louw (1926–2017)

Pluck the Strings, Blow (on) the Flute
1. *Pluk die Snare, blaas die Fluit*
[plœk di ˈsnaːrə blaːs di flœyt]

Pluck the strings, blow (on) the flute,
Pluk die snare, blaas die fluit,
[plœk di ˈsnaːrə blaːs di flœyt]

Strum out twenty little ditties
Tokkel twintig deuntjies uit
[ˈtɔkəl ˈtwəntəx ˈdjøɲkis œyt]

When I come tomorrow afternoon
As ek môremiddag kom
[as ɛk ˌmɔːrəˈmədax kɔm]

With my gardenia.
Met my katjiepieringblom.
[mɛt məj ˌkaˈkiˈpirəŋblɔm]

Come with Me to Toorberg
2. *Kom saam met my na Toorberg*[2]
[kɔm saːm mɛt məj na ˈtʊᵊrbæːrx]
Music also by: Peter James Leonard Klatzow (1945–2021)

Come with me to (the) Enchanted Mountain
Kom saam met my na Toorberg
[kɔm saːm mɛt məj na ˈtʊᵊrbæːrx]

We must climb Toorberg to the
mountaintop
Toorberg moet ons uit
[ˈtʊᵊrbæːrx mut ɔns œyt]

---

[1] Permission granted by Philip de Vos.
[2] "Toorberg" is an imaginary enchanted place for which the poet, Philip de Vos, did not have a specific location in mind. The *bamboesfluit*, translated as 'bamboo flute,' may allude to the Pied Piper.

Afrikaans Art Song Literature. Christian Bester and Bronwen Forbay, Oxford University Press. © Oxford University Press 2025.
DOI: 10.1093/oso/9780197660812.003.0008

And on the summit of Toorberg
En op die top van Toorberg
[ɛn ɔp di tɔp fan 'tʊᵊrbæ:rx]

I (will) play my bamboo flute.
Speel ek my bamboesfluit.
[speᵊl ɛk məj bam'busflœyt]

Whirlwind
3. *Warrelwind*
['varəlvənt]

Whirlwind come and whirl me
Warrelwind kom warrel my
['varəlvənt kɔm 'varəl məj]

When you tire, put me down,
As jy moeg word, sit my neer,
[as jəj mux vɔrt sət məj neᵊr]

Over the field and over the valley.
Oor die veld³ en oor die vlei.
[ʊᵊr di fæᵃlt ɛn ʊᵊr di fləj]

But (please) do it again tomorrow afternoon!
Maar doen dit môremiddag weer!
[ma:r dun dət 'mɔ:rəˌmədax veᵊr]

The Tumbleweed Is a Rolling Stone
4. *Rolbos is 'n Tolbos*
['rɔlbɔs əs ə 'tɔlbɔs]

The tumbleweed is a rolling stone,
Rolbos is 'n tolbos,
['rɔlbɔs əs ə 'tɔlbɔs]

Blown away to who knows where
Weggewaai tot wie weet waar
['væxəɣa:j tɔt vi veᵊt va:r]

A bush that runs, springs, and bolts.
'n Hardloop spring en holbos.
[ə 'ɦartlʊᵊp sprəŋ ɛn 'ɦɔlbɔs]

Across the mountain and the ledge,
Oor die berg en oor die rant,
[ʊᵊr di bæ:rx ɛn ʊᵊr di rant]

If you seek it here, it is over there
Soek jy hier is hy daar
[suk jəj ɦi:r əs ɦəj da:r]

Blown away to another land.
Weggewaai tot annerland.
['væxəɣa:j tɔt 'anərlant]

---

³ An expansive African prairie, field, or pasture, comprising a wide variety of vegetation which may be used in various ways, including agriculture or uncultivated countryside.

Take a Small Piece of (the) Sun
5. *Neem 'n stukkie Son*
[neᵊm ə ˈstœki sɔn]

Take a small piece of (the) sun,
Neem 'n stukkie son,
[neᵊm ə ˈstœki sɔn]

Take a small piece of (the) moon,
Neem 'n stukkie maan,
[neᵊm ə ˈstœki ma:n]

A droplet taken out of the big ocean.
Druppeltjie getap uit die grote oseaan.
[ˈdrœpəlki xəˈtap œyt di ˈxrʊᵊtə ʊᵊsiˈa:n]

A grain of sand
Korreltjie sand
[ˈkɔrəlki sant]

A fine grain (of sand)
Korreltjie fyn
[ˈkɔrəlki fəjn]

A grain taken from out (of) the sandy desert
Korreltjie gehaal uit die sandwoestyn
[ˈkɔrəlki xəˈɦa:l œyt di ˈsantvu ̩stəjn]

Throw it into your knapsack
Gooi dit in jou knapsak
[xo:j dət ən jœu ˈknapsak]

Keep it as collateral
Hou dit as 'n pand
[ɦœu dət as ə pant]

For the road that continues to the side of the
morning star.
*Vir die pad wat aanhou na die môrester
se kant.*
[fər di pat vat ˈa:nɦœu na di ˈmɔ:rəstær
sə kant]

If You Come to Visit Me
6. *As jy by my kom kuier*
[as jəj bəj məj kɔm ˈkœyər]

If you come to visit me
As jy by my kom kuier
[as jəj bəj məj kɔm ˈkœyər]

Then I will give you a shoe,
Dan gee ek jou 'n skoen,
[dan çeᵊ ɛk jœu ə skun]

A cake decorated with forty rats
'n Koek met veertig rotte op
[ə kuk mɛt ˈfeᵊrtəx ˈrɔtə ɔp]

And a grandma's sloppy kiss.
En 'n ou verlepte soen.
[ɛn ə œu fərˈlɛptə sun]

PHILIP DE VOS   45

You Remain Little
7. *Jy bly klein*
[jəj bləj kləjn]

You remain little,
Jy bly klein,
[jəj bləj kləjn]

(Because) of weak wine.
Van kasaterwaterwyn.
[fan ka'sa:tərɣatərvəjn]

You become tall,
Jy word groot,
[jəj vɔrt xrʊᵊt]

Because of koekmakranka bread
Van 'n koekmakrankabrood.[4]
[fan ə kukma'kraŋkabrʊᵊt]

The Mantis and the Spider
8. *Hotnotsgot en Spinnekop*
['ɦɔtnɔtsxɔt ɛn 'spənəkɔp]

The mantis and the spider,
Hotnotsgot en spinnekop,
['ɦɔtnɔtsxɔt ɛn 'spənəkɔp]

With their weird little bodies,
Met hul snaakse lyfies,
[mɛt ɦœl 'sna:ksə 'ləjfis]

The mantis and the spider
Hotnotsgot en spinnekop
['ɦɔtnɔtsxɔt ɛn 'spənəkɔp]

Also have strange little wifeys.
Het ook snaakse wyfies.
[ɦɛt ʊᵊk 'sna:ksə 'vəjfis]

The little wifey says "I love you, my darling
web-spinning-mantis-thief
*Wyfie sê "Ek het jou lief, my harte
hotnotspinnedief,*
['vəjfi sɛ: ɛk ɦɛt jœu lif məj 'ɦartə
'ɦɔtnɔt͵spənədif]

You make my heart skip a beat
Jy laat my hart so springgalop
[jəj la:t məj ɦart sʊᵊ 'sprəŋxa͵lɔp]

I could just eat you up right now!"
Ek vreet jou sommer nou-nou op!"
[ɛk freᵊt jœu 'sɔmər nœu nœu ɔp]

Were you a little insect hubby
Was jy 'n goggamannetjie
[vas jəj ə ͵xɔxa'maniki]

---

[4] "Koekmakrankabrood" (*Gethyllisis*) is one of the world's rarest fruits. It grows underground like a truffle, and only surfaces when ripe. According to the poet, the origin of the word *koekmakranka* is unknown. However, it phonetically resembles the click-click-click-click sounds of a Khoi word. The word is intentionally used by the poet in a nonsensical and humorous way.

46 AFRIKAANS ART SONG LITERATURE

And she a little insect wifey,
En sy 'n goggavroutjie,
[ɛn səj ə ˌxɔxaˈfrœuki]

Then you will perhaps on a rainy day (while
with her) have a disagreement.
*Dan loop jy op 'n reëndag dalk met haar 'n
goggabloutjie.*
[dan lʊəp jəj ɔp ə ˈreəndax dalk mɛt ɦaːr ə
ˌxɔxaˈblœuki]

And when the clouds part,
En as die wolke opklaar,
[ɛn as di ˈvɔlkə ˈɔpklaːr]

Then the little wifey might say:
Dan sê die goggavroutjie:
[dan sɛ: di ˌxɔxaˈfrœuki]

"Here in my tiny insect cage
"Hier in my goggakoutjie
[ɦiːr ən məj ˈxɔxaˌkœuki]

Is space for you, (my) little insect hubby!"
Is plek ou goggaoutjie!"
[əs plɛk œu ˈxɔxaˌœuki]

Gosh, Dang It!
9. *Gomverdorie, Poetoepap*[5]
['xɔmfərˌdʊəri ˈputupap]

Gosh, dang it,
Gomverdorie, poetoepap,
['xɔmfərˌdʊəri ˈputupap]

An ant stepped on my toe!
'n Mier het op my toon kom trap!
[ə miːr ɦɛt ɔp məj tʊən kɔm trap]

For that I beat him senseless
Toe slaan ek hom 'n pappery
[tu slaːn ɛk ɦɔm ə ˈpapərəj]

(I) trampled his toe as payback.
Oor sy toon kom trappery.
[ʊər səj tʊən kɔm ˈtrapərəj]

Poor thing,
Jitte tog,
['jətə tɔx]

When little Johnny sneezed
Toe Jannie nies,
[tu ˈjani nis]

A flea bit him on his cheek.
Byt 'n vlooi hom in sy kies.
[bəjt ə floːj ɦɔm ən səj kis]

Grab a hammer, smack him dead!
Gryp die hamer, slaat hom dood!
[xrəjp di ˈɦaːmər slaːt ɦɔm dʊət]

---

[5] The poet intentionally pairs the words *Gomverdorie, poetoepap* in a nonsensical way. The word *poetoepap*, also spelled *putu pap*, or *phuthu*, is the name of a popular South African traditional dish often found at *braais* (the South African term for barbeques). A staple food in many homes, it is made with maize and water, milk, or butter. Various cooking methods result in many different textures. For example, *poetoe* can resemble grits when in liquid form, or when its consistency hardens, a crumbly porridge called *krummel pap*.

Little Johnny grows up toothless.
Tandeloos word Jannie groot.
['tandəlʊᵊs vɔrt 'jani xrʊᵊt]

Petronella, Cockroach
10. *Petronella, Kokkerot*
['peᵊtrunɛla kɔkə'rɔt]

Petronella, cockroach,
Petronella, kokkerot,
['peᵊtrunɛla kɔkə'rɔt]

There is a dairy cow inside the pot.
Daar's 'n melkkoei in die pot.
[da:rs ə 'mæᵃlkui ən di pɔt]

I open the lid and she says:
Ek lig die deksel sy sê:
[ɛk ləx di 'dɛksəl səj sɛ:]

MOO!!
MOE!!
[mu:]

So I closed the lid again (then).
Toe maak ek weer die deksel toe.
[tu ma:k ɛk veᵊr di 'dɛksəl tu]

Grandma's Lay-Away Hen
11. *Ouma het 'n Weglêhoender*[6]
['œuma fiɛt ə 'væxlɛːˌfiundər]

Grandma chased a lay-away hen
Ouma het 'n weglêhoender
['œuma fiɛt ə 'væxlɛːˌfiundər]

Shoo-ed her out of the house.
Uit die huis uit uitgeboender.
[œyt di fiœys œyt 'œytxəˌbundər]

The hen (dared) to lay an egg
Sy't 'n ei'r gelê
[səjt ə əjr xə'lɛ:]

In the sugar bag
In die suikersak
[ən di 'sœykərsak]

And a double-yolked egg in the pantry
En 'n dubbeldoor op die spens se rak
[ɛn ə 'dœbəldʊᵊr ɔp di spɛns sə rak]

And a half-dozen in the coffee tin.
En 'n halfdosyn in die koffieblik.
[ɛn ə 'fialfduˌsəjn ən di 'kɔfiblək]

---

[6] A hen that lays eggs in hidden nests.

48 AFRIKAANS ART SONG LITERATURE

You (obstinate) lay-away hen, you're unfit!
Jou weglêding jy's ongeskik!
[jœu 'væxlɛ:dəŋ jəjs 'ɔnxəˌskək]

The Sharks in the Sea
12. *Die Haaie in die See*
[di 'ɦa:jə ən di seᵊ]

The sharks in the sea like citronella tea,
Die haaie in die see hou van sitronellatee,
[di 'ɦa:jə ən di seᵊ ɦœu fan sitru'nɛlateᵊ]

And their little Sunday afternoon snack
En hul Sondagmiddag happie
[ɛn ɦœl 'sɔndaxˌmədax 'ɦapi]

Is aunt Isabel du Preez
Is tannie Isabel du Preez
[əs 'tani 'isabæᵊl dy preᵊ]

Ahoy mister whale, how is the water?
Hallo walvis hoesie water?
['ɦælou 'valfəs 'ɦusi 'va:tər]

Wet, my friend, see you later!
Nat, ou pellie, sien jou later!
[nat œu 'pæli sin jœu 'la:tər]

Oh Golly Gosh
13. *O gits en gaats*
[ʊᵊ xəts ɛn xa:ts]

Oh golly gosh,
O gits en gaats,
[ʊᵊ xəts ɛn xa:ts]

Oh now and then,
O nou en dan,
[ʊᵊ nœu ɛn dan]

Here comes the knick-knack little man.
Hier kom die tierlantyntjieman.
[ɦi:r kɔm di 'ti:rlanˌtəjŋkiman]

He has a hat and boots on
Hy het 'n hoed en stewels
[ɦəj ɦɛt ə ɦut ɛn 'steᵊvəls]

And a pair of mismatched socks.
En 'n onpaar sokkies aan.
[ɛn ə 'ɔnpa:r 'sɔkis a:n]

I Arrived Here
14. *Ek kom hier aan*
[ɛk kɔm ɦii:r a:n]

I arrived here from here and there
Ek kom hier aan van hot en haar
[ɛk kɔm ɦii:r a:n fan ɦɔt ɛn ɦa:r]

And hop through the wheatfields with my homemade guitar.
En huppel deur die hawer met my snaarkitaar.
[ɛn 'ɦœpəl djøᵊr di 'ɦa:vər mɛt məj 'sna:rki̯ta:r]

I stamp my feet,
Ek stamp my voete,
[ɛk stamp məj 'futə]

I nod my head
Ek knik my kop
[ɛk knək məj kɔp]

And dance through the dunes with a hop, skip, and a jump.
En dans deur die duine op 'n hopgalop.
[ɛn da:ns djøᵊr di 'dœynə ɔp ə 'ɦɔpxa̯lɔp]

Dance with a hop, skip, and a jump.
Dans so op 'n hopgalop.
[da:ns sʊᵊ ɔp ə 'ɦɔpxa̯lɔp]

Devil's Children Give Me the Heebie-Jeebies
15. *Satanskinders laat my gril*
['sa:tans̬kəndərs la:t məj xrəl]

Devil's children give me the heebie-jeebes
Satanskinders laat my gril
['sa:tans̬kəndərs la:t məj xrəl]

As do iguanas and crocodiles,
Likkewaan en krokodil,
[ləkə'va:n ɛn krɔkə'dəl]

Lizards and (a) pitch black snake
Koggelman en pikswart slang
['kɔxəlman ɛn 'pəkswart slaŋ]

Geez, mommy, I'm afraid!
Gits, my mamma, ek is bang!
[xəts məj 'mama ɛk əs baŋ]

Be wary of the mamba that sambas all day,
Pas op vir die mamba[7] wat heeldag wil samba,
[pas ɔp fər di 'mamba vat 'ɦeᵊldax vəl 'samba]

---

[7] The black mamba (*Dendroaspis polylepis, Elapidae*) is generally brown or gray in color. Indigenous to sub-Saharan Africa, it is large, agile, fast moving, and highly venomous. If left untreated, its bite results in an almost 100% mortality rate. Like cobras, mambas may rear their heads and form a hood as part of their defense mechanism. The subject of numerous legends, the black mamba is considered one of the most dangerous and highly feared snakes.

Who thinks he knows all about the long-winded waltz.
Wat dink hy weet als van die langasemwals.
[vat dəŋk ɦəj veᵊt als fan di 'laŋˌa:səmvals]

His life is dull, his life is boring,
Sy lewe is vaal, sy lewe is saai,
[səj 'leᵊvə əs fa:l səj 'leᵊvə əs sa:j]

And now he wants to do the polka and swing-tickey-draai
En nou wil hy polka en swaaitiekiedraai[8]
[ɛn nœu vəl ɦəj 'pɔlka ɛn swa:jˌtiki'dra:j]

And tickey-swing, tickey-draai, draai, draai...
Tiekieswaai Tiekiedraai, draai, draai, draai...
[ˌtiki'swa:j ˌtiki'dra:j dra:j]

Twelve Little Sardines in a Can
16. *Twaalf Sardientjies in 'n Blik*
[twa:lf sar'diɲkis ən ə blək]

Twelve little sardines in a can
Twaalf sardientjies in 'n blik
[twa:lf sar'diɲkis ən ə blək]

For heaven's sake, stop pushing please!
Hemel hou tog net op met druk!
['ɦeᵊməl ɦœu tɔx nɛt ɔp mɛt drœk]

It's me and you, and me and her,
Dis jy en ek, en ek en sy,
[dəs jəj ɛn ɛk ɛn ɛk ɛn səj]

And you and her, and me and him,
En jy en sy en ek en hy,
[ɛn jəj ɛn səj ɛn ɛk ɛn ɦəj]

And him and her and you and you,
En hy en sy en jy en jy,
[ɛn ɦəj ɛn səj ɛn jəj ɛn jəj]

This shakedown is too much for me!
Dié kermisbed's te veel vir my.
['di 'kærməsbɛts tə feᵊl fər məj]

I am not going to stay here any longer.
Hier gaan ek niks langer bly.
[ɦi:r xa:n ɛk nəks 'laŋər bləj]

Your elbow (is) pushing into my side!
Jou elmboog druk in my sy!
[jœu 'æləmbʊᵊx drœk ən məj səj]

---

[8] A fast dance-movement derived from Cape square-dancing. Couples link hands, lean away from each other, and spin around on their toes while remaining on one spot.

PHILIP DE VOS   51

The Cat's Cheek
17. *Die Kat se Kies*
[di kat sə kis]

The cat's cheek,
Die kat se kies,
[di kat sə kis]

The dog's flank,
Die hond se lies,
[di fiɔnt sə lis]

The calf loves colostrum.
Koei se kind is lief vir bies.[9]
[kui sə kənt əs lif fər bis]

Twist his little neck from pillar to post
Draai sy nekkie hot om haar om
[dra:j səj 'nɛki fiɔt ɔm fia:r ɔm]

And then you tell me why.
En dan sê jy vir my waarom.
[ɛn dan sɛ: jəj fər məj va:r'ɔm]

Little Turtle Dove
18. *Tortelduifie*
['tɔrtəlˌdœyfi]

Little turtle dove in flight
Tortelduifie, in die vlug
['tɔrtəlˌdœyfi ən di flœx]

A tiny feather drops from the sky.
Val 'n veertjie uit die lug.
[fal ə 'feᵊrki œyt di lœx]

When it frolics on my hat,
As hy op my hoed rinkink,
[as fiəj ɔp məj fiut rəŋ'kəŋk]

It will remind me of your cooing.
Sal ek aan jou koerkoer dink.
[sal ɛk a:n jœu 'ku:rku:r dəŋk]

Cooing, cooing.
Koerkoer, koerkoer.
['ku:rku:r 'ku:rku:r]

[9] The milky fluid secreted by mammals who have recently given birth before breast milk production begins. It contains a high protein and antibody content.

AFRIKAANS ART SONG LITERATURE

Up in the Attic
19. *Bo in die Solder*
[bʊᵊ ən di ˈsɔldər]

Up in the topsy turvy attic
Bo in die solder holderstebolder
[bʊᵊ ən di ˈsɔldər ˈfiɔldərstəˌbɔldər]

I found an old guitar.
Kry ek 'n ou kitaar.
[krəj ɛk ə œu kiˈta:r]

(I) Play then a little of my wait-a-minute song,
Speel dan 'n bietjie my wag-'n-bietjie liedjie,
[speᵊl dan ə ˈbiki məj ˈvaxəˌbiki ˈliki]

(I) Play it from beginning to end.
Speel hom kant en klaar.
[speᵊl fiɔm kant ɛn kla:r]

If You Find Yourself Malingering
20. *Kry jy papelellekoors*
[krəj jəj papəˈlæləkʊᵊrs]

If you find yourself malingering, then you suffer for many days.
Kry jy papelellekoors ly jy baie dae.
[krəj jəj papəˈlæləkʊᵊrs ləj jəj ˈbajə ˈdaə]

You lie, you suffer, and you contract thirteen other plagues:
Lê jy, ly jy en dan kry jy dertien ander plae:
[lɛ: jəj ləj jəj ɛn krəj jəj ˈdærtin ˈandər ˈpla:ə]

Pain in your toenail, pain in your throat,
Pyn in jou toonnael, pyn in jou krop,
[pəjn ən jœu ˈtʊᵊˌna:l pəjn ən jœu krɔp]

Pain in your pinky, pain in your shell (body).
Pyn in jou pinkie, pyn in jou dop.
[pəjn ən jœu ˈpəŋki pəjn ən jœu dɔp]

Thirty days and nights of pain and complaining
Dertig dae en nagte lank is tyd van pyn en klae
[ˈdærtəx ˈda:ə en ˈnaxtə laŋk əs təjt fan pəjn ɛn ˈkla:ə]

But before you know it,
En nog voor jy jou kom kry,
[ɛn nɔx fʊᵊr jəj jœu kɔm krəj]

Better days (will) lie ahead.
Wag daar beter dae.
[vax da:r ˈbeᵊtər ˈda:ə]

Piet Fourie

21. *Piet Fourie*

[pit fu'ri]

Piet Fourie had a cramp, early on Monday morning.
Piet Fourie het 'n kramp gekry, vroeg op Maandagmôre.
[pit fu'ri ɦɛt ə kramp xə'krəj frux ɔp 'ma:ndaxˌmɔ:rə]

Turn his big toe, keep a watchful eye,
Draai sy groottoon, hou hom dop,
[dra:j səj 'xrʊᵊtʊᵊn ɦœu ɦɔm dɔp]

Put a bedbug on his head, early on Monday morning
Sit 'n weeluis op sy kop, vroeg op Maandagmôre.
[sət ə 'veᵊlœys ɔp səj kɔp frux ɔp 'ma:ndaxˌmɔ:rə]

The cramps must come to an end,
Krampe moet tog einde kry,
['krampə mut tɔx 'əjndə krəj]

No one, no one should suffer like this, on a Monday morning.
Niemand, niemand mag so ly, op 'n Maandagmôre.
['nimant 'nimant max sʊᵊ ləj ɔp 'ma:ndaxˌmɔ:rə]

Pull his hair, give him a strong drink,
Trek sy hare, gee hom dop,
[træ:k səj 'ɦa:rə çeᵊ ɦɔm dɔp]

Give (him also) moth-larva soup
Gee ook mottelarwe sop
[çeᵊ ʊᵊk 'mɔtəˌlarvə sɔp]

Early on Monday morning.
Vroeg op Maandagmôre.
[frux ɔp 'ma:ndaxˌmɔ:rə]

What Is the Difference?

22. *Wat is die verskil?*

[vat əs di fər'skəl]

What is the difference between cats and mice?
Wat is die verskil tussen katte en muise?
[vat əs di fər'skəl 'tœsən 'katə ɛn 'mœysə]

Mice have tails and cats have lice
Muise het sterte en katte het luise
['mœysə ɦɛt 'stærtə ɛn 'katə ɦɛt 'lœysə]

Although mice and cats both have tails,
Ook muise het sterte en so ook 'n kat,
[ʊᵊk 'mœysə ɦɛt 'stærtə ɛn sʊᵊ ʊᵊk ə kat]

But no louse has a mouse or a cat on his shoulder-blade.
Maar geen luis het 'n muis of 'n kat op sy blad.
[ma:r çeᵊn lœys ɦɛt ə mœys ɔf ə kat ɔp səj blat]

A mouse has a louse and a tail like a horse,
'n Muis het 'n luis en 'n stert nes 'n perd,
[ə mœys ɦɛt ə lœys ɛn ə stært nɛs ə pært]

AFRIKAANS ART SONG LITERATURE

And horses have lice, but never suffer
from mice,
En perde het luise, maar ly nooit aan muise,
[ɛn 'pærdə fiɛt 'lœysə ma:r ləj no:jt a:n
'mœysə]

And cats have lice and long silky tails,
En katte het luise en lang gladde sterte,
[ɛn 'katə fiɛt 'lœysə en laŋ 'xladə 'stærtə]

And sometimes they look dreamily into
the distance
En soms kyk hul dromerig doer in die verte
[ɛn sɔms kəjk fiɶl 'drʊᵊmərəx du:r ən di
'færtə]

At mice, and lice, and horses like houses
Na muise en luise en perde soos huise
[na 'mœysə ɛn 'lœysə ɛn 'pærdə sʊᵊs 'fiœysə]

And that's how you know,
En dis hoe jy weet,
[ɛn dəs fiu jəj veᵊt]

What cats and mice are.
Wat is katte en muise.
[vat əs 'katə ɛn 'mœysə]

Consternation
23. *Konsternasie*
[kɔnstər'na:si]

Consternation, I'm freaking out!
Konsternasie, hoenderpiep![10]
[kɔnstər'na:si 'fiundərpip]

The sea lies blue and is awfully deep.
Die see lê blou en vreeslik diep.
[di seᵊ lɛ: blœu ɛn 'freᵊslək dip]

The deep, deep blue sea (that) I have to
cross tomorrow,
Diep diep blou see moet ek môre oor,
[dip dip blœu seᵊ mut ɛk 'mɔ:rə ʊᵊr]

But the map for it
Maar die kaart daarvoor
[ma:r di ka:rt da:r'fʊᵊr]

I have already lost.
Het ek klaar verloor.
[fiɛt ɛk kla:r fər'lʊᵊr]

---

[10] The literal translation of *hoenderpiep* refers to Newcastle Disease Virus (NDV). This contagious and fatal viral disease affects the respiratory, nervous, and digestive systems in birds and poultry. In this context, the nervous symptoms of NDV describe the narrator's highly emotional state.

Susanna Viljee
24. *Susanna Viljee*
[su'sana fəl'jeᵊ]

Susanna Viljee wears mismatched shoes.
Susanna Viljee dra onpaar skoene.
[su'sana fəl'jeᵊ dra: 'ɔnpa:r 'skunə]

One was pale, the other green.
Die een was 'n vale, die ander 'n groene.
[di eᵊn vas ə 'fa:lə di 'andər ə 'xrunə]

And when she became bored, she
bought a cow.
En toe sy verveeld raak, toe koop sy 'n bees.
[ɛn tu səj fər'feᵊlt ra:k tu kʊᵊp səj ə beᵊs]

A giant of a cow,
'n Reus van 'n bees,
[ə rjøᵊs fan ə beᵊs]

But the cow died on the fourteenth day of
June, or May
*Maar die bees gee die gees op die veertiende
dag van Junie of Mei*
[ma:r di beᵊs çeᵊ di çeᵊs ɔp di 'feᵊrtində dax
fan 'juni ɔf məj]

Oh, how you should have seen Suzie suffer.
En toe moes jul sien hoe Susannatjie ly.
[ɛn tu mus jœl sin fiu su'sanaki ləj]

And when she became bored, she
bought a dog.
En toe sy verveeld raak, toe koop sy 'n hond.
[ɛn tu səj fər'feᵊlt ra:k tu kʊᵊp səj ə fiɔnt]

A lump of a dog,
'n Klont van 'n hond,
[ə klɔnt fan ə fiɔnt]

And she painted the dog: orange and yellow,
and a small dab of green
*En sy kleur sy vel bont: oranje en geel, 'n klein
tikkie groen*
[ɛn səj kljøᵊr səj fæl bɔnt ʊᵊ'ranjə ɛn çeᵊl ə
kləjn 'təki xrun]

And named him: My darling little, Orange.
En noem hom: My lieweling diertjie Lemoen.
[ɛn num fiɔm məj 'livələŋ 'di:rki lə'mun]

And when she became bored, she bought
an ant:
En toe sy verveeld raak toe koop sy 'n mier:
[ɛn tu səj fər'feᵊlt ra:k tu kʊᵊp səj ə mi:r]

A delightful little ant,
'n Plesier van 'n mier,
[ə plə'si:r fan ə mi:r]

But the animal fancied singing day and
night, night and day:
*Maar die dier het die gier om liedjies te sing
dag en nag, nag en dag:*
[ma:r di di:r fiɛt di çi:r ɔm 'likis tə səŋ dax
ɛn nax nax ɛn dax]

Beethoven and Schubert and little morsels
of Bach
Beethoven en Schubert en tikseltjies Bach
['beᵊtfiʊᵊfən ɛn'ʃubərt ɛn 'təksəlkis bax]

And when she became bored, she bought
a goat,
En toe sy verveeld raak, toe koop sy 'n bok,
[ɛn tu səj fər'feᵊlt ra:k tu kʊᵊp səj ə bɔk]

A burly goat
'n Blok van 'n bok
[ə blɔk fan ə bɔk]

Who lives in his pen but overstuffs himself
on bacon and oranges
En hy bly in sy hok, maar vreet hom half
disnis aan spek en sitroene
[ɛn ɦəj bləj ən səj ɦɔk ma:r freᵊt ɦɔm ɦalf
ˈdəsnəs a:n spɛk ɛn siˈtrunə]

And socks and pants and drab rabbit
fur shoes,
En kouse en broeke en vaal haasvel skoene,
[ɛn ˈkœusə ɛn ˈbrukə ɛn fa:l ˈɦa:sfæl ˈskunə]

And then little Suzie became bored beyond
belief…
En toe raak Susanna verveler as veeld…
[ɛn tu ra:k suˈsana fərˈfeᵊlər as feᵊlt]

And she stepped on the ant (the fun ant)
En sy trap op die mier (die mier met die gier)
[ɛn səj trap ɔp di mi:r di mi:r mɛt di çi:r]

And she thought of the spirit (the spirit of
the cow)
En sy dink aan die gees (die gees van
haar bees)
[ɛn səj dəŋk a:n di çeᵊs di çeᵊs fan ɦa:r beᵊs]

And sold off the pen (the pen and the goat)
En verkoop toe die hok (die hok met die bok)
[ɛn fərˈkuᵊp tu di ɦɔk di ɦɔk mɛt di bɔk]

And she kissed, kissed, kissed her darling
little pet, Orange
En sy soen soen soen soen liefling
diertjie Lemoen
[ɛn səj sun sun sun sun ˈlifləŋˌdi:rki ləˈmun]

And she married a man, and her last name
became Viljoen.
En sy trou met 'n man en haar van word
Viljoen.
[ɛn səj trœu mɛt ə man ɛn ɦa:r fan vɔrt
fəlˈjun]

Oh my goodness! An insect!
O togga! 'n Gogga!
[ʊᵊ ˈtɔxa ə ˈxɔxa]

BEN DREYER

(n.d.)

Little Bushveld House[1]
Bosveld[2] Huisie
['bɔsfæalt 'fiœysi]
Music: S. le Roux Marais (1896–1979), "Six Art Songs" (_Ses Kunsliedere, no. 2_)
[sɛs 'kœns͵lidərə]

There's a little house in the Bushveld with a
rugged thatched roof.
_Daar's 'n huisie in die Bosveld met sy grasdak
ru gedek._
[da:rs ə 'fiœysi ən di 'bɔsfæalt mɛt səj
'xrasdak ry xə'dɛk]

(Built) with stakes and plastered claypot
walls, licked deep by small stock animals.
_Met sy pale pot klei mure, diep deur kleinvee
uitgelek._
[mɛt səj 'pa:lə pɔt kləj 'my:rə dip djøər
'kləjnfeə 'œytxə͵lɛk]

There's a little Bushveld house consumed by
the dense bush,
_Daar's 'n huisie in die Bosveld tussen bosse
gans verdwaal,_
[da:rs ə 'fiœysi ən di 'bɔsfæalt 'tœsən 'bɔsə
xans fər'dwa:l]

With its faint oil lamp as the night's
dusk falls.
_Met sy floue olie lamplig as die nag se
donker daal._
[mɛt səj 'flœuə 'ʊəli 'lampləx as di nax sə
'dɔŋkər da:l]

By day or by night, there's always room in
the little house.
_Daar's 'n herberg in die huisie altyd daar by
dag of nag._
[da:rs ə 'fiærbærx ən di 'fiœysi 'altəjt da:r bəj
dax ɔf nax]

There is a smile, there is peace
Daar's 'n glimlag, daar is vrede
[da:rs ə 'xləmlax da:r əs 'freədə]

And forgotten pomp and circumstance.
En vergete pronk of prag.
[ɛn fər'xeətə prɔŋk ɔf prax]

---

[1] Permission granted by Van Schaik Publishers.
[2] Bosveld (_Bushveld_), an expansive African prairie consisting of mainly uncultivated countryside. It is situated in the
Limpopo and a small portion of the North West Provinces. Its grassy plains contain clusters of tall trees and shrubs.

Afrikaans Art Song Literature. Christian Bester and Bronwen Forbay, Oxford University Press. © Oxford University Press 2025.
DOI: 10.1093/oso/9780197660812.003.0009

IZAK DAVID DU PLESSIS

(1900–1981)
aka I. D. du Plessis

From Four Melancholy Songs[1]
Vier weemoedige Liedjies
[fiːr veˀˈmudəxə ˈlikis]
Arnold van Wyk (1916–1983)

In the Stillness of My Garden
3. *In die stilte van my Tuin*
[ən di ˈstəltə fan məj tœyn]
Music also by: Rosa Nepgen (1909–2001)

In the stillness of my garden
In die stilte van my tuin
[ən di ˈstəltə fan məj tœyn]

Sun and shadow flicker
Flikker son en skaduwee
[ˈfləkər sɔn ɛn ˈskaːdyveˀ]

Alternating against the wall.
Beurtelings op die muur.
[ˈbjøˀrtələŋs ɔp di myːr]

Leaves of exsanguinated roses
Blare van verbloeide rose
[ˈblaːrə fan fərˈbluidə ˈrʊˀsə]

Have been thickly strewn by the wind
Het die wind hier dikgestrooi
[ɦɛt di vənt ɦiːr ˈdəkxəˌstroːj]

In front of the open door.
Voor die ope deur.
[fʊˀr di ˈʊˀpə djøˀr]

And the moon-white butterflies float past
En die maanwit skoenlappers drywe
[ɛn di ˈmaːnvət ˈskunlapərs ˈdrəjvə]

Languidly in the fragrant sky.
Op die geurende lug lomerig verby.
[ɔp di ˈxjøˀrəndə lœx ˈlʊˀmərəx fərˈbəj]

Also, the heart that loves you
Ook die hart wat jou bemin
[ʊˀk di ɦart vat jœu bəˈmən]

Feels the bliss of the hour
Voel die vreugde van die uur
[ful di ˈfrjøˀxdə fan di yːr]

---

[1] Permission granted by NB Publishers.

Afrikaans Art Song Literature. Christian Bester and Bronwen Forbay, Oxford University Press. © Oxford University Press 2025.
DOI: 10.1093/oso/9780197660812.003.0010

As your mouth laughs just so.
As jou mond so lag.
[as jœu mɔnt sʊᵊ lax]

Cold Is the Wind
4. *Koud is die Wind*
[kœut əs di vənt]

Cold is the wind where Daphne dreams.
Koud is die wind waar Daphne droom.
[kœut əs di vənt va:r ˈdafnɛ drʊᵊm]

She who was so tender and warm …
Sy wat so teer en warm was …
[səj vat sʊᵊ teᵊr ɛn ˈvarəm vas]

And more beautiful than the laurel tree
En skoner as die lourierboom
[ɛn ˈskʊᵊnər as di lœuˈri:rbʊᵊm]

That waves over her resting place.
Wat oor haar rusplek waai.
[vat ʊᵊr ɦa:r ˈrœsplɛk va:j]

Now the bitter wind whistles for her
Nou fluit die bitter wind vir haar
[nœu flœyt di ˈbətər vənt fər ɦa:r]

And snow is packed around her door,
En sneeu pak om haar deur,
[ɛn sniu pak ɔm ɦa:r djøᵊr]

There below, as the wind subsides
Daar onder, as die wind bedaar
[da:r ˈɔndər as di vənt bəˈda:r]

You hear the waves rumble.
Hoor jy die branders dreun.
[ɦʊᵊr jəj di ˈbrandərs drjøᵊn]

Queer Love[2]
Vreemde[3] Liefde, Op. 7 [ˈfreᵊmdə ˈlifdə]
Music: Hubert du Plessis (1922–2011)

If I Have to Reveal This Queer Love of Mine
1. *As ek my vreemde Liefde bloot moes lê*
[as ɛk məj ˈfreᵊmdə ˈlifdə blʊᵊt mus lɛ:]

If I have to reveal this queer love of mine,
As ek my vreemde liefde bloot moes lê,
[as ɛk məj ˈfreᵊmdə ˈlifdə blʊᵊt mus lɛ:]

---

[2] Permission granted by NB Publishers.

[3] While the direct translation of *vreemde* means 'strange,' one of its synonyms is 'queer.' The authors have deliberately assigned the word 'queer' throughout this cycle in recognition of it being about the queer experience, and to counteract the reluctance of past reviewers and audiences to acknowledge this. While some may view this term as a historical slur, no pejorative connotation is intended.

How would the pious violators of beauty respond?
Wat sou die vrome skenders van die skoonheid sê?
[vat sœu di 'fruᵊmə 'skɛndərs fan di 'skuᵊnɦəjt sɛ:]

Would they, with holy indignation,
Sou hul, met heilige verontwaardiging,
[sœu ɦœl mɛt 'ɦəjləxə fərɔnt'va:rdəxəŋ]

Point defiling fingers towards God,
Besoedelende vingers Godswaarts steek,
[bə'sudələndə 'fəŋərs 'xɔtsva:rts steᵊk]

And after the cleansing of self-righteousness
En na díe selfregverdigende reiniging
[ɛn na 'di 'sæᵊlfræxˌfærdəxəndə 'rəjnəxəŋ]

Come to avenge their honor against me?
Hul eer aan my kom wreek?
[ɦœl eᵊr a:n məj kɔm vreᵊk]

Or would a spark from this fire that glows within me
Of sou 'n sprank van hierdie vuur wat in my gloei
[ɔf sœu ə spraŋk fan 'ɦi:rdi fy:r vat ən məj xlui]

Touch them, too, so that they will understand
Ook hulle aanraak, sodat hul verstaan
[uᵊk 'ɦœlə 'a:nra:k 'suᵊdat ɦœl fər'sta:n]

(That) Love exists in a thousand forms?
Die liefde neem 'n duisend vorme aan?
[di 'lifdə neᵊm ə 'dœysənt 'fɔrmə a:n]

I Surrendered to You
2. *Ek het my aan jou oorgegee*
[ɛk ɦɛt məj a:n jœu 'uᵊrxəˌxeᵊ]
Music also by: Dawid S. Engela (1931–1967), "Songs of a Futile Love"
(*Liedere van 'n vergeefse Liefde, no. 1*) ['lidərə fan ə fər'xeᵊfsə 'lifdə]

I surrendered to you
Ek het my aan jou oorgegee
[ɛk ɦɛt məj a:n jœu 'uᵊrxəˌxeᵊ]

So unconditionally,
So onvoorwaardelik,
[suᵊ ɔnfuᵊr'va:rdələk]

That I sometimes fear
Dat ek soms vrees
[dat ɛk sɔms freᵊs]

Ruin is the only thing that eventually
Vernietiging is al wat daar uiteindelik
[fər'nitəxəŋ əs al vat da:r œyt'əjndələk]

Awaits me;
Vir my kan wees;
[fər məj kan veᵊs]

Because in days gone by I could, in the whispering
Want voorheen kon ek in die fluistering
[vant 'fuᵊrɦeᵊn kɔn ɛk ən di 'flœystərəŋ]

Of wind and water, hear other things:
Van wind en water ander dinge hoor:
[fan vənt ɛn ˈvaːtər ˈandər ˈdəŋə fiʊᵊr]

Now my soul in quiet contemplation
Nou het my siel in stille mymering
[nœu ɦɛt məj sil ən ˈstələ ˈməjmərəŋ]

Has lost its power.
Sy krag verloor.
[səj krax fərˈlʊᵊr]

It's you that whisper to me in the trees
Dis jy wat tot my fluister in die bome
[dəs jəj vat tɔt məj ˈflœystər ən di ˈbʊᵊmə]

And float closer (to me) on the wind;
En aangesweef kom op die wind;
[ɛn ˈaːnxəˌsweᵊf kɔm ɔp di vənt]

And only in you,
En slegs in jou,
[ɛn slæxs ən jœu]

Glorified through my dreams,
Verheerlik deur my drome,
[fərˈɦeᵊrlək djøᵊr məj ˈdrʊᵊmə]

Can I find myself again.
Kan ek myself weer vind.
[kan ɛk məjˈsæᵊlf veᵊr fənt]

The Heart of Dawn
3. *Die Hart van die Daeraad*
[di ɦart fan di ˈdaːəraːt]

The two of us rode into the heart of dawn
Die hart van die daeraad het ons twee ingery
[di ɦart fan di ˈdaːəraːt ɦɛt ɔns tweᵊ ˈənxəˌrəj]

And there (we) listened
En daar geluister
[ɛn daːr xəˈlœystər]

To the clear sandgrouse and low partridges.
Ná die helder kelkiewyn⁴ van vlak patryse.⁵
[ˈna: di ˈɦæᵊldər ˈkæᵊlkivəjn fan flak paˈtrəjsə]

What can we, after this togetherness,
Wat kan ons ná díe samesyn
[vat kan ɔns ˈna: di ˈsaːməsəjn]

Still get out of the fullness of life?
Nog uit die volle lewe kry?
[nɔx œyt di ˈfɔlə ˈleᵊvə krəj]

---

[4] The sandgrouse (*Pteroclidae*) is a ground-dwelling bird that inhabits treeless landscapes, including prairies, savannahs, and arid regions. Pigeon-like in appearance, they have compact bodies with plumage in unremarkable shades such as dull brown, gray, and yellowish-beige, which enables them to blend into their dusty environment.

[5] The gray partridge (*Phasianidae*) is a foraging, seed-eating bird that inhabits agricultural fields and grasslands. Portly and chicken-like in appearance, they have rust-colored streaks on their sides and dark patches on their bellies. Found in small groups called coveys, they are known for exploding into a squawking flight when disturbed, even from afar.

Coward with a Wife and Child
4. *Swakkeling met Vrou en Kind*
['swakələŋ mɛt frœu ɛn kənt]

Coward with a wife and child,
Swakkeling met vrou en kind,
['swakələŋ mɛt frœu ɛn kənt]

You that stand safely behind the blinds,
Jy wat so veilig agter skerms staan,
[jəj vat sʊᵊ 'fəjləx 'axtər 'skærəms sta:n]

Does it ever cross your mind,
Dink jy ooit,
[dəŋk jəj o:jt]

If the bitter wind thrashes against your
shuttered windows,
*As die bitter wind teen jou beskutte
vensters slaan,*
[as di 'bətər vənt teᵊn jœu bə'skœtə
'fɛnstərs sla:n]

That single (people) with their own might
Dat enkelinge met hul eie krag
[dat 'ɛŋkələŋə mɛt fɩœl 'əjə krax]

Have to struggle up steep slopes
Die steile hellings op moet beur
[di 'stəjlə 'fɩæᵃləŋs ɔp mut bjøᵊr]

To tear free from the night's clutches
Om uit die arms van die nag
[ɔm œyt di arms fan di nax]

Their own rescue?
Hul redding los te skeur?
[fɩœl 'rɛdəŋ lɔs tə skjøᵊr]

You who share your grief with others
Jy wat jou leed met ander deel
[jəj vat jœu leᵊt mɛt 'andər deᵊl]

And easily depend on love,
En maklik op die liefde leun,
[ɛn 'maklək ɔp di 'lifdə ljøᵊn]

What do you know of the raw weeping
Wat weet jy van die rou geween
[vat veᵊt jəj fan di rœu xə'veᵊn]

That follows every unseen defeat,
Wat volg op elke ongesiene nederlaag,
[vat fɔlx ɔp 'æᵃlkə 'ɔnxəˌsinə 'neᵊdərla:x]

You, that are blessed so generously
Jy, wat so mildelik geseën
[jəj vat sʊᵊ 'məldələk xə'seᵊn]

(That) you can challenge the world?
Die wêreld uit kan daag?
[di 'væ:rəlt œyt kan da:x]

I Know That in the Calm Togetherness
5. *Ek weet dat in die kalme Samesyn*
[ɛk veᵊt dat ən di 'kalmə 'sa:məsəjn]

I know that in the calm togetherness,
Ek weet dat in die kalme samesyn,
[ɛk veᵊt dat ən di 'kalmə 'sa:məsəjn]

When the meaningful dusk deepens,
As die betekenisvolle skemering verdiep,
[as di bə'teᵊkənəsˌfɔlə 'skeᵊmərəŋ fər'dip]

A magical trembling
'n Magiese deurhuiwering
[ə 'ma:xisə djøᵊr'ɦœyvərəŋ]

For you and me lies hidden;
Vir jou en my verborge lê;
[fər jœu ɛn məj fər'bɔrgə lɛ:]

Because pure and without passion
Want rein en sonder hartstog
[vant rəjn ɛn 'sɔndər 'ɦartstɔx]

Is this togetherness
Is dié samesyn
[əs 'di 'sa:məsəjn]

When we wordlessly
Wanneer ons sprakeloos
['vaneᵊr ɔns 'spra:kəlʊᵊs]

Notice a whisper inside of ourselves,
'n Fluistering in ons gewaar,
[ə 'flœystərəŋ ən ons xə'va:r]

A quiet purification
'n Stille suiwering
[ə 'stələ 'sœyvərəŋ]

Born out of shared experiences of joy
and pain.
Gebore uit saamdeurleefde vreug en pyn.
[xə'boᵊrə œyt 'sa:mdjøᵊrˌleᵊfdə frjøᵊx ɛn pəjn]

But when the hot blaze of my blood
Maar as die hete vlae van my bloed
[ma:r as di 'ɦeᵊtə 'fla:ə fan məj blut]

Beats upward as fiery desire,
In brandende begeerte opwaarts slaan,
[ən 'brandəndə bə'xeᵊrtə 'ɔpva:rts sla:n]

Then I know that an irresistible ardor
Dan weet ek dat 'n onweerstaanbare gloed
[dan veᵊt ɛk dat ə ɔnveᵊr'sta:nba:rə xlut]

Is aroused by the lust of your loins,
Verwek word deur die wellus van jou lede,
[fər'vɛk vɔrt djøᵊr di 'væᵊləs fan jœu leᵊdə]

And my passion takes on all the glory
En neem my hartstog ál die glorie aan
[ɛn neᵊm məj 'ɦartstɔx 'al di 'xlʊᵊri a:n]

Of these blind desires.
Van dié verblindende begeerlikhede.
[fan 'di fər'bləndəndə bə'xeᵊrləkˌɦieᵊdə]

No, Rather Death
6. *Nee, liewer die Dood*
[neᵊ ˈlivər di dʊᵊt]

No, rather death called separation
Nee, liewer die dood wat skeiding heet
[neᵊ ˈlivər di dʊᵊt vat ˈskəjdəŋ ɦeᵊt]

And the corpse's garment of loneliness
En die lykgewaad van die eensaamheid
[ɛn di ˈləjkxəɣaːt fan di ˈeᵊnsaːmɦəjt]

Than the humiliating pain
As die vernederende pyn
[as di fərˈneᵊdərəndə pəjn]

Of such togetherness.
Van so 'n samesyn.
[fan sʊᵊ ə ˈsaːməsəjn]

Now that we both know the worst,
Nou dat ons albei die ergste weet,
[nœu dat ɔns ˈalbəj di ˈærxstə veᵊt]

The hours of our union are now banned,
Is die ure van ons gemeensaamheid verban,
[əs di ˈyːrə fan ɔns xəˈmeᵊnsaːmɦəjt fərˈban]

All that remains are memories for you
and me.
Al wat bly is herinnering vir jou en my.
[al vat bləj əs ɦæˈrənərəŋ fər jœu ɛn məj]

Let us forget even the joys,
Laat ons die vreugde selfs vergeet,
[laːt ɔns di ˈfrjøᵊxdə sæᵊlfs fərˈxeᵊt]

And return to loneliness.
En t'rugkeer tot die eensaamheid.
[ɛn ˈtrœxkeᵊr tɔt di ˈeᵊnsaːmɦəjt]

We have changed,
Ons het verander,
[ɔns ɦet fərˈandər]

And you understand that I must go
on alone.
En jy verstaan dat ek alleen moet verder gaan.
[ɛn jəj fərˈstaːn dat ɛk aˈleᵊn mut ˈfærdər xaːn]

At Dusk
7. *Met Skemering*
[mɛt ˈskeᵊmərəŋ]
Music also by: Arnold van Wyk (1916–1983)

At dusk, when the finches at the marsh
Met skemering, toe die vinke by die vlei
[mɛt ˈskeᵊmərəŋ tu di ˈfəŋkə bəj di fləj]

Crisscross the sky with their bright yellow,
Die lug deurweef met hul helder geel,
[di lœx djøᵊrˈveᵊf mɛt ɦœlˈɦæᵊldər çeᵊl]

I only imagined for a moment
Het ek net vir 'n oomblik my verbeel
[ɦet ɛk nɛt fər ə ˈʊᵊmblək məj fərˈbeᵊl]

That you walked again among the reeds
with me.
Jy loop weer deur die riete saam met my.
[jəj lʊᵊᵊp veᵊr djøᵊr di ˈritə saːm mɛt məj]

Everything was as when we,
Want alles was soos toe ons,
[vant 'aləs vas sʊᵊs tu ɔns]

Side by side, heard
Sy aan sy, gehoor het
[səj a:n səj xəˈɦʊᵊr ɦɛt]

How the wind played among the reeds.
Hoe die windjie deur hul speel.
[ɦu di 'vənki djøᵊr ɦœl speᵊl]

I wanted to share this hour of joy with you,
Ek wou die uur se vreugde met jou deel,
[ɛk vœu di y:r sə 'frjøᵊxtə mɛt jœu deᵊl]

I wanted to return,
Ek wou terug,
[ɛk vœu təˈrœx]

To stay with you again.
Om weer by jou te bly.
[ɔm veᵊr bəj jœu tə bləj]

But when I looked up,
Maar toe ek opkyk,
[ma:r tu ɛk 'ɔpkəjk]

The night's dark blue wings
Het die donkerblou vleuels van die nag
[ɦɛt di 'dɔŋkərblœu 'fljøᵊls fan di nax]

Had folded all around the marsh.
Al om die vlei gevou.
[al ɔm di fləj xəˈfœu]

As if he wanted to dream his whole life away
Asof hy heel sy lewe wou verdroom
[as'ɔf ɦəj ɦeᵊl səj 'leᵊvə vœu fərˈdrʊᵊm]

There was one egret standing motionless;
Was daar een reier wat nog roerloos staan;
[vas da:r eᵊn 'rəjər vat nɔx 'ru:rlʊᵊs sta:n]

And the gossamer of a willow tree
En in die ragwerk van 'n wilkerboom
[ɛn ən di 'raxværk fan ə 'vəlkərbʊᵊm]

The cold crescent of the winter moon.
Die koue sekel van die wintermaan.
[di 'kœuə 'seᵊkəl fan di 'vəntərbʊᵊm]

Oh Queer Love
8. *O vreemde*[6] *Liefde*
[ʊᵊ 'freᵊmdə 'lifdə]

Oh queer love that eventually
O vreemde liede wat my eindelik
[ʊᵊ 'freᵊmdə 'lifdə vat məj 'əjndələk]

Washed me onto this desolate shore
Gespoel het na dié afgeleë strand
[xəˈspul ɦɛt na 'di 'afxəˌle:ə strant]

Where, still intoxicated by your
slamming waves,
Waar, nog bedwelmd van jou branderslae,
[va:r nɔx bəˈdwæᵊləmt fan jœu 'brandərˌsla:ə]

I, at the threshold of a new land
Ek op die drempel van 'n nuwe land
[ɛk ɔp di 'drɛmpəl fan ə 'nyvə lant]

---

[6] See note 3.

Have to catch my breath before I go further,
Moet asem skep voordat ek verder gaan,
[mut 'a:səm skɛp 'fuᵊrdat ɛk 'færdər xa:n]

That gives me new vistas
Wat nuwe vergesigte aan my gee
[vat 'nyvə 'færxəˌsəxtə a:n məj çeᵊ]

I already feel the victorious life-giving power here
Reeds voel ek hier die lewe gewende krag
[reᵊts ful ɛk ɦi:r di 'leᵊvə 'xeᵊvəndə krax]

While still behind me the wild roaring
Terwyl nog agter my die wilde bruising
[tər'vəjl nɔx 'axtər məj di 'vəldə 'brœysən]

Of your foreign sea is heard.
Gehoor word van jou vreemde see.
[xə'ɦuᵊr vɔrt fan jœu 'freᵊmdə seᵊ]

Stand-Alone Poetry

If My Heart Now Wants to Sing[7]
As my Hart nou wil sing
[as məj ɦart nœu vəl səŋ]
Music: S. le Roux Marais (1896–1979), "New Songs"
(Nuwe Liedere, no. 11) ['nyvə 'lidərə]

If my heart now wants to sing,
As my hart nou wil sing,
[as məj ɦart nœu vəl səŋ]

I would despise myself
Myself sou ek verag
[məj'sæᵃlf sœu ɛk fər'ax]

How then, can I wait to deliver the message
Hoe kan ek dan wag om die boodskap te bring
[ɦu kan ɛk dan vax ɔm di 'buᵊtskap tə brəŋ]

To be controlled by the desire to laugh so gaily
Deur die luste bedwing om so vrolik te lag
[djøᵊr di 'lœstə bə'dwəŋ ɔm suᵊ 'fruᵊlək tə lax]

And to laugh with everyone
En met almal te lag
[ɛn mɛt 'almal tə lax]

If my heart now wants to sing,
As my hart nou wil sing,
[as məj ɦart nœu vəl səŋ]

I would despise myself
Myself sou ek verag
[məj'sæᵃlf sœu ɛk fər'ax]

To deliver the message
Om die boodskap te bring
[ɔm di 'buᵊtskap tə brəŋ]

To be controlled by the desire to sing so merrily
Deur die luste bedwing om so vrolik te sing
[djøᵊr di 'lœstə bə'dwəŋ ɔm suᵊ 'fruᵊlək tə səŋ]

How can I wait then
Hoe kan ek dan wag
[ɦu kan ɛk dan vax]

---

[7] Permission granted by NB Publishers.

To laugh with everyone
Om met almal te lag
[ɔm mɛt ˈalmal tə lax]

What will alleviate the sorrow
Wat die leed sal versag
[vat di leᵊt sal fərˈsax]

(Is) to laugh merrily.
Vrolik te lag.
[ˈfrʊᵊlək tə lax]

A Prayer[8]
'n Gebed
[ə xəˈbɛt]
Music: Heinz Hirschland (1901–1960), "Fourteen Afrikaans Songs"
(*Veertien Afrikaanse Liedere, no. 7*) [ˈfeᵊrtin afriˈkaːnsə ˈlidərə]
Anna Lambrechts-Vos (1876–1932), "Great South Africa" (*Groot Suid-Afrika*) [xrʊᵊt
sœyt ˈaːfrika], Songs in Five Volumes: Vol. 1, Op. 41, no. 3
S. le Roux Marais (1896–1979), "New Songs" (*Nuwe Liedere, no. 6*) [ˈnyvə ˈlidərə]

From base passion, deep deceit
Van lae hartstog, diep bedrog
[fan ˈlaːə ˈɦartstɔx dip bəˈdrɔx]

And jealousy
En jaloesie
[ɛn jaluˈsi]

Egotism and jealousy
Selfsugtigheid en jaloesie
[sæᵊlfˈsœxtəxɦəjt ɛn jaluˈsi]

Save me oh God
Red my o Heer
[rɛt məj ʊᵊ ɦeᵊr]

From everything that the flesh desires
Van alles wat die vlees begeer
[fan ˈaləs vat di fleᵊs bəˈxeᵊr]

Save me oh God
Red my o Heer
[rɛt məj ʊᵊ ɦeᵊr]

To remain noble, pure and strong
Om edel, rein en sterk te wees
[ɔm ˈeᵊdəl rəjn ɛn stærk tə veᵊs]

And lovingly sacrificial
En liefderyk opofferend
[ɛn ˈlifdərəjk ɔpˈɔfərənt]

Help me oh God
Help my o Heer
[ɦæᵊlp məj ʊᵊ ɦeᵊr]

And only to do Thy will
En net te doen wat U begeer
[ɛn nɛt tə dun vat y bəˈxeᵊr]

---

[8] Permission granted by the Dramatic Artistic and Literary Rights Organization (DALRO).

Help me oh God
Help my o Heer
[ɦæᵃlp məj ʊᵊ ɦeᵊr]

Help me, oh God.
Help my o Heer.
[ɦæᵃlp məj ʊᵊ ɦeᵊr]

To do, to do Thy will
Te doen te doen wat U begeer
[tə dun tə dun vat y bəˈxeᵊr]

We Said Farewell[9]
Ons het mekaar gegroet
[ɔns ɦɛt məˈka:r xəˈxrut]
Music: Dawid S. Engela (1931–1967), "Songs of a Futile Love"
(*Liedere van 'n vergeefse Liefde, no. 4*) [ˈlidərə fan ə fərˈxeᵊfsə ˈlifdə]

We said farewell
Ons het mekaar gegroet
[ɔns ɦɛt məˈka:r xəˈxrut]

And so it was, with simple words
En so, met doodgewone woorde
[ɛn sʊᵊ mɛt ˈdʊᵊtxəˌvʊᵊnə ˈvʊᵊrdə]

While surrounded by others.
Terwyl die ander om ons staan.
[tərˈvəjl di ˈandər ɔm ɔns sta:n]

And without a betraying gesture,
En geen gebaar wat kon verraai nie,
[ɛn çeᵊn xəˈba:r vat kɔn fəˈra:j ni]

The warm pulse of your blood
Die warme polsing van jou bloed
[di ˈvarmə ˈpɔlsəŋ fan jœu blut]

We said our goodbyes,
Het ons mekaar gegroet,
[ɦɛt ɔns məˈka:r xəˈxrut]

Passed over to my fingers;
Het op my vingers oorgeslaan;
[ɦɛt ɔp məj ˈfəŋərs ˈʊᵊrxəˌsla:n]

And I went away.
En ek het weggegaan.
[ɛn ɛk ɦɛt ˈvæxəˌxa:n[10]]

---

[9] Permission granted by NB Publishers.
[10] See Appendix G, Assimilation and Amalgamation of Consonants.

Tranquility and Quietness[11]

Rus en Stilte

[rœs ɛn ˈstəltə]

Music: M. L. de Villiers (1885–1977), "Six Afrikaans Art Songs"
(*Ses Afrikaanse Kunsliedere, no. 5*) [sɛs afriˈkaːnsəˈkœnsˌlidərə]
Heinz Hirschland (1901–1960), "Fourteen Afrikaans Songs"
(*Veertien Afrikaanse Liedere, no. 9*) [ˈfeᵊrtin afriˈkaːnsə ˈlidərə]
S. le Roux Marais (1896–1979), "New Songs" (*Nuwe Liedere, no. 5*)
[ˈnyvə ˈlidərə]

Cool drops of water,
Koel druppels water,
[kul ˈdrœpəls ˈvaːtər]

Quivering dew
Bewende dou
[ˈbeᵊvəndə dœu]

Whispering leaves,
Fluisterende blare,
[ˈflœystərəndə ˈblaːrə]

And people's faint voices
En mensestemme flou
[ɛn ˈmɛnsəˌstɛmə flœu]

Praying trees,
Biddende bome,
[ˈbədəndə ˈbuᵊmə]

Calm heaving seas
Stil hygend see
[stəl ˈɦəjxənd seᵊ]

Murmuring streams
Murmelende strome
[ˈmœrmələndə ˈstrʊᵊmə]

Peaceful livestock
Vreedsame vee
[ˈfreᵊtˌsaːmə feᵊ]

Milk-white little clouds that softly emerge
Melkwitte wolkies wat saggies opkom
[ˈmæᵊlkʋətə ˈvɔlkis vat ˈsaxis ˈɔpkɔm]

Tranquility on earth,
Rus op aarde,
[rœs ɔp ˈaːrdə]

And quietness all around.
En stilte alom.
[ɛn ˈstəltə alˈɔm]

---

[11] Permission granted by NB Publishers.

Snow on the Mountains[12]
Sneeu op die Berge
[sniu ɔp di 'bærgə]
Music: Doris Beyers (n.d.), "Cupid's Confetti and Five Other Songs" (*Amors Konfetti en vyf ander Liedere, no. 3*) ['aːmɔrs kɔn'fɛti ɛn fəjf 'andər 'lidərə]

White as the pearly foam
Wit soos die pêrelskuim
[vət sʊᵊs di 'pæːrəlskœym]

That dances between the rocks,
Wat tussen die rotse dans,
[va 'tœsən[13] di 'rɔtsə daːns]

Lies now the loveliness
Lê nou die lieflikheid
[lɛː nœu di 'lifləkɦəjt]

Spread across mountain and cliff
Gesprei oor berg en krans
[xə'sprəj ʊᵊr bærx ɛn kraːns]

(It is) as if He finds the beauty of His handiwork
Asof Hy skoner so
[as'ɔf ɦəj 'skʊᵊnər sʊᵊ]

More pleasing this way;
Sy skoonheids werk bevind;
[səj 'skʊᵊnɦəjts værk bə'fənt]

Pure, like a mother's soul
Rein, soos 'n moedersiel
[rəjn sʊᵊs ə 'mudərsil]

That keeps watch over her child.
Wat wag hou oor haar kind.
[vat vax ɦœu ʊᵊr ɦaːr kənt]

---

[12] Permission granted by NB Publishers.
[13] See Appendix G, Assimilation and Amalgamation of Consonants.

MORNAY ANDRÉ DU PLESSIS

(1909–1941)

Love's Grief
Liefdeswee
['lifdəsveᵊ]
Music: Mornay du Plessis (1909–1941)

Blue was the brilliance of the heavens,
Blou was die glans van die hemel,
[blœu vas di xlans fan di 'ɦeᵊməl]

Blue was the infinite sea;
Blou was die eind'lose see;
[blœu vas di 'əjntlʊᵊsə seᵊ]

And joyful was life, my darling,
En bly was die lewe, my liefling,
[ɛn bləj vas di 'leᵊvə məj 'lifləŋ]

You gave me peace.
My het jy vrede gegee.
[məj ɦɛt jəj 'freᵊdə xə'xeᵊ]

Cold was the wind from the north,
Koud was die wind uit die noorde,
[kœut vas di wənt œyt di 'nʊᵊrdə]

Cold was the mighty sea;
Koud was die magtige see;
[kœut vas di 'maxtəxə seᵊ]

And dark was my life, my darling;
En donker (my)¹ lewe, my liefling;
[ɛn dɔŋkər məj 'leᵊvə məj 'lifləŋ]

Dark (was) the night of my sorrow.
Donker die nag van my wee.
['dɔŋkər di nax fan məj veᵊ]

Again there is blue in the sky,
Weer is daar blou in die hemel,
[veᵊr əs da:r blœu ən di 'ɦeᵊməl]

Again the shimmer on the sea;
Weer is die glans op die see;
[veᵊr əs di xlans ɔp di seᵊ]

But where are you now, my darling,
Maar waar is jy nou, o my liefling,
[ma:r va:r əs jəj nœu ʊᵊ məj 'lifləŋ]

---

¹ In this score, the composer has placed the words "my" and "die" on the same note, one above the other. As there are no repeats, however, singers may choose between "my" and "die" based on their interpretation. IPA and English translations are provided for both options.

Afrikaans Art Song Literature. Christian Bester and Bronwen Forbay, Oxford University Press. © Oxford University Press 2025.
DOI: 10.1093/oso/9780197660812.003.0011

Where is the comfort of the past?
Waar is die troos van verlee?
[va:r əs di trʊᵊs fan fərˈleᵊ]

Rustle then, oh raw northerly winds!
Ruis dan o ru noordewinde!
[rœys dan ʊᵊ ry ˈnʊᵊrdəˌvəndə]

Seethe then, oh mighty sea!
Bruis dan o magtige see!
[brœys dan ʊᵊ ˈmaxtəxə seᵊ]

My lonely heart, oh my darling,
My eensame hart, o my liefling,
[məj ˈeᵊnsa:mə ɦart ʊᵊ məj ˈlifləŋ]

Weeps along with the tempests of the sea.
Ween met die seewinde mee.
[veᵊn mɛt di ˈseᵊvəndə meᵊ]

ERLANK EITEMAL

(1901–1984)

A Time to Dream[1]
Droomtyd
[ˈdrʊᵊmtəjt]
Music: Judith Brent-Wessels (1910–n.d.)

Evening's tranquility arrives unexpectedly
Awend vrede uit die blou[2]
[ˈaːvənt ˈfreᵊdə œyt di blœu]

Sky and field stand in rapture.
Lug en veld[3] staan in die vervoering.
[lœx ɛn fæᵊlt staːn ən di fərˈfuːrəŋ]

A few stars twinkle dimly
Enk'le sterre flikker flou
[ˈɛŋklə ˈstærə ˈfləkər flœu]

And they whisper softly (secretively)
about you.
En hul fluister sag van jou.
[ɛn ɦœl ˈflœystər sax fan jœu]

There's a slight quiver among the leaves
Deur die blare gaan 'n roering
[djøᵊr di ˈblaːrə xaːn ə ˈruːrəŋ]

As if doves awake
Of daar duiwe wakker word
[ɔf daːr ˈdœyvə ˈvakər vɔrt]

Dreams just as blue as doves,
Drome net soos duiwe blou,
[ˈdrʊᵊmə nɛt sʊᵊs ˈdœyvə blœu]

Like doves white and blue
Soos duiwe blank en blou
[sʊᵊs ˈdœyvə blaŋk ɛn blœu]

Return to their rest in you.
Keer na hul rus in jou.
[keᵊr na ɦœl rœs ən jœu]

Just as doves find their rest in trees,
Net soos duiwe rus in bome,
[nɛt sʊᵊs ˈdœywə rœs ən ˈbʊᵊmə]

You're the resting place of my dreams,
Jy's die rusplek van my drome,
[jəjs di ˈrœsplæk fan məj ˈdrʊᵊmə]

Exhausted from roaming through the
blue heavens,
Moeg geswerwe deur die hemel blou,
[mu xəˈswærvə[4] djøᵊr di ˈɦeᵊməl blœu]

---

[1] Permission granted by NB Publishers.
[2] The direct translation is 'out of the blue,' which is a South African idiom that means 'unexpectedly.'
[3] An expansive African prairie, field, or pasture, comprising a wide variety of vegetation which may be used in various ways, including agriculture or uncultivated countryside.
[4] See Appendix G, Assimilation and Amalgamation of Consonants.

Afrikaans Art Song Literature. Christian Bester and Bronwen Forbay, Oxford University Press. © Oxford University Press 2025.
DOI: 10.1093/oso/9780197660812.003.0012

My dreams in the evening return to you.
Keer my drome saans terug na jou.
[keᵊr məj 'drʊᵊmə sa:ns təˈrœx na jœu]

Above the mountain ridge, the moon murmurs
Bo die bergrand ruis die maan
[bʊᵊ di 'bærxrant rœys di ma:n]

Quivering with a pure delight,
Bewend van 'n blank verblyding,
['beᵊvənt fan ə blaŋk fərˈbləjdən]

While he remains poised there for a moment
Wyl hy daar 'n oomblik staan
[vəjl ɦəj da:r ə 'ʊᵊmblək sta:n]

On the lookout before continuing on his way.
Uitkyk voor hy verder gaan.
['œytkəjk fʊᵊr ɦəj 'færdər xa:n]

Through the clouds the news travels
Deur die wolke gaan die tyding
[djø̞ᵊr di 'vɔlkə xa:n di 'təjdəŋ]

That the hour of love is approaching:
Dat die liefdesuur genaak:
[dat di 'lifdəs y:r xəˈna:k]

Dreams like a caravan,
Drome soos 'n karavaan,
['drʊᵊmə sʊᵊs ə karaˈfa:n]

A caravan of clouds
'n Wolke karavaan
[ə 'vɔlkə karaˈfa:n]

Gliding white over the moon.
Wit glydend oor die maan.
[vət 'xləjdənt ʊᵊr di ma:n]

Just as light (peeks) through the seams of the clouds,
Net soos lig deur wolke some,
[nɛt sʊᵊs ləx djø̞ᵊr vɔlkə 'sʊᵊmə]

You illuminate all my dreams,
So deurlig jy al my drome,
[sʊᵊ djø̞ᵊrˈləx jəj al məj 'drʊᵊmə]

The dark night lingers before me,
Lank die donker nag wat voorlê nou,
[laŋk di 'dɔŋkər nax vat 'fʊᵊrlɛ: nœu]

Allowing me to dream of you until morning.
Laat my tot die môre droom van jou.
[la:t məj tɔt di 'mɔ:rə drʊᵊm fan jœu]

GIDEON FAGAN

(1904–1980)

The Little Dove[1]
Die Duifie
[di ˈdœyfi]
Music: Gideon Fagan (1904–1980)

I had a little dove but he's dead;
Ek het 'n duifie gehad maar hy's dood;
[ɛk ɦɛt ə ˈdœyfi xəˈɦat maːr ɦəjs dʊᵊt]

I thought it must have been from grief —
Ek het gedink dit moet van treur wees —
[ɛk ɦɛt xəˈdəŋk dət mut fan trjøᵊr veᵊs]

What could it be that made him grieve?
Wat kon hom laat treur't?
[vat kɔn ɦɔm laːt trjøᵊrt]

His feet were snared on a soft thread
Sy voet was vas aan 'n sagte draad
[səj fut vas aːn ə ˈsaxtə draːt]

That I wove myself.
Wat ek self gevleg het.
[vat ɛk sæᵃlf xəˈflæx ɦɛt]

Darling little dove, did you have to go, then?
Dierbare Duifie, moes jy dan gaan?
[ˈdiːrbaːrə ˈdœyfi mus jəj dan xaːn]

For what, oh, for what did you have to
leave me?
Waarvoor, o waarvoor moes jy my verlaat?
[ˈvaːrfʊᵊr ʊᵊ ˈvaːrfʊᵊr mus jəj məj fərˈlaːt]

You lived alone in the bush,
Jy het alleen in die bos gewoon,
[jəj ɦɛt ˈaleᵊn ən di bɔs xəˈvʊᵊn]

For what did you have to leave me here,
all alone?
Waarvoor moes jy my eensaam hier laat bly?
[ˈvaːrfʊᵊr mus jəj məj ˈeᵊnsaːm ɦiːr laːt bləj]

Your food was delicious and my
kisses sweet;
Jou kos was goed en my soene soet;
[jœu kɔs vas xut ɛn məj ˈsunə sut]

For what were you heartsore—was it
perhaps homesickness?
Waaroor jou hartseer—was dit dan heimwee?
[ˈvaːrʊᵊr jœu ˈɦartseᵊr vas dət dan ˈɦəjmveᵊ]

---

[1] Permission granted by MDS Hire & Copyright, a division of Schott Music Ltd.

Afrikaans Art Song Literature. Christian Bester and Bronwen Forbay, Oxford University Press. © Oxford University Press 2025.
DOI: 10.1093/oso/9780197660812.003.0013

HENRY ALLAN FAGAN

(1889–1963)
aka H. A. Fagan

Like the Murmuring Breeze[1]
Soos die Windjie wat suis
[sʊᵊs di ˈvəŋki vat sœys]
Music: Hans Endler (1871–1947)
Johannes J. Fagan (1898–1920)
Charles Francis Oxtoby (1912–1978), Op. 36, no. 2

Like the breeze that murmurs over the fields,
Soos die windjie wat suis oor die velde,[2]
[sʊᵊs di ˈvəŋki vat sœys ʊᵊr di ˈfæᵊldə]

Pollinated with the scents of spring,
Met geure van lente bevrug,
[mɛt ˈxjøᵊrə fan ˈlɛntə bəˈfrœx]

It is the hope that comes to whisper
Is die hoop wat kom fluister
[əs di ɦʊᵊp vat kɔm ˈflœystər]

Of labor and struggle and victory,
Van arbeid en stryd en die sege,
[fan ˈarbəjt ɛn strəjt ɛn di ˈseᵊxə]

The victory that awaits;
Die sege wat wag;
[di seᵊxə vat vax]

Like the arid rustle in the autumn
Soos die dorre geruis in die najaar
[sʊᵊs di ˈdɔrə xəˈrəjs ən di ˈna:ja:r]

Of falling and decaying leaves,
Van blare wat val en vergaan,
[fan ˈbla:rə vat fal ɛn fərˈxa:n]

The reproachful voice of squandered opportunity
Die verwytende stem van geleentheid verspeel
[di fərˈvəjtəndə stɛm fan xəˈleᵊntɦəjt fərˈspeᵊl]

And of aborted deeds.
En van dade wat sterf ongedaan.
[ɛn fan ˈda:də vat stærf ɔnxəˈda:n]

---

[1] Permission granted by NB Publishers.
[2] An expansive African prairie, field, or pasture, comprising a wide variety of vegetation which may be used in various ways, including agriculture or uncultivated countryside.

Afrikaans Art Song Literature. Christian Bester and Bronwen Forbay, Oxford University Press. © Oxford University Press 2025.
DOI: 10.1093/oso/9780197660812.003.0014

BURGER GERICKE

(1916–1989)
aka B. Gericke

The Abundant Heathlands[1]
Heideweelde
['ɦəjdəˌveˀldə]
Music: S. le Roux Marais (1896–1979), "Golden Sheaf" (*Goue Gerf, no. 25*)
['xœuə xærf]

Let us sing of our abundant heathlands,
Laat ons sing van ons heideweelde,
[laːt ɔns səŋ fan ɔns 'ɦəjdəˌveˀldə]

Let us glorify our country so beautiful,
Laat ons roem op ons land so skoon,
[laːt ɔns rum ɔp ɔns lant sʊˀ skʊˀn]

Oh land of the south, richly endowed,
O Suiderland, ryk bedeelde,
[ʊˀ 'sœydərlant rəjk bə'deˀldə]

You are the sunny country in which we live.
Jy is sonland waar ons woon.
[jəj əs 'sɔnlant vaːr ɔns vʊˀn]

Let us sing of our thousands of heathlands
Laat ons sing van ons duisend heide
[laːt ɔns səŋ fan ɔns 'dœysənt 'ɦəjdə]

In the world's largest garden,
In die wêreld se grootste tuin,
[ən di 'væːrəlt sə 'xrʊˀtstə tœyn]

The colorful paradise of the south,
Die kleurparadys van die suide,
[di 'kljøˀrparaˌdəjs fan di 'sœydə]

That stretches to the highest peak.
Wat strek tot die hoogste kruin.
[vat stræk tɔt di 'ɦʊˀxstə krœyn]

Let us sing of the hundred colors
Laat ons sing van die honderd kleure
[laːt ɔns səŋ fan ɔns 'ɦɔndərt 'kljøˀrə]

Scattered like a rainbow's cloak,
Soos 'n reënboogkleed versprei,
[sʊˀs ə 'reˀnbʊˀxkleˀt fər'sprəj]

Come and drink of the field's perfumes,
Kom drink van die velde[2] se geure,
[kɔm drəŋk fan di 'fæˀldə sə 'xjøˀrə]

Of my heathlands!
Van die heideveld van my!
[fan di 'ɦəjdəfæˀlt fan məj]

---

[1] Permission granted by the Afrikaans Volksang-en Volkspelebeweging.
[2] An expansive African prairie, field, or pasture, comprising a wide variety of vegetation which may be used in various ways, including agriculture or uncultivated countryside.

Afrikaans Art Song Literature. Christian Bester and Bronwen Forbay, Oxford University Press. © Oxford University Press 2025.
DOI: 10.1093/oso/9780197660812.003.0015

THEODORE WALTER JANDRELL

(1888–1968)
aka Theo W. Jandrell

Homeward[1]
Huistoe
['fiœystu]
Music: Johannes Joubert (1894–1958)

The day comes to an end on the Highveld;
Op die hoëveld[2] sterwe die dag;
[ɔp di 'fiʊᵊfæᵃlt 'stærvə di dax]

I am far away from home,
Ek is ver van my tuiste,
[ɛk əs fæːr fan məj 'tœystə]

Yet my heart still sings along
Maar nog sing my hart agterna
[maːr nɔx səŋ məj fiart axtər'naː]

To the tune of the ox wagon,
Op die lied van die wa,
[ɔp di lit fan di vaː]

As I ponder the rest after the journey.
As ek denk aan die rus ná die tog.
[as ɛk dɛŋk aːn di rœs 'naː di tɔx]

Oh, the road leads me homeward tonight,
O, die pad lei my huistoe vanaand,
[ʊᵊ di pat ləj məj 'fiœystu fa'naːnt]

And I long for the happy reunion;
En ek smag na ontmoeting so bly;
[ɛn ɛk smax na ɔnt'mutəŋ sʊᵊ bləj]

For the joy that awaits,
Na die vreugde wat wag,
[na di 'frjøᵊxdə vat vax]

At my arrival tonight,
By my aankoms vannag,
[bəj məj 'aːnkɔms fa'nax]

In my humble small, sod house.
In die skamel sooihuisie van my.
[ən di 'skaːməl 'soːjˌfiœysi fan məj]

Oh, the hearts full of love and faith,
O, die harte vol liefde en trou,
[ʊᵊ di 'fiartə fɔl 'lifdə ɛn troeu]

Rallying around the gleaming fireplace!
Om die gloeiende haard nou geskaar!
[ɔm di 'xluiəndə fiaːrt nœu xə'skaːr]

---

[1] Permission granted by NB Publishers.
[2] The *hoëveld*, translated as a 'high field,' is known for its cooler climate; it forms a portion of the South African inland plateau with an altitude of over 4,921 ft, but below 6,890 ft. The Highveld boasts many beautiful areas, including nature reserves and charming towns. Popular attractions include God's Window, Bourke's Luck Potholes, and the Blyde River Canyon. Lower-lying areas support both crop and livestock farming.

Afrikaans Art Song Literature. Christian Bester and Bronwen Forbay, Oxford University Press. © Oxford University Press 2025.
DOI: 10.1093/oso/9780197660812.003.0016

Oh, the sweet little smiles in the little
fire's glow!
O, die glimlaggies soet in die vuurtjies
se gloed!
[ʊᵊ di 'xləm͵laxis sut ən di 'fy:rkis sə xlut]

Not a trace of melancholy, nor worry there.
Maar geen weemoed, geen kommernis daar.
[ma:r çeᵊn 've ᵊmut çeᵊn 'kɔmərnəs da:r]

Because the road leads me homeward
tonight,
Want die pad lei my huistoe vanaand,
[vant di pat ləj məj 'fiœystu fa'na:nt]

And they yearn for a happy reunion;
En hul smag na ontmoeting so bly;
[ɛn fiœl smax na ɔnt'mutəŋ sʊᵊ bləj]

For the joy that awaits,
Na die vreugde wat wag,
[na di 'frjøᵊxdə vat vax]

At my arrival tonight,
By my aankoms vannag,
[bəj məj 'a:nkɔms fa'nax]

In my humble small, sod house.
In die skamel sooihuisie van my.
[ən di 'ska:məl 'so:j͵fiœysi fan məj]

Come Home, Beloved![3]
Kom huistoe, Liefste!
[kɔm 'fiœystu 'lifstə]
Music: Johannes Joubert (1894–1958)

Spring's happiness is upon hill and dale;
Daar's lentevreug op berg en dal;
[da:rs 'lentəfrjøᵊx ɔp bærx en dal]

Come home, beloved, come!
Kom huistoe, liefste, kom!
[kɔm 'fiœystu 'lifstə kɔm]

There is a happy awakening overall;
Daar's bly ontwaking oweral;
[da:rs bləj ɔnt'wa:kəŋ ʊᵊvər'al]

Come home, beloved, come!
Kom huistoe, liefste, kom!
[kɔm 'fiœystu 'lifstə kɔm]

It's an amorous time for you and me,
Dis minnetyd vir jou en my,
[dəs 'mənətəjt fər jœu ɛn məj]

When Spring again diffuses her scents;
As Lente weer haar geure sprei;
[as 'lentə veᵊr fia:r 'xjøᵊrə sprəj]

We have been parted for too long
Te lank is ons twee al geskei
[tə laŋk əs ɔns tweᵊ al xə'skəj]

Come home, beloved, come!
Kom huistoe, liefste, kom!
[kɔm 'fiœystu 'lifstə kɔm]

---

[3] Permission granted by NB Publishers.

Here your heart will relish rest and
peace again;
Hier smaak jou hart weer rus en vree;
[ɦi:r sma:k jœu ɦart veᵊr rœs ɛn freᵊ]

Come home, beloved, come!
Kom huistoe, liefste, kom!
[kɔm 'ɦœystu 'lifstə kɔm]

Here you will find love's happiness, like
long ago;
Hier minnevreug soos lang gelee;
[ɦi:r 'mənəfrjøᵊx suᵊs laŋ xə'leᵊ]

Come home, beloved, come!
Kom huistoe, liefste, kom!
[kɔm 'ɦœystu 'lifstə kɔm]

Through all the years ever faithful
Deur al die jare immer trou
[djøᵊr al di 'ja:rə 'əmər trœu]

I have held onto my pure love (for you);
Het ek my liefde rein behou;
[ɦɛt ɛk məj 'lifdə rəjn bə'ɦœu]

Oh (how) tenderly my heart calls to you
O teder roep my hart na jou
[ʊᵊ 'teᵊdər rup məj ɦart na jœu]

Come home, beloved, come!
Kom huistoe, liefste, kom!
[kɔm 'ɦœystu 'lifstə kɔm]

So lonely and alone, I weep;
So eensaam ween ek en alleen;
[suᵊ 'eᵊnsa:m veᵊn ɛk ɛn a'leᵊn]

Come home, beloved, come!
Kom huistoe, liefste, kom!
[kɔm 'ɦœystu 'lifstə kɔm]

I have shed so many tears over you,
So menig traan oor jou geween,
[suᵊ 'meᵊnəx tra:n ʊᵊr jœu xə'veᵊn]

Come home, beloved, come!
Kom huistoe, liefste, kom!
[kɔm 'ɦœystu 'lifstə kɔm]

In vain if pure flowers flourish,
Vergeefs as blomme rein gedy,
[fər'xeᵊfs as 'blɔmə rəjn xə'dəj]

With the sweetest scents around me
Met soetste geure rond om my
[mɛt 'sutstə 'xjøᵊrə rɔnt ɔm məj]

If we allow fate to keep us apart
As ons die noodlot langer skei
[as ɔns di 'nʊᵊtlɔt 'laŋər skəj]

Come home, beloved, come!
Kom huistoe, liefste, kom!
[kɔm 'ɦœystu 'lifstə kɔm]

Beside Still Waters[4]
Langs stille Waters
[laŋs ˈstələ ˈvaːtərs]
Music: S. le Roux Marais (1896–1979), "Two Sacred Songs" (*Twee gewyde*
Sangstukke, no. 1) [tweᵊ xəˈvəjdə ˈsaŋˌstœkə]
S. le Roux Marais (1896–1979), "Hymn, Second Choral Album"
(*Lofgesang Tweede Koor Album, no. 5*) [ˈlɔfxəˌsaŋ ˈtweᵊdə kuᵊr ˈalbəm]

Beside still waters refreshing and clear,
Langs stille waters fris en klaar,
[laŋs ˈstələ ˈvaːtərs frəs ɛn klaːr]

On pastures sweetly grazing
Op grasbeklede soete wei
[ɔp ˈxrasbəˌkleᵊdə ˈsutə vəj]

He leads me, my Shepherd and my God,
Voer Hy my Herder en my Heer,
[fuːr ɦəj məj ˈɦærdər ɛn məj ɦeᵊr]

He gently leads me, my Shepherd
Voer Hy my Herder so sag vir my
[fuːr ɦəj məj ˈɦærdər sʊᵊ sax fər məj]

If I sometimes stray over hill and dale
Verdwaal ek soms op berg en dal
[fərˈdwaːl ɛk sɔms ɔp bærx ɛn dal]

Across vast and wide plains
Oor vlaktes uitgestrek en wyd
[ʊᵊr ˈflaktəs ˈœytxəˌstræk ɛn vəjt]

He leads me back on paths,
Hy bring my weer op paaie,
[ɦəj brəŋ məj veᵊr ɔp ˈpaːjə]

On paths of righteousness.
Op paaie van geregtigheid.
[ɔ ˈpaːjə[5] fan xəˈræxtəxɦəjt]

I, poverty-stricken and lost, within
(His) love,
Ek arm verdwaalde word in liefde,
[ɛk arm fərˈdwaːldə vɔrt ən ˈlifdə]

With heavenly nourishment and
refreshment,
Met hemels spys en lafenis,
[mɛt ˈɦeᵊməls spəjs ɛn ˈlaːfənəs]

For His name's sake will be fed (and)
invigorated,
Om Sy naams wil gevoed verkwik,
[ɔm səj naːms vəl xəˈfut fərˈkwək]

There on His dish.
Daar aan Sy dis.
[daːr aːn səj dəs]

My cup runneth over
My beker word tot oor sy rand gevul
[məj ˈbeᵊkər vɔrt tɔt ʊᵊr səj rant xəˈfœl]

---

[4] Permission granted by NB Publishers.
[5] See Appendix G, Assimilation and Amalgamation of Consonants.

And my head is anointed with oil again
En my hoof gesalwe weer
[ɛn məj ɦʊᵊf xəˈsalvə veᵊr]

And at my Shepherd's feet, contentedly,
En aan my Herder voet tevree,
[ɛn aːn məj ˈɦærdər fut təˈfreᵊ]

I lay myself down.
Vly ek my neer.
[fləj ɛk məj neᵊr]

(Even if) I am encircled by danger and disaster,
Omring gevaar en rampe my,
[ɔmˈrəŋ xəˈfaːr ɛn ˈrampə məj]

Even if I in death's dark valley
As ek in donker doodsvallei,
[as ɛk ən ˈdɔŋkər dʊᵊts faˈləj]

Must go, even then, I will fear no evil,
Moet gaan, selfs dan, vrees ek g'n kwaad,
[mut xaːn sæᵊlfs dan freᵊs ɛk xən kwaːt]

Because He is with me.
Want Hy is met my.
[vant ɦəj əs mɛt məj]

However dark the shadow of frigid death
and the grave might be
*Hoe donker ook die skaduwee van kille dood
en graf*
[ɦu ˈdɔŋkər ʊᵊk di ˈskaːdyveᵊ fan ˈkələ dʊᵊt
ɛn xraf]

His support gives me courage
Sy bystand gee my moed
[səj ˈbəjstant çeᵊ məj mut]

His Shepherd's staff comforts me.
My troos Sy herderstaf.
[məj trʊᵊs səj ˈɦærdərstaf]

His goodness and mercy
Sy goedheid en weldadigheid
[səj ˈxutɦəjt ɛn væᵊlˈdaːdəxɦəjt]

Still follow me from pasture to pasture.
Loop my steeds na van wei tot wei.
[lʊᵊp məj steᵊts na fan vəj tɔt vəj]

Through all the days of my life,
Deur al my lewensdae heen,
[djøᵊr al məj ˈleᵊvəns̩daːə ɦeᵊn]

He leads me
Lei Hy vir my
[ləj ɦəj fər məj]

And at the end of my journey,
En aan die einde van my baan,
[ɛn aːn di ˈəjndə fan məj baːn]

After the cross, a golden crown awaits me;
Wag my 'n goue kroon na kruis;
[vax məj ə ˈxœuə krʊᵊn na krœys]

After bitter cold and scorching sun
Na felle kou en sonnebrand
[na ˈfælə kœu ɛn ˈsɔnəbrant]

A Father's home.
'n Vaderhuis.
[ə ˈfaːdərɦœys]

Until the Morning Glows[6]
Tot die Oggend-gloor
[tɔ di[7] 'ɔxəntxlʊᵊr]
Music: Johannes Joubert (1894–1958)

My heart returns as the dusk falls,
My hart gaan terug as die skemer val,
[məj fiart xa:n tə'rœx as di 'skeᵊmər fal]

(Across) Far-off plains and moors,
Verre vlakte en vlei,
['færə 'flaktə ɛn fləj]

'Til where, beside the stream of a
sunny valley
Tot waar langs die stroom van 'n sonnige dal
[tɔt va:r laŋs di strʊᵊm fan ə 'sɔnəxə dal]

The sweetheart of my dreams lives.
Die nooi van my drome bly.
[di no:j fan məj 'drʊᵊmə bləj]

Oh stars, shine (with) your light so clear
upon my darling,
O sterre, bestraal met jul lig so klaar my lief,
[ʊᵊ 'stærə bə'stra:l mɛt jœl ləx sʊᵊ kla:r
məj lif]

Where she slumbers peacefully now;
Waar sy sluimer nou sag;
[va:r səj 'slœymər nœu sax]

Let your light guard her against all evil,
Laat jul glans haar trou teen euwel waar,
[la:t jœl xlans fia:r trœu teᵊn 'øᵊvəl va:r]

Until the morning glows again, after
the night!
Tot die oggend weer gloor na die nag!
[tɔ di[8] 'ɔxənt veᵊr xlʊᵊr na di nax]

I see in the sparkling starlight
Ek sien in fonk'lende sterrelig
[ɛk sin ən 'fɔŋkləndə 'stærələx]

Again, the luster of (her) eyes so blue,
Weer die glans van oë so blou,
[veᵊr di xlans fan 'u:ə sʊᵊ blœu]

And I yearn for their loving, tender glances
En ek smag na hul lonkies so minlik teer
[ɛn ɛk smax na fiœl 'lɔŋkis sʊᵊ 'mənlək teᵊr]

As flowers long for refreshing dew,
Soos blomme na lawende dou,
[sʊᵊs 'blɔmə na 'la:vəndə dœu]

I think of bygone times of happy delights,
Ek dink aan die tye van vreugde verbly,
[ɛk dəŋk a:n di 'təjə fan 'frjøᵊxdə fər'bləj]

Of joyful times that await (us),
Aan tye van vreugde wat wag,
[a:n 'təjə fan 'frjøᵊxdə vat vax]

---

[6] Permission granted by NB Publishers.
[7] See Appendix G, Assimilation and Amalgamation of Consonants.
[8] Ibid.

Where a pining heart calls to me,
Waar 'n hart verlangend roep na my,
[va:r ə ɦart fər'laŋənt rup na məj]

Until the morning glows again, after the night!
Tot die oggend weer gloor na die nag!
[tɔ di⁹ 'ɔxənt ve³r xlʊ³r na di nax]

The Weary Pilgrim[10]
Vermoeide Pelgrim
[fər'muidə 'pæ³lxrəm]
Music: Johannes Joubert (1894–1958)

Listen weary pilgrim,
Vermoeide pelgrim luister,
[fər'muidə 'pæ³lxrəm 'lœystər]

Oh source of bliss,
O bron van salighede,
[ʊ³ brɔn fan 'saləxfie³də]

There comes in the quiet evening
Daar kom in stille nag
[da:r kɔm ən 'stəltə nax]

Bruised by the burden of sin,
Geknel deur sondelas,
[xə'knæl djø³r 'sɔndəlas]

A consoling word through the darkness
'n Trooswoord deur die duister
[ə 'trʊ³svʊ³rt djø³r di 'dœystər]

I come with weary steps,
Kom ek met matte skrede,
[kɔm ɛk mɛt 'matə 'skre³də]

A voice so sweet and so tender;
'n Stem so soet, so sag;
[ə stɛm sʊ³ sut sʊ³ sax]

For You to wash me clean;
Dat U my rein moet was;
[dat y məj rəjn mut vas]

"Come, child, burdened with sin,
"Kom, kind, belas met sonde,
[kɔm kənt bə'las mɛt 'sɔndə]

And through Your blood, sanctified
En deur U bloed, geheiligd
[ɛn djø³r y blut xə'ɦəjləxt]

Plagued by sorrow and grief,
Gekwel deur smart en wee,
[xə'kwæl djø³r smart ɛn ve³]

I bear my cross contentedly,
Dra ek tevree my kruis,
[dra: ɛk tə'fre³ məj krœys]

I nurture all your wounds,
Ek balsem al jou wonde,
[ɛk 'balsəm al jœu 'vɔndə]

Kept safe in (the palm of) Your faithful hand,
Trou deur U hand beveiligd,
[trœu djø³r y ɦant bə'fəjləxt]

I give you peace and rest."
Ek gee jou rus en vree."
[ɛk çe³ jœu rœs ɛn fre³]

On (the) path to (the) Father's house.
Op pad na Vadershuis.
[ɔp pat na 'fa:dərsɦœys]

---

⁹ Ibid.
¹⁰ Permission granted by NB Publishers.

INGRID JONKER

(1933–1965)

Five Songs on Texts by Ingrid Jonker, Song Cycle[1]
Vyf Liedere op Tekste van Ingrid Jonker, Sangsiklus
[fəjf ˈlidərə ɔp ˈtɛkstə fan ˈiŋgrət ˈjɔŋkər saŋˈsiklœs]
Music: Stefans Grové (1922–2014)

Song of the Rag Doll
1. *Lied van die Lappop*
[lit fan di ˈlapɔp]

I am the mute rag doll
Ek is die lappop wat nie praat
[ɛk əs di ˈlapɔp vat ni praːt]

And depend solely upon your love.
En maak net op jou liefde staat.
[ɛn maːk nɛt ɔp jœu ˈlifdə staːt]

In the evenings I am blind, quiet, and deaf,
Saans is ek blind en stil en doof,
[saːns əs ɛk blənt ɛn stəl ɛn dʊᵊf]

And I do not lift my bran-filled head.
En lig nie meer my semelhoof.
[ɛn ləx ni meᵊr məj ˈseᵊməlɦʊᵊf]

My hands do not stir,
My hande roer nie,
[məj ˈɦandə ruːr ni]

And my body becomes cold and stiff when you depart.
En my lyf word met jou weggaan koud en styf.
[ɛn məj ləjf vɔrt mɛt jœu ˈvæxaːn kœut ɛn stəjf]

I cannot walk without your help
Sonder jou hulp kan ek nie loop
[ˈsɔndər jœu ɦœlp kan ɛk ni lʊᵊp]

You bought me on a whim
Jy het my sommer sommer so gekoop
[jəj ɦɛt məj ˈsɔmər ˈsɔmər sʊᵊ xəˈkʊᵊp]

And will willfully still one Guy Fawkes Night
En sal my nog een Guy Fox nag[2] goedsmoeds
[ɛn sal məj nɔx eᵊn ˈgaə fɔks na ˈxutsmuts[3]]

---

[1] Permission granted by NB Publishers.

[2] Also known as Bonfire Night, Guy Fawkes Night is celebrated predominantly in Britain and some Commonwealth countries including South Africa, on November 5. Involving bonfires and fireworks displays, it commemorates the failed treasonous Gunpowder Plot of 1605.

[3] See Appendix G, Assimilation and Amalgamation of Consonants.

Afrikaans Art Song Literature. Christian Bester and Bronwen Forbay, Oxford University Press. © Oxford University Press 2025.
DOI: 10.1093/oso/9780197660812.003.0017

Immolate me and laugh about it
Verbrand en daaroor lag
[fər'brant ɛn 'da:rʊᵊr lax]

My pain is your loudly celebrated feast!
My pyn jou luid gevierde fees!
[məj pəjn jœu lœyt xə'fi:rdə feᵊs]

I am the rag doll without a soul;
Ek is die lappop sonder gees;
[ɛk əs di 'lapɔp 'sɔndər çeᵊs]

The Wind's Little Song
2. *Windliedjie*
['vənt‚liki]
Music also by: Hendrik Hofmeyr (b. 1957), "Words in the Wind"
(Woorde in die Wind, Op. 216, no. 1)

Where does my love, my love sleep tonight?
Waar slaap my liefde, my liefde vannag?
[va:r sla:p məj 'lifdə məj 'lifdə fa'nax]

And shall I my love, my love find again?
En sal ek my liefde, my liefde weer vinde?
[ɛn sal ɛk məj 'lifdə məj 'lifdə veᵊr 'fəndə]

Stars that rock (cradle-like) through the
pines and winds,
Sterre wat wieg in die denne en winde,
['stærə vat vix ən di 'dɛnə ɛn 'vəndə]

Winter wind lead me through bitter nights
Winterwind lei my deur bittere nagte
['vəntərvənt ləj məj djøᵊr 'bətərə 'naxtə]

Until out of the darkness I can quietly gaze
Tot uit die duister ek saggies kan staar
[tɔt œyt di 'dœystər ɛk 'saxis kan sta:r]

The dark pine tree, red road and
evening song,
Denneboom donker, rooipad en naglied,
['dɛnəbʊᵊm 'dɔŋkər 'ro:jpat ɛn 'naxlit]

How he slumbers, and slumbering my grief
Hoe hy sluimer en sluimerend my smarte
[ɦu ɦəj 'slœymər ɛn 'slœymərənt məj
'smartə]

Evening song of animals and
mysterious winds.
Naglied van diere en duistere winde.
['naxlit fan 'di:rə ɛn 'dœystərə 'vəndə]

Finally calms, deep in my heart.
Eindelik diep in my hart laat bedaar.
['əjndələk dip ən məj ɦart la:t bə'da:r]

Where does my love sleep, who calms his
distress?
Waar slaap my liefde, wie stil sy verdriet?
[va:r sla:p məj 'lifdə vi stəl səj fər'drit]

Puberty

3. *Puberteit*
['pybərtəjt]

The child in me died quietly,
Die kind in my het stil gesterf,
[di kənt ən məj ɦɛt stəl xə'stærf]

Neglected, blind, and unspoiled;
Verwaarloos blind, en onbederf;
[fər'va:rlʊᵊs blənt ɛn 'ɔnbə‚dærf]

It slowly dissipated in a puddle
In 'n klein poel stadig weggesink
[ən ə kləjn pul 'sta:dəx 'væxə‚səŋk]

And drowned somewhere in the dark,
En iewers in die duister verdrink,
[ɛn 'ivərs ən di 'dœystər fər'drəŋk]

When you unknowingly, like an animal
Toe jy onwetend soos 'n dier
[tu jəj ɔn've ᵊtənt sʊᵊs ə di:r]

Carried on laughingly celebrating your fiesta!
Nog laggend jou fiesta vier!
[nɔx 'laxənt jœu fi'ɛsta fi:r]

You did not, with the riding gesture
Jy het nie met die ry gebaar
[jəj ɦɛt ni mɛt di rəj xə'ba:r]

Foretell death or the danger,
Die dood voorspel of die gevaar,
[di dʊᵊt fʊᵊr'spæl ɔf di xə'fa:r]

But in my sleep
Maar in my slaap
[ma:r ən məj sla:p]

I see little hands,
Sien ek kleine hande,
[sin ɛk 'kləjnə 'ɦandə]

And at night the white blaze of your teeth
En snags die wit vuur van jou tande
[ɛn snaxs di vət fy:r fan jœu 'tandə]

I shudder contemplating over and over:
Wonder ek sidderend oor en oor:
['vɔndər ɛk 'sədərənt ʊᵊr ɛn ʊᵊr]

Did you murder the child in me?
Het jy die kind in my vermoor?
[ɦɛt jəj di kənt ən məj fər'mʊᵊr]

I Had Thought

4. *Ek het gedink*
[ɛk ɦɛt xə'dəŋk]

I had thought I could forget you,
Ek het gedink ek kan jou vergeet,
[ɛk ɦɛt xə'dəŋk ɛk kan jœu fər'xe ᵊt]

And could sleep alone in the soft night,
En in die sagte nag alleen kon slaap,
[ɛn ən di 'saxtə nax a'le ᵊn kɔn sla:p]

88   AFRIKAANS ART SONG LITERATURE

But in my naivety, I did not know
Maar in my eenvoud het ek nie geweet
[ma:r ən məj ˈeᵊnfœut ɦɛt ɛk ni xəˈveᵊt]

That with every gust of wind I would awake:
Dat ek met elke windvlaag sou ontwaak:
[dat ɛk mɛt ˈæᵊlkə ˈvəntfla:x sœu ɔntˈva:k]

That I the light quiver of your hand again
Dat ek die ligte trilling van jou hand weer
[dat ɛk di ˈləxtə ˈtrələŋ fan jœu ɦant veᵊr]

Over my slumbering neck would feel,
Oor my sluimerende hals sou voel,
[ʊᵊr məj ˈslœymərəndə ɦals sœu ful]

I had thought the fire that burns within me
Ek het gedink die vuur wat in my brand
[ɛk ɦɛt xəˈdəŋk di fy:r vat ən məj brant]

Had cooled off like the white arch of
the stars.
Het soos die wit boog van die sterre afgekoel.
[ɦɛt sʊᵊs di vət bʊᵊx fan di ˈstærə ˈafxə̩kul]

Now I know
Nou weet ek
[nœu veᵊt ɛk]

Our lives are like a song
Is ons lewens soos 'n lied
[əs ɔns ˈleᵊvəns sʊᵊs ə lit]

Wherein the grieving tone of our separation reverberates
Waarin die smarttoon van ons skeiding klink
[ˈva:rən di ˈsmartʊᵊn fan ɔns ˈskəjdəŋ kləŋk]

And all joys flow back in grief
En alle vreugde t'rugvloei in verdriet
[ɛn ˈalə ˈfrjøᵊxdə ˈtrœxflui ən fərˈdrit]

And are ultimately absorbed in our
loneliness.
En eind'lik in ons eensaamheid versink.
[ɛn ˈəjntlək ən ɔns ˈeᵊnsa:mɦəjt fərˈsəŋk]

Rude Awakening

5. *Ontnugtering*
[ɔntˈnœxtərəŋ]

The day awakens from its cocoon,
Die dag roer uit sy papie,
[di dax ru:r œyt səj ˈpa:pi]

The little chick from out of its shell.
Die kuiken uit sy dop.
[di ˈkœykən œyt səj dɔp]

The drowsiness leaves my being.
Die slap roer uit my wese.
[di slap ru:r œyt məj ˈveᵊsə]

I wanted to fool the world:
Ek wou die wêreld fop:
[ɛk vœu di ˈvæ:rəlt fɔp]

I wanted to introduce myself to them as a
small red-cheeked doll.
*Ek wou my aan hul voorstel as 'n klein
rooiwangpop.*
[ɛk vœu məj a:n ɦœl ˈfʊᵊrstæl as ə kləjn
ˈro:jvaŋpɔp]

This morning I am out of trickery and
my dress.
*Met hierdie oggend is ek uit my kierang en
my rok.*
[mɛt 'fiːrdi 'ɔxənt əs ɛk œyt məj 'kiraŋ en
məj rɔk]

Now they have figured me out
Nou het hul my ontsyfer
[nœu fiɛt fiœl məj ɔnt'səjfər]

And I stand in front of them
En staan ek voor hul op
[ɛn staːn ɛk fʊᵊr fiœl ɔp]

As the warped poet
As die verwrongedigter
[as di fər'vrɔŋəˌdəxtər]

Let them mock!
Laat hul spot!
[laːt fiœl spɔt]

Stand-Alone Poetry

Bitter Berry Daybreak[4]
Bitterbessie Dagbreek
['bətərˌbɛsi 'daxbreᵊk]
Music: Niel van der Watt (b. 1962)
Hendrik Hofmeyr (b. 1957)

Bitter berry daybreak
Bitterbessie dagbreek
['bətərˌbɛsi 'daxbreᵊk]

Bitter berry sun
Bitterbessie son
['bətərˌbɛsi sɔn]

A mirror broke
'n Spieel het gebreek
[ə 'spiːəl fiɛt xə'breᵊk]

Between me and him
Tussen my en hom
['tœsən məj ɛn fiɔm]

If you seek the wide path
Soek jy na die grootpad
[suk jəj na di 'xrʊᵊtpat]

To jog along
Om daarlangs te draf
[ɔm 'daːrlaŋs tə draf]

Winding little trails everywhere
Oral draai die paadjies
['ʊᵊral draːj di 'paːjkis]

(Are formed) from his words
Van sy woorde af
[fan səj 'vʊᵊrdə af]

Pine forest memories
Dennebos herinnering
['dɛnəbɔs fiæ'rənərəŋ]

Pine forest forgotten
Dennebos vergeet
['dɛnəbɔs fər'xeᵊt]

---

[4] Permission granted by NB Publishers.

I have also lost my way	Again the insults receive
Het ek ook verdwaal	*Weer die koggel kry*
[ɦɛt ɛk ʊᵊk fər'dwaːl]	[veᵊr di 'kɔxəl krəj]
Wallowing in my despair	(An) echo is not an answer
Trap ek in my leed	*Eggo is geen antwoord*
[trap ɛk ən məj leᵊt]	['ɛxu əs çeᵊn 'antvʊᵊrt]
Colorful echo like a parrot	He answers everywhere
Papegaai-bont eggo	*Antwoord hy alom*
[papə'xaːj bɔnt 'ɛxu]	['antvʊᵊrt ɦəj 'alɔm]
Hoodwink, hoodwink me	Bitter berry daybreak
Kierang kierang my	*Bitterbessie dagbreek*
['kiraŋ 'kiraŋ məj]	['bətər̩bɛsi 'daxbreᵊk]
Until I, deceived	Bitter berry sun
Totdat ek bedroë	*Bitterbessie son*
['tɔdat ɛk bə'druːə]	['bətər̩bɛsi sɔn]

The Child[5,6]

Die Kind (wat doodgeskiet is deur soldate by Nyanga)
The Child (That Was Killed by Soldiers at Nyanga)
[di kənt vat 'dʊᵊtxə̩skit əs djøᵊr sɔl'daːtə bəj 'njaːŋgaː]
Palimpses op 'Senzeni na?'[7]
Excerpts of 'What Have We Done?'
[pa'ləmpsəs ɔp sɛn'zɛːni na]
Music: Hendrik Hofmeyr (b. 1957)
"Words in the Wind" *(Woorde in die Wind, Op. 216, no. 4) to match Indexes*

The child is not dead	The child lifts his fists (in defiance) against
Die kind is nie dood nie	his mother
[di kənt əs ni dʊᵊt ni]	*Die kind lig sy vuiste teen sy moeder*
	[di kənt ləx səj 'fœystə teᵊn səj 'mudər]

---

[5] Permission granted by NB Publishers.
[6] This poem was read in full by Nelson Mandela at his inauguration on May 10, 1994.
[7] "Senzeni na?" is a South African isiXhosa anti-apartheid protest song often sung at funerals and in churches. Activist Duma Ndlovu (b. 1954) compared the influence of "Senzeni na?" to that of the American protest song, "We Shall Overcome."

Who shouts Africa! shouts the scent
Wat Afrika skreeu skreeu die geur
[vat ˈaːfrika skriu skriu di xjøˀr]

Of freedom and heathlands
Van vryheid en heide
[fan ˈfrəjɦəjt ɛn ˈɦəjdə]

In the locations (informal settlements) of
the cordoned heart
In die lokasies van die omsingelde hart
[ən di lʊˀkaːsis fan di ɔmˈsəŋəldə ɦart]

The child lifts his fists (in defiance) against
his father
Die kind lig sy vuiste teen sy vader
[di kənt ləx səj ˈfœystə teˀn səj ˈfaːdər]

In the martial procession of the generations
In die optog van die generasies
[ən di ˈɔptɔx fan di xənəˈraːsis]

Who shouts Africa! shouts the scent
Wat Afrika skreeu skreeu die geur
[vat ˈaːfrika skriu skriu di xjøˀr]

Of righteousness and blood
Van geregtigheid en bloed
[fan xəˈræxtəxɦəjt ɛn blut]

In the streets of his armed pride
In die strate van sy gewapende trots
[ən di ˈstraːtə fan səj xəˈvaːpəndə trɔts]

The child is not dead
Die kind is nie dood nie
[di kənt əs ni dʊˀt ni]

Not at Langa nor at Nyanga
Nòg by Langa nòg by Nyanga[8]
[ˈnɔx bəj ˈlaːŋga: ˈnɔx bəj ˈnjaːŋga:]
[ˈnɔx bəj ˈlaːŋga* ˈnjaːŋga*]

Neither at Orlando nor at Sharpeville
Nòg by Orlando nòg by Sharpeville
[ˈnɔx bəj ɔˈlæːndo ˈnɔx bəj ˈʃapˌvəl]
[ˈnɔx bəj ɔˈlaːndo* ˈnɔx bəj ˈʃapˌvəl*]

Nor at the police station in Philippi
Nòg by die polisiestasie in Philippi
[ˈnɔx bəj di puˈlisiˌstaːsi ən fəˈləpi:]
[ˈnɔx bəj di puˈlisiˌstaːsi ən fiˈliːpi*]

Where he lies with a bullet through his head
Waar hy lê met 'n koeël deur sy kop
[vaːr ɦəj lɛ: mɛt ə ˈkuːəl djøˀr səj kɔp]

The child is the dark shadow of the soldiers
Die kind is die skaduwee van die soldate
[di kənt əs di ˈskadyveˀ fan di sɔlˈdaːtə]

On guard with rifles Saracens and batons
Op wag met gewere sarasene en knuppels
[ɔp vax mɛt xəˈveˀrə saraˈseˀnə ɛn ˈknœpəls]

The child is present at all assemblies and
legislations
*Die kind is teenwoordig by alle vergaderings
en wetgewings*
[di kənt əs teˀnˈvʊˀrdəx bəj ˈalə fərˈxaːrdərəŋs
ɛn ˈvɛtxeˀvəŋs]

---

[8] While the pronunciation of names of the townships: Langa, Nyanga, Orlando, Sharpeville, and Philippi have been referenced from the "Nagmusiek" recording by Afrikaans mezzo-soprano Minette Du Toit-Pearce, authentic isiXhosa pronunciations (indicated by *) have also been included. Thanks are extended to Amanda Khosi for her kind assistance with the isiXhosa pronunciations.

The child peers through the windows of
houses and into the hearts of mothers
*Die kind loer deur die vensters van huise en
in die harte van moeders*
[di kənt luːr djøᵊr di 'fɛnstərs fan 'ɦœysə ɛn
ən di 'ɦartə fan 'mudərs]

This child who just wanted to play in the
sun at Nyanga is everywhere
*Die kind wat net wou speel in die son by
Nyanga is orals*
[di kənt vat nɛt vœu speᵊl ən di sɔn bəj
'njaːŋga əs 'ʊᵊrals]

The child who becomes a man, treks
throughout all (of) Africa
*Die kind wat 'n man geword het trek deur die
ganse Afrika*
[di kənt vat ə man xə'vɔrt ɦɛt træk djøᵊr di
'xansə 'aːfrika]

The child who has become a giant, journeys
through the entire world
*Die kind wat 'n reus geword het reis deur die
hele wêreld*
[di kənt vat ə rjøᵊs xə'vɔrt ɦɛt rəjs djøᵊr di
'ɦeᵊle 'væːrəlt]

Without a pass
Sonder 'n pas
['sɔndər ə pas]

ALBERTUS DANIËL KEET

(1888–1972)
aka A. D. Keet

Adoration[1]
Adoratio
[adɔˈrasiɔ]
Music: A. H. Ashworth (1895–1959)

I see your image in every flower,
Ik sien jouw beeld in elke blom,
[ɛk sin jœu beᵊlt ən ˈæᵃlkə blɔm]

And the sunlight weaves its rainbow rings,
En die sonlig vleg sij reënboog-ringe,
[ɛn di ˈsɔnləx flæx səj ˈreᵊnbʊᵊx ˈrəŋə]

Halos of glory,
Glorie-kringe,
[ˈxlʊᵊri ˈkrəŋə]

Worshipfully around you.
Aanbiddend om jou om.
[aːnˈbədənt ɔm jœu ɔm]

I hear your voice at every sea
Ik hoor jouw stem bij iedere see
[ɛk ɦʊᵊr jœu stɛm bəj ˈidərə seᵊ]

That late (in the) evening, by the starry sky,
Wat s'awends laat, bij sterrehemel,
[vat ˈsaːvənts laːt bəj ˈstærəˌɦeᵊməl]

Teems with waves,
Van branders wemel,
[fan ˈbrandərs ˈveᵊməl]

And kneel then, contentedly …
En kniel dan neer, tevree …
[ɛn knil dan neᵊr təˈfreᵊ]

When in the Evening[2]
As saans
[as saːns]
Music: Horace Barton (1872–1951)
Jan Bouws (1902–1978)
Berend Elbrecht (1883–1954)
P. W. Haasdyk (n.d.)
S. le Roux Marais (1896–1979), "The Rose and Other Afrikaans Songs"
(*Die Roos en ander Afrikaanse Liedere, no. 3*)
[di rʊᵊs ɛn ˈandər afriˈkaːnsə ˈlidərə]
M. C. Roode (1907–1967)

---

[1] Permission granted by the Keet family.
[2] Ibid.

Afrikaans Art Song Literature. Christian Bester and Bronwen Forbay, Oxford University Press. © Oxford University Press 2025.
DOI: 10.1093/oso/9780197660812.003.0018

When in the evening the sun tacitly dies
As saans die son stilwygend sterf
[as sa:ns di sɔn 'stəlɣəjxənd stærf]

There over the western ridge,
Daar oor die wester-rand,
[da:r ʊᵊr di 'vɛstərant]

Then he radiates miraculous signs
Dan straal hy wondertekens uit
[dan stra:l ɦəj 'vɔndər̩teᵊkəns œyt]

To every cloud and land.
Aan elke wolk en land.
[a:n 'æᵃlkə vɔlk ɛn lant]

When in the evening dusk's veil lowers
As saans die skemersluier sak
[as sa:ns di 'skeᵊmər̩slœyər sak]

In a quiet round of victory,
In stille segetog,
[ən 'stələ 'seᵊxətɔx]

The day continues fighting its deadly battle —
Dan veg die dag sy doodstryd voor —
[dan fæx di dax səj 'dʊᵊtstrəjt fʊᵊr]

(Until) its final breathless run.
Sy laaste ademtog.
[səj 'la:stə 'a:dəmtɔx]

When in the evening deep darkness descends —
As saans die donker duister daal —
[as sa:ns di 'dɔŋkər 'dœystər da:l]

The day's death veil —
Die doodskleed van die dag —
[di 'dʊᵊtskleᵊt fan di dax]

Then the sun's children keep
Dan hou die kinders van die son
[dan ɦœu di 'kəndərs fan di sɔn]

Their shining starry guard.
Hul ligtend sterrewag.
[ɦœl 'ləxtənt 'stærəvax]

It Is Late in the Night[3]
Dit is laat in die Nag
[dət əs la:t ən di nax]
Music: S. le Roux Marais (1896–1979), "New Songs"
(*Nuwe Liedere, no. 9*) ['nyvə 'lidərə]

It is late in the night and I wait
Dit is laat in die nag en ek wag
[dət əs la:t ən di nax ɛn ɛk vax]

For whom do I wait now, for you
Vir wie wag ek nou, vir jou
[fər vi vax ɛk nœu fər jœu]

---

[3] Permission granted by the Keet family.

It is late in the night, and I hear someone laugh,
Dit is laat in die nag en ek hoor iemand lag,
[dət əs la:t ən di nax ɛn ɛk fiʊᵊr 'imant lax]

But within you and me, (there) is regret,
only regret.
Maar in my en in jou, is berou, net berou.
[ma:r ən məj ɛn ən jœu əs bə'rœu nɛt
bə'rœu]

If I could but laugh, but laugh so deep into
the night
Kon ek maar lag, maar lag so diep in die nag
[kɔn ɛk ma:r lax ma:r lax sʊᵊ dip ən di nax]

Forget my remorse along with the
memory of you
Vergeet my beroute tesame met jou
[fər'xeᵊt məj bə'rœutə tə'sa:mə mɛt jœu]

Along with the memory of you.
Tesaam met jou.
[tə'sa:m mɛt jœu]

I Love (the Color) Blue[4]
Ek hou van blou
[ɛk fiœu fan blœu]
Music: Peter Aerts (1912–1996)
Gisela de Villiers (b. 1955)
Pieter Villiers (1924–2015)
Hennie Joubert (1926–1986)
Anton E. Kratz (1917–1980)
P. J. Lemmer (1896–1989)
Rosa Nepgen (1909–2001)
Suzanne Rentzke (b. 1982)
Francois van den Berg (b. 1954), "Two Songs for Soprano"
(*Twee liedere vir sopraan, no. 2*) [tweᵊ 'lidərə fər su'pra:n]
Peter Louis van Dijk (b. 1953)

Oh please don't ask me for my love,
O vra my nie my liefde,
[ʊᵊ fra: məj ni məj 'lifdə]

I have given it away
Ek het dit weggegee
[ɛk fiɛt dət 'væxəˌxeᵊ]

I gave it to a tiny bluebottle
Aan 'n kleine koringblommetjie
[a:n ə 'kləjnə 'kʊᵊrəŋˌblɔmiki]

And to the immense sea.
En aan die grote see.
[ɛn a:n di 'xrʊᵊtə seᵊ]

---

[4] Permission granted by the Keet family.

AFRIKAANS ART SONG LITERATURE

I love the blue flowers,
Ek hou van bloue blomme,
[ɛk ɦœu fan 'blœuə 'bləmə]

I adore the blue heavens,
'k Aanbid die hemelblou,
[ɛk a:n'bət di 'ɦeᵊməlblœu]

And I cannot elude your (blue) eyes
En jou oë vermy die kon ek nie
[ɛn jœu 'u:ə fər'məj di kən ɛk ni]

I love them more than you!
Ek min hul meer dan jou!
[ɛk mən ɦœl meᵊr dan jœu]

Mr. Sandman[5]
Klaas Vakie
[kla:s 'fa:ki]
Music: A. H. Ashworth (1895–1959)
Horace Barton (1872–1951)
Dirk Jan Brinne (1909–1974)
Cornelius Dopper (1870–1939)
Dirkie de Villiers (1920–1993)
Berend Elbrecht (1883–1954)
Marius Kerrebijn (1882–1930)
S. le Roux Marais (1896–1979), "Fifteen Afrikaans Lullabies" (*Vyftien Afrikaanse Slaapdeuntjies, no. 14*) ['fəjftin afri'ka:nsə 'sla:pˌdjøɲkis]
Harold C. Vischer (1865–1928)
J. P. J. Wierts (1866–1944), "Six Afrikaans Songs" (*Ses Afrikaanse Liedere, no. 2*)
[sɛs afri'ka:nsə'lidərə]

If I have to, I will softly
Ik[6] sal nou maar so saggies aan
[ɛk sal nœu ma:r sʊᵊ 'saxis a:n]

Go to bed —
Naar bed toe gaan —
[ma:r bɛt tu xa:n]

My little eyes are already quite drowsy,
Mij ogies is al baje vaak,
[məj 'ʊᵊxis əs al 'bajə fa:k]

I am already on the point of closing them —
Ik dwing al om hul toe te maak —
[ɛk dwəŋ al əm ɦœl tu tə ma:k]

I had better go to bed.
Ik sal maar bed toe gaan.
[ɛk sal ma:r bɛt tu xa:n]

I will now then kiss my mother goodnight,
Ik sal nou maar mij moeder kus,
[ɛk sal nœu ma:r məj 'mudər kœs]

---

[5] Permission granted by the Keet family.
[6] While various Dutch spellings occur in this poem, modern Afrikaans pronunciation rules have been utilized.

And then go rest —
En dan gaan rus —
[ɛn dan xa:n rœs]

My little eyes are already very tired,
Mij ogies is al baje moe,
[məj 'ʋᵊxis əs al 'bajə mu]

They want to close by themselves —
Hul val van self al sommer toe —
[ɦœl fal fan sæᵃlf al 'sɔmər tu]

I will then go and rest now.
Ik sal maar nou gaan rus.
[ɛk sal ma:r nœu xa:n rœs]

I will then close my little eyes;
Ik sal maar mij ogies sluit;
[ɛk sal ma:r məj 'ʋᵊxis slœyt]

The light is out,
Die lig is uit,
[di ləx əs œyt]

And yet I can still see her face,
En haar gesig die sien ik tog,
[ɛn ɦa:r xə'səx di sin ɛk tɔx]

I still think of her constantly —
Aan haar denk ik gedurig nog —
[a:n ɦa:r dɛŋk ɛk xə'dy:rəx nɔx]

Even though my little light is out.
Al is mij liggie uit.
[al əs məj 'ləxi œyt]

A Song of the Sea[7]
'n Lied van die See
[ə lit fan di seᵊ]
Music: A. H. Ashworth (1895–1959)
S. le Roux Marais (1896–1979)
Omius van Oostrum (1862–1948)

The waves break, the waves break,
Die branders breek, die branders breek,
[di 'brandərs breᵊk di 'brandərs breᵊk]

All day, all night
In die dag, in die aand
[ən di dax ən di a:nt]

Every week, every month:
Elke week, elke maand:
['æᵃlkə veᵊk 'æᵃlkə ma:nt]

Break, waves, break!
Breek, branders, breek!
[breᵊk 'brandərs breᵊk]

The waves roar, the waves roar
Die golwe dreun, die golwe dreun
[di 'xɔlvə drjøᵊn di 'xɔlvə drjøᵊn]

They moan, they groan
Hulle kreun, hulle steun
['ɦœlə krjøᵊn 'ɦœlə stjøᵊn]

---

[7] Permission granted by the Keet family.

Upon the old, old tune:
Op die ou, ou deun:
[ɔp di œu œu djøᵊn]

Roar, waves roar!
Dreun, golwe, dreun!
[drjøᵊn 'xɔlvə drjøᵊn]

The earth remains but still and quiet
Die aarde blij maar stil en swijg
[di 'a:rdə bləj ma:r stəl ɛn swəjx]

In the day, at night
In die dag, in die aand
[ən di dax ən di a:nt]

Every night, every month:
Elke nag, elke maand:
['æᵊlkə nax 'æᵊlkə ma:nt]

Remain silent, earth, silent!
Swijg, aarde, swijg!
[swəjx 'a:rdə swəjx]

Mother[8]
Moeder
['mudər]
Music: Jan Kromhout (1886–1969)
P. J. Lemmer (1862–1948)
O. A. Lewald (1905–1988)
S. le Roux Marais (1896–1979), "Six Art Songs" (*Ses Kunsliedere, no. 1*)
[sɛs 'kœnsˌlidərə]

She is old and decrepit (age-worn) now,
Nou is sy oud, en afgeleef,
[nœu əs səj œut ɛn 'afxəˌleᵊf]

Her back is stooped, and her hands tremble.
Haar rug is krom, haar hande beef.
[ɦa:r rœx əs krɔm ɦa:r 'ɦandə beᵊf]

My mother, (dearest) mother.
My moeder, moeder.
[məj 'mudər 'mudər]

I don't know what I must do now
Ek weet nie wat ek nou moet doen
[ɛk weᵊt ni vat ɛk nœu mut dun]

I send a kiss every week to my mother, my (dearest) mother.
Ek stuur maar elke week 'n soen aan moeder my moeder.
[ɛk sty:r ma:r 'æᵊlkə weᵊk ə sun a:n 'mudər məj 'mudər]

Wherever my footsteps may lead me
Waar ook my voetstap heen mag gaan
[va:r ʋᵊk məj 'futstap ɦeᵊn ma xa:n⁹]

There is but one who understands me,
Daar is maar een wat my verstaan,
[da:r əs ma:r eᵊn vat məj fər'sta:n]

---

[8] Permission granted by the Keet family.
[9] See Appendix G, Assimilation and Amalgamation of Consonants.

It's mother, my (dearest) mother;
Dis moeder, my moeder;
[dəs 'mudər məj 'mudər]

I know my mother prays for me.
Ek weet my moeder bid vir my.
[ɛk veᵊt məj 'mudər bət fər məj]

Oh God look down with compassion
O Heer sien neer in medely
[ʊᵊ ɦeᵊr sin neᵊr ən 'meᵊdələj]

Upon mother, my (dearest) mother.
Op moeder, my moeder.
[ɔp 'mudər məj 'mudər]

BESSIE KOTZÉ
(NÉE BADENHORST) (n.d.)

The Freckled Maiden[1]
Sproetenooi
['sprutəno:j]
Music: P. J. Lemmer (1896–1989), "Golden Sheaf"
(*Goue Gerf, no. 34*) ['xœuə xærf]

Every tiny freckle on her little nose
enchanted me.
Elke sproetjie op haar snoetjie het my
hart bekoor.
['æᵃlkə 'spruiki ɔp ɦa:r 'snuiki ɦɛt məj
ɦart bə'kʊᵊr]

Every tiny freckle on her little nose won me
over again and again.
Elke sproetjie op haar snoetjie wen my oor
en oor.
['æᵃlkə 'spruiki ɔp ɦa:r 'snuiki vɛn məj ʊᵊr
ɛn ʊᵊr]

Freckled little face, I swear to be faithful to
you forever.
Sproetgesiggie, ek belowe ewig trou aan jou.
['sprutxə,səxi ɛk bə'lʊᵊvə 'eᵊvəx trœu a:n jœu]

Just as long as you promise me that every
tiny freckle (will) remain.
Net solank jy my belowe elke sproetjie
te behou.
[nɛt sʊᵊ'laŋk jəj məj bə'lʊᵊvə 'æᵃlkə 'spruiki
tə bə'ɦœu]

---

[1] Permission granted by the Afrikaans Volksang en Volkspelebeweging.

Afrikaans Art Song Literature. Christian Bester and Bronwen Forbay, Oxford University Press. © Oxford University Press 2025.
DOI: 10.1093/oso/9780197660812.003.0019

CHRIS LAMPRECHT
(b. 1927)

Homage to the Northwest[1]
Aan die Noordweste
[aːn di nʊᵊrtˈvɛstə]
Texts and Music: Chris Lamprecht (b. 1927)

The Old Camel Thorn Tree
1. *Die ou Kameeldoringboom*[2]
[di œu kaˈmeᵊlˌdʊᵊrəŋbʊᵊm]

The old camel thorn tree, stands and dreams
*Die ou kameeldoringboom, die staan
en droom*
[di œu kaˈmeᵊlˌdʊᵊrəŋbʊᵊm di staːn
ɛn drʊᵊm]

For many years, he remains standing over
there and grieves alone.
Vir baie jare staan hy daar en treur alleen.
[fər ˈbajə ˈjaːrə staːn ɦəj daːr ɛn trjøᵊr aˈleᵊn]

In the Kalahari land, the lonely land,
In Kalahariland, die eensaam land,
[ən kalaˈɦarilant di ˈeᵊnsaːm lant]

An arid world where the sun's rays burn.
In dorre wêreld waar die son se strale brand.
[ən dɔrə ˈvæːrəlt vaːr di sɔn sə ˈstraːlə brant]

The old camel thorn tree, that stands
and dreams
*Die ou kameeldoringboom, die staan
en droom*
[di œu kaˈmeᵊlˌdʊᵊrəŋbʊᵊm di staːn
ɛn drʊᵊm]

Through wind and weather through many
years all alone.
In wind en weer deur baie jare heen alleen.
[ən vənt ɛn veᵊr djøᵊr ˈbajə ˈjaːrə ɦeᵊn aˈleᵊn]

In the Kalahari land, with its rusty-red
(colored) sand
In Kalahariland, se roes-rooi sand
[ən kalaˈɦarilant sə rus roːj sant]

In solitude, it moons over time and eternity.
In eensaamheid verdroom in tyd en ewigheid.
[ən ˈeᵊnsaːmɦəjt fərˈdrʊᵊm ən təjt ɛn
ˈeᵊvəxɦəjt]

---

[1] Permission granted by Chris Lamprecht.
[2] The camel thorn tree (*Acacia erioloba*) is also known as a giraffe thorn or mokala tree. A giraffe is called a *kameelperd*
in Afrikaans. Their unique tongues and lips enable them to feed off the leaves of this tree while avoiding the thorns.

Afrikaans Art Song Literature. Christian Bester and Bronwen Forbay, Oxford University Press. © Oxford University Press 2025.
DOI: 10.1093/oso/9780197660812.003.0020

The Fiscal of the Great River
2. *Die Grootrivier*[3] *se Voël*
[di ˈxrʊᵊtrəˌfiːr sə fuᵊl]

Listen to the fiscal of the Great River,
Hoor die Janfiskaal[4] *van die Grootrivier,*
[ɦʊᵊr di ˈjanfisˌkaːl fan di ˈxrʊᵊtrəˌfiːr]

Hear how he calls his mate among the whistling reeds;
Hoor hoe roep hy sy maat in die fluitjiesriet;
[ɦʊᵊr ɦu rup ɦəj səj maːt ən di ˈflœykisrit]

(It is still a) long (time) to wait before the rain comes,
Lank om te wag voor die reëntyd kom,
[laŋk ɔm tə vax fʊᵊr di ˈreᵊntəjt kɔm]

(It is still a) long (time) to wait before the marigolds bloom.
Lank om te wag voor die gousblom blom.
[laŋk ɔm tə vax fʊᵊr di ˈxœusblɔm blɔm]

As the twilight falls over Namaqualand,
As die skemering daal oor Namakwaland,[5]
[as di ˈskeᵊmərəŋ daːl ʊᵊr naˈmakwalant]

The fiscal calls near the waterfall;
Roep die Janfiskaal by die waterval;
[rup di ˈjanfisˌkaːl bəj di ˈvaːtərfal]

(It is still a) long (time) to wait before the rain comes,
Lank om te wag voor die reëntyd kom,
[laŋk ɔm tə vax fʊᵊr di ˈreᵊntəjt kɔm]

(It is still a) long (time) to wait before the marigolds bloom.
Lank om te wag voor die gousblom blom.
[laŋk ɔm tə vax fʊᵊr di ˈxœusblɔm blɔm]

Rain (Is Pouring) on the Veld
3. *Reën op die Veld*[6]
[reᵊn ɔp di fæᵊlt]

Rain (is pouring) on the veld, and the veld was drenched
Reën op die veld, en die veld was nat
[reᵊn ɔp di fæᵊlt ɛn di fæᵊlt vas nat]

And I lost my heart and I know not where.
En ek het my hart verloor en ek weet nie waar.
[ɛn ɛk ɦɛt məj ɦart fərˈlʊᵊr ɛn ɛk veᵊt ni vaːr]

---

[3] The term 'Great River' is a nickname for the Orange River, the longest river in South Africa.

[4] The Southern fiscal (*Lanius collaris*) is a populous indigenous bird of southern Africa. It is infamously referred to as the 'Jackie hangman' or 'butcher bird' as it often impales its prey on acacia thorns where food is stored for later ingestion.

[5] Namaqualand is the name of a predominantly arid region in the Northern Cape Province, derived from the Khoi word for 'Khoi people's land.' It overflows with exquisite wildflowers in a myriad of colors during the rainy spring season.

[6] An expansive African prairie, field, or pasture, comprising a wide variety of vegetation which may be used in various ways, including agriculture or uncultivated countryside.

Oh, the varicolored dress (of flowers),
O, die bonterok,
[ʊᵊ di ˈbɔntərɔk]

I would choose it above all others.
Die kies ek bowe al.
[di kis ɛk ˈbʊᵊvə al]

Namaqualand's Little Flowers
4. *Namakwaland[7] se Blommetjies*
[naˈmakwalant sə ˈblɔməkis]

The little flowers are so friendly and delighted after the rain,
Die blommetjies ná die reën is so vriend'lik en so bly,
[di ˈblɔmikis ˈna: di reᵊn əs sʊᵊ ˈfrintlək ɛn sʊᵊ bləj]

The little stars twinkle so brightly, they sparkle every evening.
Die sterretjies blink so helder, dit vonkel elke aand.
[di ˈstærikis bləŋk sʊᵊ ˈɦæᵊldər dət ˈfɔŋkəl ˈæᵊlkə a:nt]

Far and wide, the colors (are spread) over hill, veld and marsh.
Van oraloor die kleure in heuwel, veld[8] en vlei.
[fan ˈʊᵊralʊᵊr di ˈkljøᵊrə ən ˈɦjøᵊvəl fæᵊlt ɛn fləj]

So beautiful and so pristine, so fragile and so delicate,
So skoon en so rein, so broos en so fyn,
[sʊᵊ skʊᵊn ɛn sʊᵊ rəjn sʊᵊ brʊᵊs ɛn sʊᵊ fəjn]

The little sun shines so brightly here during the month of September,
Die sonnetjie skyn so helder hier in Septembermaand,
[di ˈsɔniki skəjn sʊᵊ ˈɦæᵊldər ɦii:r ən səpˈtɛmbərma:nt]

Namaqualand's floral magnificence is so dear to my heart.
Namakwaland se blommeprag so na aan my hart.
[naˈmakwalant sə ˈblɔməprax sʊᵊ na a:n məj ɦart]

Loeries Fountain
5. *Loeriesfontein[9]*
[ˈlurisfɔnˌtəjn]

Askoektrap on the little pump organ
Askoektrap[10] op die traporreltjie
[ˈaskuktrap ɔp di ˈtrapˌɔrəlki]

Plays Aunt Hessie le Roux in Loeriesfontein
Speel tant Hessie le Roux op Loeriesfontein,
[speᵊl tant ˈɦesi lə ru ɔp ˈlurisfɔnˌtəjn]

---

[7] See note 5.
[8] See note 6.
[9] A little town in the heart of Namaqualand.
[10] The "Askoektrap" is a local dance known as the 'ashcake shuffle.'

CHRISTIAN FREDERICK LOUIS LEIPOLDT

(1880–1947)
aka C. Louis Leipoldt

Four Loitering Ditties (Carousel Songs)
Vier Slampamperliedjies, Op. 23 [fiːr slamˈpampərˌlikis]
Music: Hubert du Plessis (1922–2011)

The Curly-Haired Lad
1. *Krulkop-klonkie*
[ˈkrœlkɔpˌklɔŋki]
Music also by: Judith Brent-Wessels (1910–n.d.)
Eva Noel Harvey (1900–1976), "Three New Songs" (*Drie Nuwe Liedere, no. 2*)
[dri ˈnyvə ˈlidərə]

Curly-haired lad, from whence do you arrive here so quickly?
Krulkop-klonkie, waarvandaan kom jy hierso gou-gou aan?
[ˈkrœlkɔpˌklɔŋki ˈvaːrfandaːn kɔm jəj ˈhiːrsʊᵊ xœuxœu aːn]

From heaven, curly-haired lad, from the stars, from the moon?
Van die hemel, krulkopklonkie, van die sterre, van die maan?
[fan di ˈfieməl ˈkrœlkɔpˌklɔŋki fan di ˈstærə fan di maːn]

Curly-haired lad, is your heart not yet broken, not yet black?
Krulkopklonkie, is jou hart nog nie klaar nie, nog nie swart?
[ˈkrœlkɔpˌklɔŋki əs jœu fiart nɔx ni klaːr ni nɔx ni swart]

Or is it already withered, gray from all the grief?
Of is dit lank verdor al, grys gemaak deur al die smart?
[ɔf əs dət laːŋk fərˈdɔr al xrəjs xəˈmaːk djøᵊr al di smart]

Curly-haired lad, when you laugh, darkness flees from the night
Krulkopklonkie, as jy lag, vlug die donker uit die nag
[ˈkrœlkɔpˌklɔŋki as jəj lax flœx di ˈdɔŋkər œyt di nax]

Through the backdoor to the outdoors, and it shines here like the day.
Deur die agterdeur na buite, en dit skyn hier soos die dag.
[djøᵊr di ˈaxtərdjøᵊr na ˈbœytə ɛn dət skəjn fiiːr sʊᵊs di dax]

Afrikaans Art Song Literature. Christian Bester and Bronwen Forbay, Oxford University Press. © Oxford University Press 2025.
DOI: 10.1093/oso/9780197660812.003.0021

What on earth do you want to take or
deliver now here with me, laddie?
Krulkopklonkie, wat wil jy op die wêreld
hier by my nou kom haal of lewer, klonkie?
['krɶlkɔpˌklɔŋki vat vəl jəj ɔp di 'væ:rəlt ɦi:r
bəj məj nɶu kɔm ɦa:l ɔf 'leᵊvər 'klɔŋki]

What is there to give or take?
Wat is hier te gee of kry?
[vat əs ɦi:r tə çeᵊ ɔf krəj]

Curly-haired lad, sleep peacefully, oblivious
of the dreams;
Krulkopklonkie, slaap gerus, van die drome
onbewus;
['krɶlkɔpˌklɔŋki sla:p xə'rɶs fan di 'drʊᵊmə
'ɔmbəˌɣɶs¹]

A nightmare will come soon enough;
Vroeg genoeg kry jy nagmerrie;
[fru xə'nux² krəj jəj 'naxmɛri]

Who will soothe you then, lad?
Wie sal jou dan, klonkie, sus?
[vi sal jɶu dan 'klɔŋki sɶs]

Secretary-Bird
2. *Sekretarisvoël*³
[səkrə'ta:rəsˌfu:əl]

Secretary bird with your long legs,
Sekretarisvoël met jou langebene,
[səkrə'ta:rəsˌfu:əl mɛt jɶu 'laŋəˌbeᵊnə]

With your pens stiff behind your ears,
Met jou penne agter die ore styf,
[mɛt jɶu 'pɛnə 'axtər di 'ʊᵊrə stəjf]

With your leisurely walk, what are you
doing here?
Met jou stadige stappies, wat maak jy hier?
[mɛt jɶu 'sta:dəxə 'stapis vat ma:k jəj ɦi:r]

Secretary bird with your long legs,
Sekretarisvoël met jou langebene,
[səkrə'ta:rəsˌfu:əl mɛt jɶu 'laŋəˌbeᵊnə]

With your dull gray feathers and long,
lanky body,
Met jou vaalgrys vere en lang, lang lyf,
[mɛt jɶu 'fa:lxrəjs 'feᵊrə ɛn laŋ laŋ ləjf]

With your big, big eyes, what are you
doing here?
Met jou groot, groot oë, wat maak jy hier?
[mɛt jɶu xrʊᵊt xrʊᵊt 'u:ə vat ma:k jəj ɦi:r]

---

[1] See Appendix G, Assimilation and Amalgamation of Consonants.
[2] Ibid.
[3] The secretary bird (*Sagittarius serpentarius*) is a large, mostly terrestrial bird of prey with an eagle-like body on crane-like legs. Adults have a featherless red-orange face and predominantly gray plumage.

On My Old Ramkie Guitar
3. *Op my ou Ramkietjie*[4]
[ɔp məj œu ramˈkiki]
Music also by: Peter Aerts (1912–1996)
Jan Bouws (1902–1978), "Eleven Afrikaans Songs" (*Elf Afrikaanse Liedere, no. 1*)
[æᵃlf afriˈkaːnsə ˈlidərə]
Lourens Faul (b. 1931), "Two Loitering Ditties" (*Twee Slampamperliedjies, no. 1*)
[tweᵊ slamˈpampər̩likis]
Charles Nel (1890–1983)
Rosa Nepgen (1909–2001)

On my old ramkie guitar
Op my ou ramkietjie
[ɔp məj œu ramˈkiki]

With just only one string
Met nog net een snaar
[mɛt nɔx nɛt eᵊn snaːr]

I play in the moonlight, higgledy-piggledy.
Speel ek in die maanskyn, deurmekaar.
[speᵊl ɛk ən di ˈmaːnskəjn ˈdjøᵊrməˌkaːr]

I sing of Adam and Eve's fall,
Ek sing van Adam en Eva se val,
[ɛk səŋ fan ˈadam ɛn ˈeᵊfa sə fal]

Of the forgotten paradise, almost certifiably
(halfway) mad!
Van die ou paradys, halfpad mal!
[fan di œu paraˈdəjs ˈɦalfpat mal]

So say that people that hear me play
So sê die mense wat my hoor speel
[suᵊ sɛ: di ˈmɛːnsə vat səj ɦuᵊr speᵊl]

When the dusk catches me kissing (me) like
velveteen.
As die skemer my vang soen soos ferweel.
[as di ˈskeᵊmər məj faŋ sun suᵊs fərˈveᵊl]

When the moon listens to me and the stars
beckon,
As die maan my aanhoor, en die sterre knik,
[as di maːn məj ˈaːnɦuᵊr ɛn di ˈstærə knək]

I play on bravely then, highly pleased.
Dan speel ek kordaat voort, in my skik.
[dan speᵊl ɛk kɔrˈdaːt fuᵊrt ən məj skək]

What do I care for people who say I've lost
my marbles,
Wat gee ek om mense wat sê ek's mal,
[vat çeᵊ ɛk ɔm ˈmɛnsə vat sɛ: ɛks mal]

When the ferns listen to me at the riverbank?
As die varings my aanhoor by die wal?
[as di ˈfaːrəŋs məj ˈaːnɦuᵊr bəj di val]

---

[4] An indigenous instrument developed by the Khoikhoin people during the eighteenth century, based on a similar instrument brought to the Cape by enslaved Malabaris. Made from a gourd, a large fruit with a hard skin, this early guitar likely received its name from the Portuguese word *rabequinha*, which means 'little violin.' This song "is, like 'Sekratarisvoël,' a metaphorical poem about Leipold himself as a strange and lonely figure. The unsympathetic attitude of those who fail to understand the music-maker's playing and singing in the moonlight is contrasted with the visionary inspiration of the player himself." Peter Klatzow, *Composers in South Africa Today* (Cape Town: Oxford University Press, 1987), 42.

Why bother with friends that never understand
Wat om my vrinde wat nooit verstaan
[vat ɔm məj ˈfrəndə vat noːjt fərˈstaːn]

When the stars and the moon beckon me?
As die sterre my toeknik, en die maan?
[as di ˈstærə məj ˈtuknək ɛn di maːn]

Good-for-Nothing and Sod-Off
4. *Boggom en Voertsek*
[ˈbɔxɔm ɛn ˈfurtsɛk]
Music also by: Rosa Nepgen (1909–2001)
Arnold Van Wyk (1916–1983)

Good-for-Nothing and Sod-Off lived together
Boggom en Voertsek het saam gelewe
[ˈbɔxɔm ɛn ˈfurtsɛk ɦɛt saːm xəˈleᵊvə]

Where the splendid Hantam Mountains stand forth
Waar die Hantamberge[5] pryk
[vaːr di ˈɦantamˌbærgə prəjk]

And the light snow hovers in the night air
En die dun kapok in die naglug swewe
[ɛn di dœn kaˈpɔk ən di ˈnaxlœx ˈsweᵊvə]

As the wind caresses the reeds.
As die wind die biesies stryk.
[as di vənt di ˈbisis strəjk]

Good-for-Nothing and Sod-Off roved together
Boggom en Voertsek het saam geswerwe
[ˈbɔxɔm ɛn ˈfurtsɛk ɦɛt saːm xəˈswærvə]

Where the buchu bushes blossom
Waar die boegoebossies[6] bloei
[vaːr di ˈbuxuˌbɔsis blui]

And the rugged rock, carved by the ice
En die harde klip, deur die ys gekerwe
[ɛn di ˈɦardə kləp djøᵊr di əjs xəˈkærvə]

In prehistoric times, still blooms.
In die oer-ou tyd, nog groei.
[ən di ur œu təjt nɔ xrui[7]]

Good-for-Nothing and Sod-Off whined together
Boggom en Voertsek het saam gesanik
[ˈbɔxɔm ɛn ˈfurtsɛk ɦɛt saːm xəˈsaːnək]

In the evening against the full moon:
In die aand teen die volle maan:
[ən di aːnt teᵊn di ˈfɔlə maːn]

I close my eyes today,
Sluit ek my oë vandag,
[slœyt ɛk məj ˈuːə fanˈdax]

---

[5] The Hantam Mountains form part of a mountainous, semi-desert region in the Northern Cape Province in the region of Calvinia. Known for its unusual landscape and agricultural activities including sheep farming, its name hails from a Khoi word for 'mountains where the bulbs grow.'

[6] Buchu bushes (*Osteospermum calendulaceum*) are fragrant-smelling fynbos shrubs with strongly scented lance-shaped leaves and sporadic yellow flowers. Used in traditional Indigenous remedies, rituals, and perfumes, this medicinal shrub is endemic to the Western Cape Province. Its name was first coined by the Khoikhoin people.

[7] See Appendix G, Assimilation and Amalgamation of Consonants.

Then I imagine
Dan waan ek
[dan va:n ɛk]

(That) I can understand your language.
Ek kan julle taal verstaan.
[ɛk kan 'jœlə ta:l fər'sta:n]

Good-for-Nothing and Sod-Off perished
together
Boggom en Voertsek het saam gesterwe
['bɔxɔm ɛn 'furtsɛk fiet sa:m xə'stærvə]

Where the Hantam land is outstretched.
Waar die Hantamland hom strek.
[va:r di 'fiantamlant fiɔm stræk]

There's nothing but the story to be passed on,
Daar's niks as die storie om oor te erwe,
[da:rs nəks as di 'stuᵊri ɔm ʊᵊr tə 'ærvə]

And nothing, nothing, nothing more one
can learn from it.
En niks niks niks om daaruit te trek.
[ɛn nəks nəks nəks ɔm 'da:rœyt tə træk]

Stand-Alone Poetry

The Sea Is Wild
Die See is wild
[di seᵊ əs vəlt]
Music: Joyce Loots (1907–n.d.), "Three Afrikaans Songs"
(*Drie Afrikaanse Liedere, no. 3*) [dri afri'ka:nsə 'lidərə]

The sea is wild, the sea is blind:
Die see is wild, die see is blind:
[di seᵊ əs vəlt di seᵊ əs blənt]

It pummels (so) over the rugged rocks;
Hy slaan so oor die rotse grof;
[fiəj sla:n sʊᵊ ʊᵊr di 'rɔtsə xrɔf]

From far off still the dull roar of its thunder
can be heard,
Véraf nog dreun sy donder dof,
['fæ:raf nɔx drjøᵊn səj 'dɔndər dɔf]

And the north wind howls over it.
En oor hom huil die noordewind.
[ɛn ʊᵊr fiɔm fiœyl di 'nʊᵊrdəvənt]

The wind is wild, the wind is fierce:
Die wind is wild, die wind is kwaai:
[di vənt əs vəlt di vənt əs kwa:j]

It hums through the trees
Hy gons die bome deur
[fiəj xɔns di 'buᵊmə djøᵊr]

And breaks the branches of the trunk
En breek die takke van die stam
[ɛn breᵊk di 'takə fan di stam]

And rouses the hailstorm with its
hullabaloo.
En steek die haelbui aan met sy lawaai.
[ɛn steᵊk di 'fia:lbœy a:n mɛt səj la'va:j]

The hail is wild, the hail is strong:
Die hael is wild, die hael is sterk:
[di fia:l əs vəlt di fia:l əs stærk]

It irons out the waves of the sea
Hy maak die see se branders glad
[fiəj ma:k di seᵊ sə 'brandərs xlat]

And pounds the wheat-fields flat
En stamp die koringvelde plat
[ɛn stamp di ˈkuᵊrəŋˌfæᵃldə plat]

And breaks the secretary bird's wing.
En breek die sekretaars se vlerk.
[ɛn breᵃk di ˈsəkrəta:rs sə flærk]

Even wilder than the sea and wind,
Nog wilder as die see en wind,
[nɔx ˈvəldər as di seᵃ ɛn vənt]

Even more rigid than the hailstorm's distress,
Nog strammer as die haelstormnood,
[nɔx ˈstramər as di ˈfia:lˌstɔrəmnuᵊt]

Even blinder than those three — (is) death,
Nog blinder as dié drie — die dood,
[nɔx ˈbləndər as ˈdi dri di dʊᵊt]

That appears on your forehead, old friend!
Wat op jou voorkop sit, ou vrind!
[vat ɔp jœu ˈfʊᵊrkɔp sət œu frənt]

The Little Star
Die Sterretjie
[di ˈstæriki]
Music: S. C. de Villiers (1895–1929)
Emiel Hullebroeck (1878–1965), "Six Songs" (*Zes liederen, no. 3*) [zɛs ˈlidərən]
Sydney Richfield (1882–1967), "Two Evening Songs" (*Twee aandliedere, no. 2*)
[tweᵊ ˈa:ntˌlidərə]
Wilhelm Ernst Heinrich Söhnge (1909–n.d.), titled "*Vonkel, sterretjie, vonkel*"

Twinkle, little star, twinkle, high in
the sky so blue!
*Vonkel, sterretjie, vonkel, hoog in die
lug so blou!*
[ˈfɔŋkəl ˈstæriki ˈfɔŋkəl fiʊᵊx ən di lœx
sʊᵊ blœu]

The day is short and the night is long;
Kort is die dag, en lank is die nag;
[kɔrt əs di dax ɛn laŋk əs di nax]

Your shine wanes with the sun's anticipation;
Dood is jou skyn eer die son jou verwag;
[dʊᵊt əs jœu skəjn eᵊr di sɔn jœu fərˈvax]

Your shine will grow faint quickly in the
morning
Snel sal jou glans in die môre verflou
[snæl sal jœu xlans ən di ˈmɔ:rə fərˈflœu]

Twinkle, little star, twinkle*!*
Vonkel, sterretjie, vonkel!
[ˈfɔŋkəl ˈstæriki ˈfɔŋkəl]

Twinkle, little star, twinkle, high in the
sky so high!
*Vonkel, sterretjie, vonkel, hoog in die lug
so hoog!*
[ˈfɔŋkəl ˈstæriki ˈfɔŋkəl fiʊᵊx ən di lœx
sʊᵊ fiʊᵊx]

You can almost notice the angels there,
Engele daar kan jy byna gewaar,
[ˈɛŋələ da:r kan jəj ˈbəjna: xəˈva:r]

Beneath the clouds the heavenly hosts,
Onder die wolke die hemelse skaar,
[ˈɔndər di ˈvɔlkə di ˈfieᵊməlsə ska:r]

With your silvery-white beaming eye
Elk met jou silverwit skit'rende oog
[æᵃlk mɛt jœu 'səlvərvət 'skətrəndə ʊᵃx]

Twinkle, little star, twinkle!
Vonkel, sterretjie, vonkel!
['fɔŋkəl 'stæriki 'fɔŋkəl]

Twinkle, little star, twinkle! Laughing in the sky above!
Vonkel, sterretjie, vonkel! Lag in die lug daar bo!
['fɔŋkəl 'stæriki 'fɔŋkəl lax ən di lœx da:r bʊᵃ]

It is crummy here, because the day has indeed gone;
Hier is dit sleg, want die dag is mos weg;
[ɦi:r əs dət slæx vant di dax əs mɔs væx]

The night has fastened itself over the entire field,
Oor al die veld het die nag hom geheg,
[ʊᵃr al di fæᵃlt ɦɛt di nax ɦɔm xə'ɦæx]

Till you shine again — yes, indeed one can then believe again
Tot as jy skyn — ja, dan kan 'n mens glo
[tɔt as jəj skəjn ja: dan kan ə mɛns xlʊᵃ]

Twinkle, little star, twinkle!
Vonkel, sterretjie, vonkel!
['fɔŋkəl 'stæriki 'fɔŋkəl]

Twinkle, little star, twinkle, above in the sky so blue!
Vonkel, sterretjie, vonkel, bo in die lug so blou!
['fɔŋkəl 'stæriki 'fɔŋkəl bʊᵃ ən di lœx sʊᵃ blœu]

The night is short, and the day is long,
Kort is die nag, en lank is die dag,
[kɔrt əs di nax ɛn laŋk əs di dax]

Here, where our lives and plight await us,
Hier, waar ons lewe en pligte verwag,
[ɦi:r va:r ɔns 'leᵃvə ɛn 'pləxtə fər'vax]

Illuminated by the sun, but (yet) black from mourning
Lig van die son, maar tog swart van die rou
[ləx fan di sɔn ma:r tɔx swart fan di rœu]

Twinkle, little star, twinkle!
Vonkel, sterretjie, vonkel!
['fɔŋkəl 'stæriki 'fɔŋkəl]

Dingaan, the Zulu
Dingaan, die Zoeloe
[dəŋ'ga:n di 'zulu]
Music: Jan Bouws (1902–1978)

Dingaan, the Zulu, was a devil;
Dingaan, die Zoeloe, was 'n duiwel;
[dəŋ'ga:n di 'zulu vas ə 'dœyvəl]

(The) henchman of hell was he!
Handlanger van die hel was hy!
['ɦantˌlaŋər fan di ɦæl vas ɦəj]

He devastated our people,
Hy het ons mense hard geteister,
[ɦəj ɦɛt ɔns 'mɛːnsə ɦart xə'təjstər]

Egotistical is his despotism.
Windmaker is sy dwing'landy.
['vəntˌmaːkər əs səj 'dwəŋlandəj]

Dingaan, the Zulu, was a devil;
Dingaan, die Zoeloe, was 'n duiwel;
[dəŋ'ga:n di 'zulu vas ə 'dœyvəl]

But he passed away long ago,
Maar hy is lankal dood,
[ma:r ɦəj əs 'laŋkal dʊ°t]

And we have no one who can harass us
En het ons geen mens wat ons kan teister
[ɛn ɦɛt ɔns çe°n mɛns vat ɔns kan 'tɐjstər]

Yet we still grieve!
En tog sit ons nog in die rou!
[ɛn tɔx sət ɔns nɔx ən di rœu]

Claim of the Spark
Eis van die Vonk
[əjs fan di fɔŋk]
Music: Gideon Fagan (1904–1980), "Loitering Ditties" (*Slampamperliedjies, no. 2*)
[slam'pampər̩ˌlikis]

Reclaim from the floundering spark,
Eis van die vonk wat spartel,
[əjs fan di fɔŋk vat 'spartəl]

Its gold as an adornment,
Sy goud as sieraad t'rug,
[səj 'xœut as 'sira:t trœx]

Ask of the frolicking fish,
Vra van die vis wat dartel,
[fra: fan di fəs vat 'dartəl]

A word of forgiveness or a sigh,
'n Jammerwoord of sug,
[ə 'jamərvʊ°rt ɔf sœx]

Or let the waves of the sea
Of laat die branders van die see
[ɔf la:t di 'brandərs fan di se°]

Provide an answer to your questions,
'n Antwoord op jou vrae gee,
[ə 'antvʊ°rt ɔp jœu 'fra:ə çe°]

Before you claim something from me
Eerdat jy van my eis
['e°rdat jəj fan məj əjs]

I must, for what happened long ago,
Ek moet wat lank verby is,
[ɛk mut vat laŋk fər'bəj əs]

Make amends.
Weer vergoed.
[ve°r fər'xut]

Like gold at twilight
Goud in die skemer
[xœut ən di 'ske°mər]

The magnificent firmament sparkles;
Skitter die sterreskaar se prag;
['skətər di 'stærəska:r sə prax]

The sea gleams white,
Die see blink wit,
[di se° bləŋk vət]

And whiter (is) the moon's faint
gravitational pull.
En witter die maan se dowwe krag.
[ɛn 'vətər di ma:n sə 'dɔvə krax]

And just so, in the dusk of your forgetfulness
En net so in die skemerswart van jou vergeetheid
[ɛn nɛt soᵊ ən di ˈskeᵊmərswart fan jœu fərˈxeᵊtɦəjt]

My heart shines,
Blink my hart,
[bləŋk məj ɦart]

Because whiter than the whitest sea
Want witter as die witste see
[vant ˈvətər as di ˈvətstə seᵊ]

Is what your love gives to me.
Is wat jou liefde vir my gee.
[əs vat jœu ˈlifdə fər məj çeᵊ]

I Sing of the Wind
Ek sing van die Wind
[ɛk səŋ fan di vənt]
Music: E. Amyot (n.d.)
Judith Brent-Wessels (1910–n.d.)
Leonard Brown (n.d.)
Daniel Clement (1902–1980), "South Africa Onwards, Loitering Ditty" (*Suid-Afrika vorentoe, no. 15, Slampamperliedjie*) [sœyt ˈaːfrika ˈfʊᵊrəntu slamˈpampərˌliki]
Johannes Joubert (1894–1958)
W. Spiethoff (1884–1953)
J. P. J. Wierts (1866–1944)

I sing of the blustery wind;
Ek sing van die wind wat te keer gaan;
[ɛk səŋ fan di vənt vat tə keᵊr xaːn]

I sing of the rain that is falling there;
Ek sing van die reën wat daar val;
[ɛk səŋ fan di reᵊn vat daːr fal]

I sing of our fawn-colored old Karoo land;
Ek sing van ons vaal ou Karooland;[8]
[ɛk səŋ fan ɔns faːl œu kaˈrʊᵊlant]

Of flowers that bloom on the banks;
Van blomme wat bloei by die wal;
[fan ˈblɔmə vat blui bəj di val]

Of water that bubbles over the pebbles;
Van water wat bruis oor die klippe;
[fan ˈvaːtər vat brœys ʊᵊr di ˈkləpə]

Of duikers that trot over the field;
Van duikers[9] *wat draf oor die veld;*
[fan ˈdœykərs vat draf ʊᵊr di fæᵊlt]

---

[8] The Karoo is a semi-arid desert divided into the Great Karoo and the Little Karoo, both lacking in surface water. It encompasses the Eastern, Western, and Northern Cape provinces. Its name is derived from the Khoi word for 'land of thirst.' Covering approximately one-third of the total area of South Africa, the Karoo's biodiversity includes assorted succulents and low scrub bushes, plains, fossils, and unique geographical formations.

[9] The common duiker, also known as the gray or bush duiker (*Sylvicapra grimmia*), is a small- to medium-sized brown antelope indigenous to sub-Saharan Africa.

Of birds that are singing there in the shrubs
Van voëls wat daar sing in die bossies
[fan ˈfuːəls vat daːr səŋ ən di ˈbɔsis]

But never, no, never of money!
Maar nooit nie, nee nooit nie, van geld!
[maːr noːjt ni neᵊ noːjt ni fan xæᵊlt]

Rather sing to me of flowers;
Vir my sing maar liewers van blomme;
[fər məj səŋ maːr ˈlivərs fan ˈblɔmə]

Of everything that colors the meadow;
Van al wat die vlei laat verkleur;
[fan al vat di fləj laːt fərˈkljøᵊr]

Of everything that the sunshine causes to jiggle;
Van al wat die sonskyn laat spartel;
[fan al vat di ˈsɔnskəjn laːt ˈspartəl]

Of spring and autumn's fragrance;
Van voorjaar en najaar se geur;
[fan ˈfʊᵊrjaːr ɛn ˈnaːjaːr sə xjøᵊr]

Rather sing to me of the water;
Vir my sing maar liefs van die water;
[fər məj səŋ maːr lifs fan di ˈvaːtər]

Of duikers that trot over the field;
Van duikers wat draf oor die veld;
[fan ˈdœykərs vat draf ʊᵊr di fæᵊlt]

Of rocks, and waves and clouds
Van rotse en branders en wolke
[fan ˈrɔtsə ɛn ˈbrandərs ɛn ˈvɔlkə]

Of spring and autumn's fragrance;
Van voor en najaar se geur;
[fan fʊᵊr ɛn ˈnaːjaːr sə xjøᵊr]

But never, no, never of money!
Maar nooit nie, nee nooit nie, van geld!
[maːr noːjt ni neᵊ noːjt ni fan xæᵊlt]

Whistle, Swift, Sing and Whistle
Fluit, Windswael,[10] sing en fluit
[flœyt ˈvəntswaːᵊl səŋ ɛn flœyt]
Music: Lourens Faul (b. 1931), titled *"Fluit, windswael"*
Eva Noel Harvey (1900–1976)

Whistle, swift, sing and whistle,
Fluit, windswael, sing en fluit,
[flœyt ˈvəntswaːᵊl səŋ ɛn flœyt]

High above the acorn trees!
Hoog oor die akkerbome!
[fiʊᵊx ʊᵊr di ˈakər̩bʊᵊmə]

The sun scatters gold, and green illuminates all the trees.
Die son strooi goud, en groen skyn al die bome.
[di sɔn stroːj xœut ɛn xrun skəjn al di ˈbʊᵊmə]

---

[10] The swifts (*Apodidae*) are swallow-like (*Hirundinidae*) birds that migrate to southern Africa from November through March.

And before the afternoon (comes to a) close
and the evening breeze blows cold,
*En voor die middag sluit en die aandwind
waai koud,*
[ɛn fʊᵊr di ˈmədax slœyt ɛn di ˈaːntvənt
vaːj kœut]

There is still enough time remaining, swift,
to sing and whistle:
*Daar is nog tyd genoeg, windswael, vir sing
en fluit:*
[daːr əs nɔx təjt xəˈnux ˈvəntswaːᵊl fər səŋ
ɛn flœyt]

It is still too early for night, and sleep and
dreams.
*Dit is nog alte vroeg vir nag en slaap
en droom.*
[dət əs nɔx ˈaltə frux fər nax ɛn slaːp
ɛn drʊᵊm]

Whistle, swift, whistle and sing,
Fluit, windswael, fluit en sing,
[flœyt ˈvəntswaːᵊl flœyt ɛn səŋ]

High above the acorn trees!
Hoog oor die akkerbome!
[ɦʊᵊx ʊᵊr di ˈakərˌbʊᵊmə]

The sun shines warmly, and the trees rest
quietly.
Die son skyn warm, en stil rus al die bome.
[di sɔn skəjn ˈvarəm ɛn stəl rœs al di ˈbʊᵊmə]

And before Venus delivers darkness in
his arm,
*En voor die aandster bring die donker in
sy arm,*
[ɛn fʊᵊr di ˈaːntstær brəŋ di ˈdɔŋkər ən
səj ˈarəm]

There is still enough time, swift, to whistle
and sing.
*Daar is nog tyd genoeg, windswael, vir fluit
en sing.*
[daːr əs nɔx təjt xəˈnux ˈvəntswaːᵊl fər flœyt
ɛn səŋ]

It is still too early, swift, to sleep and dream.
*Dit is nog alte vroeg, windswael, vir slaap
en droom.*
[dət əs nɔx ˈaltə frux ˈvəntswaːᵊl fər slaːp
ɛn drʊᵊm]

Give Me a Wedding Ring
Gee vir my 'n Trouring
[çeᵊ fər məj ə ˈtrœurəŋ]
Music: Daniel Clement (1902–1980), "South Africa Onwards, Loitering Ditty"
(*Suid-Afrika vorentoe, no. 14, Slampamperliedjie*) [sœyt ˈaːfrika ˈfʊᵊrəntu
slamˈpampərˌliki]

Give me a wedding ring, give me a wife;
Gee vir my 'n trouring; gee vir my 'n vrou;
[çeᵊ fər məj ə ˈtrœurəŋ çeᵊ fər məj ə frœu]

Give me a little baby—take the rest for
yourself!
Gee vir my 'n babetjie—neem die res vir jou!
[çeᵊ fər məj ə ˈbaːbiki neᵊm di rɛs fər jœu]

What do you want with a wedding ring?
Wat wil jy met trouring?
[vat vəl jəj mɛt 'trœurən]

Take the work as a wedding ring;
Neem die werk as trouring;
[neᵊm di værk as 'trœurən]

What do you want with a wife?
Wat wil jy met vrou?
[vat vəl jəj mɛt frœu]

Take your country as (your) wife;
Neem jou land as vrou;
[neᵊm jœu lant as frœu]

What do you want with a little child?
Wat wil jy met babetjie?
[vat vəl jəj mɛt 'ba:biki]

The future as your child
Die toekoms as jou babetjie
[di 'tukɔms as jœu 'ba:biki]

(With) You, still in mourning?
Jy, nog in die rou?
[jəj nɔx ən di rœu]

That's enough for you!
Die genoeg vir jou!
[di xə'nux fər jœu]

In a Hole Beneath the Sickle Bush
In 'n Gat daar onder die Sukkeldoring[11]
[ən ə xat da:r 'ɔndər di 'sœkəlˌdʊᵊrən]
Music: Pieter de Villiers (1924–2015)

In a hole beneath the sickle bush
In 'n gat daar onder die sukkeldoring
[ən ə xat da:r 'ɔndər di 'sœkəlˌdʊᵊrən]

And the lamps are little fireflies,
En die lampe is klein vuurvliegies,
[ɛn di 'lampə əs kləjn 'fy:rˌflixis]

A dwarf has his house.
Het 'n dwergieman sy huis.
[ɦɛt ə 'dwærximan səj ɦœys]

That sparkle like sunshine
Wat skitter soos sonneskyn
[vat 'skətər sʊᵊs 'sɔnəskəjn]

Its walls are made of golden yellow clay,
Die mure daarvan is goudgeel klei,
[di 'my:rə 'da:rfan əs 'xœutxeᵊl kləj]

When the green (shadows) of dusk fall
As die groen van die skemeraand val
[as di xrun fan di 'skeᵊməra:nt fal]

And the floor of silvery gravel.
En die vloer van silwergruis.
[ɛn di flu:r fan 'səlvərxrœys]

And the sun's brilliance fades,
En die son se glans verdwyn,
[ɛn di sɔn sə xlans fər'dwəjn]

---

[11] A "Sukkeldoring" does not exist. The poet may be utilizing his poetic license by referring to the sickle bush tree (*Dichrostachys cinerea*) whose flowers are lilac on top and yellow on the bottom. This color scheme gave rise to the sobriquet 'Chinese lantern trees' in other countries. The direct English translation of the Afrikaans word *sukkeldoring* is 'struggle thorn.'

The chairs are mountain crystals,
Die stoele is bergkristalle,
[di ˈstulə əs ˈbærxkrəˌstalə]

That twinkle beneath the teeny lights;
Wat onder die liggies blink;
[vat ˈɔndər di ˈləxis bləŋk]

The table, a large white mushroom,
Die tafel 'n groot wit paddastoel,
[di ˈtaːfəl ə xrʊᵊt vət ˈpadastul]

With its stem sunken in the gravel.
Met sy steel in die gruis gesink.
[mɛt səj steᵊl ən di xrœys xəˈsəŋk]

The cushions are of the most delicate (Java)
silk cotton
Die kussings is fynste wit kapok
[di ˈkœsəŋs əs ˈfəjnstə vət kaˈpɔk]

Snatched from the African warbler's nest;
Uit tinktinkienes[12] gesteel;
[œyt təŋˈtəŋkinɛs xəˈsteᵊl]

And the door curtain is an ant-cat's fur,
En die deurgordyn is 'n mierkatvel,[13]
[ɛn di ˈdjøᵊrxɔrˌdəjn əs ə ˈmiːrkatfæl]

As soft as smooth velvet.
So sag soos sag ferweel.
[sʊᵊ sax sʊᵊs sax fərˈveᵊl]

Here the dwarf resides throughout the years
Hier lewe die dwergie die jare deur
[ɦiːr ˈleᵊvə di ˈdwærxi di ˈjaːrə djøᵊr]

Where no one will ever bother him;
Waar niemand hom ooit sal stoor;
[vaːr ˈnimant ɦɔm oːjt sal stʊᵊr]

And him and his wife only come out
En hy en sy vrou kom net maar uit
[ɛn ɦəj ɛn səj frœu kɔm nɛt maːr œyt]

To draw water from the trough.
Om water te haal uit die voor.
[ɔm ˈvaːtər tə ɦaːl œyt di fʊᵊr]

And children who catch a glimpse of
them say:
En die kinders die sê as hul altwee sien:
[ɛn di ˈkəndərs di sɛː as ɦœl ˈaltweᵊ sin]

"Look, there the mice go quickly!"
"Kyk daar loop die muisies gou!"
[kəjk daːr lʊᵊp di ˈmœysis xœu]

And they do not realize (that) what they
call mice,
En hul weet nie wat hulle muisies noem,
[ɛn ɦœl veᵊt ni vat ˈɦœlə ˈmœysis num]

Are the dwarf and his wife.
Is die dwergieman en sy vrou.
[əs di ˈdwærximan ɛn səj frœu]

---

[12] The African yellow warbler (*Acrocephalidae* family, *Iduna natalensis*), also known as the Natal yellow warbler, is a foraging songbird that makes a sweet tweeting sound. Its wings have brown feathers edged with yellow, while its underside is a bright yellow color. KwaZulu-Natal Province is on the east coast of South Africa and was formerly known as Natal Province.

[13] The direct translation of *Mierkat* is 'ant-cat,' a nonsensical, imaginary animal that does not exist.

Japie

Japie

[ˈjaːpi]

Music: Daniel Clement (1902–1980), "South Africa Onwards"

(*Suid-Afrika vorentoe, no. 6*) [sœyt ˈaːfrika ˈfʊᵊrəntu]

Herre De Vos (1877–1948)

Ernst Lowenherz (1874–1958), *Op. 40*

Japie was still here this morning;
Vanmôre was Japie nog hier;
[fanˈmɔːrə vas ˈjaːpi nɔx ɦiːr]

This evening he is dead!
Vanaand is hy dood!
[fəˈnaːnt əs ɦəj dʊᵊt]

He celebrated his nuptials with a big grin
on his face
Met 'n lag om sy mond het hy bruilof gevier
[mɛt ə lax ɔm səj mɔnt ɦɛt ɦəj ˈbrœylɔf xəˈfiːr]

With a small ball of English lead.
Met 'n klein brokkie Engelse lood.
[mɛt ə kləjn ˈbrɔki ˈɛŋəlsə lʊᵊt]

Japie was still here this morning;
Vanmôre was Japie by my;
[fanˈmɔːrə vas ˈjaːpi bəj məj]

Where is he tonight?
Vanaand is hy waar?
[fəˈnaːnt əs ɦəj vaːr]

If a person can only know where he
will end up
As 'n mens maar kan weet hy eind'lik sal bly
[as ə mɛns maːr kan veᵊt ɦəj ˈəjntlək sal bləj]

Who would then see danger in the future?
Wie sien dan in die toekoms gevaar?
[vi sin dan ən di ˈtukɔms xəˈfaːr]

Japie was my friend this morning;
Vanmôre was Japie my maat;
[fanˈmɔːrə vas ˈjaːpi məj maːt]

What is he tonight?
Vanaand is hy wat?
[fəˈnaːnt əs ɦəj vat]

Will he still laugh with me, will he still
speak to me,
*Sal hy nog met my lag, sal hy nog met
my praat,*
[sal ɦəj nɔx mɛt məj lax sal ɦəj nɔx mɛt
məj praːt]

Or hold my hand in his again?
Of my hand ooit in syne weer vat?
[ɔf məj ɦant oːjt ən ˈsəjnə veᵊr fat]

Japie was a child this morning;
Vanmôre was Japie 'n kind;
[fanˈmɔːrə vas ˈjaːpi ə kənt]

Tonight he is an accomplished learner!
Vanaand is hy volleerd!
[fəˈnaːnt əs ɦəj fɔˈleᵊrt]

We often quarreled over the truth, old friend
*Ons het baie gestry om die waarheid,
ou vrind*
[ɔns ɦɛt ˈbajə xəˈstrəj ɔm di ˈvaːrɦəjt
œu frənt]

Do you now know which of us was at fault?
Weet jy nou wie van ons had verkeerd?
[ve°t jəj nœu vi fan ɔns ɦat fər'ke°rt]

This morning, Japie was … no God,
Van môre was Japie nee God,
[fan 'mɔ:rə vas 'ja:pi ne° xɔt]

He is still meant for me!
Hy is nog vir my!
[ɦəj əs nɔx fər məj]

Because death cannot separate us,
Want die dood kan nie skei nie,
[vant di dʊ°t kan ni skəj ni]

Even though it's our destiny to be alone on this earth.
Al is dit ons lot om alleen op die wêreld te bly.
[al əs dət ons lɔt ɔm a'le°n ɔp di 'væ:rəlt tə bləj]

The Choice from the Best
Keur van die Beste
[kjø°r fan di 'bɛstə]
Music: Rosa Nepgen (1909–2001)

The choice from the best that life has to offer,
Keur van die beste wat die lewe besit,
[kjø°r fan di 'bɛstə vat di 'le°və bə'sət]

I grant to you, because you abundantly gave me the best of what you had.
Gun ek vir jou wat vir my van jou beste ryklik gegee het.
[xœn ek fər jœu vat fər məj fan jœu 'bɛstə 'rəjklək xə'xe° ɦet]

The shore, in the west, shifts the color of the setting sun —
Ver in die weste, verwissel die kleur van die neerdalende son —
['fæ:r ən di 'vɛstə fər'vəsəl di kljø°r fan di ne°r'da:ləndə sɔn]

In the west richly perfumed by incense.
In die weste ryklik met wierook vergeur.
[ən di 'vɛstə 'rəjklək mɛt 'virʊ°k fər'xjø°r]

Darling, the strongest that love can claim,
Liefde, die sterkste wat liefde kan eis,
['lifdə di 'stærkstə vat 'lifdə kan əjs]

I lend you, that the weakest can demonstrate their loving service to the strongest.
Leen ek vir jou, dat die swakste die sterkste liefdevol diens kan bewys.
[le°n ek fər jœu dat di 'swakstə di 'stærkstə 'lifdəfɔl dins kan bə'vəjs]

Do not say that the least are meek and insignificant;
Sê nie die leste is luttel en klein;
[sɛ: ni di 'lɛstə əs 'lətəl ɛn kləjn]

Few were the first, but more are the least, richly refined by love.
Min was die eerste, maar meer is die leste, ryklik deur liefde verfyn.
[mən vas di 'e°rstə ma:r me°r əs di 'lɛstə 'rəjklək djø°r 'lifdə fər'fəjn]

The choice from the best of what love can gain,
Keur van die beste wat liefde kan win,
[kjøᵊr fan di ˈbɛstə vat ˈlifdə kan vən]

I shower you (with love) because I know that the very best thing is that your soul loves me.
Stort ek vir jou, want ek weet dat die beste is dat jou siel my bemin.
[stɔrt ɛk fər jœu vant ɛk veᵊt dat di ˈbɛstə əs dat jœu sil məj bəˈmən]

Trek, Trek Along the Meandering Road!
Klim op, klim op met die Slingerpad!
[kləm ɔp kləm ɔp mɛt di ˈsləŋərpat]
Music: P. J. de Villiers (1924–2015), "Three Leipoldt Songs"
(*Drie Leipoldt-liedjies, no. 3*) [dri ˈlaipɔltˈlikis]
Arthur Wegelin (1908–1995)

Trek, trek along the meandering road!
Klim op, klim op met die slingerpad!
[kləm ɔp kləm ɔp mɛt di ˈsləŋərpat]

Trek, trek along the meandering road!
Klim op, klim op langs die slingerpad!
[kləm ɔp kləm ɔp laŋs di ˈsləŋərpat]

Trek, trek, until you stand on top
Klim op, klim op, tot jy staan daar bo
[kləm ɔp kləm ɔp tɔt jəj staːn daːr bʊᵊ]

Trek, until you stand on top;
Klim op, tot jy bo-op staan;
[kləm ɔp tɔt jəj bʊᵊ ɔp staːn]

Where you survey our entire country in a moment,
Waar jy al ons land in 'n oomblik vat,
[vaːr jəj al ɔns lant ən ə ˈʊᵊmblək fat]

And observe how beautiful our world is!
En kyk hoe mooi ons wêreld is!
[ɛn kəjk ɦu moːj ɔns ˈvæːrəlt əs]

Then your soul knows the truth because you're rich!
Dan weet jou siel die waarheid want jy's ryk!
[dan veᵊt jœu sil di ˈvaːrɦəjt vant jəjs rəjk]

From Albany to the bare Karoo!
Van die Suurveld af tot die kaal Karoo![14]
[fan di ˈsyːrfæᵊlt af tɔt di kaːl kaˈrʊᵊ]

---

[14] See note 8.

120 AFRIKAANS ART SONG LITERATURE

African Corn Lilies, You Tremble and Shiver
Klossies,[15] *jul bewe en bibber*
['klɔsis jœl 'be³və ɛn 'bəbər]
Music: Maria Van der Mark (1912–n.d.)

African corn lilies, you tremble
and shiver;
Klossies, jul bewe en bibber;
['klɔsis jœl 'be³və ɛn 'bəbər]

Is the night air then so cold?
Is dan die aandlug so koud?
[əs dan di 'a:ntlœx sʊ³ kœut]

Must you cower so against the
westerly wind?
Moet julle so teen die westewind koes?
[mut 'jœlə sʊ³ te³n di 'vɛstəvənt kus]

Will he completely destroy your blue and
gold, everything?
*Sal hy vir julle die blou en die goud, alles
verwoes?*
[sal ɦəj fər 'jœlə di blœu ɛn di xœut 'aləs
fər'vus]

African corn lilies, you tremble and shiver;
Klossies, jul bewe en bibber;
['klɔsis jœl 'be³və ɛn 'bəbər]

Soak up the sun, and be joyful!
Drink maar die son, en wees bly!
[drəŋk ma:r di sɔn ɛn ve³s bləj]

Life is gold, blue, and red;
Goud, blou en rooi is die lewe;
[xœut blœu ɛn ro:j əs di 'le³və]

And our cool old westerly wind blows gently
over the marsh —
En sag waai ons ou westewind koel oor die vlei —
[ɛn sax va:j ɔns œu 'vɛstəvənt kul ʊ³r di fləj]

The day (still) remains.
Nog is die dag.
[nɔx əs di dax]

Come Dance with Me!
Kom dans met my!
[kɔm da:ns mɛt məj]
Music: Eva Noel Harvey (1900–1976)
Anna Lambrechts-Vos (1876–1932), "Great South Africa" (*Groot Suid-Afrika*)
[xrʊ³t sœyt 'a:frika:], Songs in Five Volumes: Vol. V, Op. 45, no. 21 and 22
Ernst Lowenherz (1874–1958)
Maria Van der Mark (1912–n.d.), "Six Songs to Words of Leipoldt" (*Ses liedere op
woorde van Leipoldt, no. 5*) [sɛs 'lidərə ɔp 'vʊ³rdə fan 'ləjpɔlt]

Come dance with me!
Kom dans met my!
[kɔm da:ns mɛt məj]

Come dance with me!
Kom dans met my!
[kɔm da:ns mɛt məj]

---

[15] The African corn lily (*Iridaceae*) is also known as the wand flower. Indigenous to the Western Cape Province, it has six yellow and orange-yellow star-shaped flowers. Its leaves are long and sword-like.

CHRISTIAN FREDERICK LOUIS LEIPOLDT   121

What would you rather, better do
Wat wil jy liewer, beter doen
[vat vəl jəj 'livər 'beᵊtər dun]

Than to cuddle in the springtime,
As in die lentetyd te vry,
[as ən di 'lɛntətəjt tə frəj]

When everything is beautiful,
As alles mooi is,
[as 'aləs mo:j əs]

Everything green,
Alles groen,
['aləs xrun]

And when you cuddle,
En as jy vry,
[ɛn as jəj frəj]

You kiss your love?
Jou liefde soen?
[jœu 'lifdə sun]

Come dance with me!
Kom dans met my!
[kɔm da:ns mɛt məj]

Come dance with me!
Kom dans met my!
[kɔm da:ns mɛt məj]

What would you rather, better have?
Wat wil jy liewer, beter hê?
[vat vəl jəj 'livər 'beᵊtər fiɛ:]

Than to receive in summertime
As in die somertyd te kry
[as ən di 'sʊᵊmərtəjt tə krəj]

(For) What springtime previously had put in place
Wat lente vroeër het uitgelê
[vat 'lɛntə 'fru:ər fiɛt 'œytxə‚lɛ:]

With interest, like people say?
Met rente, soos die mense sê?
[mɛt 'rɛntə sʊᵊs di 'mɛ:nsə sɛ:]

Come dance with me!
Kom dans met my!
[kɔm da:ns mɛt məj]

Come dance with me!
Kom dans met my!
[kɔm da:ns mɛt məj]

What can rather,
Wat kan jou liewer,
[vat kan jœu 'livər]

Even better, wait for you than in winter,
Beter wag as in die winter,
['beᵊtər vax as ən di 'vəntər]

After your fall out,
Ná jou stry,
['na: jœu strəj]

A time of rest, to dream the day long —
'n Tyd vir rus, vir droom 'n dag —
[ə təjt fər rœs fər drʊᵊm ə dax]

And then the very best night,
En dan die allerbeste nag,
[ɛn dan di 'alər‚bɛstə nax]

The very best night?
Die allerbeste nag?
[di 'alər‚bɛstə nax]

The Whining Little Cricket in the Attic
Kriekie, jy wat op die Solder sanik
['kriki jəj vat ɔp di 'sɔldər 'sa:nək]
Music: Maria Van der Mark (1912–n.d.)

Little cricket, you who whine in the attic,
Kriekie, jy wat op die solder sanik,
['kriki jəj vat ɔp di 'sɔldər 'sa:nək]

What can you possibly tell us?
Wat het jy tog vir ons te vertel?
[vat ɦet jəj tɔx fər ɔns tə fər'tæl]

Do you believe in old-fashioned little secrets?
Glo jy ouderwetse ou geheimpies?
[xlʊᵊ jəj 'œudərˌvɛtsə œu xə'ɦəjmpis]

Is there something which you highly regard?
Is daar iets waarop jy agting stel?
[əs da:r its va:r'ɔp jəj 'axtəŋ stæl]

Or do you just have to whine day in, and day out,
Of moet jy, dag in, dag uit, maar sanik,
[ɔf mut jəj dax ən dax œyt ma:r 'sa:nək]

Little cricket, 'till I go crazy from your monotonous drone?
Kriekie, tot ek dol word van jou dreun?
['kriki tɔt ɛk dɔl vɔrt fan jœu drjøᵊn]

Is your praise-song but a cricket elegy,
Is jou lofsang maar 'n kriekieklaaglied,
[əs jœu 'lɔfsaŋ ma:r ə 'krikiˌkla:xlit]

And your little tune, little cricket, but a whine?
En jou deuntjie, kriekie, maar 'n kreun?
[ɛn jœu 'djøɲki 'kriki ma:r ə krjøᵊn]

A Little Springtime Song
Lenteliedjie
['lɛntəˌliki]
Music: J. K. Pescod (1898–1985)

All the fields are merry, all the birdies sing;
Al die velde's[16] *vrolik; al die voëltjies sing;*
[al di 'fæᵊldəs 'frʊᵊlək al di 'fʊᵊlkis səŋ]

All the little crickets chirp outside; every grasshopper hops.
Al die kriekies kriek daar buit'; elke sprinkaan spring.
[al di 'krikis krik da:r 'bœyt 'æᵊlkə 'sprəŋka:n sprəŋ]

---

[16] An expansive African prairie, field, or pasture, comprising a wide variety of vegetation which may be used in various ways, including agriculture or uncultivated countryside.

CHRISTIAN FREDERICK LOUIS LEIPOLDT   123

All the little agama lizards come to celebrate;
Al die koggelmannetjies[17] kom om fees te vier;
[al di 'kɔxəlˌmanikis kɔm ɔm feᵊs tə fiːr]

A little bug gallops here, an ant dances over there.
Hier galop 'n goggatjie, daarso dans 'n mier.
[ɦiːr xaˈlɔp ə ˈxɔxaki ˈdaːrsɔ daːns ə miːr]

Even the little fish flounder against the bulrushes;
Selfs die vissies spartel teen die akkerskuil;[18]
[sæᵊlfs di ˈfəsis ˈspartəl teᵊn di ˈakərskœyl]

A grandfather-owl is dreaming in the big old oak tree.
In die groot ou eikeboom droom 'n oupa-uil.
[in di xrʊᵊt œu ˈəjkəbʊᵊm drʊᵊm ə ˈœupaˌœyl]

An aroma diffuses across our Karoo land:
Rond in ons Karooland[19] is 'n ruik versprei:
[rɔnt ən ɔns kaˈrʊᵊlant əs ə rœyk fərˈsprəj]

Buchu flower and apricot—can anything be better than this?
Boegoeblom en appelkoos—kan jy beter kry?
[ˈbuxublɔm ɛn ˈapəlkʊᵊs kan jəj ˈbeᵊtər krəj]

Gardenia hedges, dappled with flowers here;
Katjiepieringheinings, bont met blomme hier;
[ˌkaˈki ˈpirənˌɦəjnəns bɔnt mɛt ˈblɔmə ɦiːr]

Rose and lilac adjoining, rose and carnation.
Rose en sering daarnaas, roos en angelier.
[ˈrʊᵊsə ɛn ˈseᵊrən daːrˈnaːs rʊᵊs ɛn aɲəˈliːr]

Bind together white gardenias for me,
Binde vir my same katjiepiering wit,
[ˈbəndə fər məj ˈsaːmə ˌkaˈkiˈpirəŋ vət]

Babianas blue and multicolored, roses in the bush,
Bobbejaantjies[20] blou en bont, rose in die lit,
[bɔbəˈjaːɲkis blœu ɛn bɔnt ˈrʊᵊsə ən di lət]

Ferns (taken) from the rocks, red marigolds
Varings van die klippe, Afrikaners rooi
[ˈfaːrəns fan di ˈkləpə afriˈkaːnərs roːj]

And little turkeys from the marsh —
En kalkoentjies[21] uit die vlei —
[ɛn kalˈkuɲkis œyt di fləj]

They are all so beautiful!
Algar is so mooi!
[ˈalxaːr əs sʊᵊ moːj]

---

[17] Agama lizards (*Lacerta agama*) are small- to moderate-sized long-tailed, insectivorous lizards. They encompass at least 37 species in Africa, especially sub-Saharan Africa. Known for being polyamorous, the male often bobs his head when courting and asserting his territorial rights. This behavior has given rise to colloquial names such as *koggelmander*, which when translated into English means 'little mocking man.'

[18] This word in the original poem is highly derogatory. While the authors are aware that the word *koeraalboom* translated as 'coral tree' is sometimes used as a substitute in present-day South Africa, we have chosen to use the word *akkerskuil* (bulrushes) [ˈakərskœyl] (*Scirpoides holoschoenus*) here, to maintain the rhyming scheme. The original compound word refers to the palmiet (*Prionium serratum*), a semiaquatic, evergreen flowering bush. It can grow to about 2 m (6 ft. 7 in.) in height and is mainly found in the southwest and eastern parts of South Africa.

[19] See note 8.

[20] The babiana (*Babiana sambucina*) is a member of the Iris (*Iridaceae*) family. The origin of the name is likely derived from the Dutch word *baviaan*, referring to the Chacma baboon (*Papio ursinus*) that consumes the corms of the plant.

[21] While the direct translation of this word is 'little turkeys,' the poet may be referring to the southern bald ibis (*Geronticus calvus*), a long-legged wading bird with a featherless face and head. It is relatively quiet and makes a gobbling sound when vocalizing. This is why the Afrikaans word for this bird is the *wilde kalkoen*, which means 'wild turkey.'

African daisies from the field,
Geel gousblomme uit die veld,
[çeᵊl 'xœusˌbləmə œyt di fæᵊlt]

Irises from the water-hole —
Klossies uit die kuil —
['kləsis œyt di kœyl]

Shall we ever exchange our little flowers for
something else?
*Sal ons ooit ons blommetjies vir iets
ander ruil?*
[sal ɔns o:jt ɔns 'bləmikis fər its 'andər rœyl]

Merry is the world, happy ridge and marshes!
Vrolik is die wêreld, vrolik rand en vlei!
['frʊᵊlək əs di 'væ:rəlt 'frʊᵊlək rant ɛn fləj]

Each little agama lizard has found its mate;
Elke koggelmannetjie het sy maat gekry;
['æᵊlkə 'kɔxəlˌmaniki ɦɛt səj ma:t xə'krəj]

Every buzzing little bug is married or free —
Elke gons'rige goggatjie is getroud of vry —
['æᵊlkə 'xɔnsrəxə 'xɔxaki əs xə'trœut ɔf frəj]

The world is merry here, merry field
and marsh!
Vrolik is die wêreld hier, vrolik veld en vlei!
['frʊᵊlək əs di 'væ:rəlt ɦi:r 'frʊᵊlək fæᵊlt
ɛn fləj]

A New Song to a Familiar Tune
'n Nuwe Liedjie op 'n ou Deuntjie (Siembamba)[22]
[ə 'nyvə'liki ɔp ə œu 'djøɲki, 'simbamba:]
Music: Peter Aerts (1912–1996)
Daniel Clement (1902–1980), titled *"Siembamba"*
(Suid-Afrika vorentoe, no. 7) [sœyt 'a:frika 'fʊᵊrəntu]
Marinus De Jong (1891–1984), *Zes Zuid Afrikaanse Liederen, no. 5* [fʊᵊr di 'fɛnstər
zɛs zœyt afri'ka:nsə 'lidərən]
Roelof Willem Temmingh Sr. (1913–2001), titled "Choral Paraphrase: Siembaba"
(Koorparafrase: Siembaba) [kʊᵊrpara'fra:sə 'simbaba:]

Rockabye baby, mama's precious child!
*Siembamba, Siembamba, mamma se kindjie,
Siembamba!*
['simbamba: 'simbamba: 'mama sə 'kəɲki
'simbamba:]

Fold your tiny hands together, my child:
Vou maar jou handjies saam, my kind:
[fœu ma:r jœu 'ɦaɲkis sa:m məj kənt]

Hear how the north wind howls!
Hoor tog hoe huil die noordewind!
[ɦʊᵊr tɔx ɦu ɦœyl di 'nʊᵊrdəvənt]

Everything is calm here in the camp,
Hier in die kamp is alles stil,
[ɦi:r ən di kamp əs 'aləs stəl]

---

[22] This lullaby, sung by mothers to their children, references English-run concentration camps which imprisoned Afrikaner civilians, predominantly women and children, during the Second Anglo-Boer War (1899–1902).

Only the wind blows as it wishes;
Net maar die wind waai soos hy wil;
[nɛt ma:r di vənt va:j sʊᵊs ɦəj vəl]

Only you are allowed to groan and moan
Net maar jy self kan kreun en steun
[nɛt ma:r jəj sæᵊlf kan krjøᵊn ɛn stjøᵊn]

No one will hear you, no one, son!
Niemand sal hoor nie, niemand, seun!
['nimant sal ɦʊᵊr ni 'nimant sjøᵊn]

Everyone is (too) busy!
Almal is besig!
['almal əs 'beᵊsəx]

A cloud drifts across the land from the
north side
*Oor die land drywe 'n wolk van die
noordekant*
[ʊᵊr di lant 'drəjvə ə vɔlk fan di 'nʊᵊrdəkant]

Black as the smoke billowing from the
chimney,
Swart soos die rook uit die skoorsteen puil,
[swart sʊᵊs di rʊᵊk œyt di 'skʊᵊrsteᵊn pœyl]

Black as the night, and just as dirty as soot
Swart soos die nag, en nes roet so vuil
[swart sʊᵊs di nax ɛn nɛs rut sʊᵊ fœyl]

Fold your hands tightly together, close your
little eyes, and say amen!
*Vou maar jou handjies dig tesame, sluit maar
jou ogies, en sê ame!*
[fœu ma:r jœu 'ɦaŋkis dəx tə'sa:mə slœyt
ma:r jœu 'ʊᵊxis ɛn sɛ: 'a:mə]

You, who are the hope of our nation;
Jy, wat die hoop van ons nasie is;
[jəj vat di ɦʊᵊp fan ɔns 'na:si əs]

You, who our nation cannot do without;
Jy, wat ons volk so min kan mis;
[jəj vat ɔns fɔlk sʊᵊ mən kan məs]

You, who has to grow into a strong man;
Jy, wat moet opgroei tot 'n man;
[jəj vat mut 'ɔpxrui tɔt ə man]

You, who have to do your duty, if you can;
Jy, wat moet plig doen, as jy kan;
[jəj vat mut pləx dun as jəj kan]

You, who have no part in war;
Jy, wat geen deel aan die oorlog het;
[jəj vat çeᵊn deᵊl a:n di 'ʊᵊrlɔx ɦɛt]

You, who must sing out of pure delight
Jy, wat moet sing uit pure pret
[jəj vat mut səŋ œyt 'py:rə prɛt]

You must languish in a child's
concentration camp,
Jy moet verkwyn in 'n kinderkamp,
[jəj mut fər'kwəjn ən ə 'kəndərkamp]

You must be knocked out for the sake
of peace:
Jy moet vir vrede word uitgestamp:
[jəj mut fər 'freᵊdə vɔrt 'œytxəˌstamp]

Whooping-cough and tuberculosis,
without milk:
Kinkhoes en tering, sonder melk:
['kəŋkus ɛn 'teᵊrəŋ 'sɔndər mæᵊlk]

Bitter for you is life's milk!
Bitter vir jou is die lewensmelk!
['bətər fər jœu əs di 'leᵊvənsmæᵊlk]

Your place is there, by the tiny graves
Daar is jou plek, by die graffies
[da:r əs jœu plæk bəj di 'xrafis]

There (are) two in one coffin, a bridal pair!
Daar twee in een kissie, 'n bruilofspaar!
[da:r tweᵊ ən eᵊn 'kəsi ə 'brœylɔfspa:r]

Everything that the war holds for us
Alles vir ons wat die oorlog hou
['aləs fər ɔns vat di 'ʊᵊrlɔx fiœu]

All for us, and nothing for you:
Alles vir ons, en niks vir jou:
['aləs fər ɔns ɛn nəks fər jœu]

You inherited your duty from us
Jy het van ons jou plig geërwe
[jəj fiɛt fan ɔns jœu pləx xə'ærvə]

Duty as a child to die for our country!
Plig om as kind vir ons land te sterwe!
[pləx ɔm as kənt fər ɔns lant tə 'stærvə]

All that you win, is that we remember:
Al wat jy wen, is dat ons onthou:
[al vat jəj vɛn əs dat ɔns ɔnt'fiœu]

Liberty was worth more than a child or wife!
Meer was die vryheid as kind of vrou!
[meᵊr vas di 'frəjfiəjt as kənt ɔf frœu]

The Month of October
Oktobermaand
[ɔk'tʊᵊbərma:nt]
Music: Daniel Clement (1902–1980), "South Africa Onwards" (*Suid-Afrika vorentoe, no. 29*) [sœyt 'a:frika 'fʊᵊrəntu]
Eva Noel Harvey (1900–1976)
S. le Roux Marais (1896–1979), "New Songs" (*Nuwe Liedere, no. 1*) ['nyvə 'lidərə]
J. K. Pescod (1898–1985)
D. J. Roode (1900–1983)

It is the month of October,
Dit is die maand Oktober,
[dət əs di ma:nt ɔk'tʊᵊbər]

The most beautiful, beautiful month
Die mooiste mooiste maand
[di 'mo:jstə 'mo:jstə ma:nt]

The day is so clear, then,
Dan is die dag so helder,
[dan əs di dax sʊᵊ 'fiæᵃldər]

Every evening is so green.
So groen is elke aand.
[sʊᵊ xrun əs 'æᵃlkə a:nt]

So blue and cloudless,
So blou en sonder wolke,
[sʊᵊ blœu ɛn 'sɔndər 'vɔlkə]

The glorious heaven above —
Die hemel heerlik bo —
[di 'fieməl 'fieᵊrlək bʊᵊ]

Like a flower garden full of color
So blomtuinvol van kleure
[su̯ᵊ ˈblɔmtœynfɔl fan ˈkljø̯ᵊrə]

The ashen old Karoo.
Die asvaal ou Karoo.[23]
[di ˈasfɑ:l œu kaˈrʊ̯ᵊ]

It is the month of October
Dit is die maand Oktober
[dət əs di mɑ:nt ɔkˈtʊ̯ᵊbər]

The arum lily is in bloom,
Die varkblom is in bloei,
[di ˈfarkblɔm əs ən blui]

Over all the hippo pools
Oor al die seekoegate
[ʊ̯ᵊr al di ˈse̯ᵊkuiˌxɑ:tə]

Bulrushes are growing,
Is akkerskuil[24] *gegroei,*
[əs ˈakərskœyl xəˈxrui]

The hillocks a short while ago,
Die koppies kort gelede
[di ˈkɔpis kɔrt xəˈle̯ᵊdə]

Still as bare as a stone,
Nog as 'n klip so kaal,
[nɔx as ə kləp sʊ̯ᵊ kɑ:l]

Have now, to welcome with (a) greeting
Het nou vir welkoms-groetnis
[ɦɛt nœu fər ˈvæ̯ᵊlkɔms ˈxrutnəs]

Sported their most beautiful (attire).
Hul mooiste voorgehaal.
[ɦœl ˈmo:jstə ˈfʊ̯ᵊrxəˌɦɑ:l]

It is the month of October,
Dit is die maand Oktober,
[dət əs di mɑ:nt ɔkˈtʊ̯ᵊbər]

The acorn tree is green,
Die akkerboom is groen,
[di ˈakərbʊ̯ᵊm əs xrun]

The blue-gums (trees) along the paths
Die bloekoms langs die paaie
[di ˈblukɔms laŋs di ˈpɑ:jə]

Are all newly polished.
Is almal nuutgeboen.
[əs ˈalmal ˈny:txəˌbun]

And all around the garden you smell Persian
lilac and rose,
*En orals in die tuin rond ruik jy sering
en roos,*
[ɛn ˈʊ̯ᵊrals ən di tœyn rɔnt rœyk jəj [səˈrəŋ]
ɛn rʊ̯ᵊs]

Jasmine and gardenia
Jasmyn en katjiepiering
[jasˈməjn ɛn kaˈkiˈpirəŋ]

Orange and apricot
Lemoen en appelkoos
[ləˈmun ɛn ˈapəlkʊ̯ᵊs]

Month of October, month of October,
Oktobermaand, Oktobermaand,
[ɔkˈtʊ̯ᵊbərmɑ:nt ɔkˈtʊ̯ᵊbərmɑ:nt]

The most beautiful, most beautiful month.
Die mooiste mooiste maand.
[di ˈmo:jstə ˈmo:jstə mɑ:nt]

---

[23] See note 8.
[24] See note 18.

Sing, Little Finch, Sing!
Sing, Vinkie, sing!
[səŋ ˈfəŋki səŋ]
Music: Lourens Faul (b. 1931)
Eva Noel Harvey (1900–1976)
Heinz Hirschland (1901–1960)
Ernst Lowenherz (1874–1958)

Sing, little finch, sing,
Sing, vinkie sing,
[səŋ ˈfəŋki səŋ]

It's delightful for you to sing;
Dis heerlik vir jou om te sing;
[dəs ˈfieᵊrlək fər jœu ɔm tə səŋ]

When the sun brings forth its sunshine
As die son sy sonskyn bring
[as di sɔn səj ˈsɔnskəjn brəŋ]

Scattering gold on the road,
Om die pad met goud te saai,
[ɔm di pat mɛt xœu tə²⁵ sa:j]

Where the willow tree's branches sway,
Waar die wilgertakke swaai,
[va:r di ˈvəlxərˌtakə swa:j]

When the cool veld's breeze blows.
As die koel veldwindje waai.
[as di kul ˈfæᵊltˌvəŋki va:j]

Sing, little finch, sing!
Sing, vinkie sing!
[səŋ ˈfəŋki səŋ]

Oh how I wish that I could whistle
Ek wens maar ek kan fluit
[ɛk vɛns ma:r ɛk kan flœyt]

Like you, day in, day out
Soos jy dag in, dag uit
[suᵊs jəj dax ən dax œyt]

Across the waters and over the marsh
Oor die water oor die vlei
[uᵊr di ˈva:tər uᵊr di fləj]

Where the tiny white evening-flowers unfurl,
Waar die wit aandblompies sprei,
[va:r di vət ˈa:ntˌblɔmpis sprəj]

A white flower garden for me.
'n Blomtuin wit vir my.
[ə ˈblɔmtœyn vət fər məj]

Sing, little finch, sing,
Sing, vinkie sing,
[səŋ ˈfəŋki səŋ]

Here where your little nest sways
Hier waar jou nessie swaai
[fiːr va:r jœu ˈnɛsi swa:j]

Filled to the brim with little finch chicks!
Mit vinkietjies belaai!
[mət ˈfəŋkikis bəˈla:j]

Teach them all also to sing
Leer hulle algar ook te sing
[leᵊr ˈfiœlə ˈalxa:r uᵊk tə səŋ]

---

²⁵ See Appendix G, Assimilation and Amalgamation of Consonants.

Merrily and fluently!
Vrolik en vlot!
['frʊᵊlək ɛn flɔt]

When the sunshine brings,
As die sonskyn bring,
[as di 'sɔnskəjn brəŋ]

Gold for the morning and afternoon
Goud vir die môre en middag
[xœut fər di 'mɔːrə ɛn 'mədax]

Sing little finch, sing.
Sing vinkie sing.
[səŋ 'fəŋki səŋ]

Sing to Me Again
Sing weer vir my
[səŋ veᵊr fər məj]
Music: Hans Endler (1871–1947)

Sing again for me, sing again for me,
Sing weer vir my, sing weer vir my,
[səŋ veᵊr fər məj səŋ veᵊr fər məj]

Wind that caresses and strikes the sea's surface,
Wind wat die seevlak stryk en streel,
[vənt vat di 'seᵊflak strəjk ɛn streᵊl]

Sing of desolate far-off lands,
Sing van veraf verwoeste lande,
[səŋ fan 'fæːraf fər'vustə 'landə]

Sing of the shell-laden white beaches,
Sing van die wit geskulpte strande,
[səŋ fan di vət xə'skœlptə 'strandə]

Sing of the ice (north and south poles) and
the equator,
Sing van die ys en die ewenaar,
[səŋ fan di əjs ɛn di 'eᵊvəna:r]

Sing of everything that my heart envies,
Sing van alwat my hart beny,
[səŋ fan 'alvat məj ɦart bə'nəj]

Sing of everything that I can imagine
Sing van wat ek my kan verbeel
[səŋ fan vat ɛk məj kan fər'beᵊl]

That lurks in the west or in the east,
Daar skuil in die weste of in die oos,
[da:r skœyl ən di 'vɛstə ɔf ən di ʊᵊs]

As a balm to comfort my soul,
As lawenis om my siel te troos,
[as 'la:vənəs ɔm məj sil tə trʊᵊs]

Because I am and remain a beggar.
Want ek is en bly 'n bedelaar.
[vant ɛk əs ɛn bləj ə 'beᵊdəla:r]

Sing to me again, sing to me again,
Sing weer vir my, sing weer vir my,
[səŋ veᵊr fər məj səŋ veᵊr fər məj]

The waves of the sea that splash on the rocks,
See wat se branders op rotse spat,
[seᵊ vat sə 'brandərs ɔp 'rɔtsə spat]

Sing of the ship that devoured your strength,
Sing van die skip wat jou krag verslind het,
[səŋ fan di skəp vat jœu krax fər'slənt ɦɛt]

Sing of your color (complexion) that blinded
my eye,
Sing van jou kleur wat my oog verblind het,
[səŋ fan jœu kljø⋄r vat məj ʊᵊx fər'blənt ɦɛt]

Sing of the storm and of death's peril,
Sing van die storm en van doodsgevaar,
[səŋ fan di ˈstɔrəm ɛn fan ˈdʊᵊtsxəˌfaːr]

Sing of everything that wrestles and struggles,
Sing van alles wat stoei en stry,
[səŋ fan ˈaləs vat stui ɛn strəj]

Sing of what awaits me hereafter.
Sing van wat ek hiernamaals kry.
[səŋ fan vat ɛk ɦiːrˈnaːmaːls krəj]

I am so dirt poor that I ask for alms
Ek is so arm dat ek aalmoes vra
[ɛk əs sʊᵊ arm dat ɛk ˈaːlmus fraː]

For support and comfort to carry my burden,
Vir steun en troos om my las te dra,
[fər stjøᵊn ɛn trʊᵊs ɔm məj las tə draː]

Because I am and remain a beggar.
Want ek is en bly 'n bedelaar.
[vant ɛk əs ɛn bləj ə ˈbeᵊdəlaːr]

Like a Bubbling Finch Freeing Its Heart
Soos 'n borrelende Vink sy Hart verlos
[sʊᵊs ə ˈbɔrələndə fəŋk səj ɦart fərˈlɔs]
Music: Doris Beyers (n.d.), "Three Songs" (*Drie Liedere*) [dri ˈlidərə]
P. J. de Villiers (1924–2015), "Three Leipoldt Songs" (*Drie Leipoldt-liedjies, no. 1I*)
[dri ˈlaipɔlt ˈlikis]
Maria Van der Mark (1912–n.d.)
Rosa Nepgen (1909–2001)

Like a bubbling finch freeing its heart
Soos 'n borrelende vink sy hart verlos
[sʊᵊs ə ˈbɔrələndə fəŋk səj ɦart fərˈlɔs]

Of the song bubbling up that must be uttered
Van die sang wat opbruis en uiting moet vind
[fan di saŋ vat ˈɔbrœys ɛn ˈœytəŋ mut fənt]

As it swings on the branch of the acacia tree,
As hy swaai op die tak van die swarthoutbos,[26]
[as ɦəj swaːj ɔp di tak fan di ˈswartɦœutbɔs]

Caressed by the soft cool morning wind; Ah!
Gestreel deur die sagkoel môrewind; A!
[xəˈstreᵊl djøᵊr di ˈsaxkul ˈmɔːrəvənt aː]

Like the seagull that sings as it glides eastwards
Soos die seemeeu sing as hy ooswaarts gly
[sʊᵊs di ˈseᵊmiu səŋ as ɦəj ˈʊᵊsvaːrts xləj]

On its strong wings over the waves,
Op sy sterke wieke die branders oor,
[ɔp səj ˈstærkə ˈvikə di ˈbrandərs ʊᵊr]

Upwards, upwards in the blue sky, freely,
Omhoog, omhoog in die blou lug, vry,
[ɔmˈɦʊᵊx ɔmˈɦʊᵊx ən di blœu lœx frəj]

---

[26] The acacia tree (*Acacia melanoxylon*) belongs to about 160 species of trees and shrubs in the pea family (*Fabacea*). Indigenous to tropical and subtropical regions of the world, they are well-known landmarks in the African bushveld and in savannahs.

Enchanted by the sunshine and
the sea —
*Deur die skyn van die son en die see
bekoor —*
[djø⁹r di skəjn fan di sɔn ɛn di se⁹ bə'kʊ⁹r]

Thus sings the heart that cherishes beauty,
So sing die hart wat die skoonheid min,
[sʊ⁹ səŋ di ɦart vat di 'skʊ⁹nɦəjt mən]

Because beauty enchants like the sun and
the sea;
*Want skoonheid bekoor soos die son en
die see;*
[vant 'skʊ⁹nɦəjt bə'kʊ⁹r sʊ⁹s di sɔn ɛn di se⁹]

And he who opens his soul to beauty,
En hy wat vir skoonheid sy siel ontgin,
[ɛn ɦəj vat fər 'skʊ⁹nɦəjt səj sil ɔnt'xən]

Gives back (to) all that life gives him
through his song.
Skenk terug in sy lied wat die lewe hom gee.
[skɛŋk tə'rœx ən səj lit vat di 'le⁹və ɦɔm çe⁹]

Tirelli, Lirelli, La
Toeral, loeral, la
['tural 'lural la:]
Music: Doris Beyers (n.d.), "Three Songs" (*Drie Liedere*) [dri 'lidərə]
Lourens Faul (b. 1931)
Eva Noel Harvey (1900–1976)
Rosa Nepgen (1909–2001)

Tirelli, lirelli, la, winter is over!
Toeral, loeral, la, die winter is verby!
['tural 'lural la: di 'vəntər əs fər'bəj]

Look how the trees bloom, gardenias in
every row.
Kyk hoe bot die bome, katjies elke ry.
[kəjk ɦu bɔt di 'bʊ⁹mə 'ka ˈ kis 'æ⁹lkə rəj]

Tirelli, lirelli, la, my darling is friends
with me!
Toeral, loeral, la, my skat is maats met my!
['tural 'lural la: məj skat əs ma:ts mɛt məj]

See how her lips laugh enticingly,
caressingly, happily.
Kyk hoe lag haar lippies lokkend, strelend, bly.
[kəjk ɦu lax ɦa:r 'ləpis 'lɔkənt 'stre⁹lənt bləj]

Tirelli, lirelli, la, heaven is near!
Toeral, loeral, la, die hemel is naby!
['tural 'lural la: di 'ɦe⁹məl əs na'bəj]

Look how the bee buzzes playfully around
the flowers.
Kyk hoe om die blomme gonserig speel die by.
[kəjk ɦu ɔm di 'blɔmə 'xɔnsərəx spe⁹l di bəj]

A Weeping Song

'n Treurlied

[ə 'trjø°rlit]

Music: P. J. de Villiers (1924–2015), "Three Leipoldt Songs" (*Drie Leipoldt-liedjies, no. 2*) [dri 'laipɔlt 'likis]

Charles Nel (1890–1983)

Rosa Nepgen (1909–2001)

S. le Roux Marais (1896–1979), "Six Art Songs" (*Ses Kunsliedere, no. 6*)

[sɛs 'kœns͜lidərə]

Oh willow, that keeps vigil over the water
O wilgerboom, wat oor die water waak
[ʊ° 'vəlxərbʊ°m vat ʊ°r di 'va:tər va:k]

Set aside some of your sorrow (with) a branch, just enough to make a wreath.
Spaar van jou treur 'n tak genoeg, om kranse van te maak.
[spa:r fan jœu trjø°r ə tak xə'nux ɔm 'kransə fan tə ma:k]

Oh lily, lily flower that graces the front yard garden,
O lelie, lelie-blom wat in die voortuin pryk,
[ʊ° 'le°li 'le°li blɔm vat ən di 'fʊ°rtœyn prəjk]

Pour bridal stars that enhance the wreath with all your finery.
Skink bruilof sterre wat die krans met al jou tooi verryk.
[skəŋk 'brœylɔf 'stærə vat di krans mɛt al jœu to:j fə'rəjk]

Oh dark-green laurel that mourns the whole year long
O donkergroen lourier wat rou die hele jaar deur
[ʊ° 'dɔŋkərxrun lœu'rir vat rœu di 'ɦe°lə ja:r djø°r]

Give your foliage out of love as an adornment for the coffin's wreath.
Gee as sieraad vir die doodkiskrans jou loof uit liefde mee.
[çe° as 'sira:t fər di 'dʊ°tkəskrans jœu lʊ°f œyt 'lifdə me°]

Oh luminous sun, cast your brilliance over the grave.
O helder son, strooi oor die graf jou glans.
[ʊ° 'ɦæ°ldər sɔn stro:j ʊ°r di xraf jœu xlans]

Show sympathy with the lily blossom, and with the willow wreath.
Het meely met die lelieblom, en met die wilgerkrans.
[ɦet 'me°ləj mɛt di 'le°liblɔm ɛn mɛt di 'vəlxərkrans]

The Garden Rose Among the Tulips

Tuinroos tussen die Tulpe

['tœynrʊˀs 'tœsən di 'tœlpə]

Music: Con Lamprecht (n.d.)

Rosa Nepgen (1909–2001)

Maria Van der Mark (1912–n.d.), "Six Songs on Words by Leipoldt"

(*Ses Liedere op Woorde van Leipoldt, no. 1*) [sɛs 'lidərə ɔp 'vʊˀrdə fan 'ləjpɔlt]

The garden rose among the tulips,
Tuinroos tussen die tulpe,
['tœynrʊˀs 'tœsən di 'tœlpə]

The plumbago so blue
Vergeet-my-nie[27] so blou
[fər'xeˀt məj ni sʊˀ blœu]

As the glimmer of the sky on a
summer's day,
Soos die skyn van die lug op 'n somerdag,
[sʊˀs di skəjn fan di lœx ɔp ə 'sʊˀmərdax]

Or the color retained by the sea —
Of die kleur wat die see behou —
[ɔf di kljøˀr vat di seˀ bə'fiœu]

I pick you for my bouquet,
Ek pluk julle vir my ruiker,
[ɛk plœk 'jœlə fər məj 'rœykər]

Plumbago and rose,
Vergeet-my-nie en roos,
[fər'xeˀt məj ni ɛn rʊˀs]

As a token of my duty of love
Om 'n blyk te gee van my liefdesplig
[ɔm ə bləjk tə çeˀ fan məj 'lifdəspləx]

And to console my own grief.
En my eie smart te troos.
[ɛn məj 'əjə smart tə trʊˀs]

Garden rose among the tulips,
Tuinroos tussen die tulpe,
['tœynrʊˀs 'tœsən di 'tœlpə]

Plumbago so blue,
Vergeet-my-nie so blou,
[fər'xeˀt məj ni sʊˀ blœu]

Can I let go of my beloved without flowers,
Kan ek sonder blomme my lief laat trek,
[kan ɛk 'sɔndər 'blɔmə məj lif la:t træ:k]

And still hold on to my own treasure?
En my eie skat behou?
[ɛn məj 'əjə skat bə'fiœu]

---

[27] The plumbago (*Plumbaginbaceae*) is a scrambling shrub with trusses of white, blue, pink, red, or purple flowers. It is found widely throughout South Africa and in other warm, temperate subtropical regions.

From the Lotus Land Where the Lilies Grow, Song of Mali, the Slave
Van die Lotosland[28] *waar die Lelies groei (Lied van Mali, die Slaaf)*
[fan di ˈlʊᵊtɔslant vaːr di ˈleᵊlis xrui lit fan ˈmaːli di slaːf]
Music: Gerrit Bon Sr. (1901–1983), titled *"Lied van Mali die slaaf"*
[lit fan ˈmaːli di slaːf]
S. le Roux Marais (1896–1979), titled *"Mali, die Slaaf, se Lied"*
(Vyf Kunsliedere, no. 3) [fəjf ˈkœnsˌlidərə]

From the lotus land where the lilies grow,
Van die lotosland waar die lelies groei,
[fan di ˈlʊᵊtɔslant vaːr di ˈleᵊlis xrui]

And the hibiscus flower blooms on the
tree trunk;
En die koningsblom op die boomstam bloei;
[ɛn di ˈkʊᵊnəŋsblɔm ɔp di ˈbʊᵊmstam blui]

Where summer lives throughout the years
Waar jare deur die somer woon
[vaːr ˈjaːrə djøᵊr di ˈsʊᵊmər vʊᵊn]

And crowns every day with glory;
En elke dag met glorie kroon;
[ɛn ˈæᵊlkə dax mɛt ˈxlʊᵊri krʊᵊn]

Where the cool southeasterly wind softly
Waar sag die koel suidoostewind
[vaːr sax di kul sœytˈʊᵊstəvənt]

Greets the fertile green pasture as a friend;
Die geilgroen veld begroet as vrind;
[di ˈxəjlxrun fæᵊlt bəˈxrut as frənt]

And more gently against the white
beach break
En sagter teen die wit strand slaan
[ɛn ˈsaxtər teᵊn di vət strant slaːn]

The waves of the ocean
Die branders van die oseaan
[di ˈbrandərs fan di ʊᵊsiˈaːn]

From there, from there I come, I whose
name is Mali!
*Daarvandaan, daarvandaan kom ek wat
Mali heet!*
[ˈdaːrfandaːn ˈdaːrfandaːn kɔm ɛk vat
ˈmaːli fieᵊt]

I was free where the lotus grows
Vry was ek waar die lotos groei
[frəj vas ɛk vaːr di ˈlʊᵊtɔs xrui]

Free where the hibiscus blooms;
Vry waar die koningsblomme bloei;
[frəj vaːr di ˈkʊᵊnəŋsˌblɔmə blui]

Where every afternoon the rain gently
Waar elke middag sag die reën
[vaːr ˈæᵊlkə ˈmədax sax di reᵊn]

Weeps its ardor with immeasurable tears
Sy gloed ontel'bre trane ween
[səj xlut ɔnˈtɛlbrə ˈtraːnə veᵊn]

Over rooftops and silvery sands,
Oor ataphut[29] *en silverstrand,*
[ʊᵊr ˈaːtaphœt ɛn ˈsəlvərstrant]

---

[28] Likely the Indonesia-Malay Archipelago.
[29] Translated from Indonesian into English.

Across finely crafted rice-fields;
Oor fynbewerkte sawaland;[30]
[ʊᵊr 'fəjnbəˌværktə saˈvalant]

Where above the majestic volcano
Waar oor die statige vulkaan
[va:r ʊᵊr di 'sta:təxə fœlˈka:n]

The smoke-cloud stands in the morning
Die rookwolk in die môre staan
[di 'rʊᵊkvɔlk ən di 'mɔ:rə sta:n]

From there, from there I come, I whose name is Mali!
Daarvandaan, daarvandaan kom ek wat Mali heet!
['da:rfanda:n 'da:rfanda:n kɔm ɛk vat 'ma:li fieᵊt]

Show Me the Place
Wys my die Plek
[vəjs məj di plæk]
Music: Gideon Fagan (1904–1980), "Loitering Ditties" (*Slampamperliedjies, no. 1*)
[slamˈpampərˌliki]
Lourens Faul (b. 1931), "Two Loitering Ditties" (*Twee Slampamperliedjies, no. 2*)
[tweᵊ slamˈpampərˌlikis]
Hans Herbert Maske (1927–1976)

Show me the place where we stood together,
Wys my die plek waar ons saam gestaan het,
[vəjs məj di plæk va:r ɔns sa:m xəˈsta:n fiɛt]

Once, when you were mine —
Eens, toe jy myne was —
[eᵊns tu jəj 'məjnə vas]

Earlier, before your love for me faded,
Vroeër, voor jou liefde vir my getaan het,
['fru:ər fʊᵊr jœu 'lifdə fər məj xəˈta:n fiɛt]

Earlier, when you were mine.
Vroeër, toe jy myne was.
['fru:ər tu jəj 'məjnə vas]

Look, it's the same;
Kyk, dis dieselfde;
[kəjk dəs diˈsæᵊlfdə]

The silver sea glitters in the sunshine,
Die silwersee blink in die sonskyn,
[di 'səlvərseᵊ bləŋk ən di 'sɔnskəjn]

Like bygone days
Soos lang verlee
[sʊᵊs laŋ fərˈleᵊ]

It once shone,
Dit eenmaal geblink het,
[dət 'eᵊnma:l xəˈbləŋk fiɛt]

---

[30] Ibid.

136 AFRIKAANS ART SONG LITERATURE

A welcome greeting for our enduring love
'n Welkomsgroet vir ons liefde wat uithou
[ə ˈvæᵃlkɔmsxrut fər ɔns ˈlifdə vat ˈœytɦœu]

And all was made up for.
En alles is vergoed.
[ɛn ˈaləs əs fərˈxut]

Show me the place where we knelt together,
Wys my die plek waar ons saam gekniel het,
[vəjs məj di plæk va:r ɔns sa:m xəˈknil ɦɛt]

Once, when you were mine —
Eens, toe jy myne was —
[eᵃns tu jəj ˈməjnə vas]

Back, when one soul inspired us both,
Vroeër, toe een siel vir ons saam besiel het,
[ˈfru:ər tu eᵃn sil fər ɔns sa:m bəˈsil ɦɛt]

Back, when you were mine.
Vroeër, toe jy myne was.
[ˈfru:ər tu jəj ˈməjnə vas]

Look, it's the same;
Kyk, dis dieselfde;
[kəjk dəs diˈsæᵃlfdə]

The blue heavens laugh as before,
Die hemel, blou, lag soos voorheen,
[di ˈɦeᵃməl blœu lax sʊᵃs ˈfʊᵃrɦeᵃn]

Upon me and you;
Op my en op jou;
[ɔp məj ɛn ɔp jœu]

It still sparkles a welcome greeting
Dit skitter nog altyd 'n welkomsgroet
[dət ˈskətər nɔx ˈaltəjt ə ˈvæᵃlkɔmsxrut]

For our love that outlasts, and makes amends,
Vir ons liefde wat uithou en alles,
[fər ɔns ˈlifdə vat ˈœytɦœu ɛn ˈaləs]

For everything.
Alles vergoed.
[ˈaləs fərˈxut]

Show me the place where we walked,
Wys my die plek waar ons geloop het,
[vəjs məj di plæk va:r ɔns xəˈlʊᵃp ɦɛt]

Once, when you were mine —
Eens, toe jy myne was —
[eᵃns tu jəj ˈməjnə vas]

Earlier, when our hearts had so much hope,
Vroeër, toe ons harte soveel gehoop het,
[ˈfru:ər tu ɔns ˈɦartə ˈsʊᵃfeᵃl xəˈɦʊᵃp ɦɛt]

Back, when you were mine.
Vroeër, toe jy myne was.
[ˈfru:ər tu jəj ˈməjnə vas]

Look, it's the same!
Kyk, dis dieselfde!
[kəjk dəs diˈsæᵃlfdə]

Just not you, just not you.
Net jy nie, net jy nie.
[nɛt jəj ni nɛt jəj ni]

Ask, which of us two carries the biggest burden?
Vra, wie van ons twee die meeste dra?
[fra: vi fan ɔns tweᵃ di ˈmeᵃstə dra:]

You that have forgotten —
Jy wat vergeet het —
[jəj vat fərˈxeᵃt ɦɛt]

Or me who is punished for my love
Of ek wat boet vir my liefde
[ɔf ɛk vat but fər məj 'lifdə]

That endures and makes amends for everything?
Wat uithou en alles vergoed?
[vat 'œytɦœu ɛn 'aləs fər'xut]

WILLIAM EWART GLADSTONE LOUW

(1913–1980)
aka W. E. G. Louw

From Four Melancholy Little Songs[1]
Vier weemoedige Liedjies
[fiːr veᵊ'mudəxə 'likis]
Music: Arnold van Wyk (1916–1983)

Kestrel
1. *Vaalvalk*
['faːlfalk]
Music also by: Peter Lawrence Cohen (1937–n.d.), "Three Serious Songs"
(*Drie ernstige Liedere*) [dri 'ærənstəxə 'lidərə] Song Cycle for Baritone
and Piano, Op. 14, no. 2
Blanche Gerstman (1910–1973)

The world is (blanjketed in) white with the
woes of yesteryear
Wit is die wêreld van outyd se wee,
[vət əs di 'væːrəlt fan 'œutəjt sə veᵊ]

And a mournful melody is the early
morning tide;
En 'n treurige wys is die vroemôresee;
[ɛn ə 'trjøᵊrəxə vəjs əs di 'fruə͜mɔːreseᵊ]

Dew upon the dunes,
Dou oor die duine,
[dœu ʊᵊr di 'dœynə]

No breeze that blows,
Geen windjie wat waai,
[çeᵊn 'vəŋki vat vaːj]

Just a kestrel that sings as he circles …
Net 'n vaalvalk wat sing soos hy draai …
[nɛt ə 'faːlfalk vat səŋ sʊᵊs həj draːj]

---

[1] Permission granted by NB Publishers.

Afrikaans Art Song Literature. Christian Bester and Bronwen Forbay, Oxford University Press. © Oxford University Press 2025.
DOI: 10.1093/oso/9780197660812.003.0022

First Day of Winter
2. *Eerste Winterdag*
['eᵊrstə 'vəntərdax]
Music also by: S. Kennedy (1901–n.d.), "Five Songs for Baritone" (*Vyf Liedere vir Bariton, no. 1*) [fəjf 'lidərə fər 'baritɔn]

After all the sunshine, it is dark now;
Ná al die sonskyn is dit donker;
['na: al di 'sɔnskəjn əs dət 'dɔŋkər]

The ash-colored clouds drift by in the sky;
Vaal dryf die wolke in die lug;
[fa:l drəjf di 'vɔlkə ən di lœx]

The sparse fine rain, drizzling all day;
Vaal die ylmot-reën wat heeldag stuiwe;
[fa:l di 'əjlmɔt reᵊn 'heᵊldax 'stœyvə]

Low, whirlingly the leaves take flight.
Laag, dwarrelend die blare vlug.
[la:x 'dwarələnt di 'bla:rə flœx]

The hours drag by quietly and the fine rain is drizzling outside;
Stil sleep die ure en stuif die motreën buite;
[stəl sleᵊp di 'y:rə ɛn stœyf di 'mɔtreᵊn 'bœytə]

The drops quiver mournfully against the window pane;
Die druppels tril droewig teen die ruite;
[di 'drœpəls trəl 'druvəx teᵊn di 'rœytə]

Drip, drip monotonously, monotonously on antlers and rooftops
Drup drup eentonig, eentonig op gewei en dak
[drœp drœp eᵊn'tuᵊnəx eᵊn'tuᵊnəx ɔp xə'vəj ɛn dak]

And hang with a heavy sheen on the bare almond branch.
En hang swaarblink aan die kale amandeltak.
[ɛn haŋ 'swa:rblənk a:n di 'ka:lə a'mandəltak]

Stand-Alone Poetry

In Front of the Window[2]
Voor die Venster
[fʊᵊr di 'fɛnstər]
Music: Marinus de Jong (1891–1984), "Six South African Songs" (*Zes Zuid Afrikaanse Liederen, no. 3*) [fʊᵊr di 'fɛnstər zɛs zœyt afri'ka:nsə 'lidərən]

Again, the perfect summer moon is shining
Weer skyn die volkome somermaan
[veᵊr skəjn di fɔl'kʊᵊmə 'sʊᵊmərma:n]

And the timeless quiet stars flicker;
En blink die ewige stille sterre;
[ɛn bləŋk di 'eᵊvəxə 'stələ 'stærə]

---

[2] Permission granted by NB Publishers.

Again, the wind whispers of a distant land
Weer fluister die wind van 'n verre land
[veᵊr 'flœystər di vənt fan ə 'færə lant]

Behind the concept of laughter and tears;
Agter die begrip van lag en traan;
['axtər di bə'xrəp fan lax ɛn tra:n]

Here in the dark,
Hier in die donker,
[ɦi:r ən di 'dɔŋkər]

Against (the backdrop of which) the stars
come and go,
Waarteen die sterre kom en gaan,
['va:rteᵊn di 'stærə kɔm ɛn xa:n]

I remain lonely,
Bly ek vereensaam,
[bləj ɛk fər'eᵊnsa:m]

Standing wonder-struck.
Met wonderoë staan.
[mɛt 'vɔndər̩u:ə sta:n]

DANIËL FRANÇOIS MALHERBE

(1881–1969)
aka D. F. Malherbe

Evening Gaze
Aandblik
[ˈaːntblək]
Music: Doris Beyers (n.d.), "Cupid's Confetti and Five Other Songs"
(*Amors Konfetti en vyf ander Liedere, no. 2*) [ˈaːmɔrs kɔnˈfɛti ɛn fəjf ˈandər ˈlidərə]

Across far, far-off lands
Oor ver, verre lande
[ʊᵊr fæːr ˈfærə ˈlandə]

Across blue, blue ridges
Oor blou, bloue rande
[ʊᵊr blœu ˈblœuə ˈrantə]

I see fleecy little clouds scattered
Sien ek vliesige wolkies verspreid
[sin ɛk ˈflisəxə ˈvɔlkis fərˈsprəjt]

Across high, higher ground, softly cradled, impossible
Oor hoog, hoë gronde sag gewieg, onbegonde[1]
[ʊᵊr ɦʊᵊx ˈɦuːə ˈxrɔndə sa xəˈvix² ɔnbəˈxɔndə]

The sky's arch (is) so blue and so wide.
Die lug welf so blou en so wyd.
[di lœx væᵊlf sʊᵊ blœu ɛn sʊᵊ vəjt]

Across far, far-off lands,
Oor ver, verre lande,
[ʊᵊr fæːr ˈfærə ˈlandə]

Across blue, blue ridges,
Oor blou bloue rande,
[ʊᵊr blœu ˈblœuə ˈrantə]

Illuminated by the evening sun's beams,
Deur die aandson se strale beskyn,
[djøᵊr di ˈaːndsɔn sə ˈstraːlə bəˈskəjn]

I see free unmeasured,
Sien ek vry ongemete,
[sin ɛk frəj ɔnxəˈmeᵊtə]

Unmarked and forgotten,
Ongemerk en vergete,
[ɔnxəˈmærk ɛn fərˈxeᵊtə]

The little clouds so quietly disappearing.
Die wolkies so stil-stil verdwyn.
[di ˈvɔlkis sʊᵊ stəlstəl fərˈdwəjn]

Just as the fleeting images of the dying
Nes die vlugtige beelde van die sterwend
[nɛs di ˈflœxtəxə ˈbeᵊldə fan di ˈstærvənt]

---

[1] This word is likely "onbegonne." The spelling could possibly have been an editorial error.
[2] See Appendix G, Assimilation and Amalgamation of Consonants.

Afrikaans Art Song Literature. Christian Bester and Bronwen Forbay, Oxford University Press. © Oxford University Press 2025.
DOI: 10.1093/oso/9780197660812.003.0023

Yellow-colored clouds scattered in the sky
Vergeelde wolke in die lugte verspreid
[fər'xeᵊldə 'vɔlkə ən di 'lœxtə fər'sprəjt]

So generations sink away
So sink daar geslagte
[sʊᵊ səŋk da:r xə'slaxtə]

Like a fleeting thought
Soos 'n vlieënde gedagte
[sʊᵊs ə 'fliəndə xə'daxtə]

In the infinite realm of time.
In die eindlose ruim van die tyd.
[ən di 'əjntlʊᵊsə rœym fan di təjt]

The Rosebud
Die Roosknoppie
[di 'rʊᵊsˌknɔpi]
Music: Sydney Richfield (1882–1967)
J. K. Pescod (1898–1985)

There below in my little garden,
Daar onder in my tuintjie,
[da:r 'ɔndər ən məj 'tœyɲki]

Stands a fragile little bush;
Daar staan 'n boompie teer;
[da:r sta:n ə 'bʊᵊmpi teᵊr]

It carries only one rosebud —
Daaraan sit net één knoppie —
['da:ra:n sət nɛt 'eᵊn 'knɔpi]

One rosebud, no more.
Één roosknop, nie meer.
['eᵊn 'rʊᵊsknɔp ni meᵊr]

Every night and every morning,
Elke aand en elke môre,
['æᵊlkə a:nt ɛn 'æᵊlkə 'mɔ:rə]

I go inspect the rosebud;
Gaan ek die knoppie kyk;
[xa:n ɛk di 'knɔpi kəjk]

Hope gleams from its eyes,
Die hoop straal uit sy ogies,
[di fiʊᵊp stra:l œyt səj 'ʊᵊxis]

It will be resplendent as a little rose!
Hy sal as rosie pryk!
[fiəj sal as 'rʊᵊsi prəjk]

A gale has arrived,
Die stormwind is gekome,
[di 'stɔrəmˌʋənt əs xə'kʊᵊmə]

The branch is torn off,
Die takkie afgeskeur,
[di 'taki 'afxəˌskjøᵊr]

The little leaves have wilted and the bud has turned yellow!
Die blaartjies is verlep al die knoppie geel gekleur!
[di 'bla:rkis əs fər'lɛp al di 'knɔpi çeᵊl xə'kljøᵊr]

I see so many buds growing in the orchard of life;
Ek sien so menige knoppie in die wêreld-gaarde groei;
[ɛk sin sʊᵊ 'meᵊnəxə 'knɔpi ən di 'væ:rəlt 'xa:rdə xrui]

Hope beaming from the little eyes,
Die hoop straal uit die ogies,
[di ɦʊᵊp stra:l œyt di 'ʋᵊxis]

But alas, no little rose blooms!
Maar ag, geen, rosie bloei!
[ma:r ax çeᵊn 'rʊᵊsi blui]

Youth of My People
Jeug van my Volk
[jøᵊx fan məj fɔlk]
Music: P. J. Lemmer (1896–1989), "Golden Sheaf" (*Goue Gerf, no. 20*) ['xœuə xærf]

Youth of my people, through playing and singing,
Jeug van my volk by spel en sang,
[jøᵊx fan məj fɔlk bəj spæl ɛn saŋ]

You will remember this your whole life long:
Jul sal't onthou die lewe lang:
[jœl salt ɔnt'ɦœu di 'leᵊvə laŋ]

What you gather in gaiety,
Wat jul vergaar in vrolikheid,
[vat jœl fər'xa:r ən 'frʊᵊləkɦəjt]

Grows together to winsome solidarity.
Groei saam in mooi verbondenheid.
[xrui sa:m ən mo:j fər'bɔndənɦəjt]

Bring along the radiance of playfulness,
Bring saam die gloed van spelemei,
[brəŋ sa:m di xlut fan 'speᵊləməj]

And the pleasure of devoted voices,
En lus van stemme toegewy,
[ɛn lœs fan 'stɛmə 'tuxəyəj]

You are the future, young generation,
Jul is die toekoms, jong geslag,
[jœl əs di 'tukɔms jɔŋ xə'slax]

You are the joy of our day;
Jul is die vreugde van ons dag;
[jœl əs di 'frjøᵊxdə fan ɔns dax]

Young voices, resonate, it's your hour
Jong stemme, klink, dis julle uur
[jɔŋ 'stɛmə kləŋk dəs 'jœlə y:r]

And let your rejoicing songs endure.
En laat jul vreugdesange duur.
[ɛn la:t jœl 'frjøᵊxdəˌsaŋə dy:r]

EUGÈNE MARAIS
(1871–1936)

Of Love and Forsakenness
Van Liefde en verlatenheid
[fan 'lifdə ɛn fər'la:tənɦəjt]
Music: Arnold van Wyk (1916–1983)

The Sorceress
1. Die Towenares
[di tʊᵊvəna'rɛs]
Music also by: Arthur Wegelin (1908–1995)

What becomes of the girl who always lives alone?
Wat word van die meisie wat altyd alleen bly?
[vat vɔrt fan di 'məjsi vat 'altəjt a'leᵊn bləj]

She no longer waits for the arrival of the hunters;
Sy wag nie meer vir die koms van die jagters nie;
[səj vax ni meᵊr fər di kɔms fan di 'jaxtərs ni]

She no longer makes a fire from the sweet thorn's wood
Sy maak nie meer die vuur van swartdoringhout nie.
[səj ma:k ni meᵊr di fy:r fan 'swart͜dʊᵊrəŋɦœut ni]

The wind gusts past her ears;
Die wind waai verby haar ore;
[di vənt va:j fər'bəj ɦa:r 'ʊᵊrə]

She no longer hears the dancing song;
Sy hoor nie meer die danslied nie;
[səj ɦʊᵊr ni meᵊr di 'da:nslit ni]

The storyteller's voice is dead.
Die stem van die storieverteller is dood.
[di stɛm fan di 'stʊᵊrifər͜tælər əs dʊᵊt]

No one calls her from afar to speak beautiful words.
G'neen roep haar van ver nie om mooi woorde te praat.
['çeᵊn eᵊn rup ɦa:r fan fæ:r ni ɔm mo:j 'vʊᵊrdə tə pra:t]

She only hears the voice of the solitary wind;
Sy hoor net die stem van die wind alleen;
[səj ɦʊᵊr nɛt di stɛm fan di vənt a'leᵊn]

And the wind always weeps because it is lonely.
En die wind treur altyd om hy alleen is.
[ɛn di vənt trjøᵊr 'altəjt ɔm ɦəj a'leᵊn əs]

Afrikaans Art Song Literature. Christian Bester and Bronwen Forbay, Oxford University Press. © Oxford University Press 2025.
DOI: 10.1093/oso/9780197660812.003.0024

The Desert Lark
2. *Die Woestyn-lewerkie*
[di vu'stəjn 'leᵊvərki]

Gampta, my fawn-colored little sister, the only thing I have left in this world,
Gampta, my vaal Sussie, al wat ek in die wêreld het,
['xampta məj fa:l 'sœsi al vat ɛk ən di 'væ:rəlt ɦɛt]

Apart from my old grandmother!
Buiten my ou Ouma!
['bœjtən məj œu 'œuma]

When you sing high in the sky, you can see all the wonderful things below;
As jy hoog in die lug sing, kan jy al die wonderlike dinge onder sien;
[as jəj ɦʊᵊx ən di lœx səŋ kan jəj al di 'vɔndərləkə 'dəŋə 'ɔndər sin]

Where the bunny hides, and the little steenbuck makes its den.
Waar die hasie wegkruip en die steenbokkie sy lêplek maak.
[va:r di 'ɦa:si 'væxkrœyp ɛn di 'steᵊn bɔki səj 'lɛ:plæk ma:k]

And the maidens cannot touch you, because you are stronger than everyone
En die meide kan jou nie raak nie, want jy is sterker as almal
[ɛn di 'məjdə kan jœu ni ra:k ni vant jəj əs 'stærkər as 'almal]

Even though you are weaker than me.
Al is jy swakker dan ek.
[al əs jəj 'swakər dan ɛk]

Even the mountain-lion that scares us when roaring at night
Selfs die bergleeu wat ons bang-maak as hy snags brul
[sɛlfs di 'bærxliu vat ɔns baŋ ma:k as ɦəj snaxs brœl]

Cannot touch you.
Kan jou nie raak nie.
[kan jœu ni ra:k ni]

I will protect you, my little sister, until all your chicks have grown.
Ek sal jou oppas, my sussie, tot al jou kleintjies groot is.
[ɛk sal jœu 'ɔpas məj 'sœsi tɔt al jœu 'kləjɲkis xrʊᵊt əs]

My sleepy sister, Gampta, I see you.
My vaak sussie, Gampta, ek sien jou.
[məj fa:k 'sœsi 'xampta ɛk sin jœu]

Winter Night

3. *Winternag*

['vəntərnax]

Music also by: A. H. Ashworth (1895–1959)

L. Barnes (n.d.)

W. H. Bell (1873–1946), "Seven Afrikaans Songs for Solo Voice and Orchestra no. 1"

Daniel Clement (1902–1980), "South Africa Onwards" (*Suid-Afrika vorentoe, no. 23*)

[sœyt 'aːfrika 'fʊərəntu]

Marinus de Jong (1891–1984), "Six South African Songs" (*Zes Zuid Afrikaanse Liederen, no. 2*) [fʊər di 'fɛnstər zɛs zœyt afri'kaːnsə 'lidərən]

Dirkie de Villiers (1920–1993)

Hubert du Plessis (1922–2011), "Three Nocturnes, for Dramatic Soprano, Op. 36, no. 3"

Hendrik Hofmeyr (b. 1957), "Two Poems by Eugène Marais" (*Twee Gedigte van Eugène Marais, Op. 91, no. 1*) [tweə xə'dəxtə fan ju'dʒin marɛː]

Charles Nel (1890–1983)

Rosa Nepgen (1909–2001)

S. le Roux Marais (1896–1979)

Bosman di Ravelli (1882–1967), "Three Songs" (*Drie Liederen, no. 2*) [dri 'lidərən]

Sydney Richfield (1882–1967)

Roelof Willem Temmingh Jr. (1946–2012)

Martin Watt (b. 1970), "Five Songs on Poems by Eugène Marais, no. 4"

Judith Brent-Wessels (1910–n.d.)

Oh, (how) cold and piercing is the wind.
O koud is die windjie en skraal.
[ʊə kœut əs di 'vənki ɛn skraːl]

And gleaming in the faint light, and bleak
En blink in die doflig en kaal
[ɛn bləŋk ən di 'dɔfləx ɛn kaːl]

As wide as God's grace,
So wyd as die Heer se genade,
[sʊə vəjt as di ɦieər sə xə'naːdə]

The fields lie in starlight and shadows.
Lê die velde in sterlig en skade.
[lɛː di 'fæəldə ən 'stærləx ɛn 'skaːdə]

And high against the ridges, scattered in burnt patches of veld
En hoog teen die rande, versprei in die brande
[ɛn hʊəx teən di 'randə fər'sprəj ən di 'brandə]

The grass seeds are quivering like beckoning hands.
Is die grassaad aan roere soos winkende hande.
[əs di 'xrasaːt aːn 'ruːrə sʊəs 'vəŋkəndə 'ɦandə]

Oh how dismal (is) the tune on the east wind's beat,
O treurig die wysie op die ooswind se maat,
[ʊə 'trjøərəx di 'vəjsi ɔp di 'ʊəsvənt sə maːt]

Like the song of a maiden left by her beloved!
Soos die lied van 'n meisie in haar liefde verlaat!
[suᵊs di lit fan ə 'məjsi ən ha:r 'lifdə fər'la:t]

A dewdrop gleams,
blink 'n druppel van dou,
[bləŋk ə 'drœpəl fan dœu]

In the crease of every blade of grass
In elk' grashalm se vou
[ən æᵊlk 'xrasɦalm sə fœu]

And quickly it pales to frost in the cold.
En vinnig verbleek dit tot ryp in die kou.
[ɛn 'fənəx fər'bleᵊk dət tɔt rəjp ən di kœu]

Heart of the Dawn
4. *Hart-van-die-Dagbreek*
[ɦart fan di 'daxbreᵊk]
Music also by: Rosa Nepgen (1909–2001)
"Three Marais Songs" *(Drie Marais Liedere, no. 2)* [dri marɛ: 'lidərə]

The footprints of the heart of the dawn!
Die spore van die hart van die dagbreek!
[di 'spuᵊrə fan di ɦart fan di 'daxbreᵊk]

Nampti's tiny footprints that caused my heart to sing.
Die klein spoortjies van Nampti wat my hart laat sing.
[di kləjn 'spuᵊrkis fan 'nampti vat məj ɦart la:t səŋ]

I saw them in the dew long before the sun erased them;
Lank het ek dit in die dou gesien voor die son dit doodvee;
[laŋk ɦɛt ɛk dət ən di dœu xə'sin fuᵊr di sɔn dət 'duᵊtfeᵊ]

Deep River
5. *Diep Rivier*
[dip rə'fi:r]
Music also by: Judith Brent-Wessels (1910–n.d.)
Adolf Hallis (1896–1987)
Eva Noel Harvey (1900–1976), titled *"O Diep Rivier"*
Stewart Hylton-Edwards (1924–1987), titled *"Diep Rivier—Die Lied van Juanita Perreira"*
Hendrik Hofmeyr (b. 1957), "Two Poems by Eugène Marais" *(Twee gedigte van Eugène Marais, no. 2)* [tweᵊ xə'dəxtə fan ju'dʒin marɛ:]
Rosa Nepgen (1909–2001)
"Three Marais Songs" *(Drie Marais Liedere, no. 3)* [dri marɛ: 'lidərə]
Arnold van Wyk (1916–1983)

Oh deep river, oh dark stream,
O diep rivier, o donker stroom,
[uᵊ dip rə'fi:r uᵊ 'dɔŋkər struᵊm]

How long have I waited, how long have I dreamed,
Hoe lank het ek gewag, hoe lank gedroom,
[ɦu laŋk ɦɛt ɛk xə'vax ɦu laŋk xə'druᵊm]

The blade of love tormenting my heart?
Die lem van liefde wroegend in my hart?
[di lɛm fan lifdə 'vruxənt ən məj ɦart]

In your embrace all my grief comes to
an end.
In jou omhelsing eindig al my smart.
[ən jœu ɔm'ɦæᵃlsəŋ 'əjndəx al məj smart]

Extinguish, oh deep river, the flame of hate,
Blus uit, o diep rivier, die vlam van haat,
[blœs œyt ʊᵃ dip rə'fi:r di flam fan ɦa:t]

The great longing that never leaves me.
Die groot verlange wat my nooit verlaat.
[di xrʊᵃt fər'laŋə vat məj no:jt fər'la:t]

From afar I see the brilliance of steel and gold,
Ek sien van ver die glans van staal en goud,
[ɛk sin fan fæ:r di xlans fan sta:l ɛn xœut]

I hear the soft rumbling of water deep
and cold,
*Ek hoor die sag gedruis van waters diep
en koud,*
[ɛk ɦʊᵃr di sa xə'drœys¹ fan 'va:tərs dip
ɛn kœut]

I hear your voice as a murmur and dream.
Ek hoor jou stem as fluistering en droom.
[ɛk ɦʊᵃr jœu stɛm as 'flœystərəŋ ɛn drʊᵃm]

Come swiftly, oh deep river, oh dark stream.
Kom snel, o diep rivier, o donker stroom.
[kɔm snæl ʊᵃ dip rə'fi:r ʊᵃ 'dɔŋkər strʊᵃm]

Stand-Alone Poetry

Grim Reaper
Skoppensboer
['skɔpənsbu:r]
Music: Dirkie de Villiers (1920–1993)
Gerrit Bon Sr. (1901–1983)

There's a drop of bile in sweetest wine;
'n Druppel gal is in die soetste wyn;
[ə 'drœpəl xal əs ən di 'sutstə vəjn]

A tear upon every happy string,
'n Traan is op elk' vrolik' snaar,
[ə tra:n əs ɔp æᵃlk 'frʊᵃlək sna:r]

In every laugh a sigh of pain,
In elke lag 'n sug van pyn,
[ən 'æᵃlkə lax ə sœx fan pəjn]

In every rose a dull petal.
In elke roos 'n dowwe blaar.
[ən 'æᵃlkə rʊᵃs ə 'dɔvə bla:r]

The one that throughout the night
Die een wat deur die nag
[di eᵃn vat djø̞ᵃr di nax]

Leers at our enjoyment
Ons pret beloer
[ɔns prɛt bə'lu:r]

---

¹ See Appendix G, Assimilation and Amalgamation of Consonants.

And laughs last
En laaste lag
[ɛn 'la:stə lax]

Is the Grim Reaper.
Is Skoppensboer.
[əs 'skɔpənsbu:r]

Certain and sure is the word:
Gewis en seker is die woord:
[xə'vəs ɛn 'seᵊkər əs di vʊᵊrt]

The treasures that we amass,
Die skatte wat ons opvergaar,
[di 'skatə vat ɔns 'ɔpfərˌxa:r]

Despite the strongest lock and rope
Ondanks die sterkste slot en koord
['ɔndaŋks di 'stærkstə slɔt ɛn kʊᵊrt]

Are only preserved for moth and rust.
Word net vir mot en roes bewaar.
[vɔrt nɛt fər mɔt ɛn rus bə'va:r]

We are but tenants
Net pagters ons
[nɛt 'paxtərs ɔns]

Of dust and fluff
Van stof en dons
[fan stɔf ɛn dɔns]

To transfer
Om oor te voer
[ɔm ʊᵊr tə fu:r]

To the Grim Reaper.
Aan Skoppensboer.
[a:n 'skɔpənsbu:r]

The splendor of flesh and blood;
Die heerlikheid van vlees en bloed;
[di 'ɦeᵊrləkɦəjt fan fleᵊs ɛn blut]

The hair that the sunlight catches
Die hare wat die sonlig vang
[di 'ɦa:rə vat di 'sɔnləx faŋ]

And illuminates in a golden candescence:
En weergee in 'n goue gloed:
[ɛn 'veᵊrxeᵊ ən ə 'xœuə xlut]

The dawn on every soft cheek
Die dagbreek op elk' sagte wang
[di 'daxbreᵊk ɔp æᵃlk 'saxtə vaŋ]

And eyes filled with starry splendor
En oge vol van sterreprag
[ɛn 'ʊᵊxə fɔl fan 'stærəprax]

Are defenseless against his greater might.
Is weerloos teen sy groter mag.
[əs 'veᵊrlʊᵊs teᵊn səj 'xrʊᵊtər max]

Already the wrinkle starts to cut;
Alreeds begint die rimpel sny;
[al'reᵊts bə'xənt di 'rəmpəl snəj]

The worm keeps watch over everything
Oor alles hou die wurm wag
[ʊᵊr 'aləs ɦœu di 'vœrəm vax]

And dust and ash are all that remain:
En stof en as is al wat bly:
[ɛn stɔf ɛn as əs al vat bləj]

Because black and sadness,
Want swart en droef,
[vant swart ɛn druf]

The highest trump (card)
Die hoogste troef
[di 'ɦʊᵊxstə truf]

Over all that stirs,
Oor al wat roer,
[ʊᵊr al vat ru:r]

Is the Grim Reaper.
Is Skoppensboer.
[əs ˈskɔpənsbuːr]

Surely, everthing is only a joke!
Gewis is alles net 'n grap!
[xəˈvəs əs ˈaləs nɛt ə xrap]

We play along in the comedy
Ons speel in die komedie mee
[ɔns speˀl ən di kʊˀˈmeˀdi meˀ]

Blindfolded with a mourning cloth
Geblinddoek met 'n lamfer-lap
[xəˈblənduk mɛt ə ˈlamfərlap]

That even gives the sun a shadow.
Wat selfs die son 'n skadu gee.
[vat sæˀlfs di sɔn ˈskady çeˀ]

Why are we mourning after all?
Wat treur ons tog?
[vat trjøˀr ɔns tɔx]

Violin and flute still sound:
Viool en fluit maak nog geluid:
[fiˈʊˀl ɛn flœyt maːk nɔx xəˈlœyt]

And long is the night still ahead.
En lank die nag wat voorlê nog.
[ɛn laŋk di nax vat ˈfʊˀrlɛː nɔx]

Even though we can never touch perfection,
Al kan ons nooit volmaaktheid raak,
[al kan ɔns noːjt fɔlˈmaːktɦəjt raːk]

The eye still gleams and the skin glows
Nog blink die oog en gloei die huid
[nɔx bləŋk di ʊˀx ɛn xlui di ɦœyt]

Turning all winter into a flowering time.
Wat heel die winter blomtyd maak.
[vat ɦeˀl di ˈvəntər ˈblɔmtəjt maːk]

Thus unabashed
Dus onverlee
[dœs ˈɔnfərˌleˀ]

We laugh along
Lag ons maar mee
[lax ɔns maːr meˀ]

With every tour
Met elke toer
[mɛt ˈæˀlkə tuːr]

Of the Grim Reaper!
Van Skoppensboer!
[fan ˈskɔpənsbuːr]

Stay, Sweetie, Stay!
Staan, Poppie, staan!
[staːn ˈpɔpi staːn]
Music: Jerry Idelson (1893–n.d.)
Johannes Joubert (1894–1958)

Stay, sweetie, stay!
Staan, poppie staan!
[staːn ˈpɔpi staːn]

And let your thoughts stray,
Laat jou gedagtes gaan,
[laːt jœu xəˈdaxtəs xaːn]

So that you can tell me
Dat jy vir my kan sê
[dat jəj fər məj kan sɛ:]

How deep love lies.
Hoe diep die liefde lê.
[ɦu dip di ˈlifdə lɛ:]

Ah, tell me fearlessly,
Ag, sê my sonder vrees,
[ax sɛ: məj ˈsɔndər freᵊs]

Can this be love?
Kan dit die liefde wees?
[kan dət di ˈlifdə veᵊs]

Oh darling, sweet and tender
O liefling, soet en teer
[ʊᵊ ˈlifləŋ sut ɛn teᵊr]

Why are your eyes cast down,
Wat sak jou oë neer,
[vat sak jœu ˈu:ə neᵊr]

As dark as the night
So donker as die nag
[sʊᵊ ˈdɔŋkər as di nax]

In all its starry splendor?
Met al haar sterreprag?
[mɛt al ɦa:r ˈstærəˌprax]

Oh, tell me unequivocally,
O, sê my tog gewis,
[ʊᵊ sɛ: məj tɔ xəˈvəs²]

If this is love?
Of dit die liefde is?
[ɔf dət di ˈlifdə əs]

What causes the vivid rose
Wat maak die helder roos
[vat ma:k di ˈɦæᵊldər rʊᵊs]

To blush in your cheeks?
Wat in jou wange bloos?
[vat ən jœu ˈvaŋə blʊᵊs]

From where (comes) this great din
Vanwaar die groot rumoer
[fanˈva:r di xrʊᵊt rəˈmu:r]

That stirs within your veins?
Wat in jou are roer?
[vat ən jœu ˈa:rə ru:r]

Oh, tell me unequivocally,
O, sê my tog gewis of dit,
[ʊᵊ sɛ: məj tɔ xəˈvəs³ ɔf dət]

If this is love?
Die liefde is?
[di ˈlifdə əs]

---

[2] See Appendix G, Assimilation and Amalgamation of Consonants.
[3] Ibid.

FRANCOIS MARAIS
(n.d.)

The Star from the East
Die Ster uit die Ooste
[di stær œyt di ˈʊᵊstə]
Music: S. L. Roux Marais (1896–1979), "South African Carols"

I am the star, that shines from the East —
Ek is die ster, wat uit die Ooste skyn —
[ɛk əs di stær vat œyt di ˈʊᵊstə skəjn]

That guides the white dove home —
Die wit duif huis toe lei —
[di ˈvət dœyf ˈfiœys tu ləj]

I am the star, that over the rocky desert
Ek is die ster, wat oor die klipwoestyn
[ɛk əs di stær vat ʊᵊr di ˈkləpvusˌtəjn]

Prepares the road for you
Vir jou die pad berei
[fər jœu di pat bəˈrəj]

I am fenced in for all eternity
Tydloos is ek vasgespan
[ˈtəjtlʊᵊs əs ɛk ˈfasxəˌspan]

In the balance of black and cold.
In swart en koue ewewig.
[ən swart ɛn ˈkœuə ˈeᵊvəvəx]

Between God and His merciful heart
Tussen God en Sy genadehart
[ˈtœsən xɔt ɛn səj xəˈnaːdəfiart]

Deprived of His light.
Verstoke van Sy lig.
[fərˈstʊᵊkə fan səj ləx]

I am the star, that shines from the East —
Ek is die ster, wat uit die Ooste Skyn —
[ɛk əs di stær vat œyt di ˈʊᵊstə skəjn]

Yet (I am) unable to locate His stable —
Tog nooit Sy stal sal kry —
[tɔx noːjt səj stal sal krəj]

I am the star, that in the vast desert,
Ek is die ster, wat in die ruim woestyn,
[ɛk əs di stær vat ən di rœym vuˈstəjn]

On Christmas day, remains outside.
Op Kersdag buite bly.
[ɔp ˈkærsdax ˈbœytə bləj]

Afrikaans Art Song Literature. Christian Bester and Bronwen Forbay, Oxford University Press. © Oxford University Press 2025.
DOI: 10.1093/oso/9780197660812.003.0025

DIRK MOSTERT

(1897–1982)

Love Songs[1]
Amoreuse Liedeken
[amuˈrjøᵊsə ˈlidəkən]
Music: Gerrit Bon Sr. (1901–1983)
S. le Roux Marais (1896–1979), "Six Art Songs" (*Ses Kunsliedere, no. 5*)
[sɛs ˈkœnsˌlidərə]

There are flowers in the small garden where my sweetheart stands in the evening,
Daar is blomme in die tuintjie waar my liefste sawens staan,
[da:r əs ˈblɔmə ən di ˈtœɲki va:r məj ˈlifstə ˈsa:vəns sta:n]

As the sun in an array of glorious colors goes to rest in the sea.
As die son in kleure glorie in die see terruste gaan.
[as di sɔn ən ˈkljøᵊrə ˈxlʊᵊri ən di seᵊ təˈrœstə xa:n]

There are flowers that my darling adorns herself with early in the morning,
Daar is blomme waar my liefste smôrens vroeg haarself mee tooi,
[da:r əs ˈblɔmə va:r məj ˈlifstə ˈsmɔ:rəns frux ɦa:rˈsæᵊlf meᵊ to:j]

Where she rests in the afternoon's quietude, (with) flowers strewn all around.
Waar sy rus in middagstilte, lê daar blomme rondgestrooi.
[va:r səj rœs ən ˈmədaxˌstəltə le: da:r ˈblɔmə ˈrɔntxəˌstro:j]

There are thousands of little eyes that gaze below in the night,
Daar is duisende klein ogies wat omlaag sien in die nag,
[da:r əs ˈdœysəndə kləjn ˈʊᵊxis vat ɔmˈla:x sin ən di nax]

It is cherubs that peek down; keeping watch over her.
Dit is engeltjies wat neerkyk; en hul hou oor haar die wag.
[dət əs ˈɛɲəlkis vat ˈneᵊrkəjk ɛn ɦœl ɦœu ʊᵊr ɦa:r di vax]

As she softly wanders through (her) dreams, until daylight approaches.
As sy sag in droomgeweste wandel, tot die daglig skyn.
[as səj sax ən ˈdrʊᵊmxəˌvɛstə ˈvandəl tɔt di ˈdaxləx skəjn]

And until heaven's beams approach where the dark night disappears.
En tot hemelstrale nader waar die donker nag verdwyn.
[ɛn tɔt ˈɦeᵊməlˌstra:lə ˈna:dər va:r di ˈdɔŋkər nax fərˈdwəjn]

---

[1] Permission granted by Van Schaik Publishers.

Afrikaans Art Song Literature. Christian Bester and Bronwen Forbay, Oxford University Press. © Oxford University Press 2025.
DOI: 10.1093/oso/9780197660812.003.0026

There are birdies in the trees where my
darling rests every day,
*Daar is voëltjies in die bome waar my
liefste aldag rus,*
[da:r əs ˈfuᵊlkis ən di ˈbuᵊmə va:r məj ˈlifstə
ˈaldax rœs]

And their little songs mingle with the
breeze that caresses her.
*En hul liedjies mengel same met die
windjie wat haar kus.*
[ɛn ɦœl ˈlikis ˈmɛŋəl ˈsa:mə mɛt di ˈvəɲki
vat ɦa:r kœs]

Just as the birdies in the trees, just like
cherubs keeping watch,
*Nes die voëltjies in die lower nes die engeltjies
op wag,*
[nɛs di ˈfuᵊlkis ən di ˈluᵊvər nɛs di ˈɛŋəlkis
ɔp vax]

Just like the garland of flowers, darling, I am
with you day and night.
*Nes die blomfestoene liefste is ek by jou dag
en nag.*
[nɛs di ˈblɔmfəˌstunə ˈlifstə əs ɛk bəj jœu dax
ɛn nax]

There's a Time[2]
Daar's 'n Tyd
[da:rs ə təjt]
Music: S. le Roux Marais (1896–1979), "New Songs" (*Nuwe Liedere, no. 7*)
[ˈnyvə ˈlidərə]

There's a time to stand by and to wait
Daar's 'n tyd om te staan en te wag
[da:rs ə təjt ɔm tə sta:n ɛn tə vax]

For the dawn of the new day
Op die koms van die volgende dag
[ɔp di kɔms fan di ˈfɔlxəndə dax]

There's an hour of rest as the little campfire
dwindles,
*Daar's stonde van rus as die
kampvuurtjie blus,*
[da:rs ˈstɔndə fan rœs as di
ˈkampˌfy:rki blœs]

And an hour of prayer in the night
En 'n uur van gebed in die nag
[ɛn ə y:r fan xəˈbɛt ən di nax]

There's a time to comfort those who lament,
Daar's 'n tyd om te troos dié wat kla,
[da:rs ə təjt ɔm tə truᵊs ˈdi vat kla:]

To bear another's burden,
Om 'n ander se laste te dra,
[ɔm ə ˈandər sə ˈlastə tə dra:]

To heal his wounds,
Om sy wonde te heel,
[ɔm səj ˈvɔndə tə ɦeᵊl]

And to share your cruet,
En jou kruikie te deel,
[ɛn jœu ˈkrœyki tə deᵊl]

Without ever seeking a reward.
Sonder ooit om vergelding te vra.
[ˈsɔndər ojt ɔm fərˈxæᵃldəŋ tə vra:]

---

[2] Permission granted by Van Schaik Publishers.

There's a time to fight and to contend
Daar's 'n tyd om te veg en te stry
[da:rs ə təjt ɔm tə fæx ɛn tə strəj]

There's a purpose to seek and to find
Daar's 'n doel om te soek en te kry
[da:rs ə dul ɔm tə suk ɛn tə krəj]

There is an alluring light,
Daar's 'n lonkende lig,
[da:rs ə 'lɔŋkəndə ləx]

And a call to duty,
En 'n roepende plig,
[ɛn ə 'rupəndə pləx]

And there's often a defeat to suffer
En daar's dikwels 'n neerlaag te ly
[ɛn da:rs 'dəkvəls ə 'neᵊrla:x tə ləj]

There's time to maintain and to build,
Daar's tyd om te handhaaf en bou,
[da:rs ə təjt ɔm tə 'ɦantɦa:f ɛn bœu]

To nurture what is holy,
Om wat heilig is te hou,
[ɔm vat 'ɦəjləx əs tə ɦœu]

There's a nation that pines,
Daar's 'n nasie wat smag,
[da:rs ə 'na:si vat smax]

There's desire and there's might,
Daar's wil en daar's krag,
[da:rs vəl ɛn da:rs krax]

There's a time to be vigilant,
Daar's tyd om te waak,
[da:rs ə təjt ɔm tə va:k]

And it's now.
En dis nou.
[ɛn dəs nœu]

A Message of the Exiled[3]
Die Balling se Boodskap
[di 'baləŋ sə 'bʊᵊtskap]
Music: S. le Roux Marais (1896–1979), "New Songs"
(*Nuwe Liedere, no. 4*) ['nyvə 'lidərə]

Expect me in the eventide, my darling
Verwag my in die awend liefste
[fər'vax məj ən di 'a:vənt 'lifstə]

(In the) evenings when you feel most alone
Saans as jy die alleenste voel
[sa:ns as jəj di a'leᵊnstə ful]

Expect me where ten thousand waves
Verwag my waar tienduisend branders
[fər'vax məj va:r 'tin dœysənd 'brandərs]

Wash spuming over rocks and sand dunes
Oor rots en sandbank skuimend spoel
[ʊᵊr rɔts ɛn 'santbaŋk 'skœymənd spul]

---

[3] Permission granted by Van Schaik Publishers.

Expect me as the nocturnal sea breeze
Verwag my as die seewind sawens
[fər'vax məj as di 'seᵊvənt 'sa:vəns]

Lovingly caresses your cheeks,
Beminnig oor jou wange waai,
[bə'mənəx ʊᵊr jœu 'vaɲə va:j]

And that lock of hair playfully,
En daardie harestring baljarend,
[ɛn 'da:rdi 'ɦa:rəstrəŋ bal'ja:rənt]

In curls toys around your ears
In krulle om jou ore draai
[ən 'krœlə ɔm jœu 'ʊᵊrə dra:j]

Expect me as you alone, my darling,
Verwag my as jy eensaam, liefste,
[fər'vax məj as jəj 'eᵊnsa:m 'lifstə]

Sit there on the bare seashore
daarop die kale seestrand sit
['da:rɔp di 'ka:lə 'seᵊstrant sət]

Where waves roll (up) against your feet,
Waar golwe rol tot aan jou voete,
[va:r 'xɔlvə rɔl tɔt a:n jœu 'futə]

And what they say, believe it.
En wat hul sê, gelowe dit.
[ɛn vat ɦœl sɛ: xə'lʊᵊvə dət]

Just as the sea breeze, so will I, my darling
Net soos die seewind sal ek, liefste
[nɛt sʊᵊs di 'seᵊvənt sal ɛk 'lifstə]

Come to you across the waves.
Na jou oor die bare kom.
[na jœu ʊᵊr di 'ba:rə kɔm]

The time for waiting will be over,
Die tyd van wagte sal verby wees,
[di təjt fan 'vaxtə sal fər'bəj veᵊs]

The time for anticipation, too.
Die tyd van uitsien om.
[di təjt fan 'œytsin ɔm]

I will clasp you tightly to my breast,
Ek sal jou aan my boesem vasdruk,
[ɛk sal jœu a:n məj 'busəm 'fasdrœk]

Just as the sea breeze does
Net soos die seewind doen
[nɛt sʊᵊs di 'seᵊvənt dun]

And like the thousand waves, darling,
En soos die duisend branders, liefste,
[ɛn sʊᵊs di 'dœysənt 'brandərs 'lifstə]

I will kiss you a thousand times.
Sal ek jou duisend soene soen.
[sal ɛk jœu 'dœysənt 'sunə sun]

Slumber, Beloved[4]

Sluimer, Beminde

['slœymər bə'məndə]

Music: S. le Roux Marais (1896–1979), "Five Art Songs"

(*Vyf Kunsliedere, no. 5*) [fəjf 'kœns‿lidərə]

Come slumber beloved as the wind more
widely,
Kom sluimer as ruimer die winde beminde,
[kɔm 'slœymər as 'rœymər di 'vəndə
bə'məndə]

Strays over the far-reaching distances
of night,
Oor nagtlike vertes verdwaal,
[ʊᵊr 'naxtləkə 'færtəs fər'dwa:l]

Come and rest on my bosom 'till rays
of light,
Kom rus aan my boesem tot skigte van ligte,
[kɔm rœs a:n məj 'busəm tɔt 'skəxtə fan
'ləxtə]

Shine upon heaven's expanse,
Die hemel se wydtes bestraal,
[di 'fieᵊməl sə 'vəjtəs bə'stra:l]

Even though the heavens are teeming with
stars over there,
Al wemel die hemel van sterre daar ver,
[al 'veᵊməl di 'fieᵊməl fan 'stærə da:r fæ:r]

That hold vigil over the darkness(es),
Wat wag oor die donkertes hou,
[vat vax ʊᵊr di 'dɔŋkərtəs fiœu]

Yet I constantly keep watch as whirling
clouds,
Tog waak ek gedurig as wolke in kolke,
[tɔx va:k ɛk xə'dy:rəx as 'vɔlkə ən 'kɔlkə]

Veil the view for you.
Die uitsig besluier vir jou.
[di 'œytsəx bə'slœyər fər jœu]

The night's lamentations allow trees
in dreams
Die klagte van nagte laat bome in drome
[di 'klaxtə fan 'naxtə la:t 'buᵊmə ən 'drʊᵊmə]

To be stirred into evil phantoms,
In nare gedaantes verroer,
[ən 'na:rə xə'da:ntəs fə'ru:r]

Shaped into specters,
Tot skimme fatsoene,
[tɔt 'skəmə fat'sunə]

Which flicker through the dark,
Die donker deur flonker,
[di 'dɔŋkər djøᵊr 'flɔŋkər]

And come to peek through the curtains.
En deur die gordyne kom loer.
[ɛn djøᵊr di xɔr'dəjnə kɔm lu:r]

The horrible dangers outside the windows,
Die nare gevare daar buite die ruite,
[di 'na:rə xə'fa:rə da:r 'bœytə di 'rœytə]

Will not be able to harm my dearest,
Sal tog nie my liefste kan deer,
[sal tɔx ni məj 'lifstə kan deᵊr]

---

[4] Permission granted by Van Schaik Publishers.

Because all through the howling of the winds, beloved,
Want dwarsdeur die huiling van winde beminde,
[vant ˈdwarsdjøˀr di ˈɦœylən fan ˈvəndə bəˈməndə]

My love so tender, remains with you.
Is by jou my liefde so teer.
[əs bəj jœu məj ˈlifdə sʊˀ teˀr]

S. J. M. OSBORNE
(n.d.)

The Karoo Plain
Die Karoovlakte[1]
[di ka'rʊᵊˌflaktə]
Music: P. J. Lemmer (1896–1989)

Gently over the wide-open veld,
Sag oor die velde wyd,
[sax ʊᵊr di 'fæᵃldə vəjt]

Dreamily in solitude,
Dromend in eensaamheid,
['drʊᵊmənt ən 'eᵊnsa:mɦəjt]

Stained by the sun,
Sonstraal getint,
['sɔnstra:l xə'tənt]

Rustles with a tired sigh,
Suis met 'n moeë sug,
[sœys mɛt ə 'mu:ə sœx]

Rustles through the evening sky,
Suis deur die awendlug,
[sœys djøᵊr di 'a:vəntlœx]

Lingering, the wind.
Slepend, die wind.
['sleᵊpənt di vənt]

The grayish mountains lie in the distance,
Ver lê die berge grou,
[fæ:r lɛ: di 'bærgə xroeu]

Far (off) in a hazy blue,
Ver in 'n wasig blou,
[fæ:r ən ə 'va:səx bloeu]

Fringed with a golden luster,
Goudglans omsoomd,
['xoeutxlans ɔm'sʊᵊmt]

Calm (is) the restful scene,
Kalm die rustoneel,
['kaləm di 'rœstuˌneᵊl]

Quietness (hovers) over everything,
Stilheid oor algeheel,
['stəlɦəjt ʊᵊr 'alxəˌɦeᵊl]

Slumbering dream ...
Sluimerend droom ...
['slœymərənt drʊᵊm]

---

[1] A semi-arid desert divided into the Great Karoo and the Little Karoo, both lacking in surface water. It encompasses the Eastern, Western, and Northern Cape Provinces. Its name is derived from the Khoi word for 'land of thirst.' Covering approximately one-third of the total area of South Africa, the Karoo's biodiversity includes assorted succulents and low scrub bushes, plains, fossils, and unique geographical formations.

Afrikaans Art Song Literature. Christian Bester and Bronwen Forbay, Oxford University Press. © Oxford University Press 2025.
DOI: 10.1093/oso/9780197660812.003.0027

Bushshrike
Kokkewiet[2]
[kɔkə'vit]
Music: P. J. Lemmer (1896–1989)

Did you hear at the furrow
Het jy gehoor by die voor
[ɦɛt jəj xə'ɦʊᵊr bəj di fʊᵊr]

How the bushshrike whistles,
Hoe die kokkewiet fluit,
[ɦu di kɔkə'vit flœyt]

And charms the world with his lovely sound?
En die wêreld bekoor met sy heerlik geluid?
[ɛn di 'væ:rəlt bə'kʊᵊr mɛt səj 'ɦeᵊrlək xə'lœyt]

It's the bushshrike!
Dis kokkewiet!
[dəs kɔkə'vit]

Then he rests awhile,
Dan eers weer rus,
[dan eᵊrs veᵊr rœs]

(Rocking) back and forth lulled on a small branch,
Heen en weer op 'n takkie gesus,
[ɦeᵊn ɛn veᵊr ɔp ə 'taki xə'sœs]

And he listens and waits for his mate's coo:
En hy luister en wag op sy maatjie se koer:
[ɛn ɦəj 'lœystər ɛn vax ɔp səj 'ma:ᵎki sə ku:r]

Whee-whee-ooo!
Wiet-wiet-woer!
[vit vit vu:r]

There in the tree by the stream,
Daar in die boom by die stroom,
[da:r ən di bʊᵊm bəj di strʊᵊm]

Do you hear him?
Hoor jy hom?
[ɦʊᵊr jəj ɦɔm]

Spring's little gold-breasted herald
Borsie van goud, lentes herout
['bɔrsi fan xœut 'lɛntəs ɦæ'rœut]

Listen how he gloriously whistles his song!
Luister hoe fluit hy dit glorieryk uit!
['lœystər ɦu flœyt ɦəj dət 'xlʊᵊrirəjk œyt]

(Be) Quiet, and listen to how joyously he whistles:
Stilte, en luister hoe bly dat hy fluit:
['stəltə ɛn 'lœystər ɦu bləj dat ɦəj flœyt]

Spring is coming!
Lente kom!
['lɛntə kɔm]

---

[2] "Kokkewiet" (*Telophorus zeylonus*) are a type of shrike indigenous to southern Africa. Their loud antiphonal bird-song resembles the pronunciation of their colloquially known name "bok-ma-kierie." A distinctive feature of their yellow-green plumage is a narrow black stripe that starts at their eyes, runs past the base of their beaks, and resembles a collar across their throats.

Boulder by the Sea
Rots by die See
[rɔts bəj di seˀ]
Music: P. J. Lemmer (1896–1989)

Come along with me to the far-off sea,
Kom met my na die verre see,
[kɔm mɛt məj na di ˈfærə seˀ]

There where the waves tussle,
Daar waar die branders stoei,
[daːr vaːr di ˈbrandərs stui]

There where the waters rumble and groan.
Daar waar die waters dreun en kreun.
[daːr vaːr di ˈvaːtərs drjøˀn ɛn krjøˀn]

(Where) swells become waves.
 Deining tot golwe groei.
[ˈdəjnəŋ tɔt ˈxɔlvə xrui]

Come along with me to the far-off sea,
Kom met my mee na die verre see,
[kɔm mɛt məj meˀ na di ˈfærə seˀ]

There where the waves splash!
Daar waar die golwe klots!
[daːr vaːr di ˈxɔlvə klɔts]

There where the waters swish and foam,
Daar waar die waters ruis en bruis,
[daːr vaːr di ˈvaːtərs rœys en brœys]

There upon a high boulder.
Daar op 'n hoë rots.
[daːr ɔp ə ˈɦuːə rɔts]

Let us go stand at the ocean
Kom ons gaan staan by die oseaan
[kɔm ɔns xaːn staːn bəj di ʊˀsiˈaːn]

Just the two of us alone.
Net maar ons twee alleen.
[nɛt maːr ɔns tweˀ aˈleˀn]

There we will listen and understand;
Daar sal ons luister en verstaan;
[daːr sal ɔns ˈlœystər ɛn fərˈstaːn]

There our souls become one.
Daar word ons siele een.
[daːr vɔrt ɔns ˈsilə eˀn]

PETER JOHN PHILANDER

(1921–2006)
aka Piet Philander or P. J. Philander

Eclipse[1]

Sonsverduistering
['sɔnsfər‚dœystərəŋ]
Music: P. J. de Villiers (1924–2015), "Four Songs of Doubt and Faith"
(*Vier Liedere van Twyfel en Geloof, no.1*) [fir 'lidərə fan 'twəjfəl ɛn xə'lʊᵊf]

Gradually, noiselessly, the patch of shadow shifts
Langsamerhand, geruisloos skuif die vlek van skadu
['laŋsamərfiant xə'rœyslʊᵊs skœyf di flæk fan 'ska:dy]

And shrink the sun's crescent
En verklein die sekelboog van son
[ɛn fər'kləjn di 'seᵊkəlbʊᵊx fan sɔn]

Until threateningly, black the spot on high
Tot dreigend swart die kol daar hoog
[tɔt 'drəjxənt swart di kɔl da:r fiʊᵊx]

Causes a cold strange gloaming to extend
'n Koue vreemde skemerte laat trek
[ə 'kœuə 'freᵊmdə 'skeᵊmərtə la:t træk]

Wide over the plain from which, taciturn,
Wyd oor die vlakte waarvandaan, swygsaam,
[vəjt ʊᵊr di 'flaktə 'va:rfanda:n 'swəjxsa:m]

An ashen line of donkeys on the shortest route
'n Vaal streep donkies met die kortste pad
[ə fa:l streᵊp 'dɔŋkis mɛt di 'kɔrtstə pat]

Swerves hurriedly to the stable, before
Oorhaastig stalwaarts swingel nog voordat
[ʊᵊr'fia:stəx 'stalva:rts 'swəŋəl nɔx 'fʊᵊrdat]

The sheep baa-baaing return to the corral.
Die skape blêr-blêr na die kraal toe gaan.
[di 'ska:pə blæ:rblæ:r na di kra:l tu xa:n]

Over all humanity hangs a shadow
Oor gans die mensdom hang 'n skaduwee
[ʊᵊr xans di 'mɛnsdɔm fiaŋ ə 'ska:dyveᵊ]

That so eclipses all light of God and Christ
Wat alle lig van God en Christus so verduister
[vat 'alə ləx fan xɔt ɛn 'xrəstəs sʊᵊ fər'dœystər]

That His path becomes invisible.
Dat Sy pad onsigbaar is.
[dat səj pat ɔn'səxba:r əs]

And we, subjugated to this darkness,
En ons, aan hierdie duisternis gedwee,
[ɛn ɔns a:n 'fii:rdi 'dœystərnəs xə'dweᵊ]

---

[1] Permission granted by NB Publishers.

Afrikaans Art Song Literature. Christian Bester and Bronwen Forbay, Oxford University Press. © Oxford University Press 2025.
DOI: 10.1093/oso/9780197660812.003.0028

Don't have a sheep's sense of foreboding or
believe
Het nie 'n skaap se voorgevoel of glo
[ɦɛt ni ə ska:p sə ˈfʊᵊrxəˌful ɔf xlʊᵊ]

That we must (also) return home in time
for rest.
Dat ons moet tydig Huiswaarts keer vir rus.
[dat ɔns mut ˈtəjdəx ˈɦœysva:rts keᵊr fər rœs]

HILDA POSTMA

(1895–1993)

To Stella[1]
Aan Stella
[aːn ˈstæla]
Music: P. J. Lemmer (1896–1989), "Golden Sheaf"
(*Goue Gerf, no. 103*) [ˈxœuə xærf]

The turtledove on the tree branch,
Die tortel op die boomtak,
[di ˈtɔrtəl ɔp di ˈbʊᵊmtak]

Oh dear how pitiful there —
Aitog hoe droewig daar —
[ˈajtɔx ɦu ˈdruvəx daːr]

The turtledove on the tree branch,
Die tortel op die boomtak,
[di ˈtɔrtəl ɔp di ˈbʊᵊmtak]

Who can explain its sorrow?
Wie kan sy leed verklaar?
[vi kan səj leᵊt fərˈklaːr]

The melancholy in your eyes,
Die weemoed in jou oë,
[di ˈveᵊmut ən jœu ˈuːə]

Oh dear how poignant it is,
Aitog hoe gryp dit aan,
[ˈajtɔx ɦu xrəjp dət aːn]

The melancholy in your eyes,
Die weemoed in jou oë,
[di ˈveᵊmut ən jœu ˈuːə]

If there was but a tear —
Was daar tog maar 'n traan —
[vas daːr tɔx maːr ə traːn]

The turtledove on the tree branch,
Die tortel op die boomtak,
[di ˈtɔrtəl ɔp di ˈbʊᵊmtak]

Reaches the ear (already) from afar —
Vang al die oor van ver —
[faŋ al di ʊᵊr fan fæːr]

Your sorrow is as quiet as the night,
Jou hartseer is so nagstil,
[jœu ˈɦartseᵊr əs sʊᵊ ˈnaxstəl]

Your smile, your smile but a star.
Jou glimlag, jou glimlag net 'n ster.
[jœu ˈxləmlax jœu ˈxləmlax nɛt ə stær]

---

[1] Permission granted by the Afrikaans Volksang-en Volkspelebeweging.

Afrikaans Art Song Literature. Christian Bester and Bronwen Forbay, Oxford University Press. © Oxford University Press 2025.
DOI: 10.1093/oso/9780197660812.003.0029

TOTIUS

(1877–1953)
Pseudonym of Jacob Daniël du Toit

The Gardener
Die Howenier
[di ɦʊᵊvəˈniːr]
Music: Bosman di Ravelli (1882–1967), "Three Songs" (*Drie Liederen, no. 1*)
[dri ˈlidərən]
Note: Various Dutch words have been transcribed into the IPA using
modern Afrikaans pronunciation.

An urchin sees a little rose standing
'n Knapie sag 'n rosie staan
[ə ˈknaːpi sax ə ˈrʊᵊsi staːn]

A little rose in the garden;
'Rosie in die gaarde;
[ˈrʊᵊsi ən di ˈxaːrdə]

Now, he thought, his plans can come to fruition,
Nou, dag hij, kom sij planne reg,
[nœu dax ɦəj kɔm səj ˈplanə ræx]

The gardener is finally gone,
Die howenier is eindlik weg,
[di ˈɦʊᵊvəniːr əs ˈəjntlək væx]

Now I will go there and pluck her (the rose),
Nou sal ik haar gaan plukke daar,
[nœu sal ɛk ɦaːr xaːn ˈplœkə daːr]

The valuable little flower.
Die blommetje van waarde.
[di ˈblomiki fan ˈvaːrdə]

The urchin slowly approached
Die knapie naakte langsaam
[di ˈknaːpi ˈnaːktə ˈlaŋsaːm]

The little rose of the garden.
Aan die rosie van die gaarde.
[aːn di ˈrʊᵊsi fan di ˈxaːrdə]

Oh leave me alone, oh leave me alone,
Og laat mij staan, og laat mij staan,
[ax laːt məj staːn]

The gardener has gone away.
Die howenier is weggegaan.
[di ˈɦʊᵊvəniːr əs ˈvæxəˌxaːn]

Have compassion, so she begged
Heb medelij, so smeekte sij
[ˈɦɛt ˈmeᵊdələj sʊᵊ ˈsmeᵊktə səj]

The valuable little flower.
Die blommetje van waarde.
[di ˈblomiki fan ˈvaːrdə]

Afrikaans Art Song Literature. Christian Bester and Bronwen Forbay, Oxford University Press. © Oxford University Press 2025.
DOI: 10.1093/oso/9780197660812.003.0030

Alas no, he did not want to leave
her alone,
Maar nee, hij wou haar nie laat staan,
[ma:r neᵊ ɦəj vœu ɦa:r ni la:t sta:n]

The little rose of the garden.
Die rosie van die gaarde.
[di 'rʊᵊsi fan di 'xa:rdə]

The rough urchin broke her stem
Die ruwe knapie brak haar steel
[di 'ryvə 'kna:pi breᵊk ɦa:r steᵊl]

And hurled his mud upon
her pistil.
En wierp sijn modder op haar geel.
[ɛn værp səj 'mɔdər ɔp ɦa:r çeᵊl]

Stay down, I am leaving again,
Blijf nou maar lê, ik gaan weer weg,
[bləj nœu mar lɛ: ɛk xa:n veᵊr væx]

So said he, the degenerate.
So sprak hij, die ontaarde.
[sʊᵊ spra:k ɦəj di ɔnt'a:rdə]

The gardener then visited again
Die howenier besog toen weer
[di ɦʊᵊvə'ni:r bə'suk tu veᵊr]

His little rose and his garden.
Sijn rosie en sijn gaarde.
[səj 'rʊᵊsi ɛn səj 'xa:rdə]

There she lay on the winding path
Daar lag sij op die slingerpad
[da:r lax səj ɔp di 'sləŋərpat]

And sobbing, the floral angel said:
En snikkend sei die blommeskat:
[ɛn 'snəkənt səj di 'blɔməskat]

Oh if only you were here, oh gardener,
Ag was u hier, o howenier,
[ax vas y ɦi:r ʊᵊ ɦʊᵊvə'ni:r]

Then I would still have had my worth.
Dan had ik nog mijn waarde.
[dan ɦat ɛk nɔx məj 'va:rdə]

The flower's words pierced his heart,
Die blommetaal sijn hart doorsneed,
[di 'blɔməta:l səj ɦart dʊᵊr'sneᵊt]

He stood a long time and stared.
Hij lange stond en staarde.
[ɦəj 'laŋə stɔnt ɛn 'sta:rdə]

My rose-child, I had to leave here,
Mijn rosekind ik moes van hier,
[məj 'rʊᵊsəkənt ɛk mus fan ɦi:r]

I had to, thus spoke the gardener,
Ik moes, so sprak die howenier,
[ɛk mus sʊᵊ sprak di ɦʊᵊvə'ni:r]

And picked her up, his rosebud
En nam haar op, sijn roseknop
[ɛn nam ɦa:r ɔp səj 'rʊᵊsəknɔp]

Valuable little flower.
Blommetje van waarde.
['blomiki fan 'va:rdə]

With a tender glance he saw
Met tedere oogstraal sag hij
[mɛt 'teᵊdərə 'ʊᵊxstra:l sax ɦəj]

How the urchin did not spare his flower,
Hoe die knaap sijn blom nie spaarde,
[ɦu di kna:p səj blɔm ni 'spa:rdə]

But alas, no gardener's skill could heal (her),
Maar ag geen tuinmanskuns kon heel,
[ma:r ax çeᵊn 'tœynmanskœns kɔn fieᵊl]

No (amount of) tears could cleanse her mud,
Geen traneplas haar modder was,
[çeᵊn 'tra:nəplas fia:r 'mɔdər vas]

Her once broken stem,
Haar eenmaal afgebroke steel,
[fia:r 'eᵊnma:l afxə'brʊᵊkə steᵊl]

And give her back her worth.
En geef haar weer haar waarde.
[ɛn çeᵊ fia:r veᵊr fia:r 'va:rdə]

JAN REINDER LEONARD VAN BRUGGEN

(1895–1948)
aka J. R. L. van Bruggen

Outside the Breeze Rustles Softly
Buite suis die sagte Windjie
['bœytə sœys di 'saxtə 'vəŋki]
Music: S. le Roux Marais (1896–1979), "Fifteen Afrikaans Lullabies"
(*Vyftien Afrikaanse Slaapdeuntjies, no. 4*) ['fəjftin afri'ka:nsə 'sla:pˌdjøŋkis]
S. le Roux Marais (1896–1979), "Fifteen Afrikaans Lullabies" (*Vyftien Afrikaanse Slaapdeuntjies, no. 6*) ['fəjftin afri'ka:nsə 'sla:pˌdjøŋkis]
Both arrangements use the same text.

Outside the breeze rustles softly,
Buite suis die sagte windjie,
['bœytə sœys di 'saxtə 'vəŋki]

Inside lies a dear little child,
Binne lê 'n liewe kindjie,
['bənə lɛ: ə 'livə 'kəŋki]

Sleep my dearest sleep
Slaap my liefie slaap
[sla:p məj 'lifi sla:p]

Already the little moon peeks through
the window
Maantjie kyk al deur die ruit
['maŋki kəjk al djøˀr di rœyt]

My little child must close her eyes,
Kindjie moet haar ogies sluit,
['kəŋki mut fia:r 'ʊˀxis slœyt]

Sleep my darling sleep gently now,
Slaap my liefling slaap nou sag,
[sla:p məj 'lifləŋ sla:p nœu sax]

Sleep my darling sleep.
Slaap my liefling slaap.
[sla:p məj 'lifləŋ sla:p]

Afrikaans Art Song Literature. Christian Bester and Bronwen Forbay, Oxford University Press. © Oxford University Press 2025.
DOI: 10.1093/oso/9780197660812.003.0031

Give Me

Gee my

[çeᵊ məj]

Music: Joyce Loots (1907–n.d.), "Three Afrikaans Songs, no. 1"
S. le Roux Marais (1896–1979), "To the Bushveld and Two Other Songs"
(*Bosveldtoe*[1] *en Twee ander Liedere, no. 2*) ['bɔsfæᵊltu ɛn tweᵊ 'andər 'lidərə]

Give me sunlight, give me roses,
Gee my sonlig, gee my rose,
[çeᵊ məj 'sɔnləx çeᵊ məj 'rʊᵊsə]

Give me lilies white and pure,
Gee my lelies blank en rein,
[çeᵊ məj 'leᵊlis blaŋk ɛn rəjn]

Give me clear children's eyes in which the
light of heaven shines.
*Gee my klare kinderoë waar die hemellig
in skyn.*
[çeᵊ məj 'kla:rə 'kəndər‚u:ə va:r di 'ɦeᵊmələx
ən skəjn]

I am tired of this life,
Ek is moeg vir hierdie lewe,
[ɛk əs mux fər 'ɦi:rdi 'leᵊvə]

Tired of all the unrest and pain,
Moeg vir onrus, en van pyn,
[mux fər 'ɔnrəs ɛn fan pəjn]

Tired of wandering in the dark,
Moeg van ronddwaal in die duister,
[mux fan 'rɔntdwa:l ən di 'dœystər]

Tired of glitz and tired of glamor.
Moeg van glans en moeg van skyn.
[mux fan xlans ɛn mux fan skəjn]

When the dusk with its wings
As die skemer met sy vlerke
[as di 'skeᵊmər mɛt səj 'flærkə]

Casts shadows over veld and marsh,
Skadu's gooi oor veld[2] *en vlei,*
['ska:dys xo:j ʊᵊr fæᵊlt ɛn fləj]

I feel how forgotten things
Voel ek hoe vergete dinge
[ful ɛk ɦu fər'xeᵊtə 'dəŋə]

And old grief stir within me.
En ou smarte roer in my.
[ɛn œu 'smartə ru:r ən məj]

Oh, my heart can bear nothing more,
O, my hart kan niks meer dra nie,
[ʊᵊ məj ɦart kan nəks meᵊr dra: ni]

And when dusk's beauty speaks,
En as skemerskoonheid praat,
[ɛn as 'skeᵊmər‚skʊᵊnhəjt pra:t]

The most tender love in me battles
Veg die teerste van my liefde
[fæx di 'teᵊrstə fan məj 'lifdə]

With the cruelest of my hate.
Met die wreedste van my haat.
[mɛt di 'vreᵊtstə fan məj ɦa:t]

---

[1] An expansive African prairie consisting of mainly uncultivated countryside. It is situated in the Limpopo and a small portion of the North West Provinces. Its grassy plains contain clusters of tall trees and shrubs.

[2] An expansive African prairie, field, or pasture, comprising a wide variety of vegetation which may be used in various ways, including agriculture or uncultivated countryside.

Therefore, I pray, give me roses,
Daarom bid ek, gee my rose,
['da:rɔm bət ɛk çeᵊ məj 'rʊᵊsə]

Give me pure children's eyes,
Gee my kinderoë rein,
[çeᵊ məj 'kəndəɾ̩u:ə rəjn]

Give me kindness and love,
Gee my vriend'likheid en liefde,
[çeᵊ məj 'frintləkɦəjt ɛn 'lifdə]

Give me purifying sunshine.
Gee my suiw'rend' sonneskyn.
[çeᵊ məj 'sœyvrɛnt 'sɔnəskəjn]

Homesickness/Nostalgia
Heimwee[3]
['ɦəjmveᵊ]
Music: Anna Lambrechts-Vos (1876–1932), "Songs of Anna Lambrecht-Vos"
(*Liederen van Anna Lambrechts-Vos, Op. 51, no. 3*)
['lidərən fan 'ana 'lambræxts fɔs]
S. le Roux Marais (1896–1979)

My heart longs for the silence,
My hart verlang na die stilte,
[məj hart fər'laŋ na di 'stəltə]

Of the wide-open undulating veld[4]
Van die wye wuiwende veld
[fan di 'vəjə 'vœyvəndə fæᵊlt]

Far from the city's din,
Ver van die stadsgeluide,
[fæ:r fan di 'statsxə‚lœydə]

And the jingle-jangle of money.
En die klinkende klank van geld.
[ɛn di 'kləŋkəndə klaŋk fan xæᵊlt]

I am tired of the restless life
Ek is moeg vir die rustelose lewe
[ɛk əs mux fər di 'rœstəlʊᵊsə 'leᵊvə]

Of people that come and go
Van mense wat kom en gaan
[fan 'mɛnsə vat kɔm ɛn xa:n]

I want to return to the free expanse,
k'Wil terug na die vrye ruimte,
[kvəl tə'rəx na di 'frəjə 'rœymtə]

Where a soul lives that understands.
Waar 'n siel in woon, wat verstaan.
[va:r ə sil ən vʊᵊn vat fər'sta:n]

Oh, I see again, the sun on the veld (fields)
O, ek sien weer die son op die velde
[ʊᵊ ɛk sin veᵊr di sɔn ɔp di 'fæᵊldə]

And the eternal blue above.
En die ewige blou daar bo.
[ɛn di 'eᵊvəxə blœu da:r bʊᵊ]

And my heart is overcome with homesickness,
En my hart skiet vol van heimwee,
[ɛn məj hart skit fɔl fan 'ɦəjmveᵊ]

---

[3] Translated as 'longing, nostalgia, or homesickness.' It refers to a profound, intense longing for one's homeland or the past.
[4] See note 2.

And my dreams swim in my eyes.
En my drome swem in my oë.
[ɛn məj 'drʊᵊmə swɛm ən məj 'uːə]

I see the pale blue mountains again.
Ek sien weer die ylbloue berge.
[ɛk sin veᵊr di 'əjl̩ blœuə 'bærgə]

There, far over the western horizon
Daar ver oor die westerkim
[daːr fæːr ʊᵊr di 'vɛstərkəm]

And (I) don't wonder anymore why melancholy,
En wonder nie meer waarom weemoed,
[ɛn 'vɔndər ni meᵊr 'vaːrɔm 'veᵊmut]

Rises so softly from out of my songs.
So sag uit my liedere klim.
[sʊᵊ sax œyt məj 'lidərə kləm]

Climbing to the gray skies above.
Klim na die grys lug bowe.
[kləm na di xrəjs lœx 'bʊᵊvə]

Where the sun dissolves into the mists,
Waar die son in die miste kwyn,
[vaːr di sɔn ən di 'məstə kwəjn]

Because oh, I dearly long for the veld (fields)
Want o, ek verlang na die velde
[vant ʊᵊ ɛk fər'laŋ na di 'fæᵊldə]

For the eternal sunshine.
Na die ewige sonneskyn.
[na di 'eᵊvəxə 'sɔnəskəjn]

Spring Song
Lentelied
['lɛntəlit]
Music: S. le Roux Marais (1896–1979)

Flutter, flutter little butterfly,
Fladder, fladder vlindertjie,
['fladər 'fladər 'fləndərki]

Round and round a rose,
Om en om 'n roos,
[ɔm ɛn ɔm ə rʊᵊs]

Flitter here and flitter there,
Kuier hier en kuier daar,
['kœyər ɦiːr ɛn 'kœyər daːr]

Flutter to you know not where,
Fladder na jy weet nie waar,
['fladər na jəj veᵊt ni vaːr]

Let the flowers blush,
Laat die blomme bloos,
[laːt di 'blɔmə blʊᵊs]

You're spring's darling,
Jy's die lentelieweling,
[jəjs di ˌlɛntə'livələŋ]

You inspire songs sung everywhere
Jy laat liedjies oral sing
[jəj laːt 'likis 'ʊᵊral səŋ]

Spring is here, spring is here,
Lente is hier, lente is hier,
['lɛntə əs ɦiːr 'lɛntə əs ɦiːr]

Everything rejoices together from pure delight,
Alles juig same van puur plesier,
['aləs jœyx 'sa:mə fan py:r plə'si:r]

Oh my dear little butterfly,
O my liewe vlindertjie,
[ʊᵃ məj 'livə 'fləndərki]

Flutter in my heart,
Fladder in my hart,
['fladər ən məj ɦart]

Whisper all your ditties there,
Fluister al jou liedjies daar,
['flœystər al jœu 'likis da:r]

And dispel my grief.
En verjaag my smart.
[ɛn fər'ja:x məj smart]

Who wants to be moping around
Wie wil nou ook nukke hê
[vi vəl nœu ʊᵃk 'nœkə ɦɛ:]

When spring sings
As die lente sing
[as di 'lɛntə səŋ]

Flutter, flutter little butterfly, spring's
darling
Fladder, fladder vlindertjie, lentetroeteling
['fladər 'fladər 'fləndərki ˌlɛntə'trutələŋ]

Flutter, flutter little butterfly,
Fladder, fladder vlindertjie,
['fladər 'fladər 'fləndərki]

Round and round a rose ...
Om en om 'n roos ...
[ɔm ɛn ɔm ə rʊᵃs]

Little butterfly, flutter from pure delight!
Vlindertjie fladder, van puur plesier!
['fləndərki 'fladər fan py:r plə'si:r]

My Soul Is Sick with Longing
My Siel is siek van Heimwee[5]
[məj sil əs sik fan 'ɦəjmveᵃ]
Music: P. J. Lemmer (1896–1989)
S. le Roux Marais (1896–1979), titled
"Heimwee na die See"

My soul is sick with longing,
My siel is siek van heimwee,
[məj sil əs sik fan 'ɦəjmveᵃ]

With longing for the sea,
Van heimwee na die see,
[fan 'ɦəjmveᵃ na di seᵃ]

The blue light upon the waves
Die blou lig op die branders
[di blœu ləx ɔp di 'brandərs]

That rejuvenates your life,
Wat jou weer lewe gee,
[vat jœu veᵃr 'leᵃvə çeᵃ]

The horizon of water,
Die horison van water,
[di 'ɦʊᵃrisɔn fan 'va:tər]

Of water, light and air,
Van water, lig en lug,
[fan 'va:tər ləx ɛn lœx]

---

[5] See note 3.

The salty breeze in your lungs,
Die soutbries in jou longe,
[di ˈsœutbris ən jœu ˈlɔŋə]

The seagulls in (their) flight.
Die seevoëls in hul vlug.
[di ˈseᵊfʊᵊls ən ɦœl flœx]

I'm tired of the city's throngs,
'k is moeg van stadsgewemel,
[k əs mux fan ˈstatsxəˌveᵊməl]

Noise and grit and pretense,
Rumoer en stof en skyn,
[rəˈmu:r ɛn stɔf ɛn skəjn]

Of soulless people
Van mense sonder siele
[fan ˈmɛnsə ˈsɔndər ˈsilə]

And their hollow sapped spirits.
En geeste voos verfyn.
[ɛn ˈçeᵊstə fʊᵊs fərˈfəjn]

Roar through my heart, oh waves!
Dreun deur my hart, o branders!
[drjøᵊn djøᵊr məj ɦart ʊᵊ ˈbrandərs]

Let your song beat against my chest!
Beuk in my bors jul lied!
[bjøᵊk ən məj bɔrs jœl lit]

Laugh horizon of water,
Lag horison van water,
[lax ˈɦʊᵊrisɔn fan ˈva:tər]

Dispel my grim sorrow!
Verdryf my fel verdriet!
[fərˈdrəjf məj fɛl fərˈdrit]

Because oh, the salty breeze calls again!
Want o, die soutbries roep weer!
[vant ʊᵊ di ˈsœutbris rup veᵊr]

The voice that gives life
Die stem wat lewe gee
[di stɛm vat ˈleᵊvə çeᵊ]

Arises from my being sick with yearning
Klim uit my siek verlange
[kləm œyt məj sik fərˈla:ŋə]

And longing for the sea.
En heimwee na die see.
[ɛn ˈɦəjmveᵊ na di seᵊ]

Lullaby

Slaapdeuntjie
[ˈsla:pˌdjøɲki]
Music: S. le Roux Marais (1896–1979), "Fifteen Afrikaans Lullabies"
(*Vyftien Afrikaanse Slaapdeuntjies, no. 2 and no. 3*)
[ˈfəjftin afriˈka:nsə ˈsla:pˌdjøɲkis]

Go to sleep my lambkin,
Doedoe my skapie,
[ˈdudu məj ˈska:pi]

Close your little eyes,
Sluit jou ogies toe,
[slœyt jœu ˈʊᵊxis tu]

Fold your tiny hands together.
Vou jou handjies same.
[fœu jœu ˈɦaɲkis ˈsa:mə]

Go to sleep little one, sleep,
Doedoe baba, doedoe,
[ˈdudu ˈba:ba ˈdudu]

Sleep, go to sleep little one, sleep.
Doedoe, doedoe baba, doedoe.
['dudu 'dudu 'ba:ba 'dudu]

Sleep little child, go to sleep,
Slaap kindjie, slaap nou,
[sla:p 'kəɲki sla:p nœu]

Mister Sandman is knocking outside.
Buite klop Klaas Vaak.
['bœytə klɔp kla:s fa:k]

Cherubs are hovering above you
Bowe jou sweef engeltjies
['bʊᵊvə jœu sweᵊf 'ɛɲəlkis]

And your mother keeps watch.
En jou mama waak, waak, waak.
[ɛn jœu 'mama va:k va:k va:k]

Dream sweetheart, keep dreaming,
Droom hartjie, droom maar,
[drʊᵊm 'ɦarki drʊᵊm ma:r]

Dreams, oh so tender,
Drome, o so teer,
['drʊᵊmə ʊᵊ sʊᵊ teᵊr]

Descend from the Heavens,
Daal vanuit die Hemel,
[da:l fan'œyt di 'ɦeᵊməl]

From the loving Lord.
Van die liewe Heer.
[fan di livə ɦeᵊr]

Go to sleep.
Doedoe, doedoe, doedoe.
['dudu 'dudu 'dudu]

CHRISTIAN MAURITS VAN DEN HEEVER

(1902–1957)

aka C. M. van den Heever

Autumn Evening[1]

Herfsaand

['ɦærfs a:nt]

Music: S. le Roux Marais (1896–1979)

The city is so quiet in the autumn evening,
Die stad is so stil in die herfsaand,
[di stat əs sʊᵊ stəl ən di 'ɦærfs a:nt]

The hustle-and-bustle of the day is gone,
Die gewoel van die dag is verby,
[di xə'vul fan di dax əs fər'bəj]

And my heart, it shouts full of joy,
En my hart die jubel vol vreugde,
[ɛn məj ɦart di 'jybəl fɔl 'frjøᵊxdə]

It's autumn evening, it's autumn evening
for me.
Dis herfsaand, dis herfsaand vir my.
[dəs 'ɦærfs a:nt dəs 'ɦærfs a:nt fər məj]

Oh autumn evening, my soul is full
of love,
O herfsaand my siel is vol liefde,
[ʊᵊ 'ɦærfs a:nt məj sil əs fɔl 'lifdə]

The night is so vast and so beautiful,
Die nag is so groot en so mooi,
[di nax əs sʊᵊ xrʊᵊt ɛn sʊᵊ mo:j]

The moon that circles there in the
silvery (sky),
Die maan wat daar sirkel in die silwer,
[di ma:n vat da:r 'sərkəl ən di 'səlvər]

Has decorated the world in luxury.
Het die wêreld in weelde getooi.
[ɦet di 'væ:rəlt ən 've'ldə xə'to:j]

The breeze blows cooler than yesterday,
Die windjie waai koeler as gister,
[di 'vəɲki va:j 'kulər as 'xəstər]

Is summer's heat gone?
Is somer se hitte verby?
[əs 'sʊᵊmər sə 'ɦətə fər'bəj]

I don't know, I feel only contentment,
Ek weet nie ek voel net tevrede,
[ɛk veᵊt ni ɛk ful net tə'freᵊdə]

For me it's autumn evening, it's autumn
evening.
Dis herfsaand, dis herfsaand vir my.
[dəs 'ɦærfs a:nt dəs 'ɦærfs a:nt fər məj]

---

[1] Permission granted by NB Publishers.

Afrikaans Art Song Literature. Christian Bester and Bronwen Forbay, Oxford University Press. © Oxford University Press 2025.
DOI: 10.1093/oso/9780197660812.003.0032

The autumn evening is part of my life,
Die herfsaand is deel van my lewe,
[di 'fiærfs a:nt əs deˀl fan məj 'leˀvə]

I still remember the night there alone,
Ek onthou nog die aand daar alleen,
[ɛk ɔnt'fiœu nɔx di a:nt da:r a'leˀn]

Your heart was devastated with grief,
Jou hart was stukkend van smarte,
[jœu fiart vas 'stœkənt fan 'smartə]

You cried so softly.
So saggies het jy geween.
[sʊˀ 'saxis fiɛt jəj xə'veˀn]

Oh, extinguish the memories of yesterday,
O blus die gedagtes van gister,
[ʊˀ blœs di xə'daxtəs fan 'xəstər]

The pains that gnaw at the heart,
Die pyne wat vreet aan die hart,
[di 'pəjnə vat freˀt a:n di fiart]

I kiss your tear-stained face,
Ek soen jou gelaat so vol trane,
[ɛk sun jœu xə'la:t sʊˀ fɔl 'tra:nə]

The autumn evening plates despair
with silver,
Die herfsaand versilwer die smart,
[di 'fiærfs a:nt fər'səlvər di smart]

It's all lost, the past,
Dis alles verloor die verlede,
[dəs 'aləs fər'lʊˀr di fər'leˀdə]

Yet my soul still burns now, like fire,
Maar my siel brand nou nog soos vuur,
[ma:r məj sil brant nœu nɔx sʊˀs fy:r]

Even as the autumn evening so hesitantly
shudders,
As die herfsaand so grillerig huiwer,
[as di 'fiærfs a:nt sʊˀ 'xrələrəx 'fiœyvər]

And the moonbeams are embroidered with
shadows,
En maanskyn met skaadwees borduur,
[ɛn 'ma:nskəjn mɛt 'ska:tveˀs bɔr'dy:r]

Allow the moon through wrinkly clouds,
Laat die maan deur gerimpelde wolke,
[la:t di ma:n djøˀr xə'rəmpəldə 'vɔlkə]

Like a prince riding past palaces,
Soos 'n vors langs paleise heen ry,
[sʊˀs ə fɔrs laŋs pa'ləjsə fieˀn rəj]

My soul feels full and happy,
My siel voel groot en gelukkig,
[məj sil ful xrʊˀt ɛn xə'lœkəx]

It's autumn evening, it's autumn evening for me.
Dis herfsaand, dis herfsaand vir my.
[dəs 'fiærfs a:nt dəs 'fiærfs a:nt fər məj]

STEVEN VAN VENE

(n.d.)

A Lullaby
Slaapliedjie
['slaːpˌliki]
Music: Arthur Ellis (b. 1931)

Beddy-bye, beddy-bye, my lovely little baby,
Slapedoe, slapedoe, my lief klein kindjie,
['slaːpədu 'slaːpədu məj lif kləjn 'kəɲki]

Eyes so blue as the heavens above.
Ogies so blou soos die hemel daarbo.
['ʊᵊxis sʊᵊ blœu sʊᵊs di 'ɦeᵊməl daːr'bʊᵊ]

The sun is already asleep,
Sonnetjie slaap al,
['sɔniki slaːp al]

The little stars twinkle,
Sterretjies flikker,
['stærikis 'fləkər]

Your little eyes are closing, that I can believe.
Ogies val toe, dit kan ek glo.
['ʊᵊxis fal tu dət kan ɛk xlʊᵊ]

Your soft little pillow and your warm
little crib,
Kussinkie sag en jou bedjie so warm,
['kœsəɲki sax ɛn jœu 'bɛːki sʊᵊ 'varəm]

Sleep just as if you were in mother's arms.
Slaap maar net soos in moeder se arm.
[slaːp maːr nɛt sʊᵊs ən 'mudər sə 'arəm]

Beddy-bye, beddy-bye, my lovely little baby,
Slapedoe, slapedoe, my lief klein kindjie,
['slaːpədu 'slaːpədu məj lif kləjn 'kəɲki]

Eyes as blue as the heavens above.
Ogies so blou soos die hemel daarbo.
['ʊᵊxis sʊᵊ blœu sʊᵊs di 'ɦeᵊməl daːr'bʊᵊ]

Afrikaans Art Song Literature. Christian Bester and Bronwen Forbay, Oxford University Press. © Oxford University Press 2025.
DOI: 10.1093/oso/9780197660812.003.0033

NICOLAAS PETRUS VAN WYK LOUW

(1906–1970)
aka N. P. van Wyk Louw

Four Seasonal Prayers in the Boland[1]
Vier Gebede by Jaargetye in die Boland[2]
[fir xəˈbeᵊdə bəj ˈjaːrxəˌtəjə ən di ˈbuᵊlant]
Music: Hendrik Hofmeyr (b. 1957)

Early Autumn
1. *Vroegherfs*
[ˈfruxɦærfs]
Music also by: Peter Klatzow (1945–2021)

The year ripens in golden acorn leaves,
Die jaar word ryp in goue akkerblare,
[di jaːr vɔrt rəjp ən ˈxœuə ˈakərˌblaːrə]

In vineyards turned bronze, and the paler sky
In wingerd wat verbruin, en witter lug
[ən ˈvəŋərt vat fərˈbrœyn ɛn ˈvətər lœx]

All day long, washed by the new wind and bright
Wat daglank van die nuwe wind en klare
[vat ˈdaxlaŋk fan di ˈnyvə vənt ɛn ˈklaːrə]

Sunlight; every flower becomes fruit,
Son deurspoel word; elke blom word vrug,
[sɔn djøᵊrˈspul vɔrt ˈæᵃlkə blɔm vɔrt frœx]

Even the most stagnant; and the first leaves fall
Tot selfs die traagstes; en die eerste blare val
[tɔt sæᵃlfs di ˈtraːxstəs ɛn di ˈeᵊrstə ˈblaːrə fal]

Quite unnoticed in the smoky-blue wood and lane,
So stilweg in die rookvaal bos en laan,
[suᵊ ˈstəlvæx ən di ˈruᵊkfaːl bɔs ɛn laːn]

(So) that the branches of the lanky poplars already,
Dat die takke van die lang populiere al,
[dat di ˈtakə fan di laːŋ pɔpəˈliːrə al]

With each radiant morning, stand a bit whiter.
Met elke ligte môre witter staan.
[mɛt ˈæᵃlkə ˈləxtə ˈmɔːrə ˈvətər staːn]

Oh God, let these days become sanctified:
O Heer, laat hierdie dae heilig word:
[ʊᵊ ɦeᵊr laːt ˈɦiːrdi ˈdaːə ˈɦəjləx vɔrt]

---

[1] Permission granted by NB Publishers.
[2] The "Boland," translated as 'highland,' is a wine-making region in the Western Cape Province with an elevated, highly fertile terrain.

Afrikaans Art Song Literature. Christian Bester and Bronwen Forbay, Oxford University Press. © Oxford University Press 2025.
DOI: 10.1093/oso/9780197660812.003.0034

Let everything fall (away) that was glitter and adornment
Laat alles val wat pronk en sieraad was
[la:t 'aləs fal vat prɔŋk ɛn 'sira:t vas]

Or simply youth, and far removed from pain;
Of enkel jeug, en vér was van die pyn;
[ɔf 'ɛŋkəl jøˀx ɛn 'fæ:r vas fan di pəjn]

Let it ripen, Lord, let Your wind blow,
Laat ryp word, Heer, laat U wind waai,
[la:t rəjp vɔrt ɦeˀr la:t y vənt va:j]

Let my illusion fall, until all the grandeur finally appears
Laat stort my waan, tot al die hoogheid eindelik vas
[la:t stɔrt məj va:n tɔt al di 'ɦʊˀxɦəjt 'əjndələk vas]

Solid and bare out of the tenderness of my youth.
En nakend uit my teerder jeug verskyn.
[ɛn 'na:kənt œyt məj 'teˀrdər jøˀx fər'skəjn]

Out of This Light-Filled Autumn
2. *Uit hierdie ligte Herfs*
[œyt 'ɦi:rdi 'ləxtə ɦærfs]

Out of this light and wide autumn radiates
Uit hierdie ligte en wye herfstyd straal
[œyt 'ɦi:rdi 'ləxtə ɛn 'vəjə 'ɦærfstəjt stra:l]

A new, nameless joy within me
'n Nuwe, namelose vreug in my
[ə 'nyvə 'na:məlʊˀsə frjøˀx ən məj]

That I bewildered roam through a world,
Dat ek verwilderd deur 'n wêreld dwaal,
[dat ɛk fər'vəldərt djøˀr ə 'væ:rəlt dwa:l]

Where things daily reach their fulfillment:
Waar dinge daeliks hul vervulling kry:
[va:r 'dəŋə 'daˀləks ɦœl fər'fœləŋ krəj]

The marshes are filled again every morning to the brim, and white
Die vleie staan weer soggens vol, en wit
[di 'fləjə sta:n veˀr 'sɔxəns fɔl ɛn vət]

With Cape-pondweeds; and twilights white like wheat
Van waterblomme;[3] en skemerings wit soos graan
[fan 'va:tərˌblɔmə ɛn 'skeˀmərəŋs vət sʊˀs xra:n]

That hold the riches of much of the summer-filled air,
Wat die rykheid van veel somerlug besit,
[vat di 'rəjkɦəjt fan feˀl 'sʊˀmərlœx bə'sət]

Arrive across the yellow orchards and harvested fields.
Kom oor die geel boorde en stoppellande aan.
[kɔm ʊˀr di çeˀl 'bʊˀrdə ɛn 'stɔpəlˌlandə a:n]

Why then (does) the grief silently ache again now,
Waarom die smart wat nou weer stilweg skryn,
['va:rɔm di smart vat nœu veˀr 'stəlvæx skrəjn]

---

[3] The Cape-pondweed (*Aponogeton distachyos*) is an aquatic pond plant indigenous to the Western Cape and Mpumalanga provinces. Its sweetly scented flowers and mottled leaves float on standing water surfaces.

And this muttering of new words,
En hierdie preweling van nuwe woorde,
[ɛn 'ɦi:rdi 'preᵊvələŋ fan 'nyvə 'vuᵊrdə]

This sense of loss? Has all become pain,
Dié gemis? Is alle wording pyn,
['di xəˈmᵊs əs 'alə 'vɔrdəŋ pəjn]

And all prayer the quest of our unsettled
En alle bid die tas van ons verstoorde
[ɛn 'alə bət di tas fan ɔns fərˈstuᵊrdə]

(For the) Heart (to find) new names for
the grief
Hart na nuwe name vir die leed
[ɦart na 'nyvə 'na:mə fər di leᵊt]

Of the wondrous flourishing within
our souls?
*Van die wondre uitbloei wat hy in
hom weet?*
[fan di 'vɔndrə 'œytblui vat ɦəj ən ɦɔm veᵊt]

Winter
3. *Winter*
['vəntər]

Now the earth lies soaking for nights on end
Nou lê die aarde nagtelank en week
[nœu lɛ: di 'a:rdə 'naxtəlaŋk ɛn veᵊk]

In the dark, quiet grace of the rain,
In die donker, stil genade van die reën,
[ən di 'dɔŋkər stəl xəˈna:də fan di reᵊn]

And dusky houses and branches pale
every day
En skemer huise en takke daeliks bleek
[ɛn 'skeᵊmər 'ɦœysə ɛn 'takə 'daᵊləks bleᵊk]

Through the white fogginess and rustling.
Deur die wit mistigheid en suising heen.
[djøᵊr di vət 'məstəxɦəjt ɛn 'sœysəŋ ɦeᵊn]

It's all rich and peaceful with the heavy
Dis alles ryk en rustig van die swaar
[dəs 'als rəjk ɛn 'rœstəx fan di swa:r]

Secret growth that finds its paths
Geheime wasdom wat sy paaie vind
[xəˈɦəjmə 'vasdɔm vat səj 'pa:jə fənt]

Through the warm earth to every shoot
and leaf,
Deur warm aarde na elke skeut en blaar,
[djøᵊr 'varəm 'a:rdə na 'æᵊlkə skjøᵊt en bla:r]

And obscurely binds everything near
and far
En ver en naby alles duister bind
[ɛn fæ:r ɛn naˈbəj 'aləs 'dœystər bənt]

In moisture and fruitfulness and great
yearning;
In vog en vrugbaarheid en groot verlange;
[ən fɔx ɛn 'frœxba:rɦəjt ɛn xruᵊt fərˈlaŋə]

Until on a bright afternoon we suddenly see
Tot ons 'n helder middag skielik sien
[tɔt ɔns ə 'ɦæᵊldər 'mədax 'skilək sin]

The grass gleaming, and the young wheat
against the slopes,
*Die gras blink, en die jong graan teen
die hange,*
[di xras bləŋk ɛn di jɔŋ xra:n teᵊn di 'ɦaŋə]

And know that all rest serves life:
En weet dat alle rus die lewe dien:
[ɛn veᵊt dat 'alə rœs di 'leᵊvə din]

How could I have thought that summer was richer (more fertile)
Hoe kon ek dink dat somer ryker is
[ɦu kɔn ɛk dəŋk dat 'suᵊmər 'rəjkər əs]

Than the silent mystery of this growth?
As hierdie groei se stil geheimenis?
[as 'ɦiːrdi xrui sə stəl xə'ɦəjmənəs]

First Snow
4. *Eerste Sneeu*
[eᵊrstə sniu]

Joy has overnight, like new snow
Die blydskap het oornag soos nuwe sneeu
[di 'bləjtskap ɦɛt ʊᵊr'nax suᵊs 'nyvə sniu]

Transformed the lowest slopes of my earlier sorrow
Die laagste hellings van my vroeë smartr
[di 'laːxstə 'ɦæləŋs fan məj 'fruːə smart]

To beauty, where every cry
Tot skoonheid omgeskep waar elke skreeu
[tɔt 'skuᵊnɦəjt 'ɔmxəˌskep vaːr 'æᵃlkə skriu]

Like a loud whip in the bright air of the kloofs[4]
Soos 'n sweep in die blink lug van die klowe hard
[suᵊs ə sweᵊp ən di bləŋk lœx fan di 'klʊᵊvə ɦart]

And clearly resounds. The round earth stands
En helder klink. Die ronde aarde staan
[ɛn 'ɦæᵃldər kləŋk die 'rɔndə 'aːrdə staːn]

White, blooming and pure like a flower —
Wit oopgekelk en suiwer soos 'n blom —
[vət 'ʊᵊpxəˌkæᵃlk ɛn 'sœyvər suᵊs ə blɔm]

One shimmer where (the) new waters go,
Een glinstering waar die nuwe waters gaan,
[eᵊn 'xlənstərəŋ vaːr di 'nyvə 'vaːtərs xaːn]

Without expectation, since everything has arrived.
Verwagtingloos, want alles het gekom.
[fər'vaxtəŋlʊᵊs vant 'aləs ɦɛt xə'kɔm]

Oh heart, will joy reach greater heights,
O hart, sal vreugde hoër gaan,
[ʊᵊ ɦart sal 'frjøᵊxdə 'ɦʊᵊr xaːn]

Without you dying? Within me a quiet impression occurs,
En jy nie sterf? Daar kom in my 'n stil vermoede,
[ɛn jəj ni stærf daːr kɔm ən məj ə stəl fər'mudə]

That all life finds fulfillment in this way
Dat alle lewe só sy volheid kry
[dat 'alə 'leᵊvə 'suᵊ səj 'fɔlɦəjt krəj]

---

[4] Kloof(s) are canyon-like deep glens or ravines in South Africa that may be wooded.

And blissfully submits to the refuge of a
reposeful death,
En heerlik gaan in die rustige dood se hoede,
[ɛn ˈfieᵊrlək xaːn ən di ˈrœstəxə dʊᵊt sə ˈfiudə]

That you will be washed, smashed, and
poured out
Dat jy sal spoel en breek en uitgestort
[dat jəj sal spul ɛn breᵊk ɛn ˈœytxəˌstɔrt]

Into this white wave of joy.
*In hierdie wit golf van die vreugde
word.*
[ən ˈfiiːrdi vət xɔlf fan di ˈfrjøᵊxdə
vɔrt]

Stand-Alone Poetry

The Little Chisel[5]
Die Beiteltjie
[di ˈbəjtəlki]
Music: Rosa Nepgen (1909–2001)

I get a tiny little chisel,
Ek kry 'n klein klein beiteltjie,
[ɛk krəj ə kləjn kləjn ˈbəjtəlki]

A chisel has to be able to break a rock
'n Beitel moet kan klip breek
[ə ˈbəjtəl mut kan kləp breᵊk]

I tap it and it sounds;
Ek tik hom en hy klink;
[ɛk tək fiɔm ɛn fiəj kləŋk]

If it is a chisel —
As hy 'n beitel is —
[as fiəj ə ˈbəjtəl əs]

So I sharpen it and sharpen it
Toe slyp ek en ek slyp hom
[tu sləjp ɛk ɛn ɛk sləjp fiɔm]

I bash it with my little chisel
Ek slaat hom met my beiteltjie
[ɛk słaːt fiɔm mɛt məj ˈbəjtəlki]

Until it sounds and shines.
Totdat hy klink en blink.
[ˈtɔdat fiəj kləŋk ɛn bləŋk]

Which proved to be strong enough:
En dié was sterk genoeg:
[ɛn ˈdi vas stærk xəˈnux]

I place a pebble on a rock:
Ek sit 'n klippie op 'n rots:
[ɛk sət ə ˈkləpi ɔp ə rɔts]

And so the pebble burst
Daar spring die klippie stukkend
[daːr sprəŋ di ˈkləpi ˈstœkənt]

One must be certain: —
Mens moet jou vergewis: —
[mɛns mut jœu fərxəˈvəs]

And cut clean like along a seam:
En skoon soos langs 'n voeg:
[ɛn skʊᵊn sʊᵊs laŋs ə fux]

---

[5] Permission granted by NB Publishers.

Then, under my ten fingers splits
Toe, onder my tien vingers bars
[tu 'ɔndər məj tin 'fəŋərs bars]

Then, with two golden chasms
Dan, met twee goue afgronde
[dan mɛt tweᵊ 'xœuə 'afˌxrɔndə]

The gray rock down the middle
Die grys rots middeldeur
[di xrəjs rɔts 'mədəldjøᵊr]

Splitting the planet in two
Val die planeet aan twee
[fal di pla'neᵊt a:n tweᵊ]

And next to my feet I feel
En langs my voete voel ek
[ɛn laŋs məj 'futə ful ɛk]

And across the cliffs, boiling,
En oor die kranse, kokend,
[ɛn ʊᵊr di 'kra:nsə 'kʊᵊkənt]

The soft earth tear,
Die sagte aarde skeur,
[di 'saxtə 'a:rdə skjøᵊr]

The shallow green sea disappears
Verdwyn die vlak groen see
[fər'dwəjn di flak xrun seᵊ]

The dark seam runs through my country
Die donker naat loop deur my land
[di 'dɔŋkər na:t lʊᵊp djøᵊr məj lant]

And on the day I see the night
En op die dag sien ek die nag
[ɛn ɔp di dax sin ɛk di nax]

And cleaves it to its very roots —
En kloof hom wortel toe —
[ɛn klʊᵊf ɦɔm 'vɔrtəl tu]

There on other side, open up
Daar anderkant gaan oop
[da:r 'andərkant xa:n ʊᵊp]

A chisel must cut in this way
Só moet 'n beitel slaan
['sʊᵊ mut ə 'bəjtəl sla:n]

With a rupture that from my chisel
Met 'n bars wat van my beitel af
[mɛt ə bars vat fan məj 'bəjtəl af]

Like a chisel should, not so?
Wat beitel is, of hoe?
[vat 'bəjtəl əs ɔf ɦu]

Runs right through the stars.
Dwarsdeur die sterre loop.
['dwarsdjøᵊr di 'stærə lʊᵊp]

The Love Within Me[6]
Die Liefde in my
[di 'lifdə ən məj]
Music: Dirkie de Villiers (1920–1993), titled "Winter Trees"
"Winterbome" ['vəntərˌbʊᵊmə]
Rosa Nepgen (1909–2001)

It's always you, just always you,
Dis altyd jy, net altyd jy,
[dəs 'altəjt jəj nɛt 'altəjt jəj]

The one thought that remains with me
Die een gedagte bly my by
[di eᵊn xə'daxtə bləj məj bəj]

---

[6] Permission granted by NB Publishers.

Like shadows that linger underneath the trees,
Soos skadu's onder bome bly,
[sʊᵊs ˈska:dys ˈɔndər ˈbʊᵊmə bləj]

Just always you, just always you.
Net altyd jy, net altyd jy.
[nɛt ˈaltəjt jəj nɛt ˈaltəjt jəj]

My sorrow travels along many roads,
Langs baie weë gaan my smart,
[laŋs ˈbajə ˈveᵊə xa:n məj smart]

My eyes are blind, and confused
Blind is my oë en verward
[blənt əs məj ˈu:ə ɛn fərˈvart]

Are all (the) things in my heart.
Is alle dinge in my hart.
[əs ˈalə ˈdəŋə ən məj ɦart]

But it will remain one and only,
Maar dit sal een en enkeld bly,
[ma:r dət sal eᵊn ɛn ˈɛŋkəlt bləj]

And finds its relief both deep and mundane,
En aards en diep sy laafnis kry,
[ɛn a:rts ɛn dip səj ˈla:fnəs krəj]

Even if winter manifests (itself), nakedly
within me,
Al staan dit winter, kaal in my,
[al sta:n dət ˈvəntər ka:l ən məj]

The love in me, the love in me.
Die liefde in my, die liefde my.
[di ˈlifdə ən məj di ˈlifdə ən məj]

<h2 style="text-align:center">Boundaries[7]</h2>

Grense
[ˈxrɛnsə]
Music: Dirkie de Villiers (1920–1993)

Without diffidence my exposed soul
My naakte siel wil sonder skrome
[məj ˈna:ktə sil vəl ˈsɔndər ˈskrʊᵊmə]

Wants to approach you in all simplicity,
In alle eenvoud tot jou gaan,
[ən ˈalə ˈeᵊnfœut tɔt jœu xa:n]

Like our dreams out of a deep sleep,
Soos uit diepe slaap ons drome,
[sʊᵊs œyt ˈdipə sla:p ɔns ˈdrʊᵊmə]

Like the trees against the twilight
Soos teen skemerlug die bome
[sʊᵊs teᵊn ˈskeᵊmərlœx di ˈbʊᵊmə]

Reach up, reach up, to the blue moon;
Opreik, opreik, opreik na die bloue maan;
[ˈɔprəjk ɔprəjk ˈɔprəjk na di ˈblœuə ma:n]

Approach (you) with all its dark wishes,
Gaan met al sy donker wense,
[xa:n mɛt al səj ˈdɔŋkər ˈvɛnsə]

And say the holy
En die heil'ge
[ɛn di ˈɦəjlxə]

Things never heard before,
Nooitgehoorde dinge sê,
[ˈno:jtxəˌɦʊᵊrdə ˈdəŋə sɛ:]

---

[7] Permission granted by NB Publishers.

For which folks hesitate,
Waarvoor die mense huiwer,
['vaːrfʊᵊr di 'mɛnsə 'ɦœyvər]

And which flicker around the edges,
En wat om die grense flikker,
[ɛn vat ɔm di 'xrɛnsə 'fləkər]

Flicker from my dark words.
Flikker van my duister woorde.
['fləkər fan məj 'dœystər vʊᵊrdə]

Come Tonight in My Dreams[8]
Kom vannag in my Drome
[kɔm fa'nax ən məj 'drʊᵊmə]
Music: Anton Hartman (1918–1982)

Come tonight in my dreams
Kom vannag in my drome
[kɔm fa'nax ən məj 'drʊᵊmə]

When it is dark and quiet;
As dit donker is en stil;
[as dət 'dɔŋkər əs ɛn stəl]

Reach out (to me) your hand through the dreams,
Reik my jou hand deur die drome,
[rəjk məj jœu ɦant djøᵊr di 'drʊᵊmə]

And we will roam wherever we please.
En ons sal dwaal waar ons wil.
[ɛn ɔns sal dwaːl vaːr ɔns vəl]

Come, in the starry labyrinth
Kom, in die sterreduister
[kɔm ən di 'stærə͜dœystər]

I will recognize your soul;
Sal ek jou siel herken;
[sal ɛk jœu sil ɦær'kɛn]

Like every night in the dark
Soos elke nag in die duister
[sʊᵊs 'æᵊlkə nax ən di 'dœystər]

I will know your eyes.
Sal ek jou oë ken.
[sal ɛk jœu 'uːə kɛn]

Like smoke our souls will glide
Soos rook sal ons siele swewe
[sʊᵊs rʊᵊk sal ɔns 'silə 'sweᵊvə]

Precipitously though the starry night
Steil deur die sterrenag
[stəjl djøᵊr di 'stærənax]

Across the dark mountains,
Bo oor die donker berge,
['bʊᵊ ʊᵊr di 'dɔŋkər 'bærgə]

Across the dark night.
Bo oor die donker nag.
[bʊᵊ ʊᵊr di 'dɔŋkər nax]

Across happiness and love
Bo oor blydskap en liefde
[bʊᵊ ʊᵊr 'bləjtskap ɛn 'lifdə]

---

[8] Permission granted by NB Publishers.

That this world knows,
Wat hierdie wêreld ken,
[vat 'ɦi:rdi 'væ:rəlt kɛn]

(There) we will, in undisturbed radiance
Sal ons in roerlose straling
[sal ɔns ən 'ru:rlʊᵊsə 'stra:ləŋ]

Know eternal beauty.
Die ewige skoonheid ken,
[di 'eᵊvəxə 'skʊᵊnɦəjt kɛn]

The beauty that we
Die skoonheid wat ons
[di 'skʊᵊnɦəjt vat ɔns]

For a moment see sparkle and perish
'n Oomblik sien flikker en vergaan
[ə 'ʊᵊmblək sin 'fləkər ɛn fər'xa:n]

Between the dark things
Tussen die donker dinge
['tœsən di 'dɔŋkər 'dəŋə]

Through which our lives wander
Waardeur ons lewes gaan
['va:rdjø̞ᵊr ɔns 'leᵊvəs xa:n]

With perpetual serene sadness half the recollection
Met ewigstille weemoed en halwe herinnering
[mɛt 'eᵊvəxˌstələ 've̞ᵊmut ɛn 'ɦalvə ɦæ'rənərəŋ]

Of something that was,
Van iets wat was,
[fan its vat vas]

And still hovers above our reminiscences;
En nog swewe oor ons herinnering;
[ɛn nɔx 'sweᵊvə ʊᵊr ɔns ɦæ'rənərəŋ]

Of something that we can never have,
Van iets wat ons nooit kan kry nie,
[fan its vat ɔns 'no:jt kan krəj ni]

Of something that we cannot see,
Van iets wat ons nie kan sien,
[fan its vat ɔns ni kan sin]

The heart filled with dreams and yearning,
Die hart van droom en verlange,
[di ɦart fan drʊᵊm ɛn fər'laŋə]

That our souls will see,
Dié sal ons siele sien,
['di sal ɔns 'silə sin]

Love, when you come in my dreams,
Lief, as jy kom in my drome,
[lif as jəj kɔm ən məj 'drʊᵊmə]

Come in the starry night,
Kom in die sterrenag,
[kɔm ən di 'stærənax]

And the two of us will wander through the dreams
En ons twee dwaal deur die drome
[ɛn ɔns tweᵊ dwa:l djø̞ᵊr di 'drʊᵊmə]

Across the dark night.
Bo oor die donker nag.
['bʊᵊ ʊᵊr di 'dɔŋkər nax]

Command[9]

Opdrag
['ɔpdrax]
Music: Dawid Engela (1931–1967), "Two Songs"
(*Twee Liedere, no. 1*) [tweᵊ 'lidərə]

You were my youth,
Jy was my jeug,
[jəj vas məj jøᵊx]

All that I knew of joy and sorrow you gave
(to me)!
*Al wat ek ken van vreugde en leed het
jy gegee!*
[al vat ɛk kɛn fan 'frjøᵊxdə ɛn leᵊt ɦɛt jəj
xə'xeᵊ]

And now remains of our plentitude,
En nou bly van ons volheid,
[ɛn nœu bləj fan ɔns 'fɔlɦəjt]

Only silences,
Nog net stiltes,
[nɔx nɛt 'stəltəs]

That know no words.
Wat geen woorde weet.
[vat çeᵊn 'vʊᵊrdə veᵊt]

I then had to find new words,
Toe moes ek nuwe woorde vind,
[tu mus ɛk 'nyvə 'vʊᵊrdə fənt]

Full of heavy surmises,
Vol swaar vermoede,
[fɔl swa:r fər'mudə]

As a prayer for one who passionately
still wanted
As gebed vir een wat driftig nog die jeug,
[as xə'bɛt fər eᵊn vat 'drəftəx nɔx di jøᵊx]

To rescue youth and the beauty of life!
En skoonheid om te leef, wou red!
[ɛn 'skʊᵊnɦəjt ɔm tə leᵊf vœu rɛt]

Take this for yourself,
Neem dié vir jou,
[neᵊm 'di fər jœu]

But I who go,
Maar ek wat gaan,
[ma:r ɛk vat xa:n]

Where higher, colder paths lie,
Waar hoër, kouer paaie lê,
[va:r 'ɦʊᵊr 'kœuər 'pa:jə lɛ:]

Want scant comfort and no prayers, and few,
Wil weinig troos en geen gebed, en min,
[vəl 'vəjnəx trʊᵊs ɛn çeᵊn xə'bɛt ɛn mən]

Yet pure (truthful) words!
Maar suiwer woorde hê!
[ma:r 'sœyvər 'vʊᵊrdə ɦɛ:]

---

[9] Permission granted by NB Publishers.

Panic-Stricken Angst[10]

Paniese Angs

['pa:nisə aŋs]

Music: Marinus de Jong (1891–1984), "Six South African Songs" (*Zes Zuid-Afrikaanse Liederen, no. 1*) [zɛs zœyt afriˈka:nsə ˈlidərən]

God, this angst, this angst,
God, hierdie angs, hierdie angs,
[xɔt ˈfiirdi aŋs ˈfiirdi aŋs]

This cannot be Your utmost revelation:
Dít kan nie U uiterste openbaring wees:
[ˈdət kan ni y ˈœytərstə ˌʊᵊpənˈba:rəŋ veᵊs]

This confusion of my eyes,
Hierdie verwarring van my oë,
[ˈfiirdi fərˈvarəŋ fan məj ˈu:ə]

This white-eyed fear.
Hierdie wit-ogige vrees.
[ˈfiirdi vət ˈʊᵊxəxə freᵊs]

That I do not fear the demolition of
my body,
Dat ek vrees nie die breek van my liggaam,
[dat ɛk freᵊs ni di breᵊk fan məj ˈləxa:m]

But within me Your enormous struggle;
Maar in my U geweldige beure;
[ma:r ən məj y xəˈvæᵃldəxə ˈbjøᵊrə]

How will You break my resistance,
Hoe sal U my weerstand breek,
[fiu sal y məj ˈveᵊrstant breᵊk]

How You pummel and pummel on
my doors.
Hoe slaat U en slaat U op my deure.
[fiu sla:t y ɛn sla:t y ɔp məj ˈdjøᵊrə]

Till I shrink back like the water of the sea
before You in my great need:
*Tot ek terugkrimp soos die see se water voor U
in my grote nood:*
[tɔt ɛk təˈrœxkrəmp sʊᵊs di seᵊ sə ˈva:tər fʊᵊr
y ən məj ˈxrʊᵊtə nʊᵊt]

You rise, Oh God, to my lips.
U styg, O God, tot my lippe.
[y stəjx ʊᵊ xɔt tɔt məj ˈləpə]

With the salty taste of Your death.
Met die soutsmaak van U dood.
[mɛt di ˈsœutsma:k fan y dʊᵊt]

---

[10] Permission granted by NB Publishers.

Daybreak[11]
Rooidag
['ro:jdax]
Music: S. le Roux Marais (1896–1979), "New Songs"
(*Nuwe Liedere, no. 10*) ['nyvə 'lidərə]
Maria van der Mark (1912–n.d.), "Eight Songs on Words by N. P. van Wyk Louw"
(*Agt Liedere op Woorde van N. P. van Wyk Louw, no. 4*)
[axt 'lidərə ɔp 'vʊᵊrdə fan ɛn 'pi:ə fan vəjk lœu]
Henk van Eck (n.d.), "Seven Songs on Words by N. P. van Wyk Louw"
(*Sewe Liedere op Woorde van N. P. van Wyk Louw, no. 1*)
[seᵊvə 'lidərə ɔp 'vʊᵊrdə fan ɛn 'piə fan vəjk lœu]

Daybreak, daybreak what do you bring
Rooidag, rooidag wat bring jy
['ro:jdax 'ro:jdax vat brəŋ jəj]

My heart is palpitating and it feels to me,
My hart dit klop en dit voel vir my,
[məj ɦart dət klɔp ɛn dət ful fər məj]

I don't know why I feel so happy
Ek weet nie waarom voel ek so bly
[ɛk veᵊt ni 'va:rɔm ful ɛk sʊᵊ bləj]

Truly, truly, today he'll come!
Sowaar, sowaar vandag kom hy!
[sʊᵊ'va:r sʊᵊ'va:r fan'dax kɔm ɦəj]

---

[11] Permission granted by NB Publishers.

ANDRIES GERHARDUS VISSER

(1879–1929)
aka A. G. Visser

Noah's Ark
Noag se Ark
[ˈnuːax sə ark]
Music: Lourens Faul (b. 1931)

The Elephant
1. *Die Olifant*
[di ˈʊᵊlifant]

This rubbery rogue	Roly —
Hierdie gomlastiekkalant	*Rolie —*
[ˈɦiːrdi ˈxɔmlastikaˌlant]	[ˈrʊᵊli]
With a tail at both ends,	Poly —
Met 'n stert aan elke kant,	*Polie —*
[mɛt ə stært aːn ˈæᵃlkə kant]	[ˈpʊᵊli]
With his peaty skin naked and rough,	Kitten-like —
Met sy turfvel kaal en skurf,	*Katjie —*
[mɛt səj ˈtœrfæl kaːl ɛn skœrf]	[ˈka ⁱ ki]
Is the	Stealthy —
Is die	*Poetjie —*
[əs di]	[ˈpu ⁱ ki]
Slippery —	Elephant.
Olie —	*Olifant.*
[ˈʊᵊli]	[ˈʊᵊlifant]

Afrikaans Art Song Literature. Christian Bester and Bronwen Forbay, Oxford University Press. © Oxford University Press 2025.
DOI: 10.1093/oso/9780197660812.003.0035

The Rhinoceros
2. *Die Renoster*
[di 'rənɔstər]

The deserter with its ashen skin rug (kaross),
Die droster met sy vaal karos,
[di 'drɔstər mɛt səj fa:l ka'rɔs]

It is indeed
Dit is mos
[dət əs mɔs]

There by the buffalo thorn (tree),
Daar by die wag-'n-bietjie-bos,[1]
[da:r bəj di 'vaxəˌbikibɔs]

The tail-ender (hindmost ox) —
Die Agteros —
[di 'axtərɔs]

With the thick tucks in its hide,
Met die dik opnaaisels in sy huid,
[mɛt di dək 'ɔpna:jsəls ən səj ɦœyt]

Horse whipped —
Sambok —
[sam'bɔk]

With a toothpick on its snout —
Met 'n tandestoker op sy snuit —
[mɛt ə 'tandəˌstʊᵊkər ɔp səj snœyt]

Rhino-ox.
Renosteros.
[rə'nɔstərɔs]

The Hump-Backed Camel
3. *Die Dromedaris*[2]
[di ˌdrɔmə'da:rəs]

The furry old harlequin,
Die harige ou harlekyn,
[di 'ɦa:rəxə œu 'ɦarləkəjn]

That has always been sparkling clean and clear,
Wat nog altyd silwerskoon en klaar is,
[vat nɔx 'altəjt 'səlvərskʊᵊn ɛn kla:r əs]

The Ford car of the sandy desert,
Die Fordkar van die sandwoestyn,
[di 'fɔrtkar fan di 'santˌvustəjn]

Is the
Is die
[əs di]

With a barrel of water in his inventory,
Met 'n rolvat water in sy inventaris,
[mɛt ə 'rɔlfat 'va:tər ən səj ənfən'ta:rəs]

---

[1] The buffalo thorn (*Ziziphus mucronata)* is a small- to medium-sized tree with an extended canopy. Found throughout southern Africa, its leaves are a favorite food of giraffes (*Giraffa*) and impala (*Aepyceros*). Its hooked thorns give the tree its Afrikaans name, *wag-'n-bietjie*, which means 'wait-a-minute.' The Zulu people have used them historically as grave markers for deceased Zulu chiefs and call them *umLahlankosi*, translated as 'that which buries the chief.'
[2] The hump-backed camel *(Camelus dromedarius)* is also known as the Somali or Arabian camel.

Kalahari — *Kalaharie* — [kala'ɦa:ri]	Flat-canary — *Blikkanarie* — [bləka'na:ri]
Sari — *Sarie* — ['sa:ri]	Hump-backed- *Drome-* ['drɔmə]
Hari — *Harie* — ['ɦa:ri]	Camel. *Daris.* ['da:rəs]

The Hippopotamus
4. *Die Seekoei*
[di 'seᵊkui]

The old stumpy that furiously roars over there, *Die ou vetsak wat daar woedend brul,* [di œu 'fɛtsak vat da:r 'vudənt brœl]	The *Die* [di]
	Hip-hip-hip *Hiep-hiep-hiep* ['ɦipɦipɦip]
Is the bitty old hippopotamus bull. *Is die bitsige ou seekoeibul.* [əs di 'bətsəxə œu 'seᵊkuibœl]	
	Hooray — *Hoerê* — ['ɦurɛ:]
What say you, most learned reverend? *Wat sê u, hooggeleerde dominee?* [vat sɛ: y 'ɦʊᵊxəˌleᵊrdə 'dʊᵊmini]	
	Po — *Po* — [pɔ]
Is it a contradiction in terms? *Is dit 'n contradictio in terminee?* [əs dət ə kɔntra'diktsiœu ən 'tærmini]	
	Hippopotamus *Potamus.* ['pɔtaməs]
Oh no, I know he has been baptized thus: *O nee, ek weet hy is gedoop aldus:* [ʊᵊ neᵊ ɛk veᵊt ɦəj əs xə'dʊᵊp al'dəs]	

The Giraffe
5. *Die Kameelperd*
[di ka'meᵊlpært]

The old long-necked up-and-down,
Die ou langenekker op-en-af,
[di œu 'laŋə‚nɛkər 'ɔpɛnaf]

With his both-sides, same-sides run,
Met sy alkant-selfkant-draf,
[mɛt səj 'alkant‚sæᵃlfkantdraf]

With his small head lost (above)
Met sy klein verdwaalde koppie
[mɛt səj kləjn fər'dwa:ldə 'kɔpi]

In the highest tree's canopy,
In die hoogste boom se toppie,
[ən di 'fiʊᵊxstə bʊᵊm sə 'tɔpi]

Is old
Is ou
[əs œu]

Fourteen —
Veertien —
['feᵊrtin]

Foot —
Voet —
[fut]

Of —
Van —
[fan]

Sore throat —
Seerkeel —
['seᵊrkeᵊl]

When —
As —
[as]

He gets a sore throat —
Hy-keelseer-kry —
[fiəj'keᵊlseᵊr krəj]

Giraffe.
Giraf.
[çi'raf]

And-So-Forth
6. *Ensovoorts*
['ɛnsʊᵊfʊᵊrts]

There are even more things with
crueler names:
Daar's nog goed met wreder name:
[da:rs nɔ xut[3] mɛt 'vreᵊdər 'na:mə]

Quaggas from the Kragga Kamma,
Kwaggas[4] uit die Kraggakame,[5]
['kwaxas œyt di 'kraxa‚ka:mə]

---

[3] See Appendix G, Assimilation and Amalgamation of Consonants.
[4] Quaggas (*Equus quagga quagga*) were an unusual subspecies of zebra native to South Africa that became extinct in the late nineteenth century. They only had stripes on the front half of their bodies, while their rear halves were brown.
[5] An area in the Eastern Cape Province consisting of lush coastal forests and grasslands.

Saucer-sized-palm-nut-cane-chutney-
orangutans,
Piering-pinang-rottang-blatjang[6]-
oerangoetangs,
['pirəŋ 'pinaŋ 'rɔtaŋ 'blatjaŋ uraŋ'utaŋs]

Mediterranean sea's
Reuben-Simeon-Leviathans.
*Middellandse-see-se-ruben-simeon-
leviatangs.*[7]
['mədəlantsə se° sə 'rubən 'simiɔn lə'fiataŋs]

If you return in a week's time, then perhaps
Kom jul môre oor 'n week weer, dan miskien
[kɔm jœl 'mɔ:rə ʋ°r ə ve°k ve°r dan məs'kin]

You will see all the brothers of the ark and
they will see you.
*Sal al die arkebroeders jul vir hul en hul vir
julle sien.*
[sal al di 'arkəbrudərs jœl fər ɦœl ɛn ɦœl fər
'jœlə sin]

Stand-Alone Poetry

The Dark Stream
Die Donker Stroom
[di 'dɔŋkər strʋ°m]
Music: Doris Beyers (n.d.), "Three Songs" (*Drie Liedere*) [dri 'lidərə]
Lily Lapin (1893–n.d.), "Two Songs for Bass Voice, no. 2"
S. le Roux Marais (1896–1979), "New Songs" (*Nuwe Liedere, no. 2*) ['nyvə 'lidərə]
Rosa Nepgen (1909–2001)
Sydney Richfield (1882–1967)
M. C. Roode (1907–1967)

I wonder still if we one day,
Ek wonder steeds of ons eendag,
[ɛk 'vɔndər ste°ts ɔf ɔns 'e°ndax]

There (on the) other side of the dark stream,
Daar anderkant die donker stroom,
[da:r 'andərkant di 'dɔŋkər strʋ°m]

If we will know and feel and laugh
Of ons sal weet en voel en lag
[ɔf ɔns sal ve°t ɛn vul ɛn lax]

And dream while sleeping soundly.
En in die lange slaap nog droom.
[ɛn ən di 'laŋə sla:p nɔx drʋ°m]

If I could dream and fantasize
As ek kon droom en fantaseer
[as ɛk kɔn drʋ°m ɛn fantə'se°r]

In the shadowy hereafter, then would —
In skadu-ryk hierna, dan sou —
[ən 'ska:dyrəjk ɦi:r'na: dan sœu]

---

[6] *Blatjang* is a tangy chutney-like sauce made of dried fruit (usually apricots) and chilies cooked in vinegar, sugar, and spices. It is traditionally served as a condiment with South African meat and curry dishes.
[7] A sea serpent from the Hebrew tradition that served as one of God's first beasts.

Then would I desire no happiness
Dan sou ek geen geluk begeer
[dan sœu ɛk çeᵊn xəˈlœk bəˈxeᵊr]

Than, dearest, just to dream of you.
As, liefste, net te droom van jou.
[as ˈlifstə nɛt tə druᵊm fan jœu]

The Little Bells of Paarl
Die Pêrel se Klokkies
[di ˈpæːrəl sə ˈklɔkis]
Music: Fannie Edith Starke Eagar (1920–n.d.)
Arthur Ellis (b. 1931)

The little bells of Paarl have a delightful ring,
Die Pêrel se klokkies het 'n mooie geluid,
[di ˈpæːrəl sə ˈklɔkis ɦɛt ə ˈmoːjə xəˈlœyt]

And the maidens of the Boland look really dainty!
En die Bolandse[8] nooientjies sien liefies daaruit La-la!
[ɛn di ˈbuᵊlantsə ˈnoːjɲkis sin ˈlifis daːrˈœyt lala]

The Berg River flows through there as clear as glass.
Die bergrivier vloei daar so helder as glas.
[di ˈbærxrəfiːr flui daːr suᵊ ˈɦæᵊldər as xlas]

And I cannot deny that I fell head-over-heels for you all!
En ek kan nie ontken nie, hoe lief jul my was — La-la!
[ɛn ɛk kan ni ɔntˈkɛn ni ɦu lif jœl məj vas lala]

A pinch of love, a pinch of fidelity;
'n Klein bietjie liefde, en 'n klein bietjie trou;
[ə kləjn ˈbiki ˈlifdə ɛn ə kləjn ˈbiki trœu]

And a touch of treachery and there you have it, a wife!
En 'n klein bietjie valsheid en daar het jy 'n vrou! La-la!
[ɛn ə kləjn ˈbiki ˈfalsɦəjt ɛn daːr ɦɛt jəj ə frœu lala]

Alas, the Onderveld calls me, I have to say my farewells;
Maar die Onderveld[9] roep my dis nou oulaas se sien;
[maːr di ˈɔndərfæᵊlt rup məj dəs nœu ˈœulaːs sə sin]

I will be sick of longing for you all, perhaps!
Ek sal treur van verlange na julle miskien! La-la!
[ɛk sal trjøᵊr fan fərˈlaŋə na ˈjœlə məsˈkin lala]

---

[8] The "Boland," which means 'highland,' is a wine-making region in the Western Cape Province with an elevated, highly fertile terrain.

[9] The "Onderveld," which means 'under field,' initially formed part of the original Cape Province. Situated east and north of the Hex River Mountains, these lower-lying grassy prairies and plains were later expanded to include portions of the former Orange Free State (Free State) and Transvaal provinces, which previously included parts of the Limpopo, Mpumalanga, Gauteng, and North-West provinces.

The Rose
Die Roos
[di rʊᵊs]
Music: Gerrit Bon Sr. (1901–1983)
Arthur Ellis (b. 1931)
S. le Roux Marais (1896–1979), "The Rose and Other Afrikaans Songs" (*Die Roos en ander Afrikaanse Liedere, no. 1*) [di rʊᵊs ɛn ˈandər afriˈkaːnsə ˈlidərə]

Too short (was) the duration of your beauty,
Te kort jou skoonheids-duur,
[tə kɔrt jœu ˈskʊᵊnɦəjts dy:r]

Rose of my garden
Roos van my hof
[rʊᵊs fan məj ɦɔf]

(Yet) For your hour of perfection
Vir jou volmaakte uur
[fər jœu fɔlˈma:ktə y:r]

We praise the Giver!
Die gewer lof!
[di ˈxeᵊvər lɔf]

Too short-lived was our romance:
Te kort ons liefdestyd:
[tə kɔrt ɔns ˈlifdəstəjt]

Too long our grief.
Te lank die rou.
[tə laŋk di rœu]

Though — 'till the end of time
Tog — tot in Ewigheid
[tɔx tɔt ən ˈeᵊvəxɦəjt]

I thank God for you!
Goddank vir jou!
[ˈxɔdaŋk fər jœu]

The Roses of Remembrance
Die Rose van Herinnering
[di ˈrʊᵊsə fan ɦæˈrənərəŋ]
Music: Doris Beyers (n.d.)
Gerrit Bon Sr. (1901–1983)
Rosa Nepgen (1909–2001), titled "Be for Me, My Song, a Golden Chalice"
"Wees jy, my Lied, 'n goue Kelk" [veᵊs jəj məj lit ə ˈxœuə kæᵊlk]

Be my song,
Wees jy, my lied,
[veᵊs jəj məj lit]

For me a golden chalice
Vir my 'n goue kelk
[fər məj ə ˈxœuə kæᵊlk]

Wherein with blossoms unwithered
Waarin met bloesems onverwelk
[ˈva:rən mɛt ˈblusəms ˈɔnfərʋæᵊlk]

The deep red rose of my grief
Die donkerrooie roos van my verdriet
[di ˈdɔŋkəˌro:jə rʊᵊs fan məj fərˈdrit]

For only too short, too beautiful an hour
Nog een te kort, te skone uur
[nɔx eᵊn tə kɔrt tə ˈskʊᵊnə y:r]

Of heartache-filled joy
Van smartelik' geluk
[fan ˈsmartələk xəˈlœk]

Torn from time —
Die tyd ontruk —
[di təjt ɔnt'rœk]

Will last.
Sal Duur.
[sal dy:r]

Be a priceless vase wherein
Wees jy 'n kostelike vaas waarin
[veᵊs jəj ə 'kɔstələkə fa:s 'va:rən]

Still lovingly is preserved
Nog liefd'rik word bewaar
[nɔx 'lifdrək vɔrt bə'va:r]

Every poor wilted leaf
Elk arm' verwelkte blaar
[æᵊlk 'arəm fər'væᵊlktə bla:r]

Aforetime caressed and loved by me;
Deur my weleer geliefkoos en bemin;
[djøᵊr məj 'væleᵊr xə'lifkʊᵊs en bə'mən]

That whoever might pass by henceforth,
Dat wie ook al hierna verby mag gaan,
[dat vi ʊᵊk al 'ɦi:rna: fər'bəj ma xa:n¹⁰]

Star-struck will perceive
Beswymend sal ontwaar
[bə'swəjmənt sal ɔnt'va:r]

The sweet pot-pourri
Die soete allegaar
[di 'sutə alə'xa:r]

Knowing that once upon a time a rose
stood here.
*En weet: hier — eenmaal — het 'n roos
gestaan.*
[ɛn veᵊt ɦi:r 'eᵊnma:l ɦɛt ə rʊᵊs xə'sta:n]

Be, my song, the urn of precious stone
Wees jy, my lied, die urn van edelsteen
[veᵊs jəj məj lit di œrn of fan 'eᵊdəlsteᵊn]

In which the cherished ash,
Waarin die kosb're as,
['va:rən di 'kɔsbrə as]

That once was beauty,
Wat eenmaal skoonheid was,
[vat 'eᵊnma:l 'skʊᵊnɦəjt vas]

Is still kept safe and mourned by me
Deur my nog steeds bewaak word en beween
[djøᵊr məj nɔx steᵊts bə'va:k vɔrt ɛn bə'veᵊn]

Until the bittersweet memories
Totdat die bittersoet geheuenis
['tɔdat di 'bətərsut xə'ɦjøᵊənəs]

Of deep love and mourning
Van diepe liefde en leed
[fan 'dipə 'lifdə ɛn leᵊt]

Have perished and (been) forgotten,
Vergaan is en vergeet,
[fər'xa:n əs ɛn fər'xeᵊt]

And (he) who cherished the rose ... no
longer is there.
En wie die roos bemin het ... nie meer is.
[ɛn vi di rʊᵊs bə'mən ɦɛt ni meᵊr əs]

---

¹⁰ See Appendix G, Assimilation and Amalgamation of Consonants.

Be, my song, a chord so fine,
Wees jy, my lied, 'n snaar so fyn,
[veᵊs jəj məj lit ə sna:r sʊᵊ fəjn]

Of exquisite gold, pure and immaculate,
Van louter goud, klinkklaar en rein,
[fan 'lœutər xœut 'kləŋkla:r en rəjn]

On which my thanks
Waarop my dank
['va:rɔp məj daŋk]

For each miraculous day
Vir elke wonderdag
[fər 'æᵊlkə 'vɔndərdax]

Of life, love and laughter —
Van lewe, liefde en lag —
[fan 'leᵊvə 'lifdə en lax]

The mission and the blessings:
Die sending en die seëning:
[di 'sɛndəŋ ɛn di 'se:ənəŋ]

The roses of remembrance —
Die rose van herinnering —
[di 'rʊᵊsə fan ɦæ'rənərəŋ]

Will quiver and die with your last sound!
Sal tril en sterwe met jou laaste klank!
[sal trəl ɛn 'stærvə mɛt jœu 'la:stə klaŋk]

The Black Oxen
Die swarte Osse
[di 'swartə 'ɔsə]
Music: Horace Barton (1872–1951)

The years advance over the hills
Die jare kom die bulte oor
[di 'ja:rə kɔm di 'bœltə ʊᵊr]

Like heavy, black oxen;
Soos sware, swarte osse;
[sʊᵊs 'swa:rə 'swartə 'ɔsə]

Across my heart lie their tracks —
Dwarsoor my hart lê hulle spoor —
['dwarsʊᵊr məj ɦart lɛ: 'ɦœlə spʊᵊr]

The faded track through the bushes.
Die vaalstreep deur die bosse.
[di 'fa:lstreᵊp djø̞ᵊr di 'bɔsə]

The years come, the years go,
Die jare kom, die jare gaan,
[di 'ja:rə kɔm di 'ja:rə xa:n]

Even deeper dig the grooves;
Al dieper sny die groewe;
[al 'dipər snəj di 'xruvə]

I am broken and exhausted
Gebroke is ek en gedaan
[xə'brʊᵊkə əs ɛk en xə'da:n]

Because of their heavy hooves.
Deur hulle sware hoewe.
[djø̞ᵊr 'ɦœlə 'swa:rə 'ɦuvə]

The Gardener
Die Tuinman
[di 'tœynman]
Music: Rosa Nepgen (1909–2001)
Maria van der Mark (1912–n.d.)

Dig, oh Gardener, dig deep, 'till the earth's lips clutch,
Spit, o Tuinman, spit diep, tot die aardlippe klou,
[spət ʊᵊ 'tœynman spət dip 'tɔt di 'a:rt̩ləpə klœu]

Saturating the mellowest soil with the most refreshing dew
Drenk die vetste van aarde met lawendste dou
[drɛŋk di 'fɛtstə fan 'a:rdə mɛt 'la:vəntstə dœu]

And then wait. At night He brings fragile calyxes,
En dan wag. In die nag bring Hy blomkelkies broos,
[ɛn dan vax ən di nax brəŋ ɦəj 'blɔm̩kæᵊlkis brʊᵊs]

Because He knows the mystery of the rose's form.
Want Hy ken die geheim van die vorm van die roos.
[vant ɦəj ken di xə'ɦəjm fan di fɔrm fan di rʊᵊs]

Prune, oh Gardener, prune briskly — keep the buds guided
Snoei, o Tuinman, snoei flink — hou die knoppe gerig
[snui ʊᵊ 'tœynman snui fləŋk ɦœu di 'knɔpə xə'rəx]

Towards the sun, because a rose is a child of the light:
Na die son, want die roos is 'n kind van die lig:
[na di sɔn vant di rʊᵊs əs ə kənt fan di ləx]

Let a sunbeam wake them with a kiss from the east —
Laat 'n sonstraal hul wek met 'n kus uit die Oos —
[la:t ə 'sɔnstra:l ɦœl vɛk mɛt ə kœs œyt di ʊᵊs]

He also knows the mystery of the color of the rose.
Hy ken ook die geheim van die kleur van die roos.
[ɦəj kɛn ʊᵊk di xə'ɦəjm fan di kljøᵊr fan di rʊᵊs]

Wash, oh Gardener, wash well — keep the enemies out,
Spoel, o Tuinman, spoel goed — hou die vyande weg,
[spul ʊᵊ 'tœynman spul xut ɦœu di 'fəjandə væx]

Pure of blossom and leaf, the rose blooms to its potential.
Rein van bloesem en blad kom die roos tot sy reg.
[rəjn fan 'blusəm ɛn blat kɔm di rʊᵊs tɔt səj ræx]

Sleep softly then, because He arrives even before the blush of dawn
Slaap dan sag, want Hy kom voor die môre nog bloos
[sla:p dan sax vant ɦəj kɔm fuᵊr di ˈmɔ:rə nɔx bluᵊs]

And He knows the mystery of a rose's perfume.
En Hy ken die geheim van die geur van die roos.
[ɛn ɦəj kɛn di xəˈɦəjm fan di xjøᵊr fan di ruᵊs]

Capture, o Gardener, the attar that drips in the night
Vang, o Tuinman, die attar wat drup in die nag
[faŋ uᵊ ˈtœynman di ˈatar vat drœp ən di nax]

And enjoy your carnival of color every day;
En geniet van jou kleur-karnaval elke dag;
[ɛn xəˈnit fan jœu ˈkljøᵊrˌkarnafal ˈæᵊlkə dax]

And when winter approaches and your garden withers away,
En as winter dan kom en jou tuin alles derf,
[ɛn as ˈvəntər dan kɔm ɛn jœu tœyn ˈaləs dærf]

Ponder: He knows the mystery of beauty that dies.
Dink: Hy ken die geheim van die skoonheid wat sterf.
[dəŋk ɦəj kɛn di xəˈɦəjm fan di ˈskuᵊnɦəjt vat stærf]

Pray, oh Gardener, continue to pray that your garden will not languish,
Bid, o Tuinman, bid steeds, dat jou gaarde nie kwyn,
[bət uᵊ ˈtœynman bət steᵊts dat jœu ˈxa:rdə ni kwəjn]

That her splendor does not vanish from the earth,
Dat haar heerlikheid nie van die aarde verdwyn,
[dat ɦa:r ˈɦeᵊrləkɦəjt ni fan di ˈa:rdə fərˈdwəjn]

Before He (will) also one day — and this will be your consolation —
Voor Hy eendag ook jou — en dit sy jou tot troos —
[fuᵊr ɦəj ˈeᵊndax uᵊk jœu ɛn dət səj jœu tɔt truᵊs]

Rake you ever so softly away, together with the rose.
O so saggies sal weghark tesaam met die roos.
[uᵊ suᵊ ˈsaxis sal ˈvæxɦark təˈsa:m mɛt di ruᵊs]

The Road Is My Dwelling
Die Wapad is my Woning
[di va:pat əs məj ˈvuᵊnəŋ]
Music: Daniel Clement (1902–1980), titled "South Africa Onwards,"
"Die Wapad" (Suid-Afrika vorentoe, no. 19) [sœyt ˈa:frika ˈfuᵊrəntu]
Arthur Ellis (b. 1931)

Ah, had I but my own little house,
Ag, had ek 'n eie ou huisie,
[ax hat ɛk ə ˈəjə œu ˈɦœysi]

Even if it were wretched and small —
Al was dit armoedig en klein —
[al vas dət ˈarəmudəx ɛn kləjn]

A little lounge with a kitchenette,
'n Voorhuisie met 'n kombuisie,
[ə 'fʊˀrˌfiœysi mɛt ə kɔmˈbœysi]

A small bedroom warm and chaste.
'n Slaapplekkie warm en rein.
[ə 'slaːplæki 'varəm ɛn rəjn]

And a fireplace in the kitchenette,
En in die kombuisie 'n essie,
[ɛn ən di kɔmˈbœysi ə 'ɛsi]

On which I can cook my food —
Waarop ek my ete kan kook —
['vaːrɔp ɛk məj 'eˀtə kan kʊˀk]

A kettle, a brazier, and a firepan,
'n Ketel, komfoor en 'n tessie,
[ə 'keˀtəl 'kɔmfʊˀr ɛn ə 'tɛsi]

A chimney that smokes before dawn.
'n Skoorsteen wat voordag al rook.
[ə 'skʊˀrsteˀn vat 'fʊˀrdax al rʊˀk]

A table, and on it my little book,
'n Tafel en daarop my boekie,
[ə 'taːfəl ɛn 'daːrɔp məj 'buki]

And (a) Bible — a gift from my husband;
En bybel — my man se geskenk;
[ɛn 'bəjbəl məj man sə xəˈskɛŋk]

I'm sitting in a little corner just off the road,
Ek sit van die pad, in 'n hoekie,
[ɛk sət fan di pat ən ə 'fiuki]

Reminiscing about love and heartache.
Die lief en die leed te herdenk.
[di lif ɛn di leˀt tə fiærˈdɛŋk]

A window with two tiny geraniums —
'n Venster met twee malvaplantjies —
[ə 'fɛnstər mɛt tweˀ 'malfaˌplaɲkis]

How pretty are the red and the green!
Hoe mooi is die rooi en die groen!
[fiu moːj əs di roːj ɛn di xrun]

Where I sit in the afternoon crocheting my lace
Waar ek smiddags sit hekel my kantjies
[vaːr ɛk 'smədaxs sət 'fieˀkəl məj 'kaɲkis]

And tying-up all my loose-end jobs.
En al my ou werkies kan doen.
[ɛn al məj œu 'værkis kan dun]

A small wooden cupboard with a few things,
'n Muurkassie met 'n paar goedjies,
[ə 'myːrˌkasi mɛt ə paːr 'xœykis]

And next to it, a clock on the wall;
En langsaan 'n klok teen die muur;
[ɛn 'laŋsaːn ə klɔk teˀn di myːr]

I sing while I dust, so sweetly,
Ek sing wyl ek afstof, so soetjies,
[ɛk səŋ vəjl ɛk 'afstɔf sʊˀ 'su ˈkis]

And I keep everything shiny by scouring it!
En blink hou ek alles geskuur!
[ɛn bləŋk fiœu ɛk 'aləs xəˈskyːr]

A tiny porch where I in the evening, carefree,
'n Stoepie waar'k saans, vry van sôre,
[ə 'stupi vaːrk saːns frəj fan 'sɔːrə]

Can look upon the lengthening shadows;
Kan kyk hoe die skadu's verleng;
[kan kəjk fiu di 'skaːdys fərˈlɛŋ]

Thank God they point to the morning,
Goddank hulle wys na die môre,
['xɔdaŋk 'fiœlə vəjs na di 'mɔːrə]

202   AFRIKAANS ART SONG LITERATURE

Which will bring joy in reunion.
Wat weersien in blydskap sal breng.
[vat 'veᵊrsin ən 'bləjtskap sal brɛŋ]

A little garden with vegetables and herbs,
'n Tuintjie met groente en kruie,
[ə 'tœyŋki mɛt 'xruntə ɛn 'krœyə]

Have I desired all my life;
Het lewenslank ek al begeer;
[ɦɛt 'leᵊvənslaŋk ɛk al bə'xeᵊr]

Who can explain to others
Wie kan tog aan andere beduie
[vi kan tɔx a:n 'andərə bə'dœyə]

What a person lacks on the road?
Wat 'n mens op die wapad ontbeer?
[vat ə mɛns ɔp di 'va:pat ɔnt'beᵊr]

And when death finally comes as a blessing,
En kom eens die Dood in genade,
[ɛn kɔm eᵊns di dʊᵊt ən xə'na:də]

(And) The storms of life subsided,
Die storm van die lewe gesus,
[di 'stɔrəm fan di 'leᵊvə xə'sœs]

How I would like to lie in your shade,
Hoe graag sou ek dan in jou skade,
[ɦu xra:x sœu ɛk dan ən jœu 'ska:də]

Oh dear marula tree, (and) rest!
O liewe maroelaboom,[11] *rus!*
[ʊᵊ 'livə ma'rulabʊᵊm rœs]

Because it is the end of the striving,
Want dit is die end van die strewe,
[vant dət əs di ɛnt fan di 'streᵊvə]

Of all that a mother had to endure:
Van al wat 'n moeder moes ly:
[fan al vat ə 'mudər mus ləj]

Too long have I lived, already,
Te lank het ek nou al gelewe,
[tə laŋk ɦɛt ɛk nœu al xə'leᵊvə]

There is no more space for me.
Geen ruimte is daar meer vir my.
[çeᵊn 'rœymtə əs da:r meᵊr fər məj]

I am tired, oh so tired of roaming;
Ek is moeg, O so moeg al van swerwe;
[ɛk əs mux ʊᵊ sʊᵊ mux al fan 'swærvə]

For my body and soul I implore rest.
Rus smeek ek vir liggaam en gees.
[rœs smeᵊk ɛk fər 'ləxa:m ɛn çeᵊs]

Would there not be for me, ere I die,
Sou daar nie vir my eer ek sterwe,
[sœu da:r ni fər məj eᵊr ɛk 'stærvə]

Be somewhere, a standing place (of remembrance), too?
Ook êrens 'n staanplekkie wees?
[ʊᵊk 'æ:rəns ə 'sta:nplæki veᵊs]

---

[11] Marula trees (*Sclerocarya birrea*) are medium-sized deciduous dioecious trees indigenous to southern Africa. They are single stemmed with a wide-spreading crown. The trunk is characterized by gray mottled bark. Giraffes (*Giraffa*), rhinoceroses (*Rhinocerotidae*), and elephants (*Elephantidae*) are known for grazing on marula fruit, which is edible, succulent, tart, and has a distinct nutty flavor. This fruit is also the key ingredient of marula beer and the world-famous Amarula Cream Liqueur.

But ahead, across the highway, there are always,
Maar voor oor die wapad staan immer,
[ma:r fʊᵊr ʊᵊr di ˈva:pat sta:n ˈəmər]

The high blue mountains of Never
Die hoë blou berge van Nimmer
[di ˈfiu:ə blœu ˈbærgə fan ˈnəmər]

Crowned with a twinkling star,
Bekroon deur 'n lonkende ster,
[bəˈkrʊᵊn djø°r ə ˈlɔnkəndə stær]

That block the path to the land of Fortune!
Wat die weg na Geluksland versper!
[vat di væx na xəˈlœkslant fərˈspær]

A Thousand-and-One
Duisend-en-een
['dœysənt ɛn eᵊn]
Music: Arthur Ellis (b. 1931)
Rosa Nepgen (1909–2001)
S. le Roux Marais (1896–1979), "New Songs" (*Nuwe Liedere, no. 3*) ['nyvə 'lidərə]

Night has a thousand eyes:
Die nag het duisend oë:
[di nax fiet ˈdœysənt ˈu:ə]

The soul knows a thousand stars:
Die Gees ken duisend sterre:
[di çeᵊs kɛn ˈdœysənt ˈstærə]

Day, just one.
Net één die Dag.
[nɛt ˈeᵊn di dax]

The heart, just one.
Net één die Hart.
[nɛt ˈeᵊn di fiart]

Yet it retreats from the heavens,
Tog wyk dié uit die hoë,
[tɔx vəjk ˈdi œyt di ˈfiu:ə]

Yet (if) that does not wink from afar,
Tog lonk dié nie van verre,
[tɔx lɔŋk ˈdi ni fan ˈfærə]

And a starry night ensues.
Volg 'n wêreldnag.
[fɔlx ə ˈvæ:rəltnax]

A life of suffering ensues.
Volg 'n lewensmart.
[fɔlx ə ˈleᵊvənsmart]

The Birth of Spring
Geboorte van die Lente
[xəˈbʊᵊrtə fan di ˈlɛntə]
Music: J. S. Manca (1908–1985)
S. le Roux Marais (1896–1979), "Five Art Songs" (*Vyf Kunsliedere, no. 2*)
[fəjf ˈkœnsˌlidərə]

Happy and joyful was the day
Gelukkig en bly was die dag
[xəˈlœkəx ɛn bləj vas di dax]

When the Rain married the Sunshine,
Toe die Reent met die Sonskyn gaan trou het,
[tu di reᵊnt mɛt di ˈsɔnskəjn xa:n trœu fiet]

Multi-colored the arch of the sky
Veelverwig die boog wat die lug
['feᵊlfərˌʋəx di buᵊx vat di lœx]

Artistically built for them a wedding present.
Vir 'n troupresent kunstig gebou het.
[fər ə 'trœuprəˌsent 'kœnstə xə'bœu¹² fiɛt]

One day they quarreled
Getwis het hul eens op 'n dag
[xə'twəs fiɛt fiœl eᵊns ɔp ə dax]

With a storm of reproachful words.
Met 'n storm verwytende woorde.
[mɛt ə 'stɔrəm fər'vəjtəndə 'ʋuᵊrdə]

The Sunshine disappeared,
Die Sonskyn verdwyn,
[di 'sɔnskəjn fər'dwəjn]

And the Rain became a cold shower of hail from the north.
En die Reent word 'n haelbui koud uit die Noorde.
[ɛn di reᵊnt vɔrt ə 'fiaːlbœy kœut œyt di 'nuᵊrdə]

They reconciled again,
Versoen raak hul weer,
[fər'sun raːk fiœl veᵊr]

And paid with interest, the overdue debt owed to Love.
En betaal met rente, agterstallige Liefde.
[ɛn bə'taːl mɛt 'rɛntə ˌaxtər'staləxə 'lifdə]

And Sunshine and Rain rejoice together,
En Sonskyn en Reent, die juig tesaam,
[ɛn 'sɔnskəjn ɛn reᵊnt di jœyx tə'saːm]

Over a dear little daughter, Spring.
Oor 'n liewe klein dogtertjie Lente.
[uᵊr ə 'livə kləjn 'dɔxtərki 'lɛntə]

Little Ground Fellow, My Shadow
Grondmannetjie my Skaduwee
['xrɔntˌmaniki]
Music: Jan Kromhout (1886–1969)

Little Ground Fellow, I will get you!
Grondmannetjie, ek sal jou kry!
['xrɔntˌmaniki ɛk sal jœu krəj]

You mock and you tease me.
Jy koggel en jy terg vir my.
[jəj 'kɔxəl ɛn jəj tærx fər məj]

You are a nuisance to me.
Jy is my tot 'n las.
[jəj əs məj tɔt ə las]

Even if I thrash you with the horsewhip,
Al klop ek jou met die karwats,
[al klɔp ɛk jœu mɛt di kar'vats]

Even if I jump away, you're too nimble for me,
Al spring ek weg, jy's veels te rats,
[al sprəŋ ɛk væx jəjs feᵊls tə rats]

You clutch my feet tightly.
Jy klou my voete vas.
[jəj klœu məj 'futə fas]

---

¹² See Appendix G, Assimilation and Amalgamation of Consonants.

You think you're funny, you play the fool,
Jy dink jy's snaaks, jy speel die gek,
[jəj dəŋk jəjs sna:ks jəj speᵊl di xæk]

You're only silly to stretch like that
Jy's net verspot om so te rek
[jəjs nɛt fər'spɔt ɔm sʊᵊ tə ræk]

Every morning and evening.
Al oggende en saans.
[al 'ɔxəndə ɛn sa:ns]

I roll the heaviest chunk onto you,
Ek rol op jou die swaarste kluit,
[ɛk rɔl ɔp jœu di 'swa:rstə klœyt]

It's of no use to me, you still slip out,
Dit help my niks, jy glip tog uit,
[dət ɦæᵊlp məj nəks jəj xləp tɔx œyt]

Even if there were a cliff.
Al was dit ook 'n krans.
[al vas dət ʊᵊk ə krans]

Little Ground Fellow, who are you then?
Grondmannetjie, wie is jy dan?
['xrɔntˌmaniki vi əs jəj dan]

Do you have a name, what is your surname?
Het jy 'n naam, voer jy 'n van?
[ɦɛt jəj ə na:m fu:r jəj ə fan]

I know: your name is Scared!
Ek weet: jou naam is Bang!
[ɛk veᵊt jœu na:m əs baŋ]

You're brave in the sunshine
Jy's dapper in die sonneskyn
[jəjs 'dapər ən di 'sɔnəskəjn]

But when night falls you've disappeared —
Maar donkeraand het jy verdwyn —
[ma:r 'dɔŋkəra:nt ɦɛt jəj fər'dwəjn]

You don't ever allow anyone to catch you.
Jy laat jou nooit nie vang.
[jəj la:t jœu no:jt ni faŋ]

Little Ground Fellow, my grandfather says:
Grondmannetjie, my oupa sê:
['xrɔntˌmaniki məj 'œupa sɛ:]

You want to have him in the earth,
Jy wil hom in die aarde hê,
[jəj vəl ɦɔm ən di 'a:rdə ɦɛ:]

You are warping him already now;
Jy trek hom nou al krom;
[jəj træk ɦɔm nœu al krɔm]

He toiled his whole life through,
Hy het die lewe deur geswoeg,
[ɦəj ɦɛt di 'leᵊvə djøᵊr xə'swux]

He wants to rest now, he is weary now,
Nou wil hy rus, nou word hy moeg,
[nœu vəl ɦəj rəs nœu vɔrt ɦəj mux]

Soon you will get him.
Netnou kry jy vir hom.
['nɛtnœu krəj jəj fər ɦɔm]

But two of us still want to play,
Maar ons twee wil nog lekker speel,
[ma:r ɔns tweᵊ vəl nɔx 'lækər speᵊl]

Climb trees (and steal fruit!),
Nog bome klim (en vrugte steel!),
[nɔx 'bʊᵊmə kləm ɛn 'frœxtə steᵊl]

Roll around, jump and laugh!
Nog rol en spring en lag!
[nɔx rɔl ɛn sprəŋ ɛn lax]

Just one thing you should understand well:
Net een ding moet jy goed verstaan:
[nɛt eᵊn dəŋ mut jəj xut fər'sta:n]

(If) you think I will come to you —
Dink jy ek sal na jou toe gaan —
[dəŋk jəj ɛk sal na jœu tu xaːn]

Then you will have to wait a long time!
Dan sal jy lank moet wag!
[dan sal jəj laŋk mut vax]

Puppy Love
Kalwerliefde
['kalvərˌlifdə]
Music: Daniel Clement (1902–1980), "South Africa Onwards"
(*Suid-Afrika vorentoe, no. 34*) [sœyt 'aːfrika 'fʊᵊrəntu]

Over there in (the) Transvaal,
Daar oorkant in Transvalia,[13]
[daːr 'ʊᵊrkant ən trans'vaːlia]

There lives a beloved child (girl);
Daar woon 'n liefste kind;
[daːr vʊᵊn ə 'lifstə kənt]

She is the apple of my eye
Sy is die appel van my oog
[səj əs di 'apəl fan məj ʊᵊx]

And I (am) her best friend!
En ek haar beste vrind!
[ɛn ɛk ɦaːr 'bɛstə frənt]

Oh my Dina! How can you be so pretty?
O my Diena! Hoe is jy tog so fraai?
[ʊᵊ məj 'dina ɦu əs jəj tɔx sʊᵊ fraːj]

I feel as if I am already in Canaan,
Ek voel my reeds in Kanaän,
[ɛk ful məj reᵊts ən 'kaːnan]

When the two of us *tickey-draai* (traditional dance).
As ons twee tiekiedraai.
[as ɔns tweᵊ 'tikidraːj]

You live there, halfway to the heavens
Jy woon daar halfpad na die lug
[jəj vʊᵊn daːr 'ɦalfpat na di lœx]

So unattainably far;
So onbereikbaar ver;
[sʊᵊ ɔnbə'rəjkbaːr fæːr]

The little light in your window is
Die liggie in jou venster is
[di 'ləxi ən jœu 'fɛnstər əs]

My evening and morning star!
My aand- en môre-ster!
[məj aːnt ɛn 'mɔːrə stær]

Oh my Lina! You're as beautiful as a star
O my Liena! Jy's as 'n ster so skoon
[ʊᵊ məj 'lina jəjs as ə stær sʊᵊ skʊᵊn]

---

[13] One of the original four provinces of South Africa that existed from the founding of the Union of South Africa (1910), through it being recognized formally as the Republic of South Africa (1961) and its democratization (1994). While this province no longer exists, its territory now occupies the northeastern portion of the country, forming all or part of the Gauteng, North-West, Limpopo, and Mpumalanga provinces.

But unfortunately, you live in the sky,
Net jammer dat jy in die lug,
[nɛt ˈjamər dat jəj ən di lœx]

And I live on earth.
En ek op aarde woon.
[ɛn ɛk ɔp ˈaːrdə vʊᵊn]

And do you know what Concordia (goddess of Harmony)
En weet jy wat Concordia
[ɛn veᵊt jəj vat kɔnˈkɔrdia]

Means in Afrikaans?
Wil sê in Afrikaans?
[vəl sɛː ən afriˈkaːns]

Two little hearts that beat as one
Twee hartjies wat net eners klop
[tweᵊ ˈɦarkis vat nɛt ˈeᵊnərs klɔp]

From early morning till night!
Van smôrens vroeg tot saans!
[fan ˈsmɔːrəns frux tɔt saːns]

Oh my Meena! How can you be so loving?
O my Miena! Hoe is jy tog so lief?
[ʊᵊ məj ˈmina ɦu əs jəj tɔx sʊᵊ lif]

You've stolen my heart long ago,
Jy't lankal reeds my hart gesteel,
[jəjt ˈlaŋkal reᵊts məj ɦart xəˈsteᵊl]

You (are) the sweetest thief of hearts.
Jou soetste hartedief.
[jœu ˈsutstə ˈɦartədif]

Every night before I can fall asleep
Elk' aand voor ek aan slaap kan raak
[æᵊlk aːnt fʊᵊr ɛk aːn slaːp kan raːk]

I think of you just once more;
Dink ek nog eens aan jou;
[dəŋk ɛk nɔx eᵊns aːn jœu]

Of untied golden locks
Aan goue lokkies ongebind
[aːn ˈxœuə ˈlɔkis ˈɔnxəˌbənt]

And of two little blue eyes!
En aan twee ogies blou!
[ɛn aːn tweᵊ ˈʊᵊxis blœu]

Oh my Nina! How can you be so beautiful?
O my Niena! Hoe is jy tog so mooi?
[ʊᵊ məj ˈnina ɦu əs jəj tɔx sʊᵊ moːj]

Is there a lily-white like you,
Is daar 'n leliewit soos jy,
[əs daːr ə ˈleᵊlivət sʊᵊs jəj]

A rose as red as you?
'n Roos as jy so rooi?
[ə rʊᵊs as jəj sʊᵊ roːj]

Outside on the football field
Daar buite op die voetbalveld
[daːr ˈbœytə ɔp di ˈfutbalfæᵊlt]

I play till I (bruise) black and blue;
Speel ek my pers en blou;
[speᵊl ɛk məj pærs ɛn blœu]

And at school I study till I'm gray
En in die skool leer ek my grys
[ɛn ən di skʊᵊl leᵊr ɛk məj xrəjs]

And everything just for you!
En alles net vir jou!
[ɛn ˈaləs nɛt fər jœu]

Oh my Seena! How can you look so fine?
O my Siena! Hoe lyk jy so piekfyn?
[ʊə məj 'sina ɦu ləjk jəj sʊə 'pikfəjn]

What is the world without you?
Wat is die wêreld sonder joui?
[vat əs di 'væ:rəlt 'sɔndər jœu]

Like a mine without gold!
Soos sonder goud 'n myn!
[sʊəs 'sɔndər xœut ə məjn]

And if I became president one day
En word ek eendag president
[ɛn vɔrt ɛk 'eəndax prəsə'dɛnt]

Of the whole of South Africa.
Van heel Suid Afrika.
[fan ɦeəl sœyt 'a:frika]

Then we will go to the capital
Dan gaan ons na die hoofstad toe
[dan xa:n ɔns na di 'ɦʊəfsta tu¹⁴]

Us two, on a wagon!
Ons tweetjies op 'n wa!
[ɔns 'tweəkis ɔp ə va:]

Oh my Tina! You're the one who takes
the crown;
O my Tiena! Jy span tog maar die kroon;
[ʊə məj 'tina jəj span tɔx ma:r di krʊən]

Here is my heart so tender and faithful
Hier is my hart so teer en trou
[ɦi:r əs məj ɦart sʊə teər ɛn trœu]

For you to live in!
Vir jou om in te woon!
[fər jœu ɔm ən tə vʊən]

Little Ray of Sunshine
Klein Sonneskyn
[kləjn 'sɔnəskəjn]
Music: Gideon Fagan (1904–1980)

Just as a loving lambkin,
Net soos 'n lammetjie so lief,
[nɛt sʊəs ə 'laməki sʊə lif]

So playful and so gay,
So dartel en so bly,
[sʊə 'dartəl ɛn sʊə bləj]

He played around me the entire day
Het hy aldag om my gespeel
[ɦɛt ɦəj 'aldax ɔm məj xə'speəl]

Constantly at my side.
Gedurig aan my sy.
[xə'dy:rəx a:n məj səj]

Just as a lambkin freezes to death
Net soos 'n lammetjie verkluim
[nɛt sʊəs ə 'laməki fər'klœym]

During a bitterly cold winter's night,
In bitt're winternag,
[ən 'bətrə 'vəntərnax]

---

¹⁴ See Appendix G, Assimilation and Amalgamation of Consonants.

So bleak, so cold was he at last,
So kil, so koud was hy oplaas,
[sʊᵊ kəl sʊᵊ kœut vas ɦəj ɔp'la:s]

So quiet his happy laughter.
So stil sy blye lag.
[sʊᵊ stəl səj 'bləjə lax]

They say he will be happy:
Hulle sê hy sal gelukkig wees:
['ɦœlə sɛ: ɦəj sal xə'lœkəx veᵊs]

There is no grief where he is (now);
Waar hy is, is geen smart;
[va:r ɦəj əs əs çeᵊn smart]

But who will now nurture Little Sunshine
Maar wie sal nou Klein Sonneskyn
[ma:r vi sal nœu kləjn 'sɔnəskəjn]

Softly against her heart?
Sag troetel aan haar hart?
[sax 'trutəl a:n ɦa:r ɦart]

I only know — through the long night,
Ek weet net — deur die lange nag,
[ɛk veᵊt nɛt djøᵊr di 'laŋə nax]

Until light returns —
Totdat die lig weer kom —
['tɔ dat¹⁵ di ləx veᵊr kɔm]

I know how my arms ache
Ek weet hoe my arms pyn
[ɛk veᵊt ɦu məj 'arəms pəjn]

From his emptiness.
Met ledigheid van hom.
[mɛt 'leᵊdəxɦəjt fan ɦɔm]

Protect also my lamb, Oh Lamb of God,
Hoed ook my lam, O Lam van God,
[ɦut ʊᵊk məj lam ʊᵊ lam fan xɔt]

Oh Friend of children and Guardian.
O Kindervriend en Hoeder.
[ʊᵊ 'kəndərfrint ɛn 'ɦudər]

Who can love him in the great universe
Wie kan hom in die Groot Heelal
[vi kan ɦɔm ən di xrʊᵊt 'ɦeᵊlal]

As much as his mother?
So liefhê soos sy moeder?
[so: 'liffɛ sʊᵊs səj 'mudər]

Country, Nation, and Language
Land, Volk en Taal
[lant fɔlk ɛn ta:l]
Music: Daniel Clement (1902–1980), "South Africa Onwards"
(*Suid-Afrika vorentoe, no. 4*) [sœyt 'a:frika 'fʊᵊrəntu]

Land of the oaks with vivid green leaves,
Land van die eike met helder groen lower,
[lant fan di 'əjkə mɛt 'fiæᵊldər xrun 'lʊᵊvər]

Rustling wheat fields and pearlescent wine,
Ruisende graanveld en pêr'lende wyn,
['rœysəndə 'xra:nfæᵊlt ɛn 'pæ:rləndə vəjn]

---

¹⁵ See Appendix G, Assimilation and Amalgamation of Consonants.

Where every morning is enchanted
with gold,
Waar elke môre met sonne goud tower,
[va:r 'æᵃlkə 'mɔ:rə mɛt 'sɔnə xœut 'tʊᵊvər]

The Southern Cross appears sparkling
at night.
Skitt'rend die Suiderkruis nagt'liks verskyn.
['skətrənt di 'sœydərkrœys 'naxtləks fər'skəjn]

Oh blissful sunny Country,
O heerlik sonnig' Land,
[ʊᵊ 'fieᵊrlək 'sɔnəx lant]

On your shores of hospitality
Aan U gasvrye strand
[a:n y 'xas‚frəjə strant]

We pay tribute with heart and mind.
Bring ons die hulde van hart en verstand.
[brəŋ ɔns di 'fiœldə fan fiart ɛn fər'stant]

Nation issued from the loins of the heroes,
Volk uit die lende van helde gesprote,
[fɔlk œyt di 'lɛndə fan 'fiæᵊldə xə'sprʊᵊtə]

Tolerating no tyrant, strengthened in danger,
Duldend geen dwing'land, gehard in gevaar,
['dœldənt çeᵊn 'dwəŋlant xə'fiart ən xə'fa:r]

Worthy forefathers, the Protestants and
Huguenots
Waardig die vaad're, die Geus' en Hug'note
['va:rdəx di 'fa:drə di xjøᵊs ɛn 'fiyx‚nʊᵊtə]

Who can match your courageous deeds?
Wie kan U dade van durf ewenaar?
[vi kan y 'da:də fan dœrf 'eᵊvəna:r]

Oh hardy ancestors,
O stoere voorgeslag,
[ʊᵊ 'sturə 'fʊᵊrxə‚slax]

Your bravery and strength
U mannemoed en krag
[y 'manəmut ɛn krax]

We honor here with thanksgiving.
Word hier ons dankbare hulde gebrag.
[vɔrt fii:r ɔns 'daŋkba:rə 'fiœldə xə'brax]

The language of my mother, her love and
prayers
Taal van my moeder, haar liefd' en gebede
[ta:l fan məj 'mudər fia:r lift ɛn xə'beᵊdə]

Lisped while stuttering as a child at her knee,
Staam'lend gelispel as kind aan haar knie,
['sta:mlənt xə'ləspəl as kənt a:n fia:r kni]

What I believed, loved, and suffered
Wat ek geloof het, gelief en gelede
[vat ɛk xə'lʊᵊf fiet xə'lif ɛn xə'leᵊdə]

Murmurs in Your sounds like a sweet
melody.
Ruis in U klanke as 'n soet melodie.
[rœys ən y 'klaŋkə as ə sut mɛlu'di]

Oh beloved mother tongue,
O dierb're Moedertaal,
[ʊᵊ 'di:rbrə 'mudərta:l]

If my final day should come
As eens my dag ook daal
[as eᵊns məj dax ʊᵊk da:l]

I will hear you still for the last loving time!
Hoor ek U nog vir die laas liewe maal!
[fiʊᵊr ɛk y nɔx fər di la:s 'livə ma:l]

Song of the Miracle Tree (Sycamore-Fig Tree)
Lied van die Wonderboom[16]
[lit fan di ˈvɔndərbʊᵊm]
Music: Doris Beyers (n.d.)
Gideon Fagan (1904–1980)
S. le Roux Marais (1896–1979), "Six Art Songs" (*Ses Kunsliedere, no. 4*)
[sɛs ˈkœnsˌlidərə]

Come to my shade, noble lady,
Kom na my skaduwee, edele vrou,
[kɔm na məj ˈska:dyveᵊ ˈeᵊdələ frœu]

Red like rubies my fruit glows for you,
Rooi soos saffier[17] gloei my vrugte vir jou,
[ro:j sʊᵊs saˈfi:r xlui məj ˈfrœxtə fər jœu]

Green like papyrus my leaves
Groen soos papirus my blare
[xrun sʊᵊs paˈpirəs məj ˈbla:rə]

All together faint, my trunk shimmers with the color of opal
Altemaal dof glim my stam met die kleur van opaal
[ˈaltəma:l dɔf xləm məj stam mɛt di kljøᵊr fan ʊᵊˈpa:l]

Send then to him, whom your heart already loves,
Send dan aan hom wat jou hart reeds bemin,
[sɛnt dan a:n ɦɔm vat jœu ɦiart reᵊts bəˈmən]

Secretly a letter with a message that reads:
Heimlik 'n brief met die boodskap daarin:
[ˈɦəjmlək ə brif mɛt di ˈbʊᵊtskap da:rˈən]

Cool is the shade, quietly flows the stream
Koel is die skaduwee, sag vloei die stroom
[kul əs di ˈskadyveᵊ sax flui di strʊᵊm]

Sweeter the reality here than the dream.
Soeter die werklikheid hier as die droom.
[ˈsutər di ˈværkləkɦəjt ɦi:r as di drʊᵊm]

Bread to break, wine to drink
Brood om te breek, wyn om te drink
[brʊᵊt ɔm tə breᵊk vəjn ɔm tə drəŋk]

Drink love from the chalice of my bosom
Liefde uit die kelk van my boesem te drink
[ˈlifdə œyt di kæᵊlk fan məj ˈbusəm tə drəŋk]

Come, my beloved, because love alone
Kom, my beminde, want liefde alleen
[kɔm məj bəˈməndə vant ˈlifdə aˈleᵊn]

Can make these moments last.
Kan aan die oomblikke duurte verleen.
[kan a:n di ˈʊᵊmbləkə ˈdy:rtə fərˈleᵊn]

Noble lady, only my leaves whisper here,
Edele vrou, net my blare hier fluister,
[ˈeᵊdələ frœu nɛt məj ˈbla:rə ɦi:r ˈflœystər]

---

[16] "This poem loosely reproduces the general meaning of the original text of an ancient Egyptian poem from around 3000 BC. The 'Miracle Tree' belongs to the same family as the sycamore (*Ficus sycomorus*). This tree is also known as the sycamore fig or fig-mulberry as its fruit resemble figs while its leaves remind one of mulberry leaves. It is well-known from North Africa through to Pretoria. In the poem, the tree sings to the lady who owns the garden in which it stands." Gideon Fagan, "Lied van die Wonderboom," in *Sing sag menig' lied—'n Versameling toonsettings van die verse van A. G. Visser,* compiled by Anna Bender (Johannesburg: DALRO, 1978), 64.

[17] While the direct translation of this word is 'sapphire,' red sapphires are also known as rubies. This refers to the ripened fruit of the miracle tree which turns from green to red when ripened.

No one that sneaks or eavesdrops on love,
Niemand wat liefde beloer of beluister,
['nimant vat 'lifdə bə'lu:r ɔf bə'lœystər]

Here you are guarded safely by my foliage,
Hier is jy veilig beskerm deur my loof,
[ɦi:r əs jəj 'fəjləx bə'skærm djø³r məj lʊ³f]

Blind am I, seeing, and willfully deaf.
Blind is ek, siende, en horende, doof.
[blənt əs ɛk 'sində ɛn 'fiʊ³rəndə dʊ³f]

Man and Wife
Man en Vrou
[man ɛn frœu]
Music: M. C. Roode (1907–1967)

The woman was made for the man,
Die vrou is vir die man gemaak,
[di frœu əs fər di man xə'ma:k]

The man again for the woman:
Die man weer vir die vrou:
[di man ve³r fər di frœu]

Like the leg of lamb roast for the hook,
Soos die braaiboud vir die haak,
[sʊ³s di 'bra:ibœut fər di ɦa:k]

Like the boot for the squeak,
Soos die stewel vir die kraak,
[sʊ³s di 'ste³vəl fər di kra:k]

The monkey for the sleeve,
Die apie vir die mou,[18]
[di 'a:pi fər di mœu]

The tail-feather for the peacock —
Die stertveer vir die pou —
[di 'stærtfe³r fər di pœu]

The woman was made for the man,
Die vrou is vir die man gemaak,
[di frœu əs fər di man xə'ma:k]

The man again for the woman!
Die man weer vir die vrou!
[di man ve³r fər di frœu]

Just like the sweet cake for taste buds,
Nes die soetkoek vir die smaak,
[nɛs di 'sutkuk fər di sma:k]

Just like small talk for drowsiness,
Nes die praatjies vir die vaak,
[nɛs di 'prajkis fər di fa:k]

Jaws for chewing,
Die kake vir die kou,
[di 'ka:kə fər di kœu]

The front ox for the rope —
Die trekos vir die tou —
[di 'trɛkɔs fər di tœu]

The woman was created for the man,
Die vrou is vir die man gemaak,
[di frœu əs fər di man xə'ma:k]

The man again for the woman!
Die man weer vir die vrou!
[di man ve³r fər di frœu]

---

[18] "Die aap is uit die mou" is the Afrikaans equivalent of the English saying, 'Let the cat out of the bag.'

Are her eyes green or gray,
Is haar ogies groen of grou,
[əs ɦa:r 'ʊᵊxis xrun ɔf xrœu]

Slightly squinting, brown or deep blue,
Soetskeel, bruin of baftablou,
['sutskeᵊl brœyn ɔf 'baftablœu]

Still, she is the girl for you!
Tog is sy die nooi vir jou!
[tɔx əs səj di no:j fər jœu]

The woman was made for the man
Die vrou is vir die man gemaak,
[di frœu əs fər di man xə'ma:k]

The man again for the woman!
Die man weer vir die vrou!
[di man veᵊr fər di frœu]

With a Little Basket of Roses
Met 'n Mandjie Rose
[mɛt ə 'maɲki 'rʊᵊsə]
Music: S. le Roux Marais (1896–1979), "The Rose and Other Afrikaans Songs"
(*Die Roos en ander Afrikaanse Liedere, no. 5*) [di rʊᵊs ɛn 'andər afri'ka:nsə 'lidərə]

Dearest Auntie, we bring roses,
Liefste Tannie, ons bring rosies,
['lifstə 'tani ɔns brəŋ 'rʊᵊsis]

Roses shining with morning dew,
Rosies blink met môredou,
['rʊᵊsis bləŋk mɛt 'mɔ:rədœu]

Pretty colors, sweet fragrances,
Mooie kleurtjies, soete geurtjies,
['mo:jə 'kljøᵊrkis 'sutə 'xjøᵊrkis]

And it's all just for you!
En dis alles net vir jou!
[ɛn dəs 'aləs nɛt fər jœu]

Roses whisper: 'love, little kisses' —
Rosies fluister: 'Liefde, soentjies' —
['rʊᵊsis 'flœystər 'lifdə 'suɲkis]

In veiled flower's language;
In verbloemde blommetaal;
[ən fər'blumdə 'blɔmməta:l]

Roses from our little garden,
Rosies wat ons uit ons tuintjie,
['rʊᵊsis vat ɔns œyt ɔns 'tœyɲki]

Love that we take from our hearts.
Liefde uit ons hartjies haal.
['lifdə œyt ɔns 'ɦarkis ɦa:l]

But the kisses … in no basket,
Maar die soentjies … in geen mandjie,
[ma:r di 'suɲkis ən çeᵊn 'maɲki]

Nowhere will it success to fit in —
Nêrens in wil dit geluk —
['næ:rəns ən vəl dət xə'lœk]

Dearest Auntie, we are at (our) wit's end —
Liefste Tannie, ons is raad-op —
['lifstə 'tani ɔns əs 'ra:tɔp]

You will have to pick your own little kisses!
Soentjies moet jy self maar pluk!
['suɲkis mut jəj sæᵊlf ma:r plœk]

Afternoon Nap
Middagslapie
['mədax͵sla:pi]
Music: P. J. de Villiers (1924–2015)
Lettie Joubert (1894–1966)
Ernst Lowenherz (1874–1958), *Op. 27, no. 2*
S. le Roux Marais (1896–1979), "Fifteen Afrikaans Lullabies" (*Vyftien Afrikaanse Slaapdeuntjies, no. 13*) ['fəjftin afri'ka:nsə 'sla:p͵djøɲkis]

On the clothesline above the green grass
Aan die lyn oor die groene gras
[a:n di ləjn ʊᵊr di 'xrunə xras]

Hang all her freshly washed little clothes;
Hang al haar kleertjies skoon gewas;
[ɦaŋ al ɦa:r 'kleᵊrkis skʊᵊn xə'vas]

Seven pieces all hang in a row;
Sewe stuks hang hulle daar op 'n ry;
['seᵊvə stœks ɦaŋ 'ɦœlə da:r ɔp ə rəj]

Wide open little eyes still peek at me.
Wyd ope ogies loer nog vir my.
[vəjt 'ʊᵊpə 'ʊᵊxis lu:r nɔx fər məj]

Would my lambkin
Wil my klein skapie
[vəl məj kləjn 'ska:pi]

Still not want to go to sleep?
Dan nog nie slaap nie?
[dan nɔx ni sla:p ni]

The hen makes her nest in the sand;
In die sand maak die hen haar bed;
[ən di sant ma:k di ɦɛn ɦa:r bɛt]

The spider spins her web in the nook;
In die hoek span die spin haar net;
[ən di ɦuk span di spən ɦa:r nɛt]

A little butterfly descends on the calyx,
Vlindertjie daal op die blomkelk neer,
['fləndərki da:l ɔp di 'blɔmkæᵃlk neᵊr]

Fluttering its wings to and fro.
Wikkel sy vlerkies heen en weer.
['vəkəl səj 'flærkis ɦeᵊn ɛn veᵊr]

Would my lambkin
Wil my klein skapie
[vəl məj kləjn 'ska:pi]

Still not want to go to sleep?
Dan nog nie slaap nie?
[dan nɔx ni sla:p ni]

Doo-doo-doo, doo-doo-doo murmurs the wind;
Dóédoedoe, Dóédoedoe, suis die wind;
['dududu 'dududu sœys di vənt]

Dimly look the little eyes of my child,
Flou lyk die kykertjies van my kind,
[flœu ləjk di 'kəjkərkis fan məj kənt]

Weary, too weary to keep them open;
Moeg, alte moeg om hul oop te hou;
[mux 'altə mux ɔm ɦœl ʊᵊp tə ɦœu]

Sleep casts its veil over both (eyes) now.
Slaap werp sy sluier oor albei nou.
[sla:p værp səj 'slœyər ʊᵊr 'albəj nœu]

Just one more yawn …
Net nog 'n gapie …
[nɛt nɔx ə ˈxa:pi]

My lambkin sleeps soundly.
Sag slaap my skapie.
[sax sla:p məj ˈska:pi]

Now or Never
Nimmer of nou
[ˈnəmər ɔf nœu]
Music: Gerrit Bon Sr. (1901–1983), "Voortrekker/Pioneer Festival Songs"
(*Voortrekker-Feessange, no. 2*) [ˈfʊᵊr trækər ˈfeᵊˌsaŋə]
John Lea-Morgan (n.d.)
Sydney Richfield (1882–1967)

Listing little ships on gyrating waves,
Wank'lende skepies op went'lende bare,
[ˈvaŋkləndə ˈskeᵊpis ɔp ˈvɛntləndə ˈba:rə]

But an unwavering hand on the rudder —
Maar 'n standvastige hand aan die roer —
[ma:r ə stantˈfastəxə fiant a:n di ru:r]

That is how the Almighty through a
thousand dangers
So het die Almag deur duisend gevare
[sʊᵊ fiɛt di ˈalmax djøᵊr ˈdœysənt xəˈfa:rə]

Brought our ancestors here long ago.
Voortyds ons voorsate hierheen gevoer.
[ˈfʊᵊrtəjts ɔns ˈfʊᵊrsa:tə ˈfii:rfieᵊn xəˈfu:r]

We recognise His hand over the years
Kennelik sien ons Sy hand deur die jare
[ˈkɛnələk sin ɔns səj fiant djøᵊr di ˈja:rə]

Even in the variable fate of the farmer:
Nog in die wiss'lende lot van die boer:
[nɔx ən di ˈvəsləndə lɔt fan di bu:r]

His wagon jolting in a sea of barbarians,
Wag'lend sy wa in 'n see van barbare,
[ˈvaxlənt səj va: ən ə seᵊ fan barˈba:rə]

Firm his trust in God and his musket.
Vas sy vertroue op God en sy roer.
[fas səj fərˈtrœuə ɔp xɔt ɛn səj ru:r]

Will we safeguard the pioneer's imprint —
Sal ons die Voortrekkerstempel[19] bestendig —
[sal ɔns di ˈfʊᵊrtrækərˌstɛmpəl bəˈstɛndəx]

Lord of his holding and master of
his farm —
Heer van sy hoewe en baas van sy plaas —
[fieᵊr fan səj ˈfiuvə ɛn ba:s fan səj pla:s]

Or through complacency degenerate and
become listless
Of deur verslapping ontaard en lamlendig
[ɔf djøᵊr fərˈslapəŋ ɔntˈa:rt ɛn lamˈlɛndəx]

---

[19] A journey of Afrikaners known as "Voortrekkers," translated as 'forerunners' or 'pioneers,' who migrated through the interior of the country from the mid-1830s onward in hopes of creating their own independent communities, due to dissatisfaction with British colonization and conflicts with Indigenous ethnic groups at the Cape. The term "Afrikaner" was originally associated with urban-based descendants of the Dutch, German, and French Huguenots who settled at the Cape, while the term "Boers," translated as 'farmers,' referred to rural settlers. The "Boers" later became part of the Afrikaner ethnic group during the Great Trek. These designations are somewhat interchangeable in modern-day South Africa.

A servant and subordinate on our
birthground? —
Op ons geboortegrond kneg word en klaas? —
[ɔp ɔns xə'bʊᵊrtəxrɔnt knæx vɔrt ɛn kla:s]

If we have the unity—the strength—from
our motto;
*Had ons die Eendrag—die Mag—van
ons leuse;*
[ɦat ɔns di 'eᵊndrax di max fan ɔns 'ljøᵊsə]

If we have the will to maintain and retain …
Had ons die Wil om te handhaaf, te hou …
[ɦat ɔns di vəl ɔm tə 'ɦantɦa:f tə ɦœu]

Here lie the crossroads, and limited is the
choice,
Hier lê die kruispad, en kort is die keuse,
[ɦi:r lɛ: di 'krœyspat ɛn kɔrt əs di 'kjøᵊsə]

Easy to go astray, but … long the remorse!
*Maklik die dwaalweg, maar … lank
die berou!*
['maklək di 'dwa:lvæx ma:r laŋk di bə'rœu]

Because Death
Omdat die Dood
['ɔmda di dʊᵊt][20]
Music: Gideon Fagan (1904–1980)

Because Death so early
Omdat die dood so vroeg vir jou
['ɔmda di dʊᵊt sʊᵊ vrux fər jœu][21]

Tore you from my side,
Geskeur het van my sy,
[xə'skjøᵊr ɦɛt fan məj səj]

You will always retain your beauty
Sal jy jou skoonheid steeds behou
[sal jəj jœu 'skʊᵊnɦəjt steᵊts bə'ɦœu]

And remain youthful forever.
En ewig jeugdig bly.
[ɛn 'eᵊvəx 'jøᵊxdəx bləj]

But I will become old, stiff, and gray
Maar ek sal oud word, stram en grys
[ma:r ɛk sal œut vɔrt stram ɛn xrəjs]

And gradually become cold —
En koud van liewerlee —
[ɛn kœut fan 'livərleᵊ]

The contribution that life claims,
Die skatting wat die lewe eis,
[di 'skatəŋ vat di 'leᵊvə əjs]

Pays toward grief and woe.
Betaal aan leed en wee.
[bə'ta:l a:n leᵊt ɛn 'veᵊ]

Why do I lament over lost youth?
Wat klaag ek oor verlore jeug?
[vat kla:x ɛk ʊᵊr fər'lʊᵊrə jøᵊx]

What is there to preserve?
Wat is daar te behou?
[vat əs da:r tə bə'ɦœu]

---

[20] See Appendix G, Assimilation and Amalgamation of Consonants.
[21] Ibid

After all, desire and happiness were buried
Begrawe is tog begeerte en vreug
[bəˈxraːvə əs tɔx bəˈxeᵊrtə ɛn frjøᵊx]

Long ago … with you!
Al lank gelee … met jou!
[al laŋk xəˈleᵊ mɛt jœu]

The Distant Princess
Prinses van verre
[prənˈsɛs fan ˈfærə]
Music: Gerrit Bon Sr. (1901–1983)
Johannes Joubert (1894–1958)
P. J. Lemmer (1898–1989)

Were you a rose blossom
Was jy 'n rosebloesem
[vas jəj ə ˈrʊᵊsəˌblusəm]

And I, the rose's fragrance.
En ek die roos se geur.
[ɛn ɛk di rʊᵊ sə xjøᵊr]

And I the rose's fragrance,
En ek die roos se geur,
[ɛn ɛk di rʊᵊs ə xjøᵊr]

Were you the lyrics of a song
Was jy 'n lied se woorde
[vas jəj ə lit sə ˈvʊᵊrdə]

How lovely it would be to go through life
Hoe heerlik deur die lewe
[ɦu ˈɦeᵊrlək djøᵊr di ˈleᵊvə]

And I the melody,
En ek die melodie,
[ɛn ɛk di mɛluˈdi]

Floating all around you,
Steeds rondom jou te swewe,
[steᵊts ˈrɔntɔm jœu tə ˈsweᵊvə]

How the day would extol
Hoe sou die dag verheerlik
[ɦu sœu di dax fərˈɦeᵊrlək]

Swooning at your bosom,
Beswymend aan jou boesem,
[bəˈswəjmənt aːn jœu ˈbusəm]

Your desirable beauty;
Jou skoonheid so begeerlik;
[jœu ˈskʊᵊnɦəjt sʊᵊ bəˈxeᵊrlək]

Bewitched by your color.
Betower deur jou kleur.
[bəˈtʊᵊvər djøᵊr jœu kljøᵊr]

The night trilling with chords
Die nag tril van akkoorde
[di nax trəl fan aˈkʊᵊrdə]

Were you a rose blossom
Was jy 'n rosebloesem
[vas jəj ə ˈrʊᵊsəˌblusəm]

And the sweetest harmony.
En soetste harmonie.
[ɛn ˈsutstə ɦarmʊᵊˈni]

Were you the lyrics of a song,
Was jy 'n lied se woorde,
[vas jəj ə lit sə 'voˑrdə]

And I, the melody.
En ek die melodie.
[ɛn ɛk di mɛlu'di]

Were you the highest cliffs
Was jy die hoogste kranse
[vas jəj di 'fiʊˑxstə 'kransə]

And I, the glow of the sun,
En ek die sonnegloed,
[ɛn ɛk di 'sɔnəxlut]

Your cheeks would then paint
Jou wange sou dan verwe
[jœu 'vaŋə sœu dan 'færvə]

And on your lips die
En op jou lippe sterwe
[ɛn ɔp jœu 'ləpə 'stærvə]

My first morning's irradiance
My eerste môreglanse
[məj 'eˑrstə 'mɔːrəˌxlansə]

And last dusk's farewell;
En laaste awendgroet;
[ɛn 'laːstə 'aːvəntxrut]

Were you the highest cliff,
Was jy die hoogste kranse,
[vas jəj di 'fiʊˑxstə 'kransə]

And I, the glow of the sun.
En ek die sonnegloed.
[ɛn ɛk di 'sɔnəxlut]

But you're the distant princess
Maar jy's prinses van verre
[maːr jəjs prən'sɛs fan 'færə]

And I ... a troubadour;
En ek ... 'n troebadoer;
[ɛn ɛk ə 'trubaduːr]

Even if my songs glow
Al gloei ook my gesange
[al xlui ʊˑk məj xə'saŋə]

From love and longing
Van liefde en verlange
[fan 'lifdə ɛn fər'laŋə]

The firefly for the stars —
Die vuurvlieg vir die sterre —
[di 'fyːrflix fər di 'stærə]

That transports me to heaven;
Wat my ten hemel voer;
[vat məj tɛn 'fieˑməl fuːr]

You remain the distant princess
Jy bly prinses van verre
[jəj bləj prən'sɛs fan 'færə]

And I ... a troubadour.
En ek ... 'n troebadoer.
[ɛn ɛk ə 'trubaduːr]

A Love Letter
Salut d'Amour
[sa'ly da'mu:r]
Music: M. L. De Villiers (1885–1977)
Eva Noel Harvey (1900–1976), "Three New Songs" (*Drie nuwe Liedere, no. 1*)
[dri 'nyvə 'lidərə]
S. le Roux Marais (1896–1979), "Six Art Songs" (*Ses Kunsliedere, no. 3*)
[sɛs 'kœnsˌlidərə]
Rosa Nepgen (1909–2001)
J. K. Pescod (1898–1985)

I ride through the bush in the morning,
Ek ry in die veld in die môre,
[ɛk rəj ən di fæᵃlt ən di 'mɔ:rə]

I drink from the chalice of the night
Ek drink uit die kelk van die nag
[ɛk drəŋk œyt di kæᵃlk fan di nax]

A toast created by Aurore,
'n Heildronk geskep deur Aurore,
[ə 'ɦəjldrɔŋk xə'skɛp djø̞ᵊr au'rɔ:rə]

From the bubbling source of the day.
Uit die bruisende bron van die dag.
[œyt di 'brœysəndə brɔn fan di dax]

How it gleams all around
Hoe glinster dit al in die ronde
[ɦu 'xlənstər dət al ən di 'rɔndə]

With pearl-shaped tears of dew …
Met per'lende trane van dou …
[mɛt 'pærləndə 'tra:nə fan dœu]

Dreamed during the nightly hour,
Gedroom het, in nagt'like stonde,
[xə'druᵊm ɦɛt ən 'naxtləkə 'stɔndə]

The flowers, my dearest, my dearest of you.
Die blomme, my liefste, my liefste, van jou.
[di 'blɔmə məj 'lifstə məj 'lifstə van jœu]

How all the leaves whisper it,
Hoe fluister dit al die blare,
[ɦu 'flœystər dət al di 'bla:rə]

So happily during the clear noontide …
So bly op die heldere noen …
[suᵊ bləj ɔp di 'ɦæᵃldərə nun]

The wind played with your hair,
Die wind het gespeel met jou hare,
[di vənt ɦɛt xə'speᵊl mɛt jœu 'ɦa:rə]

Your lips, my dearest, kissed.
Jou lippe, my liefste, gesoen.
[jœu 'ləpə məj 'lifstə xə'sun]

Return, oh fortunate winds,
Keer weer, o bevoorregte winde,
[keᵊr veᵊr ʊᵊ bə'fʊᵊˌræxtə 'vəndə]

And as the western horizon is colored, bring
En bring, as die weste verkleur,
[ɛn brəŋ as di 'vɛstə fər'kljø̞ᵊr]

A greeting from the veld, my beloved —
'n Groet van die veld my beminde —
[ə xrut fan di fæᵃlt məj bə'məndə]

My message with the scent of flowers.
My boodskap met blomme se geur.
[məj 'bʊᵊtskap mɛt 'blɔmə sə xjø̞ᵊr]

(Pretty) Susie
Sannie
['sani]
Music: Daniel Clement (1902–1980), "South Africa Onwards"
(*Suid-Afrika vorentoe, no. 33*) [sœyt 'a:frika 'fʊᵊrəntu]

In my eyes, there was no young man so fine,
Daar was in my oë geen jonkman so flink,
[da:r vas ən məj 'u:ə çeᵊn 'jɔŋkman sʊᵊ fləŋk]

So friendly as so pleasant as Johnny.
So gaaf en so prettig as Jannie.
[sʊᵊ xa:f ɛn sʊᵊ 'prɛtəx as 'jani]

"For him I will wait," I thought secretly,
"Vir hom sal ek wag," het ek heimlik gedink,
[fər ɦɔm sal ɛk vax ɦɛt ɛk 'ɦəjmlək xə'dəŋk]

"Even if I don't end up with any other man!"
"Al kry ek ook anders geen man nie!"
[al krəj ɛk ʊᵊk 'andərs çeᵊn man ni]

But he only had eyes for pretty Susie du Toit
Maar hy had net oë vir Sannie du Toit
[ma:r ɦəj ɦat nɛt 'u:ə fər 'sani dy tɔj]

(And who has a smile as she has?).
(En wie het 'n glimlag soos sy het?).
[ɛn vi ɦɛt ə 'xləmlax sʊᵊs səj ɦɛt]

A darling she was, so amiable, so pretty,
'n Skatjie was sy, so lieftallig, so mooi,
[ə 'ska ˈki vas səj sʊᵊ lif'taləx sʊᵊ mo:j]

Don't ask (me) if I was envious of Susie!
Moenie vra of ek Sannie beny het!
['muni fra: ɔf ɛk 'sani bə'nəj ɦɛt]

I will never forget ... neither the day nor
the year
Vergeet sal ek nooit ... nie die dag of die jaar
[fər'xeᵊt sal ɛk no:jt ni di dax ɔf di ja:r]

When Johnny got married to pretty Susie,
Toe Jannie gaan trou het met Sannie,
[tu 'jani xa:n trœu ɦɛt mɛt 'sani]

Goodness me, but they were a beautiful
couple,
My liewe, maar dit was 'n prag van 'n paar,
[məj 'livə ma:r dət vas ə prax fan ə pa:r]

A perfect image of a groom — Johnny!
'n Beeld van 'n bruidegom — Jannie!
[ə beᵊlt fan ə 'brœydəxɔm 'jani]

The reverend could barely contain himself,
Die dominee self kon dit byna nie hou,
[di 'dʊᵊməni sæᵊlf kɔn dət 'bəjna ni ɦœu]

I thought: "What if it wasn't her,
Ek dink: "Sê nou maar dit was sy nie,
[ɛk dəŋk se: nœu ma:r dət vas səj ni]

But rather myself that was getting married
to Johnny."
*Maar liewer ek self wat met Jannie
gaan trou."*
[ma:r 'livər ɛk sæᵊlf vat mɛt 'jani xa:n trœu]

Oh, didn't I begrudge her then?!
O, het ek haar toe nie beny nie?!
[ʊᵊ ɦɛt ɛk ɦa:r tu ni bə'nəj ni]

Two years passed, and pretty Susie was there
no more,
*Twee jaar was verby, en mooi Sannie
nie meer,*
[tweᵊ ja:r vas fər'bəj ɛn mo:j 'sani ni meᵊr]

Poor Johnny (was) so inconsolable and lonely.
Arme Jannie so droef en allenig.
['arəmə 'jani sʊᵊ druf ɛn a'leᵊnəx]

(But) Old love does not rust, it's my turn this time.
Die ou liefde roes nie, dis my beurt dié keer.
[di œu 'lifdə rus ni dəs məj bjø̞ᵊrt 'di keᵊr]

We are now united in matrimony!
Nou is ons in die huwelik verenig!
[nœu əs ɔns ən di 'ɦyvələk fər'eᵊnəx]

I think about her peaceful grave in the gorge …
Ek dink aan haar rustige graf in die kloof …
[ɛk dəŋk a:n ɦa:r 'rœstəxə xraf ən di klʊᵊf]

Without the burden of a child or husband …
Geen oorlas van kind of van man nie …
[çeᵊn 'ʊᵊrlas fan kənt ɔf fan man ni]

Climbing roses grow around her headstone —
Die rankrosies rondom die steen aan haar hoof —
[di 'raŋkˌrʊᵊsis 'rɔntɔm di steᵊn a:n ɦa:r ɦʊᵊf]

For the first time I am truly envious of Susie!
Nou beny ek eers regtig vir Sannie!
[nœu bə'nəj ɛk eᵊrs 'ræxtəx fər 'sani]

Dedication
Toewyding
['tuvəjdəŋ]
Music: J. S. Manca (1908–1985)
Rosa Nepgen (1909–2001)
Maria van der Mark (1912–n.d.)

A harp hanged
'n Harp het gehang
[ə ɦarp ɦɛt xə'ɦaŋ]

Unnoticed, in front of the door,
Voor die deur ongeag,
[fʊᵊr di djø̞ᵊr 'ɔnxəˌax]

The wind played
Die wind het gespeel
[di vənt ɦɛt xə'speᵊl]

Through the strings at night.
Deur die snare by nag.
[djø̞ᵊr di 'sna:rə bəj nax]

Through the strings, the wind
Die wind deur die snare
[di vint djø̞ᵊr di 'sna:rə]

Softly sang many a song:
Sing sag menig' lied:
[səŋ sax 'meᵊnəx lit]

The homage falteringly
Die hulde wat huiw'rig
[di 'ɦœldə vat 'ɦœyvrəx]

Presented to You, (by) the singer!
Die sanger U bied!
[di 'saŋər y bit]

If the song becomes soundless
Word klankloos die lied
[vɔrt 'klaŋklʊᵊs di lit]

Because of joy or sorrow,
Van geluk of van smart,
[fan xə'lœk ɔf fan smart]

The image of your beauty
Die beeld van U skoonheid
[di beᵊlt fan y 'skʊᵊnɦəjt]

Remains alive in his heart.
Leef voort in sy hart.
[leᵊf fʊᵊrt ən səj ɦart]

From the Forlorn Marsh
Van Verlore-vlei
[fan fər'lʊᵊrə fləj]
Music: Rosa Nepgen (1909–2001)

You are the skylark,
Jy is die leeurik,
[jəj əs di 'liurək]

I am the marsh;
Ek is die vlei;
[ɛk əs di fləj]

High in the blue sky
Hoog in die bloute
[ɦʊᵊx ən di 'blœutə]

You fly (away) from me.
Vlug jy vir my.
[flœx jəj fər məj]

Waiting, yearning,
Wagtende, Smagtende,
['vaxtəndə 'smaxtəndə]

I gaze until you, far from the blue sky,
Staar ek tot jy ver uit die bloue lug,
[sta:r ɛk tɔt jəj fæ:r œyt di 'blœuə lœx]

Hither(ward) from the cold air
Her uit die koue lug
[ɦær œyt di 'kœuə lœx]

Return to me.
T'rugkeer tot my.
['trœxkeᵊr tɔt məj]

You are the skylark,
Jy is die leeurik,
[jəj əs di 'liurək]

I am the marsh.
Ek is die vlei.
[ɛk əs di fləj]

Sungold and stardust,
Son-goud en ster-stof,
['sɔnxœut ɛn 'stærstɔf]

The luster of the moon,
Glans van die maan,
[xlans fan di ma:n]

Fervent and appeased,
Vuurlik en vérlig,
['fy:rlək ɛn fər'ləx]

This attracts you,
Dié trek jou aan,
['di træk jœu a:n]

Fearing, fleeing,
Dugtende, Vlugtende,
['dœxtəndə 'flœxtəndə]

Still unsatisfied.
Steeds onvoldaan.
[ste°ts ɔnfɔl'da:n]

This distresses you yet again,
Dié verontrus jou weer,
['di fər'ɔntrəs jœu ve°r]

I alone calm you, again.
Ek alleen sus jou weer.
[ɛk a'le°n sœs jœu ve°r]

Everything is an illusion: Sungold and stardust,
Alles is waan: Son-goud en ster-stof,
['aləs əs va:n 'sɔnxœut ɛn 'stærstɔf]

The luster of the moon,
Glans van die maan.
[xlans fan di ma:n]

Come my beloved,
Kom, my beminde,
[kɔm məj bə'məndə]

Unlimited joy,
Vreugd' onbeperk,
[frjø°xt 'ɔmbə,pærk[22]]

Heaving bosom,
Hygende boesem,
['fiəjxəndə 'busəm]

Gravitating wing,
Neigende vlerk,
['nəjxəndə flærk]

Heaving, gravitating,
Hygende, neigende,
['fiəjxəndə 'nəjxəndə]

High from the heavens,
Hoog uit die swerk,
[fiʊ°x œyt di swærk]

Continually rocking, again,
Immer weer wiegende,
['əmər ve°r 'vixəndə]

Nevermore flying,
Nimmermeer vliegende,
['nəmərme°r 'flixəndə]

Love too strong —
Liefde te sterk —
['lifdə tə stærk]

Come, my beloved,
Kom, my beminde,
[kɔm məj bə'məndə]

Delight unlimited.
Vreugd' onbeperk.
[frjø°xt 'ɔmbə,pærk[23]]

---

[22] See Appendix G, Assimilation and Amalgamation of Consonants.
[23] Ibid.

A Light Shines Ahead on the Wagon Trail
Voor in die Wapad brand 'n Lig
[fʊᵊr ən di 'va:pat brant ə ləx]
Music: Arthur Ellis (b. 1931)

Freedom, the word above all words
Vryheid, woord van alle woorde
['frəjɦəjt vʊᵊrt fan 'alə vʊᵊrdə]

That stirs the human heart,
Wat die mensehart beroer,
[vat di 'mɛnsəɦart bə'ru:r]

Responding to your call to the north
Op jou wekroep na die noorde
[ɔp jœu 'vɛkrup na di 'nʊᵊrdə]

Treks sturdy, small farmer.
Trek die stoere, kleine boer.
[træk di 'stu:rə 'kləjnə bu:r]

In the school of life filled with danger —
In die leerskool van gevare —
[ən di 'leᵊrskʊᵊl fan xə'fa:rə]

Wild animals and barbarians —
Wilde diere en barbare —
['vəldə 'di:rə ɛn bar'ba:rə]

His childhood years are toughened.
Word gebrei sy kinderjare.
[vɔrt xə'brəj səj 'kəndərˌja:rə]

Under burdensome conditions, undescribed
Onder swaarkry nooit beskrywe
['ɔndər 'swa:rkrəj no:jt bə'skrəjvə]

A man grows up on the road,
Groei 'n man op, langs die pad,
['xrui ə man ɔp laŋs di pat]

Who can lead his own team (of oxen)
Wat die eie span kan drywe
[vat di 'əjə span kan 'drəjvə]

Taking the leading thong safely:
En die voortou veilig vat:
[ɛn di 'fʊᵊrtœu 'fəjləx fat]

Knuckling under no drift (ford) or
darkness ...
Vir g'n drif of duister swig ...
[fər xən drəf ɔf 'dœystər swəx]

A light shines ahead on the wagon trail.
Voor in die wapad brand 'n lig.
[fʊᵊr ən di 'va:pat brant ə ləx]

The young man approaches from the north
Kom die jonkman uit die noorde
[kɔm di 'jɔŋkman œyt di 'nʊᵊrdə]

While dusk's shadows lengthen;
Wyl die awendskadu's val;
[vəjl di 'a:vəntˌska:dys fal]

The foaming stream laps against its edges:
Skuimend lek die stroom sy boorde:
['skœymənt læk di strʊᵊm səj 'bʊᵊrdə]

The Vaal River is in spate.
Vaalrivier[24] lê kant en wal.
['fa:lrəˌfi:r le: kant ɛn val]

---

[24] The Vaal River is the largest tributary of the Orange River and the third largest river in South Africa. It is 700 miles in length. The Afrikaans word "Vaal" means 'dull.' It refers to the color of the water, especially during flood season.

In the waters of the Vaal
In die waters van die Vaal
[ən di 'va:tərs fan di fa:l]

Where the dark whirlpool swirls,
Waar die donker draaikolk maal,
[va:r di 'dɔŋkər 'dra:jkɔlk ma:l]

Brightly gleams a ray (of light)!
Helder skitter daar 'n straal!
['ɦæᵃldər 'skətər da:r ə stra:l]

Eyes misty with longing,
Oë mistig van verlange,
['u:ə 'məstəx fan fər'laŋə]

Reflecting a beautiful dream:
Weerskyn van 'n skone droom:
['veᵃrskəjn fan ə 'skʊᵃnə drʊᵃm]

Soft arms, red cheeks …
Sagte arms, rooie wange …
['saxtə 'arəms 'ro:jə 'vaŋə]

And he hurls himself into the stream!
En hy werp hom in die stroom!
[ɛn ɦəj værp ɦɔm ən di strʊᵃm]

Love keeps his vision fixed …
Liefde hou sy blik gerig …
['lifdə ɦœu səj blək xə'rəx]

Across the water shines a light!
Oorkant die water brand 'n lig!
['ʊᵃrkant di 'va:tər brant ə ləx]

Heroism and contempt of death,
Heldemoed en doodsveragting,
['ɦæᵃldəmut ɛn 'dʊᵃtsfərˌaxtən]

Makapan, your cave is called
Makapan,[25] *spel jou spelonk*
['makapan spæl jœu spə'lɔŋk]

On the day of the cruel massacre
Op die dag van wrede slagting
[ɔp di dax fan 'vreᵃdə 'slaxtən]

Of your warriors drunk from bloodlust.
Van jou stryders bloedlusdronk.
[fan jœu 'strəjdərs 'blutləsdrɔŋk]

At the mouth of the cave
Reg voor die spelonk se mond
[ræx fʊᵃr di spə'lɔŋk sə mɔnt]

Severely wounded the leader falls,
Val die voorman swaar gewond,
[fal di 'fʊᵃrman swa:r xə'vɔnt]

Drenching the ground with his blood.
Drenkend met sy bloed die grond.
['drɛŋkənt mɛt səj blut di xrɔnt]

With the outcry: "Help! oh God,"
Met die uitroep: "Help! o Here,"
[mɛt di 'œytrup ɦæᵃlp ʊᵃ 'ɦeᵃrə]

Wild as the wind,
Onweerstaanbaar soos die wind,
[ˌɔnveᵃr'sta:nba:r sʊᵃs di vənt]

---

[25] This mountainous area in the Limpopo Province is known as the Waterberg Biosphere Reserve. Previously called *Makapansgat*, the Makapan Valley was declared a South African Heritage site, as it contains a rich biodiversity of vegetation with over 5,500 species of plants. Part of the Cradle of Humankind, a UNESCO World Heritage Site, it has the world's largest cluster of fossilized human ancestral remains. Various archaeological findings predating the Stone Age have been discovered in the area.

Out of the guns' mouths
Uit die mond van die gewere
[œyt di mɔnt fan di xə'veᵊrə]

He saves his wounded friend!
Red hy sy gewonde vrind!
[rɛt ɦəj səj xə'vɔndə frənt]

Brotherly love and patriotic duty —
Broederliefde en burgerplig —
['brudər‚lifdə ɛn 'bœrgərpləx]

Deep within his breast glows the light.
Diep in sy boesem gloei die lig.
[dip ən səj 'busəm 'xlui di ləx]

After the campaign, rest and peace —
Ná die veldtog, rus en vrede —
['na: di 'fæᵊltɔx rœs ɛn 'freᵊdə]

Peace in the fatherland;
Vrede in die vaderland;
['freᵊdə ən di 'fa:dərlant]

Every stride brings him closer
Nader bring hom elke skrede
['na:dər brəŋ ɦɔm 'æᵊlkə 'skreᵊdə]

To the little house against the ridge.
Na die huisie teen die rant.
[na di 'ɦœysi teᵊn di rant]

With the faithful spouse
Met die troue eggenoot
[mɛt di 'trœuə 'æxənuᵊt]

And the children around her lap,
En die kleintjies om haar skoot,
[ɛn di 'kləŋkis ɔm ɦa:r skuᵊt]

All (are) precious, small and big,
Dierbaar almal, klein en groot,
['di:rba:r 'almal kləjn ɛn xrʊᵊt]

And he hums: "Thank You, Father,"
En hy neurie: "Dank U, Vader,"
[ɛn ɦəj 'njøᵊri daŋk y 'fa:dər]

While his heart beats ever faster —
Wyl sy hart al sneller klop —
[vəj səj ɦart al 'snælər klɔp]

"That the hour of reuniting is dawning!"
"Dat die uur van weersien nader!"
[dat di y:r fan 'veᵊrsin 'na:dər]

He directs his horse into a gallop;
Trek sy perd weer op galop;
[træ:k səj pært veᵊr ɔp xa'lɔp]

Joy brightens his countenance:
Vreug verklaar sy aangesig:
[frjøᵊx fər'kljøᵊr səj 'a:nxə‚səx]

Ahead on the wagon trail shines a light!
Voor in die wapad brand 'n lig!
[fʊᵊr ən di 'va:pat brant ə ləx]

Black, heavy ominous clouds
Swarte, sware onweerswolke
['swartə 'swa:rə 'ɔnveᵊrs‚vɔlkə]

Gather together across the youthful state,
Trek saam oor die jonge staat,
[træ:k sa:m ʊᵊr di 'jɔŋə sta:t]

Benjamin of all the nations
Benjamin van al die volke
['bɛnjamən fan al di 'fɔlkə]

Victim of greed, malice and hate.
Prooi van hebsug, nyd en haat.
[ˈproːj fan ˈɦɛpsəx nəjt ɛn ɦaːt]

"Here," he says, "no tyranny!"
"Hier," spreek hy, "g'n dwing(e)landy,"
[ɦiːr spreᵊk ɦəj xən ˈdwəŋlandəj]

"Here no foreign dominion,
"Hier g'n vreemde heerskappy,
[ɦiːr xən ˈfreᵊmdə ˈɦeᵊrskapəj]

"The world knows: We are free!
"Weet' die wêreld: Ons is vry!
[veᵊ di ˈvæːrəlt ɔns əs frəj]

"Tremble for no war trumpets,
"Bewe vir g'n krygsbasuine,
[ˈbeᵊvə fər xən ˈkrəjxsbaˌsœynə]

No oppressor's vengefulness;
G'n geweldenaar se wrok;
[xən xəˈvæᵊldənaːr sə vrɔk]

Never will he bring our country to ruin
Nooit lê hy ons land in puine
[ˈnoːjt lɛ ɦəj ɔns lant ən ˈpœynə]

Before us we shock all of mankind!
Voor ons heel die mensdom skok!
[fʊᵊr ɔns ɦeᵊl di ˈmɛnsdɔm skɔk]

Fall freely, flashing thunderbolt:
"Val vry, felle bliksemskig:
[fal frəj ˈfælə ˈbləksəmskəx]

On Majuba's crest burns a light!"
Bo-op Majoeba²⁶ brand 'n lig!"
[bʊᵊ ɔp maˈjuba brant ə ləx]

In the land of snow and bitter cold
In die land van sneeu en koue
[ən di lant fan sniu ɛn ˈkœuə]

The gray hero is overset with contemplation,
Peins oorstelp die gryse held,
[pəjns ˈʊᵊrstæᵊlp di ˈxrəjsə ɦæᵊlt]

Alone in his unwavering trust in God
Enkel met sy Godsvertroue
[ˈɛŋkəl mɛt səj ˈxɔtsfərˌtrœuə]

And longing for his bushveld!
En verlange na sy veld!²⁷
[ɛn fərˈlaŋə na səj fæᵊlt]

Hear him plead: "God, it's enough;
Hoor hom smeek: "Heer, dis genoeg;
[ɦʊᵊr ɦɔm smeᵊk ɦeᵊr dəs xəˈnux]

"Call the farmer from the plow:
"Roep die landman van die ploeg:
[rup di ˈlantman fan di plux]

"He's exhausted, God, he is tired!
"Hy's gedaan, Heer, hy is moeg!
[ɦəjs xəˈdaːn ɦeᵊr ɦəj əs mux]

"You who know all hearts,
"U, die Kenner van die harte,
[y di ˈkɛnər fan di ˈɦartə]

---

[26] The Battle of Majuba Hill occurred near Volksrust, in the KwaZulu-Natal Province, on February 27, 1881. This final battle of the First Anglo-Boer War (1880–1881) resulted in victory for the Boers and the subsequent signing of a peace treaty between the Afrikaners (Boers) and the English.

[27] An expansive African prairie, field, or pasture, comprising a wide variety of vegetation which may be used in various ways, including agriculture or uncultivated countryside.

"Know what each heart can endure.
"Weet wat elke hart kan dra.
[veᵊt vat 'æᵃlkə ɦart kan dra:]

"Alleviate, Man of Sorrow, the sorrows
"Lenig, Man van Smart, die smarte
['leᵊnəx man fan smart di 'smartə]

"Of (a) wounded South Africa."
"Van verwond' Suid-Afrika."
[fan fər'vɔnt sœyt 'a:frika]

His countenance beams as he dies:
Sterwend straal sy aangesig:
['stærvənt stra:l səj 'a:nxəˌsəx]

"Ahead on the wagon trail shines a light!"
"Voor in die wapad brand 'n lig!"
[fʊᵊr ən di 'va:pat brant ə ləx]

Question and Answer
Vraag en Antwoord
[fra:x ɛn 'antvʊᵊrt]
Music: Daniel Clement (1902–1980)

I asked the golden sun:
Die goue son het ek gevra:
[di 'xœuə sɔn ɦɛt ɛk xə'fra:]

Do you know what love is?
Weet jy wat liefde is?
[veᵊt jəj vat 'lifdə əs]

His answer was … a stream of light
Sy antwoord was … 'n stroom van lig
[səj 'antvʊᵊrt vas ə strʊᵊm fan ləx]

Through deep darkness.
Deur diepe duisternis.
[djøᵊr 'dipə 'dœystərnəs]

I asked the red rose:
Die rooie roos het ek gevra:
[di 'ro:jə rʊᵊs ɦɛt ɛk xə'fra:]

Is love a child of beauty?
Is liefde skoonheidskind?
[əs 'lifdə 'skʊᵊnɦəjtskənt]

Her answer was … a sweet perfume
Haar antwoord was … 'n soete geur
[ɦa:r 'antvʊᵊrt vas ə 'sutə xjøᵊr]

On the wings of the wind.
Op wieke van die wind.
[ɔp 'vikə fan di vənt]

I asked the joyful stream:
Die blye stroom het ek gevra:
[di 'bləjə strʊᵊm ɦɛt ɛk xə'vra:]

Is love bliss or misery?
Is liefde wel of wee?
[əs 'lifdə væl ɔf veᵊ]

His answer was … a melody
Sy antwoord was … 'n melodie
[səj 'antvʊᵊrt vas ə mɛlu'di]

Softly singing from the sea.
Sag singend van die see.
[sax 'səŋənt fan di seᵊ]

I asked the night wind once:
Die nagwind het ek eens gevra:
[di ˈnaxvənt ɦɛt ɛk eᵊns xəˈfra:]

Is love joy or sorrow?
Is liefde vreugde of smart?
[əs ˈlifdə ˈfrjøᵊxdə ɔf smart]

A sigh of pain softly murmured
Toe suis daar sag 'n sug van pyn
[tu sœys da:r sax ə sœx fan pəjn]

Quietly gnawing at my heart.
Stilknaend aan die hart.
[stəlˈkna:ənt a:n di ɦart]

I asked Goodness itself
Die Goedheid self het ek gevra
[di ˈxutɦəjt sæᵃlf ɦɛt ɛk xəˈfra:]

What love would be:
Wat of die liefde sy:
[vat ɔf di ˈlifdə səj]

Is it holy solemnity or mere frivolity?
Of heil'ge erns òf louter skerts?
[ɔf ˈɦəjlxə ærns ˈɔf ˈlœutər skærts]

He then gave you to me.
Toe gee hy jou aan my.
[tu çeᵊ ɦəj jœu a:n məj]

And now that I may read your heart
En nou ek jou hart mog lees
[ɛn nœu ɛk jœu ɦart mɔx leᵊs]

Your sweet secrets,
Jou soet geheimenis,
[jœu sut xəˈɦəjmənəs]

Now my heart knows—now I don't ask …
Nou weet my hart—nou vra ek nie …
[nœu veᵊt məj ɦart nœu fra: ɛk ni]

Anymore what love is!
Nie meer wat liefde is!
[ni meᵊr vat ˈlifdə əs]

If I Were a Singer
Was ek 'n Sanger
[vas ɛk ə ˈsaŋər]
Music: Gerrit Bon Sr. (1901–1983)
Lettie Joubert (1894–1966)
Con Lamprecht (n.d.)
Ernst Löwenherz (1874–1958)

If I were a singer I would celebrate
Was ek 'n sanger sou ek besing
[vas ɛk ə ˈsaŋər sœu ɛk bəˈsəŋ]

The laughter and life that spring brings;
Die lag en lewe wat lente bring;
[di lax ɛn ˈleᵊvə vat ˈlɛntə brəŋ]

The rosy clouds in the blue skies;
Die rosewolke in bloue lug;
[di ˈrʊᵊsəˌvɔlkə ən ˈblœuə lœx]

The golden wonder when shadows flee;
Die goue wonder as skadu's vlug;
[di ˈxœuə ˈvɔndər as ˈska:dys flœx]

The morning glory on dew drops:
Die môreglorie op druppels dou:
[di ˈmɔ:rəˌxlʊᵊri ɔp ˈdrœpəls dœu]

Your smile, darling, and your blue eyes!
Jou glimlag, liefste, en oë blou!
[jœu ˈxləmlax ˈlifstə ɛn ˈu:ə blœu]

If I were a singer my song would resound,
Was ek 'n sanger sou klink my lied,
[vas ɛk ə 'saŋər sœu kləŋk məj lit]

Empress Summer, over your kingdom!
Vorstinne Somer, oor u gebied!
[fɔr'stənə 'sʊᵊmər ʊᵊr y xə'bit]

A song of opulence, a crowning glory,
'n Lied van weelde,'n Son-sieraad,
[ə lit fan 've⁹ldə ə 'sɔn͜sira:t]

Of fields and gardens in bridal attire:
Van velde en tuine in bruidsgewaad:
[fan 'fæᵊldə ɛn 'tœynə ən 'brœytsxə͜va:t]

Your rosy cheeks oh darling mine,
Jou rose wange o liefste myn,
[jœu 'rʊᵊsə 'vaŋə ʊᵊ 'lifstə məjn]

Your soft lips incarnate!
Jou sagte lippe inkarnadyn!
[jœu 'saxtə 'ləpə ən'karnadəjn]

If I were a singer, over mountain and valley
Was ek 'n sanger, oor berg en dal
[vas ɛk ə 'saŋər ʊᵊr bærx en dal]

I would sing about autumn's riches before
leaves fall;
Sing'k najaarsrykdom eer blare val;
[səŋk 'na:ja:rs͜rəjkdɔm eᵊr 'bla:rə fal]

When all the trees are hanging full of fruit,
As al die bome vol vrugte hang,
[as al di 'bʊᵊmə fɔl 'frœxtə ɦaŋ]

The orchard echoes with birdsong —
Die boord weergalm van voëlsang —
[di bʊᵊrt veᵊr'xalm fan 'fʊᵊlsaŋ]

Afternoon bliss, free—light-hearted:
Namiddagvreugde, vry—onbeklem:
['na:͜mədax'frjøᵊxdə frəj ɔmbə'klɛm²⁸]

Your mature beauty, your sweet voice!
Jou rype skoonheid, jou soete stem!
[jœu 'rəjpə 'skʊᵊnɦəjt jœu 'sutə stɛm]

If I were a singer, as winter approaches
Was ek 'n sanger, as winter kom
[vas ɛk ə 'saŋər as 'vəntər kɔm]

I would sing of roses in full bloom!
Sou'k sing van rose in volle blom!
[sœuk səŋ fan 'rʊᵊsə ən 'fɔlə blɔm]

It's not only spring that brings beauty:
Dis nie net lente wat skoonheid bring:
[dəs ni nɛt 'lɛntə vat 'skʊᵊnɦəjt brəŋ]

The sweet evening-flower is a reminder!
Die aandblom²⁹ soet is herinnering!
[di 'a:ntblɔm sut əs ɦæ'rənərəŋ]

The fire within—becomes cold
outdoors, too,
Die vuur van binne—word buite ook koud
[di fy:r fan 'bənə vɔrt 'bœytə ʊᵊk kœut]

Glow then first brightly: your heart of gold!
Gloei dan eers helder: Jou hart van goud!
[xlui dan eᵊrs 'ɦæᵊldər jœu ɦart fan xœut]

---

[28] See Appendix G, Assimilation and Amalgamation of Consonants.

[29] The evening-flower *(Geophyte)* is a species of *Hesperanthus, Gladiolus, Freesia,* and *Iridacae.* It has soft hairy leaves and petals that range in color from dark purple, nearly black, to an occasional pale yellow. Found in various regions of the Western Cape Province, these flowers are very fragrant at nighttime. Their scent resembles cinnamon.

CORNELIUS FRANCOIS VISSER

(1882–1965)
aka C. F. Visser

I Love the Morning[1]
Ek hou van die Môre
[ɛk ɦœu fan di ˈmɔːrə]
Music: Johannes Joubert (1894–1958)

Which approaches with an erubescent and
radiant sun,
Wat nader van blosende, stralende son,
[vat ˈnaːdər fan ˈblʊᵊsəndə ˈstraːləndə sɔn]

Of love and life (from) the Father,
Van liefde en lewe die Vader,
[fan lifdə ɛn ˈleᵊvə di ˈfaːdər]

Oh wondrous source of light.
O wonderbaar ligtende bron.
[ʊᵊ ˈvɔndərbaːr ˈləxtəndə brɔn]

I adore the fields and ridges,
Ek hou van die velde en rande,
[ɛk ɦœu fan di ˈfæᵃldə ɛn ˈrandə]

Gently kissed by the morning sun's rays,
Deur môreson sag gekus,
[djøᵊr ˈmɔːrəsɔn sa xəˈkœs]

And far over the pastures and fields
En ver op die wei en die lande
[ɛn fæːr ɔp di vəj ɛn di ˈlandə]

The silence and blissful rest.
Die stilte en saalgerus.
[di ˈstəltə ɛn ˈsaːlxəˌrœs]

I like the clear spring days
Ek hou van die skoon lentedae
[ɛk ɦœu fan di skʊᵊn ˈlentəˌdaːə]

Decorated and adorned with flowers,
Met blomme versier en getooi,
[mɛt ˈblɔmə fərˈsiːr ɛn xəˈtoːj]

The world is brimming with contentment,
Die wêreld so vol selfbehae,
[di ˈvæːrəlt sʊᵊ fɔl ˈsæᵃlfbəˌɦaːə]

---

[1] Permission granted by the Federasie van Afrikaanse Kultuurvereniginge (FAK).

Afrikaans Art Song Literature. Christian Bester and Bronwen Forbay, Oxford University Press. © Oxford University Press 2025.
DOI: 10.1093/oso/9780197660812.003.0036

Life, so young and so beautiful.
Die lewe so jong en so mooi.
[di 'leᵊvə sʊᵊ jɔŋ ɛn sʊᵊ mo:j]

It's the time for longing,
Dis tyd van verlange,
[dəs təjt fan fər'laŋə]

For dreaming, that silently stirs within the soul.
Van drome, wat stil in die siel verrys.
[fan 'drʊᵊmə vat stəl ən di sil fə'rəjs]

Upon everything, streams of sunlight,
Op alles die sonlig in strome,
[ɔp 'aləs di 'sɔnləx ən 'strʊᵊmə]

And all around me one Paradise.
En om my een Paradys.
[ɛn ɔm məj eᵊn para'dəjs]

Come Dance Klaradyn[2]
Kom dans Klaradyn
[kɔm da:ns klara'dəjn]
Music: S. le Roux Marais (1896–1979)

Come dance Klaradyn, come and dance again with me,
Kom dans Klaradyn, kom en dans weer met my,
[kɔm da:ns klara'dəjn kɔm ɛn da:ns veᵊr met məj]

In time (tact) to the evening breeze that sways over the meadow,
Op maat van die aandwind wat wieg oor die wei,
[ɔp ma:t fan di 'a:ntvənt vat vix ʊᵊr di vəj]

The flowers invite us, the feast is ready
Die blomme hul nooi ons die feesmaal is klaar
[di 'blɔmə fiœl no:j ɔns di 'feᵊsma:l əs kla:r]

The little stars (are) all twinkling, the moon is already there.
Die sterretjies brand al, die maan is al daar.
[di 'stærikis brant al di ma:n əs al da:r]

Come dance Klaradyn, come dance Klaradyn,
Kom dans Klaradyn, kom dans Klaradyn,
[kɔm da:ns klara'dəjn kɔm da:ns klara'dəjn]

Come and dance again with me, again with me
Kom en dans weer met my, weer met my
[kɔm ɛn da:ns veᵊr met məj veᵊr met məj]

In time to the evening breeze that wafts over the meadow,
Op maat van die aandwind wat wieg oor die wei,
[ɔp ma:t fan di 'a:ntvənt vat vix ʊᵊr di vəj]

Come dance Klaradyn, come dance Klaradyn,
Kom dans Klaradyn, kom dans Klaradyn,
[kɔm da:ns klara'dəjn kɔm da:ns klara'dəjn]

---

[2] Permission granted by the Die Afrikaanse Volksang-en Volkspelebeweging.

Tell me Klaradyn, come and tell me
that you,
Vertel Klaradyn, kom vertel my dat jy,
[fər'tæl klara'dəjn kɔm fər'tæl məj dat jəj]

Will also remain the bridal queen of
my heart.
Die koningin bruid van my hart ook gaan bly.
[di kʊᵊnəŋ'xən brœyt fa məj hart ʊᵊk xa:n bləj][3]

Even if flowers wilt and the opulence
disappears,
As blomme verwelk en die weelde vergaan,
[as 'blɔmə fər'væᵊlk ɛn di 'veᵊldə fər'xa:n]

Even if stars fade and the moon dims.
As sterre verbleek en verduister die maan.
[as 'stærə fər'bleᵊk ɛn fər'dœystər di ma:n]

Tell me Klaradyn, tell me Klaradyn,
Vertel Klaradyn, vertel Klaradyn,
[fər'tæl klara'dəjn fər'tæl klara'dəjn]

Come and tell me that you, tell me that you
Kom vertel my dat jy, vertel my dat jy
[kɔm fər'tæl məj, fər'tæl məj dat jəj]

Will also remain the bridal queen of
my heart,
Die koningin bruid van my hart ook gaan bly,
[di kʊᵊnəŋ'xən brœyt fa məj[4] hart ʊᵊk
xa:n bləj]

Tell me Klaradyn, tell me Klaradyn
Vertel Klaradyn, vertel Klaradyn
[fər'tæl klara'dəjn fər'tæl klara'dəjn] ... etc.

Oh, (Beloved) Farmstead[5]

O, Boereplaas
[ʊᵊ 'bu:rəpla:s]
Music: Daniel Clement (1902–1980), "South Africa Onwards"
(*Suid-Afrika vorentoe, no. 5*) [sœyt 'a:frika 'fʊᵊrəntu]
Johannes Joubert (1894–1958)

Oh, (beloved) farmstead, native soil!
O, boereplaas, geboorte grond!
[ʊᵊ 'bu:rəpla:s xə'bʊᵊrtə xrɔnt]

I love you (dearly) above all.
Jou het ek lief bo alles.
[jœu ɦet ɛk lif bʊᵊ 'aləs]

Though I traverse the whole world,
Al dwaal ek heel die wêreld rond,
[al dwa:l ɛk ɦeᵊl di 'væ:rəlt rɔnt]

Where (can I find) more bliss, more
wholesomeness?
Waar so gelukkig, so gesond?
[va:r sʊᵊ xə'lœkəx sʊᵊ xə'sɔnt]

Oh my mother's house, where else so
at home?
O moederhuis, waar ooit so tuis?
[ʊᵊ 'mudərɦœys va:r o:jt sʊᵊ tœys]

---

[3] See Appendix G, Assimilation and Amalgamation of Consonants.
[4] Ibid.
[5] Permission granted by NB Publishers.

I love you (dearly) above all.
Jou het ek lief bo alles.
[jœu ɦɛt ɛk lif bʊᵊ 'aləs]

The world, its riches, pomp, and ceremony
Die wêreld, rykdom, prag en praal
[di 'væ:rəlt 'rəjkdɔm prax ɛn pra:l]

Can never repay me for your loss.
Kan jou verlies my nooit betaal.
[kan jœu fər'lis məj no:jt bə'ta:l]

Oh mother tongue, oh dulcet language!
O moedertaal, o soetste taal!
[ʊᵊ 'mudərta:l ʊᵊ 'sutstə ta:l]

I love you (dearly) above all.
Jou het ek lief bo alles.
[jœu ɦɛt ɛk lif bʊᵊ 'aləs]

Of all the languages that I hear,
Van al die tale wat ek hoor,
[fan al di 'ta:lə vat ɛk ɦʊᵊr]

Nothing enchants my soul like you.
Niks wat my siel ooit so bekoor.
[nəks vat məj sil o:jt sʊᵊ bə'kʊᵊr]

THEO WASSENAAR

(1892–1982)

Sea Sonnet[1]
See-Sonnet
[se^ə sɔˈnɛt]
Music: P. J. de Villiers (1924–2015)

Oh mighty ocean,
O magtige oseaan,
[ʊ^ə ˈmaxtəxə ʊ^əsiˈa:n]

You, far-flung,
Jy wyd gestrekte,
[jəj vəjt xəˈstræktə]

Encircled by the unfathomable,
Omsirkel deur die ongemetenheid,
[ɔmˈsərkəl djø^ər di ɔnxəˈme^ətənɦəjt]

Deep in your bosom
Diep in jou boesem
[dip ən jœu ˈbusəm]

Rests the undiscovered;
Rus die onontdekte;
[rœs di ɔnɔnˈdæktə]

Only your heavy heaving notices the time.
Alleen jou swaar gehyg verneem die tyd.
[aˈle^ən jœu swa:r xəˈɦəjx fərˈne^əm di təjt]

Oh inexhaustible sea
O nooitvermoeidesee
[ʊ^ə no:jtfərˈmuidəse^ə]

That continuously bustles,
Wat immerwoelend,
[vat ˈəmər̩ʋulənt]

Regulating tides by the course of the moon
Getye reël na gange van die maan
[xəˈtəjə re^əl na ˈxaŋə fan di ma:n]

And tempestuously washing by the voice of
the storm,
En op die storm se stem onstuimig spoelend,
[ɛn ɔp di ˈstɔrəm sə stɛm ɔnˈstœyməx
ˈspulənt]

Your waves break against the rocks!
Jou branders op die rotse stukkend slaan!
[jœu ˈbrandərs ɔp di ˈrɔtsə ˈstœkənt sla:n]

Oh never-ending swell of the Great and
Omnipotent!
O eew'ge deining van die Grote en Magt'ge!
[ʊ^ə ˈe^əvxə ˈdəjnəŋ fan di ˈxrʊ^ətə ɛn ˈmaxtxə]

So surges the broad strong stream
So dein die breed sterk stroom
[sʊ^ə dəjn di bre^ət stærk strʊ^əm]

---

[1] Permission granted by NB Publishers.

Afrikaans Art Song Literature. Christian Bester and Bronwen Forbay, Oxford University Press. © Oxford University Press 2025.
DOI: 10.1093/oso/9780197660812.003.0037

Of a full life in my little heart.
Van volle lewe in my klein hart.
[fan 'fɔlə 'leᵊvə ən məj kləjn ɦart]

I the most insignificant crystal,
Ek nietigste kristal,
[ɛk 'nitəxstə krə'stal]

May also play with the resplendence
Ek mag ook speel met glans
[ɛk max ʊᵊk speᵊl mɛt xlans]

Of the eternal beauty (Paradise).
Van die ewigpragt'ge.
[fan di 'eᵊvəxˌpraxtxə]

The Creation has also given me its purpose:
Die skepping het ook my sy doel gegewe:
[di 'skɛpəŋ ɦɛt ʊᵊk məj səj dul xə'xeᵊvə]

One pulse beating in the rhythm of the universe!
Een polsslag in die ritme van die heelal!
[eᵊn 'pɔlslax ən di 'rətmə fan di 'ɦeᵊlal]

C. H. WEICH

(1892–1973)

Song Cycle for Soprano and Piano[1]
Sangsiklus vir Sopraan en Klavier
['saŋˌsikləs fər su'pra:n ɛn kla'fi:r]
Music: Blanche Gerstman (1910–1973)

I Barely Know You
1. *Ek ken jou skaars*
[ɛk kɛn jœu ska:rs]

I barely know you,
Ek ken nou skaars,
[ɛk kɛn jœu ska:rs]

And yet I, early this morning
En tog het ek vanoggend nog vroeg
[ɛn tɔx fiɛt ɛk fan'ɔxənt nɔx frux]

Before the first dew drops vanished
Voor die eerste druppels dou verdwyn het
[fʊ°r di 'e°rstə 'drœpəls dœu fər'dwəjn fiɛt]

All my love and fidelity
Al my liefde trou
[al məj 'lifdə trœu]

Poured out in silence before you:
In stilte uitgestort voor jou:
[ən 'stəltə 'œytxəˌstɔrt fʊ°r jœu]

Quietly kneeling,
Stil neergekniel,
[stəl 'ne°rxəˌknil]

And softly asked, that God may grant me the strength
En sag gevra, dat God my krag mag gee
[ɛn sa xə'fra:[2] dat xɔt məj krax max çe°]

To make you understand;
Om jou te laat verstaan;
[ɔm jœu tə la:t fər'sta:n]

The love that exists in my soul that will never perish!
Die sieleliefde wat bestaan om nimmer te vergaan!
[di 'siləˌlifdə vat bə'sta:n ɔm 'nəmər tə fər'xa:n]

---

[1] Permission granted by the Federasie van Afrikaanse Kultuurvereniginge (FAK).
[2] See Appendix G, Assimilation and Amalgamation of Consonants.

Afrikaans Art Song Literature. Christian Bester and Bronwen Forbay, Oxford University Press. © Oxford University Press 2025.
DOI: 10.1093/oso/9780197660812.003.0038

238   AFRIKAANS ART SONG LITERATURE

I Know You Now
2. *Ek ken jou nou*
[ɛk kɛn jœu nœu]

I know you now, but alas,
Ek ken jou nou, maar ag,
[ɛk kɛn jœu nœu ma:r ax]

It's as if my soul longs for those first
blissful days,
Dis of my siel so smag na daardie eerste
vreugdedae,
[dəs ɔf məj sil sʊᵊ smax na 'da:rdi 'eᵊrstə
'frjøᵊxdəˌda:ə]

When you, so gorgeous, were dumbfounded
by my overzealous romantic questions.
Toe jy, so wonderskoon verslae was oor my
strenge liefdesvrae.
[tu jəj sʊᵊ 'vɔndərskʊᵊn fər'sla: vas ʊᵊr məj
'strɛŋə 'lifdəsˌfra:ə]

Now I love you,
Nou min ek jou,
[nœu mən ɛk jœu]

And you, so ice-cold, are happy over your
victory.
En jy so yskoud is bly oor jou oorwinning.
[ɛn jəj sʊᵊ 'əjskœut əs bləj ʊᵊr jœu ʊᵊr'vənəŋ]

Though you will, I know it
Dog jy sal, ek weet dit
[dɔx jəj sal ɛk veᵊt dət]

And I feel it already,
En ek voel dit al,
[ɛn ɛk ful dət al]

You will still love me!
Jy sal my nog bemin!
[jəj sal məj nɔx bə'mən]

You will!
Jy sal!
[jəj sal]

Why?
3. *Waarom?*
[va:r'ɔm]

You came to rescue my soul from its grief,
Jy't gekom om my siel uit sy smart te haal,
[jəjt xə'kɔm ɔm məj sil œyt səj smart tə ɦa:l]

To soften my heart, so depraved.
Om my hart, so ontaard, te versag.
[ɔm məj ɦart sʊᵊ ɔnt'a:rt tə fər'sax]

You came with a soul like a sun beam,
Jy't gekom met 'n siel soos 'n sonnestraal,
[jəjt xə'kɔm mɛt ə sil sʊᵊs ə 'sɔnəstra:l]

That illuminates after a pitch-dark night.
Wat verlig na 'n stikdonkernag.
[vat fər'ləx na ə 'stəkˌdɔŋkərnax]

I am intoxicated, oh so intoxicated with
love's wine,
Ek is dronk, o so dronk van die liefdeswyn,
[ɛk əs drɔŋk ʊᵊ sʊᵊ drɔŋk fan di 'lifdəsvəjn]

I am blinded by the luster of your soul.
Van die glans van jou siel is ek blind.
[fan di xlans fan jœu sil əs ɛk blənt]

You enchant me, you stupefy me when
you appear
Jy bekoor my, bedwelm my as jy verskyn
[jəj bə'kʊᵊr məj bə'dwæᵊlm məj as jəj
fər'skəjn]

Binding me tighter and tighter (to you).
Om my vaster en vaster te bind.
[ɔm məj 'fastər ɛn 'fastər tə bənt]

You came, but how short-lived was the
blissful delight,
Jy't gekom, maar hoe kort was die vreuggenot,
[jəjt xə'kɔm ma:r ɦu kɔrt vas di 'frjøᵊxəˌnɔt]

That love was nothing but a farce.
Daardie liefde was alles maar skyn.
['da:rdi 'lifdə vas 'aləs ma:r skəjn]

You came, and now I ask you:
Jy't gekom, en nou vra ek:
[jəjt xə'kɔm ɛn nœu fra: ɛk]

"Why? oh God!
"Waarom? o God!
[va:r'ɔm ʊᵊ xɔt]

She came only to leave again."
Sy't gekom net om weer te verdwyn."
[səjt xə'kɔm nɛt ɔm veᵊr tə fər'dwəjn]

ANONYMOUS

A Lullaby
Sluimerlied
['slœymərlit]
Music: S. le Roux Marais (1896–1979)

Cradle me while slumbering, oh night wind,
Wieg my in sluimer, o wind van die nag,
[vix məj ən 'slœymər ʋᵊ vənt fan di nax]

Forgotten (are) the worries and woes of
the day,
Vergete die sorge en wee van die dag,
[fər'xeᵊtə di 'sɔrgə ɛn veᵊ fan di dax]

Weary are my hands, and mournful
my heart;
Moeg is my hande, en treurend my hart;
[mux əs məj 'ɦandə ɛn 'trjøᵊrənt məj 'ɦart]

Lonesome (is) my life, and dark my grief.
Eensaam my lewe, en donker my smart.
['eᵊnsa:m məj 'leᵊvə ɛn 'dɔŋkər məj smart]

Far away are the mountains and valleys
of peace,
Ver is die berge en vlaktes van rus,
[fæ:r əs di 'bærgə ɛn 'flaktəs fan rœs]

And far away lull the waves of
eternity's shore.
En ver sus die golwe van ewigheidskus.
[ɛn fæ:r sœs di 'xɔlvə fan 'eᵊvəxɦəjtskœs]

Afrikaans Art Song Literature. Christian Bester and Bronwen Forbay, Oxford University Press. © Oxford University Press 2025.
DOI: 10.1093/oso/9780197660812.003.0039

BIBLICAL TEXTS

Nehemia

If I Have to Perish, Beloved
As ek moet sterwe, liefste
[as ɛk mut ˈstærvə]
Music: S. le Roux Marais (1896–1979), "New Songs" (*Nuwe Liedere, no. 8*)
[ˈnyvə ˈlidərə]

If I have to perish, beloved,
As ek moet sterwe, liefste,
[as ɛk mut ˈstærvə ˈlifstə]

Lay a wreath on my grave
Lê op my graf 'n krans
[lɛː ɔp məj xraf ə kraːns]

With (the) color of blue cyan,
Met kleur van blou siane,
[mɛt kljøˀr fan blœu siˈaːnə]

And starlight of the firmament.
En sterlig van die trans.
[ɛn ˈstærləx fan di traːns]

Shed no tears over me beloved,
Stort oor my lief geen trane,
[stɔrt ʊˀr məj lif çeˀn ˈtraːnə]

Let joy reign supreme.
Laat blydskap hoogty vier.
[laːt ˈbləjtskap ˈfiʊˀxtəj fiːr]

And let me rest in peace,
En laat my rus in vrede,
[ɛn laːt məj rœs ən ˈfreˀdə]

After my final hour.
Ná my bestemmingsuur.
[ˈnaː məj bəˈstɛməŋsyːr]

All I ask are flowers,
Al wat ek vra is blomme,
[al vat ɛk fraː əs ˈblɔmə]

A wreath of beautiful roses,
'n Krans van rose skoon,
[ə kraːns fan ˈrʊˀsə skʊˀn]

So that always, over my resting place,
Dat altyd oor my rusplek,
[dat ˈaltəjt ʊˀr məj ˈrœsplæk]

The perfume of spring (may) live.
Die geur van lente woon.
[di xjøˀr fan ˈlɛntə vʊˀn]

Afrikaans Art Song Literature. Christian Bester and Bronwen Forbay, Oxford University Press. © Oxford University Press 2025.
DOI: 10.1093/oso/9780197660812.003.0040

Psalms

In the Lord I Take Refuge
Ek skuil by die Here
[ɛk skœyl bəj di 'ɦeᵊrə]
Words: Psalm XI
Music: P. J. de Villiers (1924–2015), "Four Songs of Doubt and Faith"
(*Vier Liedere van Twyfel en Geloof, no. 2*) [fiːr 'lidərə fan'twəjfəl ɛn xə'lʊᵊf]

In the Lord I take refuge
Ek skuil by die Here
[ɛk skœyl bəj di 'ɦeᵊrə]

How dare you say to me:
Hoe durf julle vir my sê:
[ɦu dœrf 'jœlə fər məj sɛ:]

"Flee to the mountains like a bird!
"Vlug na die berge toe soos 'n voël!
[flœx na di 'bærgə tu sʊᵊs ə 'fʊᵊl]

(For) Look, the ungodly bend their bows;
Kyk, die goddeloses span hulle boë;
[ləjk di xɔdə'lʊᵊsəs span 'ɦœlə 'bu:ə]

And they place their arrow upon the string;
En hulle lê aan met die pyl op die snaar;
[ɛn 'ɦœlə lɛ: a:n mɛt di pəjl ɔp di sna:r]

They stand ready, out of the darkness
Hulle staan reg om uit die donker
['ɦœlə sta:n ræx ɔm œyt di 'dɔŋkər]

To pierce the righteous of heart.
Die opregtes van hart te tref.
[di ɔp'ræxtəs fan ɦar təˡ trɛf]

As the foundations are undermined
As die fondamente ondermyn word
[as di fɔnda'mɛntə ɔndər'məjn vɔrt]

What can the righteous do about it?"
Wat kan die regverdige daaraan doen?"
[vat kan di ræx'færdəxə 'da:ra:n dun]

The Lord is in His holy temple!
Die Here is in sy heilige tempel!
[di 'ɦeᵊrə əs ən səj 'ɦəjləxə 'tɛmpəl]

The Lord is on His throne in the heavens!
Die Here is op sy troon in die hemel!
[di 'ɦeᵊrə əs ɔp səj trʊᵊn ən di 'ɦeᵊməl]

His eyes are open
Sy oë is oop
[səj 'u:ə əs ʊᵊp]

His eyes judge the children of men.
Sy oë keur die mensekinders.
[səj 'u:ə kjøᵊr di 'mɛnsə‚kəndərs]

---

[1] See Appendix G, Assimilation and Amalgamation of Consonants.

The Lord distinguishes between the righteous and unrighteous.
Die Here onderskei tussen regverdige en goddelose.
[di 'fieᵊrə ɔndər'skəj 'tœsən ræx'færdəxə ɛn xɔdə'lʊᵊsə]

Those who love violence, He hates.
Wie geweld liefhet, haat Hy.
[vi xə'væᵊlt 'lifɦet 'fia:t ɦəj]

He rains down fire and sulfur on the ungodly,
Hy laat vuur en swael reën op die goddeloses,
[ɦəj la:t fy:r ɛn 'swa:l reᵊn ɔp di xɔdə'lʊᵊsəs]

A scorching wind: that is the chalice that they shall drink.
'n Skroeiende wind: dit is die beker wat hulle sal drink.
[ə 'skruiəndə vənt dət əs di 'beᵊkər vat 'ɦœlə sal drəŋk]

The Lord is righteous.
Die Here is regverdig.
[di 'fieᵊrə əs ræx'færdəx]

He loves those who are righteous and upright in their dealings,
Hy het die mense lief wat regverdig en opreg handel,
[ɦəj ɦet di 'mɛnsə lif vat ræx'færdəx ɛn ɔp'ræx 'ɦandəl]

And He will dwell with them.
En Hy sal by hulle wees.
[ɛn ɦəj sal bəj 'ɦœlə veᵊs]

You Forgave My Debt
U het my Skuld vergewe
[y ɦet məj skœlt fər'xeᵊvə]
Words: Psalm XXXII

Music: P. J. de Villiers (1924–2015), "Four Songs of Doubt and Faith" (*Vier Liedere van Twyfel en Geloof, no. 4*) [fi:r 'lidərə fan'twəjfəl ɛn xə'lʊᵊf]

Blessed is the man
Dit gaan goed met die mens
[dət xa:n xut mɛ di² mɛns]

Who is not punished for their sin,
Wie se oortredings nie gestraf word nie,
[vi sə ʊᵊr'treᵊdəŋs ni xə'straf vɔrt ni]

Whose transgressions are forgiven.
Wie se sondes vergewe word.
[vi sə 'sɔndəs fər'xeᵊvə vɔrt]

Blessed is the man
Dit gaan goed met die mens
[dət xa:n xut mɛt di mɛns]

---

[2] See Appendix G, Assimilation and Amalgamation of Consonants.

Unto whom the Lord does not impute for his iniquity
Vir wie die Here die oortreding nie toereken nie
[fər vi di 'fie³rə di ʊ³r'tre³dəŋ ni 'ture³kən ni]

And in whose spirit there is no duplicity.
En in wie se gees daar geen valsheid meer is nie.
[ɛn ən vi sə çe³s da:r çe³n 'falsfiəjt me³r əs ni]

When I kept silent about my sin,
Toe ek oor my sonde geswyg het,
[tu ɛk ʊ³r məj 'sɔndə xə'swəjx fiɛt]

My body was emaciated
Het my liggaam uitgeteer
[fiɛt məj 'ləxa:m 'œytxə̩te³r]

From calling for help all day long.
Soos ek heeldag om hulp geroep het.
[sʊ³s ɛk 'fie³ldax ɔm fiœlp xə'rup fiɛt]

Thy hand day and night
U hand het dag en nag
[y fiant fiɛt dax ɛn nax]

Pressed heavily upon me,
Swaar op my gedruk,
[swa:r ɔp məj xə'drœk]

My strength dried up
My krag het opgedroog
[məj krax fiɛt 'ɔpxə̩drʊ³x]

Like water in summer heat.
Soos water in somerhitte.
[sʊ³s 'va:tər ən 'sʊ³mər̩fiətə]

Then I confessed my sin,
Toe het ek my sonde bely,
[tu fiɛt ɛk məj 'sɔndə bə'ləj]

I did not hide my transgressions.
My oortreding nie weggesteek nie.
[məj ʊ³r'tre³dəŋ ni 'væxə̩ste³k ni]

I said:
Ek het gesê:
[ɛk fiɛt xə'sɛ:]

"Before the Lord, I confess my rebelliousness"
"Voor die Here bely ek my opstandigheid"
[fʊ³r di 'fie³rə bə'ləj ɛk məj ɔp'standəxfiəjt]

And You forgave my sin
En U het my skuld vergewe
[ɛn y fiɛt məj skœlt fər'xe³və]

That is why every believer
Dit is waarom elke gelowige
[dət əs 'va:rɔm 'æ³lkə xə'lʊ³vəxə]

In a time of need, prays to You;
In 'n tyd van nood tot U bid;
[ən ə təjt fan nʊ³t tɔt y bət]

Not even floodwaters shall suddenly overcome him.
Selfs vloedwaters sal hom nie skielik oorval nie.
[sæ³lfs 'flutɣa:tərs sal fiɔm ni 'skilək ʊ³r'fal ni]

You are for me, a refuge,
U is vir my 'n skuilplek,
[y əs fər məj ə 'skœylplæk]

You guard me against onslaughts,
U beskerm my teen aanvalle,
[y bə'skærm məj te³n 'a:nfalə]

You let me sing songs of victory.
U laat my oorwinningsliedere sing.
[y laːt məj ʊᵊrˈvənəŋsˌlidərə səŋ]

Rejoice in the Lord and be glad, ye righteous,
Verbly julle in die Here en juig, regverdiges,
[fərˈbləj ˈjœlə ən di ˈɦeᵊrə ɛn jœyx ræxˈfærdəxəs]

Shout for joy, all (you) righteous.
Jubel, alle opregtes.
[ˈjybəl ˈalə ɔpˈræxtəs]

BIBLIOGRAPHY

Afrikaanse Taal en Kultuurvereeniginge (ATKV). *2011 Musiqanto Classical Voice Competition English Brochure*. Randburg (Gauteng): ATKV, 2011.

Bester, Christian. "The Influence of Indigenous Bushmen Musical Elements and Significant Compositional Traits on Niel Van Der Watt's Song Cycle, Die Wind Dreun Soos 'n Ghoera, 'n Siklus Boesman-Mites." Dissertation (D.M.A.), University of North Texas, 2014. https://digital.library.unt.edu/ark:/67531/metadc699878/ (accessed July 14, 2024).

Bester, Christian, and Bronwen Forbay. "An Introduction to Afrikaans Art Songs: A Guide to Lyric Diction." *Journal of Singing* 78, no. 4 (2022): 497–506. https://doi.org/10.53830/tstu7 308 (accessed July 14, 2024).

———. "An Introduction to Afrikaans Art Song Literature: Origins and Repertoire." *Journal of Singing* 78, no. 4 (2022): 471–482. https://doi.org/10.53830/qxmd1468 (accessed July 14, 2024).

Bouws, Jan. *Die Volkslied, Deel van ons Erfenis*. Kaapstad: Human & Rousseau, 1969.

———. *Die Afrikaanse Volkslied*. Johannesburg: Voortrekkerpers Bpk. (FAK), 1957.

———. *Komponiste van Suid-Afrika*. Stellenbosch: Albertyn (C.F.), 1971.

———. "Sestig Jaar Afrikaanse Kunslied (1908–1968) deur Jan Bouws." In *Tydskrif vir Geesteswetenskappe* 9, no. 1. Pretoria: Suid-Afrikaanse Akademie vir Wetenskap en Kuns, March 1969: 68–80.

———. *Solank daar Musiek is … Musiek en musiekmakers in Suid-Afrika (1652–1982)*. Kaapstad: Tafelberg-Uitgewers Beperk, 1982.

———. *Suid-Afrikaanse Komponiste van Vandag en Gister*. Kaapstad: A.A. Balkema, 1957.

———. *Woord en Wys van die Afrikaanse Lied*. Kaapstad: H.A.U.M., 1961.

Brukman, Jeffrey. "Aspects of Musical Modernism: The Afrikaans Song Cycles of Cromwell Everson." *Journal of the Musical Arts in Africa* 8, no. 1 (2012): 1–21. https://doi.org: 10.2989/18121004.2011.652353 (accessed July 14, 2024).

Burgers, M. P. O. *Teach Yourself Afrikaans*. London: English Universities Press, 1957.

Combrink, J. G. H., and L. G. De Stadler. *Afrikaanse Fonologie*. Johannesburg: Macmillan Suid-Afrika, 1987.

Cupido, Conroy. "Significant Influences in the Composition of Hendrik Hofmeyr's Song Cycle, Alleenstryd." Dissertation (D.M.A.), University of North Texas, 2009. Academia.edu, September 28, 2021. https://www.academia.edu/53707861 (accessed July 14, 2024).

Donaldson, Bruce. "Afrikaans." In *The Germanic Languages*, edited by Johan van der Auwera and Ekkehard König. New York: Routledge, 1994, 478–504.

———. *Colloquial Afrikaans: The Complete Course for Beginners*. London: Routledge, 2000.

———. *A Grammar of Afrikaans*. Mouton de Gruyter. Berlin; New York, 1993.

248   BIBLIOGRAPHY

Du Plessis, Madaleine, Fred Pheiffer, Wanda Smith-Müller, and Jana Luther. *Pharos Afrikaans-Engels, Engels-Afrikaans Woordeboek.* Kaapstad: Pharos Dictionaries, 2005.

Ferguson, Howard. "Arnold Van Wyk." In *Composers in South Africa Today*, edited by Peter Klatzow. Cape Town: Oxford University Press, 1987, 1–31.

Forbay, Bronwen Michelle. "Afrikaans Art Song: A Stylistic Study and Performance Guide." Dissertation (D.M.A.), University of Cincinnati, 2011. http://rave.ohiolink.edu/etdc/view?acc_num=ucin1307322705 (accessed July 14, 2024).

Gerber, Marelize. *'n Kritiese Waardebepaling van Mimi Coertse (1932–) se bydrae tot die Uitvoering van die Afrikaanse Kunslied.* Thesis (M. Mus.), University of South Africa, 2005.

Graaff-Reinet, Gem of the Karoo. "Graaff Reinet: Richly Imbued with History, Nature & Beauty." http://www.graaffreinet.co.za/ (accessed April 15, 2011).

Grové, I. J. *Arnold van Wyk, 1916–1983: Opstelle oor sy lewe en werk.* Bloemfontein: Universiteit van die Oranje Vrystaat, 1984.

Grové, I. J., Elna Van der Merwe, Minette Du Toit-Pearce, André Howard, and Vanessa TaitJones. *'n Eeu van Afrikaanse liedkuns.* South Africa: s.n., 2009.

Haarhoff, T. J. *Afrikaans, Its Origins and Development: Lectures Delivered Before the University of Oxford on the 19th and 20th February, 1936.* Oxford: Clarendon Press, 1936.

Holzapfel, Helmut. *Die Liedere van S. le Roux Marais: 'n Geannoteerde Katalogus.* Thesis (D. Phil.), Universiteit van Stellenbosch, 1992.

Kannemeyer, Johan Christoffel. *A History of Afrikaans Literature: Die Beiteltjie.* Pietermaritzburg: Shuter and Shooter (Pty) Ltd., 1993.

Kimberley, South Africa. "What Kimberley, South Africa, Has to Offer." http://www.bdb.co.za/kimberley/ (accessed July 14, 2024).

Klatzow, Peter. *Composers in South Africa Today.* Cape Town: Oxford University Press, 1987.

Kotzé, Ernst F. *Essential English-Afrikaans Dictionary (Based on the Afrikaans-Japannese Woordeboek met Engelse Vertalings).* n.d.

Kotzé, Ernst F., and Cor de Ruyter. "Oor Austro-Nederlands en die oorsprong van Afrikaans." *Literator* 23, no. 3 (November 2002): 139–160.

Kotzé, Ernst F., and Takashi Sakurai. *Afrikaans-Japannese Woordeboek met Engelse vertalings.* Tokyo: Institute for the Study of Languages and Cultures of Asia and Africa, 2001.

Kritzinger, Matthys Stephanus Benjamin. *Groot Woordeboek: Afrikaans-Engels*, 13th ed. Edited by L. C. Eksteen, M. S. B. Kritzinger, P. C. Schoonees, and U. J. Cronje. Pretoria: J. L. van Schaik, 1986.

Kromhout, Jan., Matthys Stefanus Benjamin Kritzinger, and H. A. Steyn. *Skoolwoordeboek: Afrikaans-Engels—School Dictionary: English-Afrikaans.* Kaapstad: Pharos, 2004.

Lange, Margreet de. *The Muzzled Muse: Literature and Censorship in South Africa.* Amsterdam: John Benjamins, 1997.

Language (Magazine). "Sign Officially Becomes South Africa's 12th Language." https://www.languagemagazine.com/2023/10/16/sign-officially-becomes-south-africas-12th-language/ (accessed July 10, 2024).

Leipoldt, Christiaan Louis, and compiler Anna Bender, *So Sing ook die Hart: Getoonsette verse van C. Louis Leipoldt/versamel deur Anna Bender in opdrag*. Johannesburg: Dalro, 1980.

Le Roux, T. H., and P. De Villiers Pienaar. *Uitspraakwoordebook Van Afrikaans*, 4th ed. Pretoria: J. L. Van Schaik Publishers, 1971.

Lockwood, W. B. *An Informal History of the German Language: With Chapters on Dutch and Afrikaans, Frisian and Yiddish*. London: Andre Deutsch, 1976.

Lucia, Christine. *The World of South African Music: A Reader*. Newcastle-upon-Tyne: Cambridge Scholars, 2005.

Lutrin, Beryl. *Afrikaans Handbook and Study Guide: An English Student's Guide to Afrikaans*. 3rd ed. Birnam Park, South Africa: Berlut Books, 1999.

Malan, Jacques P. *South African Music Encyclopedia*, Vol. 1, *A–D*. Cape Town: Oxford University Press, 1979.

———. *South African Music Encyclopedia*, Vol. 2, *E–I*. Cape Town: Oxford University Press, 1982.

———. *South African Music Encyclopedia*, Vol. 3, *J–O*. Cape Town: Oxford University Press, 1984.

———. *South African Music Encyclopedia*, Vol. 4, *P–Z*. Cape Town: Oxford University Press, 1986.

Marais, S. le Roux. *Heimwee*. Kaapstad: R. Müller, 1930.

———. *Geboorte van die Lente*. Kaapstad: R. Müller, 1932.

———. *Kom dans Klaradyn*. Kaapstad: R. Müller, 1935.

———. *Lentelied*. Kaapstad: R. Müller, 1936.

———. *Rooidag*. Johannesburg: FAK, 1970.

May, James. "Some Aspects of Unity in Arnold van Wyk's Works Between 1940 and 1952." *Musicus* 24, no. 1 (1996): 92–98.

———. "Pitch Organization in Hendrik Hofmeyr's Alleenstryd." *South African Journal of Musicology* 23 (2003): 43–53. http://hdl.handle.net/11427/21523 (accessed on July 12, 2024).

Muller, Stephanus. "Apartheid Aesthetics and Insignificant Art." *Journal of Musicology* 33, no. 1 (2016): 45–69. https://doi.org/10.1525/jm.2016.33.1.45 (accessed July 14, 2024).

Pescod, John K. *Oktobermaand: A Tribute to Mimi* (hand-written score), 1925.

Ponelis, Friedrich Albert. *The Development of Afrikaans*. Frankfurt am Main: P. Lang, 1993.

Potgieter, Johann Hendrik. *'n Analitiese Oorsig van die Afrikaanse Kunslied met klem op die werke van Nepgen, Van Wyk en du Plessis*. Proefskrif (D.Mus.), Universiteit van Pretoria, 1967.

———. "Die Afrikaanse liedere van Arnold Van Wyk." In *Arnold Van Wyk, 1916–1983: Opstelle oor sy lewe en werk*, edited by I. J. Grové. Bloemfontein: Universiteit van die Oranje-Vrystaat (1984), 78–83.

South Africa.info: Gateway to the Nation. "The Eleven Languages of South Africa." https://southafrica-info.com/arts-culture/11-languages-south-africa/ (accessed July 13, 2024).

South African History Online. "The Cape Malay." https://www.sahistory.org.za/article/cape-malay (accessed July 1, 2024).Statistics South Africa. "Census 2022." https://census.statssa.gov.za/#. (accessed January 2, 2025).

Van Blerk, M. E.. *Afrikaanse Verklarende Musiekwoordeboek*. Kaapstad: Vlaeberg Uitgewers, 1994.

Van der Merwe, C. N. *Breaking Barriers: Stereotypes and the Changing of Values in Afrikaans Writing 1875–1990*. Amsterdam: Rodopi, 1994.

Van Rensburg, Christo, and Achmat Davids. *Afrikaans in Afrika*. Pretoria: J. L. van Schaik, 1997.

Van Schalkwyk, Helena. *Afrikaans*. Chicago: NTC Publishing Group, 1992.

Van Wyk, Arnold. *Van Liefde en Verlatenheid. Von Liebe und Verlassenheit. Of Love and Forsakenness*. London: Boosey & Hawkes, 1956.

———. *Vier Weemoedige Liedjies*. Amsterdam: Heuwekemeijer, 1947.

Villiers, Pieter de. *Boerneef sing: Komposisies van Uitgesoekte verse: 10 siklusse*. Pretoria: Litera, 2004.

Walton, C. R. "Bond of *Broeders*: Anton Hartman and Music in an Apartheid State." *Musical Times* 145, no.1887 (2004): 63–74.

Walton, Chris. "Composing Africa: Stefans Grové at 85." *The Musical Times* 148, no. 1899 (2007): 19. https://doi.org/10.2307/25434455 (accessed July 14, 2024).

Wet, Wouter de. Liner notes and CD, *Onse Mimi* [Our Mimi]. Mimi Coertse (soprano), Hennie Joubert (piano), Pieter de Villiers (piano), Albie Van Schalkwyk (piano), National Symphony Orchestra of the SABC, Richard Cock (director). Johannesburg: BMG Records, Africa. 1999. CDCLA (WM) 001.

Wissing, Daan. "Afrikaans Phonology Segment Inventory Lists." Category: Afrikaans Phonology, Version: 1.0, May 2020. https://taalportaal.org/taalportaal/topic/pid/topic-14610909940908011 (accessed April 10, 2024).

Appendix A
MUSICAL ANTHOLOGIES

F. A. K. Kunsliedbundel. Johannesburg: Federasie van Afrikaanse Kultuurvereniginge, 1984. (ISBN: 0620065206, 9780620065207).

Goue Gerf—Nasionale Raad vir Volksang en Volkspele. Germiston, 1970. (OCLC: 216931220).

Kersliedere uit Suid-Afrika. Compiled by Jo Ross, Voortrekkerpers, 1967. (OCLC: 664600224).

Liefdeswee—'n Keur van Afrikaanse Kunsliedere. Anna Bender-Brink, Johannesburg: DALRO en SAMRO, 1983. (ISBN 086964440, 9780869644447).

Sing sag menig' lied—'n Versameling toonsettings van die verse van A. G. Visser, Johannesburg: DALRO, 1978. (ISBN: 0869642707, 9780869642702).

So sing ook die hart—Getoonsette verse van C. Louis Leipoldt. Anna Bender, Johannesburg: DALRO 1980. (ISBN: 0869642626, 9780869642627; OCLC 1102726591).

Appendix B

RESOURCES FOR OBTAINING MUSICAL SCORES

Dramatic, Artistic and Literary Rights Organization (DALRO): https://dalro.co.za (accessed on July 14, 2024).

Furman University Maxwell Music Library: https://libguides.furman.edu/music/home (accessed on July 14, 2024).

National Afrikaans Literary Museum and Research Centre of South Africa: https://www.sacr.fs.gov.za/?page_id=4017 and https://museumexplorer.co.za/national-afrikaans-literary-museum-and-research-centre/ (accessed on July 14, 2024).

North-West University Music Library: https://libguides.nwu.ac.za/music (accessed on July 14, 2024).

South African Music Rights Organization (SAMRO): https://www.samro.org.za (accessed on July 14, 2024).

Stellenbosch University Music Library: https://libguides.sun.ac.za/music (accessed on July 14, 2024).

University of KwaZulu-Natal: https://libguides.ukzn.ac.za/c.php?g=771188 (accessed on July 14, 2024).

University of Pretoria Music Library: https://library.up.ac.za/music (accessed on July 14, 2024).

University of South Africa: https://libguides.sun.ac.za/SAMusicCollections/UNISA (accessed on July 14, 2024).

Worldcat.org: https://search.worldcat.org/ (accessed on July 14, 2024).

Appendix C

SOUND RECORDINGS: A DISCOGRAPHY

Aan blomme [To flowers]. Ina Snyman (soprano), Anna Bender (piano). Pretoria: Musica Activa Trust. 1981. (OCLC Number: 638656634). https://youtu.be/NWRszz3yvL0?si=03C-uLBAA3YVMgxF (accessed on July 14, 2024).

Afrikaanse Kunsliedfees [Afrikaans Art Song Festival] 28 en [and] 30 Mei [May] 1983. Dawie Couzyn, Werner Nel (baritones); Rina Hugo, Ina Snyman, Hanna van Niekerk (sopranos); Hester Stander (mezzo-soprano), Evelyn Green, Truida van der Walt, Pieter de Villiers, Anna Bender, Heinrich van der Mescht, Derik van der Merwe (piano). Musaion, Pretoria: Universiteit van Pretoria Kultuurburo. 1983. (OCLC Number: 660092513).

Alleenstryd—Ses Gedigte deur SV Petersen, vir bariton en klavier [Lonely struggle/outcast—Six poems by SV Petersen, for baritone and piano] 2. *Die veles* [The many]. André Howard (baritone) and Hendrik Hofmeyr (composer and piano). https://www.youtube.com/watch?v=qubssBoNDiE (accessed on July 14, 2024). 4. *Kinderland* [The land of children]. André Howard (baritone) and Hendrik Hofmeyr (composer and piano). https://www.youtube.com/watch?v=PGOMCI6a_mM&list=PLTKGF-LiWgsuSvrlbAiMOnhwlloKmqnId&index=4 (accessed on July 14, 2024).

Bronwyn Basson Sing Twee Liedere van S. le Roux Marais "Rus en Stilte" [Bronwyn Basson sings two songs by S. le Roux Marais "Rest and Stillness"]. Bronwyn Basson (soprano), Diane Coutts (piano). https://www.youtube.com/watch?v=OSkf8pQehQg (accessed on July 14, 2024).

Bronwyn Basson Sing Twee Liedere van S. le Roux Marais [Bronwyn Basson sings two songs by S. le Roux Marais], *As ek moet sterwe liefste* [If I have to perish, beloved], *Dit is laat in die nag* [It is late in the night]. Bronwyn Basson (soprano), Diane Coutts (piano). https://www.youtube.com/watch?v=ANpXYeLD-Gg&list=RDOSkf8pQehQg&index=4 (accessed on July 14, 2024).

Die Afrikaanse Lied: Historiese SAUK-opnames deur Suid-Afrikaanse sangers [The Afrikaans art song: Historic SABC-recordings by South African singers]. Sydney Richfield, Walter Spiethoff, P. J. Lemmer, Dirkie De Villiers, Theo Wendt, Ernest Lowenherz, S. le Roux Marais, Gawie Fagan, Mornay Du Plessis, M. L. De Villiers, Arthur Ellis, C. G. S. De Villiers, Emiel Hullebroeck (composers), Anton Hartman (conductor), Arnold Van Wyk (piano), Cecilia Wessels (soprano), Dirk Lourens (tenor), Albina Bini (soprano), Louis Knobel (baritone), Betsy De la Porte (soprano), Stephen H. Eyssen (baritone), Jean Gluckman (mezzo-soprano), Gladys Hugo (soprano), David Tidboald (conductor), Jossie Boshoff (soprano), Anna Bender-Brink (piano), Pieter De Villiers (piano). Johannesburg: South African Broadcasting Corporation (SABC) Records. 1976. (OCLC: 788234634).

Die skaduwee van die son—Ses gedigte van Lina Spies vir mezzo-sopraan en klavier [The shadow of the sun—Six poems by Lina Spies for mezzo-soprano and piano] 4. *Musiek* [music]. Minette Du Toit-Pierce (mezzo-soprano), Esthea Kruger (piano). https://youtu.be/cDB7T-XGa9s (accessed on July 14, 2024).

Die stil avontuur [The quiet adventure]: *Sewe Liedere op tekstes van Elizabeth Eybers* [Seven songs on texts by Elisabeth Eybers [a version in English translation also exists as *The Quiet Adventure*]. Hendrik Hofmeyr (composer and piano), Zanne Stapelberg (soprano). 4. Nocturne [Evening Song] https://www.youtube.com/watch?v=GY6P2Qb6nZQ&list=PLTKGF-LiWgsuSvrlbAiMOnhwlloKmqnId&index=5 (accessed on July 14, 2024).

Drie Orkesliedere oor gedigte van Ingrid Jonker [Three orchestral songs on poems of Ingrid Jonker.] Bongani Ndodana-Breen (composer), Goitsemang Lehobye (soprano), Perry So (conductor), Cape Town Philharmonic Orchestra. Live performance October 22, 2015. Settings of *Die Kind* [The child], *Ek Herhaal Jou* [I repeat you], and *Met Hulle Is Ek* [I am with them] by Afrikaans poet Ingrid Jonker. https://www.youtube.com/watch?v=HG6bi0jQ9h0 (accessed July 14, 2024).

Ek maak 'n hek oop in my hart—Vyf gedigte deur Uys Krige, Op. 126, vir middel stem en klavier [I open a gate in my heart—Five poems by Uys Krige, for medium voice and piano. Also arranged for high voice]. Hendrik Hofmeyr (composer).

6. *Plaashek* [Farmgate]. LeOui Rendsburg (mezzo-soprano), Mikey Pandya (piano). https://www.youtube.com/watch?v=B7QwPzC09dM (accessed on July 14, 2024).

En Skielik is dit aand—Vyf gedigte deur Deon Knobel vir stem en klavier [And suddenly it is evening—five poems by Deon Knobel for voice and piano]. Hendrik Hofmeyr (composer). 2. *Elegie* [elegy]. Milena Gurova (mezzo-soprano), Corneli Smit (piano). https://www.youtube.com/watch?v=vOtqSv7dL7Q (accessed on July 14, 2024). 3. *Gedig vir Klein Estie* [Poem for little Estie]. André Howard (baritone), Hendrik Hofmeyr (piano). https://www.youtube.com/watch?v=ivlM2dh1ucc (accessed on July 14, 2024). 5. *Op slag gedood* [Killed on sight]. Milena Gurova (mezzo-soprano), Corneli Smit (piano). https://youtu.be/n_8Qb3BZbr0?si=8m1QlgOfp_9Ti9SG (accessed on July 14, 2024).

Hendrik Hofmeyr—Lieder [Hendrik Hofmeyr—Art songs], *Vier gebede by jaargetye in die Boland—Sangsiklus vir stem en klavier* [Four seasonal prayers in the Boland—Song cycle for voice and piano]. Hendrik Hofmeyr (composer and piano), Zanne Stapelberg (soprano), André Howard (baritone). Cape Town: CD Xpress, 2007.

Ina Snyman—Opera Singer. YouTube page. Ina Snyman (soprano), Anna Bender (piano). Repertoire consists of many songs set to poems within this Translation and Performance Guide, including: *Van Kirstenbosch tot in Namaqualand* [From Kirstenbosch until Namaqualand], *Die Duifie* [The little dove], *Die Pêrel se Klokkies* [The little bells of pearl], *Gee my* [Give me], *Oktobermaaand* [The month of October], *Krymekaar* [Love nest], *Fluit windswael, sing en fluit* [Whistle, swift, sing and whistle], *Klein Sonneskyn* [Little ray of sunshine], etc. https://www.youtube.com/watch?v=W6lmE_2JP9Y&list=PLAnvUodn0AvdO0ram6ooqikiFqZLUdH2A (accessed on July 14, 2024).

Live in Concert, O Boereplaas [O farmstead]. Mimi Coertse (soprano). https://www.youtube.com/watch?v=2L1gvd0PkU0 (accessed on July 14, 2024).

Mimi Coertse en die Afrikaanse Lied [Mimi Coertse and the Afrikaans song]. Repertoire includes many songs set to poems within this Translation and Performance Guide, including: *Op my ou Ramkiekie* [On my old ramkie guitar], *'n Doornekroon* [A crown of thorns], *Oktobermaand* [The month of October], *My siel is siek van Heimwee* [My soul is sick with longing], *Mali, Die Slaaf se Lied* [Mali, the slave's song], *Rooidag* [Daybreak], *Sluimer beminde* [Slumber, beloved], *Sewe Boerneef Liedjies* [Seven farmer/nephew songs], *Ek hou van die môre* [I love the morning], *Staan Poppie Staan* [Stay, sweetheart, stay], etc. Mimi Coertse (soprano), with accompanying musicians. Gallo South Africa. 2007. (OCLC Number: 173599111). https://www.youtube.com/playlist?list=OLAK5uy_nT0VTsfCBI xUUpmaeZrWYcVoscLUV6IN8 (accessed on July 14, 2024).

Mimi Coertse Sing [Mimi Coertse sings]. Repertoire includes many songs set to poems within this Translation and Performance Guide, including: *Lentelied* [Spring song], *Heimwee* [Homesickness/nostalgia], *Kom dans Klaradyn* [Come dance, Klaradyn], *Dis al* [That's all], *Die Roos* [The rose], *Sluimerlied* [Slumber song], My Moeder [My mother], *Met 'n Mandjie Rose* [With a little basket of roses], *Kokkewiet* [Bush shrike], *Vier weemoedige Liedjies* [Four melancholy little songs], etc. Mimi Coertse (soprano), Victor Graef (piano). London: Decca. 1960. (OCLC Number: 660109983). https://www.youtube.com/watch?v=9GgCvIIJzlw&list=PLiW3Z8FaoSsrPGROC66vq9ATc_IWaL2Xt (accessed on July 14, 2024).

'n Eeu van Afrikaanse Liedkuns [A century of Afrikaans art songs]. Minette Du Toit-Pearce (mezzo-soprano), André Howard (baritone), Vanessa Tait-Jones (soprano), Elna Van der Merwe (piano). South Africa: [publisher not identified]. 2010. (OCLC Number: 646412214).

Nagmusiek [Night music]. Minette Du Toit-Pierce (mezzo-soprano), Marika Hofmeyr (piano). [Place of publication not identified]: Hortus, 2023. (OCLC Number: 1394910358). https://www.youtube.com/watch?v=mkkmA8Xt_Xo&list=OLAK5uy_kHjvvTvzjCgAydOeIK F0Vp5oxnxbHmvY4 (accessed on July 14, 2024).

Onse Mimi [Our Mimi]. Mimi Coertse (soprano), Hennie Joubert (piano), Pieter de Villiers (piano), Albie Van Schalkwyk (piano), National Symphony Orchestra of the SABC, Richard Cock (conductor). Repertoire consists of operatic arias for lyric coloratura /dramatic coloratura soprano. Johannesburg: BMG Records, Africa. 1999. CDCLA (WM) 001. (OCLC Number: 870558400) https://www.youtube.com/watch?v=EJZmyWNkPck&list=OLAK5uy_lSNL5hYM9mDMhjr3OxzoSyNMp023FVos4&index=2 (accessed on July 14, 2024).

Onse Mimi, vol. 2 [Our Mimi, vol. 2]. Repertoire includes lyric-coloratura soprano operatic arias and Afrikaans art songs including *Die sterretjie* [The little star], *Gebedjie* [Little prayer], *Winterbome* [Winter tree], *Geboorte van die Lente* [The birth of spring], *Amors Konfetti* [Cupid's confetti], etc. https://www.youtube.com/watch?v=ObU-nBHAbIE&list=OLA K5uy_mn-iK6wkjVrTqGKpyxEBh5MTN3jgISbis&index=2 (accessed on July 14, 2024).

Rose van Herinnering: Liedere op gedigte van A. G. Visser. [Roses of remembrance: Songs to poems by A. G. Visser]. Repertoire includes *Rose Van Herrinering* [Rose of remembrance], *Middagslapie* [Afternoon nap], *Duisend-en-een* [A thousand-and-one], *Omdat die Dood* [Because death], *Salut d'amour* by Rosa Nepgen and Eva Harvey [A love letter], *Princess van Verre* [The distant princess], *Van Verlorevlei* [From the forlorn marsh], *Toewyding* [Dedication], etc. Hanli Stapela (soprano), Tessa Rhoodie (piano). Provided to YouTube by Catapult Reservatory, LLC. 2020. https://www.youtube.com/watch?v=MkYMpO-IQBE&list=OLAK5uy_nrsJVWvBoRMe52fggu8tu3sG01Vm78cf8&index=2 (accessed on July 14, 2024).

South Africa NATS Chapter Inaugural Conference: "The relevance of Afrikaans folk songs presented as art songs: A lecture recital of ten Afrikaans folksongs—arranged by Xander Kritzinger." Repertoire includes *Tien Afrikaanse Volksliedere* [Ten Afrikaans folksongs] by X. Kritzinger (composer) (b. 1985) 1. *Magaliesburgse aandlied* [Magalies Mountain evening song], 2. *Hulle sê daar's 'n man in die maan* [They say there's a man in the moon] 3. *Die Overbergse liefdesliedjies* [The Overberg's little love songs] 4. *Siembamba* [Lullaby] 5. *Vervul my hart met dankbaarheid (Môregesang)* [Fill my heart with thankfulness (morning song)] 6. *Kolperd* [Bat-horse] 7. *Ma daar kom die jong soldaat* [But there came the young soldier] 8. *Vaarwel my eie soetelief* [Farewell my sweet love] 9. *Mamma, 'k wil 'n man hê!* [Mamma, I want a man!] 10. *Voortrekker aandgesang* [Pioneer evening song]. Lauren Dasappa (soprano), Xander Kritzinger (tenor), Elna van der Merwe (piano). Live 2023. https://www.youtube.com/watch?v=uCSM9mUmkF0.

The Worlds behind the Words—Art Songs of Hendrik Hofmeyr. Twee gedigte van Eugène Marias [Two poems by Eugène Marais], *Allenstryd* [Lonely struggle/outcast], *Die skaduwee van die son* [The shadow of the sun], *Wintersprokie* [Winter fairytale]. Paulina Malefane, Brittany Smith, Ané Pretorius (sopranos), Minette du Toit-Pierce, (mezzo-soprano), Van Wyk Venter (baritone), Esthea Kruger (piano)]. Cape Town, South Africa: SACM Productions. 2021. (OCLC Number: 1353595843).

Twee verjaarsdagliedere [Two birthday songs]. Hendrik Hofmeyr (composer), Minette Du Toit-Pearce (mezzo-soprano), Marika Hofmeyr (piano). From Nagmusiek [Night Music]. Hortus: 2023. 1. *Die moeder* [The mother] (accessed July 14, 2024). https://www.youtube.com/watch?v=mkkmA8Xt_Xo&list=PLkAnu8HWZyrK3D0MYdrtdWHvFkGZiR7d6&index=1&pp=iAQB8AUB (accessed on July 14, 2024). 2. *Geluk* [Good fortune] https://www.youtube.com/watch?v=mnlCaOpb_QI&list=PLkAnu8HWZyrK3D0MYdrtdWHvFkGZiR7d6 (accessed on July 14, 2024).

Twee gedigte van Eugène Marias [extract]: *Winternag vir stem en klavier* [Two poems by *Eugène Marias* [extract]: Winter night for voice and piano] and *Swewe en Swerwe: Poetiese Liedere oor en uit Suid-Afrika* [Floating and roaming: Poetical songs about and from South Africa]. Julia Bronkhorst (soprano), Jacco Lamfers (piano). Eindhoven, Netherlands: Q Disk, 2003. Q 97042. Barcode: 8 713309 970425.

Wintersprokie—Drie Liedere op gedigte van Petra Müller [Winter's fairytale—Three songs on poems by Petra Müller]. Henrik Hofmeyr (composer). 3. *Persephone.* Ané Pretorius (soprano), Esthea Kruger (piano) https://www.youtube.com/watch?v=vpznQRN4VrU (accessed on July 14, 2024).

Woorde in die wind—Vier gedigte deur Ingrid Jonker [Words in the wind—Four poems of Ingrid Jonker]. Hendrik Hofmeyr (composer), Minette Du Toit-Pearce (mezzo-sopran), Marika Hofmeyr (piano). From Nagmusiek [Night Music]. Hortus: 2023. 1. *Windliedjie* [Little song of the breeze] https://www.youtube.com/watch?v=QNdgQGlq9A4 (accessed on July 14, 2024). 2. *Toemaar die donker man* [Fear not the shadow man] https://www.youtube.com/watch?v=8PPMaU9XCwo. 3. *Bitterbessie dagbreek* [Bitter berry daybreak] https://www.youtube.com/watch?v=ckRyHLzSrdg (accessed on July 14, 2024). 4. *Die kind* [The child] https://www.youtube.com/watch?v=3rL4tACFECA (accessed on July 14, 2024).

Vier gebede by jaargetye in die Boland [Four seasonal prayers in the Boland]
André Howard (baritone), Hendrik Hofmyer (composer and piano) 1. *Vroegherfs* [Early Autumn] https://soundcloud.com/hendrik-hofmeyr/vier-gebede-by-jaargetye-in-die-bol and-1-vroegherfs-andre-howard-hendrik-hofmeyr.

Recommended Afrikaans Art Song Music Subscription Channels on YouTube

An increasing number of Afrikaans art song recordings are available on YouTube.

Many can be found by typing in the song title, composer, and poet's name in the search engine.

Hendrik Hofmeyr@hendrikhofmeyr4491: https://www.youtube.com/@hendrikhofmeyr4491 (accessed on July 15, 2024).

Johan Kotze@SA_OperaSingers: www.youtube.com/@SA_OperaSingers (accessed on July 15, 2024).

Mimi Coertse Topic: www.youtube.com/channel/UC60YpFsEXp0f1FmRefe2exg (accessed on July 15, 2024).

Thula Mhlope@ThulaMhlope: https://www.youtube.com/watch?v=9GgCvIIJzlw&list=PLiW3Z8FaoSsrPGROC66vq9ATc_IWaL2Xt (accessed on January 2, 2025).

Franco Prinsloo@MrFrancoprinsloo:

https://www.youtube.com/results?search_query=franco+prinsloo (accessed on January 2, 2025).

Recommended Afrikaans Poetry Recitation Channels

Boggom en Voertsek [Good for nothing and sod off] by C. L. Leipoldt https://www.youtube.com/watch?v=p9nMEAHdC2U&list=PLU4Rg6xwhuHGcGKTjJ5r6jPFlv4W4mwKV&index=4 (accessed on July 15, 2024).

Douglas Vale@douglasvale8860: www.youtube.com/@douglasvale8860 (accessed on July 15, 2024).

Twee gedigte van Eugène Marias: *Winternag* [From two poems by *Eugène Marias*: Winter night] https://www.youtube.com/watch?v=0HKdTH2afaM&list=PLU4Rg6xwhuHGcGKTjJ5r6jPFlv4W4mwKV&index=1 (accessed on July 15, 2024).

Other Pronunciation Recordings

A growing number of Afrikaans poetry recitation recordings are available on YouTube. Many can be found by typing in the poem title and the poet's name in the search engine.

Die Kind [The child] by Ingrid Jonker, read in Afrikaans: https://www.youtube.com/watch?v=kPr7gfUoFt0 (accessed on July 15, 2024).

The Child, read by Nelson Mandela: https://www.youtube.com/watch?v=A0pmjGj8BFE (accessed on July 15, 2024).

Appendix D

RESOURCES FOR OBTAINING INFORMATION ON AFRIKAANS ART SONGS, SONG CYCLES, COMPOSERS, PERFORMERS, AND LYRIC DICTION IN ENGLISH

Bester, Christian. "The Influence of Indigenous Bushmen Musical Elements and Significant Compositional Traits on Niel Van Der Watt's Song Cycle, Die Wind Dreun Soos 'n Ghoera, 'n Siklus Boesman-Mites." Dissertation (D.M.A.), University of North Texas, 2014. https://digital.library.unt.edu/ark:/67531/metadc699878/ (accessed on July 14, 2024).

Bester, Christian, and Bronwen Forbay. "An Introduction to Afrikaans Art Songs: A Guide to Lyric Diction." *Journal of Singing* 78, no. 4 (2022): 497–506. https://doi.org/10.53830/tstu7308 (accessed on July 12, 2024).

———. "An Introduction to Afrikaans Art Song Literature: Origins and Repertoire." *Journal of Singing* 78, no. 4 (2022): 471–82. https://doi.org/10.53830/qxmd1468.

Brukman, Jeffrey. "Aspects of Musical Modernism: The Afrikaans Song Cycles of Cromwell Everson." *Journal of the Musical Arts in Africa*, 8, no. 1 (2012): 1–21. https://doi.org: 10.2989/18121004.2011.652353 (accessed on July 12, 2024).

Cupido, Conroy. "Significant Influences in the Composition of Hendrik Hofmeyr's Song Cycle, Alleenstryd." Dissertation (D.M.A.), University of North Texas, 2009. Academia.edu, September 28, 2021. https://www.academia.edu/es/53707861/Significant_Influences_in_the_Composition_of_Hendrik_Hofmeyrs_Song_Cycle_Alleenstryd (accessed on July 12, 2024).

Forbay, Bronwen Michelle. "Afrikaans Art Song: A Stylistic Study and Performance Guide." Dissertation (D.M.A.), University of Cincinnati, 2011. https://etd.ohiolink.edu/acprod/odb_etd/etd/r/1501/10?clear=10&p10_accession_num=ucin1307322705 (accessed on July 12, 2024).

Klatzow, Peter. *Composers in South Africa Today*. Cape Town: Oxford University Press, 1987. (ISBN: 0195704312, 9780195704310).

May, James. "Some Aspects of Unity in Arnold van Wyk's Works Between 1940 and 1952." *Musicus* 24, no. 1 (1996): 92–98.

———. "Pitch Organization in Hendrik Hofmeyr's Alleenstryd." *South African Journal of Musicology* 23 (2003): 43–53. http://hdl.handle.net/11427/21523 (accessed on July 12, 2024).

Muller, Stephanus. "Apartheid Aesthetics and Insignificant Art." *Journal of Musicology* 33, no. 1 (2016): 45–69. https://doi.org/10.1525/jm.2016.33.1.45 (accessed on July 14, 2024).

South Africa Chapter, National Association of Teachers of Singing (NATS), established in 2022. http://natsinternationalregion.org/index.php/chapters/south-africa.

South African Music Encyclopedia (SAME). (ISBN 0195703634 9780195703634)

Vol. 1, A–D (1979) (OCLC 874857820); Cape Town: Oxford University Press, 1979.

Vol. 2, E–I (1982) (ISBN 0195702867 9780195702866 0195702859 9780195702859; OCLC 59176920); Cape Town: Oxford University Press, 1982.

Vol. 3, J–O (1984) (ISBN 0195703111 9780195703115; OCLC 59176927); Cape Town: Oxford University Press, 1984.

Vol. 4, P–Z (1986) (ISBN 0195703634 9780195703634; OCLC 830186261). Cape Town: Oxford University Press, 1986.

South African Music Encyclopedia (SAME) volumes by Jacques P. Malan are currently available in the United States at https://search.worldcat.org/.

Walton, Chris. "Composing Africa: Stefans Grové at 85." *The Musical Times* 148, no. 1899 (2007): 19. https://doi.org/10.2307/25434455 (accessed on July 14, 2024).

Appendix E

AFRIKAANS LANGUAGE, CULTURE, AND HISTORY INSTITUTIONS

ATKV: Afrikaanse Taal-en Kultuurvereniging (Afrikaans Language and Culture Association): https://atkv.org.za (accessed on July 15, 2024).

F.A.K.: Federasie van Afrikaanse Kultuurvereniginge (Federation of Afrikaans Cultural Associations): https://fak.org.za (accessed on July 15, 2024).

NALN: National Afrikaans Literary Museum and Research Center: https://www.musicinafrica.net/directory/national-afrikaans-literary-museum-naln (accessed on July 15, 2024).

SABC: South African Broadcasting Corporation (formerly also known as the SAUK: Suid-Afrikaanse Uitsaaikorporasie) has archival, historical recordings of Afrikaans art song performances by South African singers: https://www.sabc.co.za/sabc/ (accessed on July 15, 2024).

Appendix F

RESEARCH PROJECTS IN PROGRESS

Ilse Keet, granddaughter of poet A. D. Keet, is compiling scores of musical settings of Keet's poems.

Ongoing and future Afrikaans art song literature research projects by Drs. Christian Bester (baritone) and Bronwen Forbay (soprano) include:

- Continued IPA and English translations of poetry not yet covered in this anthology.
- Afrikaans lyric-diction clinics.
- Lecture-recitals on Afrikaans art song literature covering topics commonly addressed in the traditional art song canon, as well as innovative program offerings such as "Illuminating I.D.E.A. (Inclusion, Diversity, Equity and Anti-racism) in Afrikaans Art Song Literature," which focused specifically on repertoire on this topic, presented at the 2024 NATS National Conference (Knoxville, TN).
- A recording project for high, medium, and low voices.

Appendix G

AFRIKAANS LYRIC DICTION SUMMARY

Fronting Vowels			
[i]	*ie* is [i] in all positions: *iets* [its], *treurlied* ['trjøªrlit], *kierie* ['kiri] When followed by another consonant: *kiertsregop* ['kirts͵ræxɔp]	[iː]	*ie* + *r* when final in a word: *dier* [diːr] *ie* + *r* when followed by a schwa in the next syllable: *miere* [miːrə] In words of foreign origin when followed by another consonant: *Ierland* ['iːrlant]
[e]	*e* in a stressed syllable when followed by a single consonant: *gelede* [xəˈleªdə] *ee* spellings: *geen* [çeªn] Exceptions: Other options for *e* spellings include [ɛ], [æ] and [ə]. Check pronunciation rules.[1]		
[ɛ]	*e* + single consonant in monosyllabic words: *wet* [vɛt] Pronunciation for the pronoun *ek* varies by region. The authors recommend using [ɛ] instead of [æ] for lyric diction. Exception: *lekker* ['lækər][2] *e* + two or more consonants in an unstressed syllable: *ekskuus* [ɛkˈskys] *e* + two consonants in a stressed syllable: *emmer* ['ɛmmər] In polysyllabic words of foreign origin, *e* is: *energie* [ɛnərˈxi], *ekspo* ['ɛkspu] *è* in monosyllabic words: *nè* [nɛ]	[ɛː]	Final *-ê*: *lê* [lɛː] Exception: Polysyllabic words with final unstressed *-ens*, *-end*, *-eld* all sound [ə]: *nêrens* ['næːrəns], *gewapend* [xəˈvaːpənt], *wêreld* ['væːrəlt][3]
[æ]	*e* + *g, k, l*, in a stressed closed syllable: *geld* [xæªlt], *melk* [mæªlk], *lekker* ['lækər] *e* + *r* + a consonant cluster in a stressed syllable: *ernstig* ['ærənstəx] *e* + *rr*: *sterre* ['stærə]	[æː]	*ê* + *r* within a stressed syllable: *wêreld* ['væːrəlt] Monosyllabic *ver* is pronounced ['fæːr] 'far' when used as an adjective or adverb. When used in a prefix, however, as in *vertel* [fərˈtæl] 'to tell,' it becomes an unstressed schwa.

[1] See Pronunciation Guide.
[2] See [æ] explanation.
[3] See [æː] explanation.

268   APPENDIX G

[a]	The authors recommend using only bright [a] vowels to facilitate lyric diction. *a* + single consonant within monosyllabic words: *pak* [pak] *a* + two or more consonants: *vars* [fars]	[a:]	*a* + single consonant in polysyllabic words or when final: *blare* [ˈbla:rə], *pa* [pa:] *aa* spellings: *aand* [a:nt] *ae* spellings in a stressed syllable: *hael* [ˈɦa:l]
Backing Vowels			
[ɔ]	*o* + single consonant in monosyllabic words: *kop* [kɔp] *o* + double consonants: *rokkie* [ˈrɔki] Final	[ɔ:]	*ô*: *môre* [ˈmɔ:rə]
[u]	*oe* spellings: *groet* [xrut] *u* spellings in foreign or borrowed words: *rubato* [ruˈba:tu] In unstressed syllables ending in *o* spellings, the tongue raises toward [u]: *melodie* [mɛluˈdi]	[u:]	*oe* + *r*: *loer* [lu:r]
[ʊᵊ]	*o* when final: *bo* [bʊᵊ] *oo* spellings: *verloop* [fərˈlʊᵊp] *o* + single consonant in polysyllabic words: *bome* [ˈbʊᵊmə]		
Note: *oë* spellings followed by a consonant result in the superscript schwa [ᵊ]: *hoëveld* [ˈɦʊᵊfæᵊlt]			
Note: *oë* spellings in monosyllabic words, or when *oë* is final in polysyllabic words, result in the regular schwa [ə]: *oë* [ˈu:ə]			
Mixed Vowels (Also known as rounded front vowels)			
[œ]	*u* spellings: *hulle* [ˈɦœlə] Exceptions: Other sounds for *u* spellings including [u], [y] and [y:].[4]	[œ:]	*û* spellings: *brûe* [ˈbrœ:ɦə] (rare)
[ø]	*eu* spellings: *kleur* [kljøᵊr][5]		
[y]	*uu* spellings: *minuut* [məˈnyt] *u* spellings in open syllables: *minute* [məˈnytə]	[y:]	*uu* + *r* spellings: *muur* [my:r]

Schwa: Occurs in Both Stressed and Unstressed Positions
Note: Tips for singing the Afrikaans schwa [ə]: The authors recommend the vowel substitution of [œ] for [ə] but without lip rounding. The tip of the tongue needs to still be relaxed and touch the bottom front teeth.

---

[4] See Pronunciation Guide.
[5] Ibid.

[ə]⁶	[ə:]
Unstressed prefixes include: *ge-*: *gespeel* [xəˈspeᵊl] *be-*: *beproef* [bəˈpruf] *ver-*: *verlede* [fərˈleᵊdə]	*î* spellings: *wîe* [ˈvəːꟸə] (rare)
Final *-e* or *-er* spellings: *se* [sə], *beter* [ˈbeᵊtər]	
Final unstressed *-ens, end, -eld*: *nêrens* [næːrəns], *geheimhoudend* [xəˈꟸəjmˌꟸœudənt], *wêreld* [ˈvæːrəlt]	
A schwa is inserted between *l* or *r* + *m* or *n*: *elmboog* [ˈæləmbʊᵊx], *ferm* [ˈfærəm]	
A schwa is inserted when vowels other than *e* occur before *r* or *l*: *kalm* [ˈkaləm], *film* [ˈfələm]	

More on Diacritical Marks

Acute Accents are sometimes added to words that don't originally contain accents to indicate that the word is of greater importance and should be pronounced more emphatically. Note that a primary stress mark has been added in front of the IPA transcriptions to demonstrate emphasis.

- On final vowels in monosyllabic words, the vowel is stressed and long. Example: *ná*, [ˈnaː] Note: *á* in the word *ná* distinguishes the meaning of the word: *ná* 'after' vs. *na* 'close/to.'
- On vowels in monosyllabic words ending in a consonant, the vowel is stressed and short. Example: *kán* [ˈkan].
- In monosyllabic words ending in a diphthong, both the consonant and initial vowel are emphasized. Example: *sý* [ˈsəj].
- When on two adjacent vowel letters in the same word, a similar emphasis occurs. Example: *vóór* [ˈfʊᵊr].
- Exception: When on vowels in loan words and proper nouns, a similar emphasis does not occur. Examples: *née* [nəj], *André* [ˈandrəj].

Grave accent results in a stressed vowel sound that is short in duration.
- Occurs on only four indigenous Afrikaans words. Examples: *dè* [dɛ] 'here, take it!', *nè* [nɛ] 'really?' (Likely from the French *n'est-ce pas?*), *hè* [ꟸɛ] 'what did you say?', and *appèl* [aˈpæl] 'to appeal.'
- Distinguishes between which syllables are stressed, while also disambiguating the meanings of words. Examples: *appel* [ˈapəl] 'apple' vs. *appèl* [aˈpæl] 'to appeal.'
- Otherwise it is only found in loanwords or proper nouns from languages such as French and Italian. Examples: *Eugène* and *Pietà*.⁷

Diaresis
- Indicates the start of a new syllable if it could otherwise be mistaken as forming part of a diphthong. Examples: *geïn* [xəˈən] 'collected,' *geüiter* [xəˈœytər] 'uttered.'
- A diaresis is not required in combinations of *a* and *e* since they cannot constitute a diphthong. In cases such as *haël*, the *aë* spelling "indicates the deletion of an erstwhile Dutch *g* [x] and is pronounced as a long [a:]." Example: *haël* [ˈꟸaːl].⁸
- Can indicate a glide. Example: *pasiënt* [pasiˈjɛnt].
- *aä* indicates that the second [a] is stressed. The insertion of a glottal stop (a 'breath lift' is recommended by the authors for singers) is required between the *aä*. Example: *Aäron* [aˈaːrɔn]
- *oë* and *eë* (in addition to marking the start of a new syllable) are reminiscent of the intervocalic *g* in Dutch. Example: *reën* [ˈriən] 'rain,' *bewoë* [bəˈvuːə] 'moved.'

---

⁶ See Pronunciation Guide.
⁷ Ernst Kotzé, email message to the authors, October 22, 2023.
⁸ Ibid.

Diphthongs			
Authentic		**Inauthentic**	
[əj]	*ei, y - meisie* ['məjsi]	[aj]	*ai - baie* ['bajə]
[œu]	*ou - koud* [kœut]	[ɔːj]	*ôi - nôi* [nɔːj]
[œy]	*ui - uit* [œyt]	[jøˀ]	*eu - kleur* [kljøˀr]
		[oːj]	*ooi - gooi* [xoːj]
		[ui]	*oei - koei* [kui]
		[aːj]	*aai - waai* [vaːj]
		[iu]	*eeu - leeu* [liu]
			ieu - Nieu-Seeland [niu'seˀlant]

Diminutive Diphthongs	
[aⁱ]	*katjie* ['kaⁱki]
[aːⁱ]	*maatjie* ['maːⁱki]
[oⁱ]	*pootjie* ['poⁱki]
[ɔⁱ]	*potjie* ['pɔⁱki]
[əⁱ]	*pitjie* ['pəⁱki]
[ɛ]	*prentjie* ['prɛɲki]
[ɔ]	*hondjie* ['hɔɲki]
[oey]	*fluitjie* ['flœyki]
[œ]	*muntjie* ['mœɲki]
[ø]	*deuntjie* ['djøɲki]

Diminutive Suffixes	
-djie [ki]	*hondjie* ['hɔɲki]
-tjie [ki]	*katjie* ['kaⁱki]
-kie [ki]	*koekie* ['kuki]
-pie [pi]	*oompie* ['ʋˀmpi]
–ie [i]	*liefie* ['lifi]

Plosive Consonants			
[b]	*b* spellings: *beveel* [bə'feˀl]	[p]	*p* spellings: *pa* [paː] Final *b*: *Job* [jɔp] *b + s*: *absorbeer* [apsɔr'beˀr]
[d]	*d* spellings: *bedien* [bə'din] *d* + unstressed neutral *e* [ə]: *honde* ['hɔndə]	[t]	*t* spellings: *tak* [tak] Final *d* or *ds*: *hard* [hart], *gids* [xəts]

[k]	*k* spellings: *knie* [kni] *-djie* suffix: *liedjie* ['liki] *c + a* spellings: *cabaletta* [kabaˈlɛta] *c* spellings in foreign or loanwords can represent [k] or [s]: *chroom* [krʊᵊm] *Cirene* [siˈreᵊnə].	[g]	Initial *gh*: *gholf* [gɔlf] *r + g* + unstressed *e*: *berge* ['bærgə]
[kw]	*qu* spellings: *quisling* ['kwəsliŋ] Exceptions: *quiche* [kiʃ], *Qur'aan* [kurˈa:n]		
[ks]	Exceptions: Final *x*: *Xerox* ['zeᵊrɔks]		
[ɛks]	Initial *x*: *X-straal* ['ɛkstra:l]. *x* spellings can result in various pronunciations: [k], [ks], [ɛks], [z].		

Fricative Consonants			
[f]	*f* spellings: *familie* [faˈmili] *v* spellings: *vandag* [fanˈdax] Exceptions: Some foreign or loan words containing *v + i* + vowel spellings sound [f]: *viool* [fiˈjʊᵊl] *v + u* spellings: [f]: *vurk* [fœrk] Exception: *vuvuzela* [vuvuˈze:la] (isiZulu origin) *v + y* spellings: *vyf* [fəjf]	[v]	*w* spellings: *water* ['va:tər] Exceptions: combinations of *dw*: *dwaal* [dwa:l], *kw*: *kwaad* [kwa:t], *sw*: *swaai* [swa:i], *tw*: *twee* [tweᵊ] Exceptions: Some foreign or loan words containing *v + i* + consonant spellings sound [v]: *televisie* [tɛləˈvisi]
[s]	*s* spellings: *ses* [sɛs] *sch* spellings in proper nouns of Dutch origin: *Stellenbosch* [stɛlənˈbɔs] *-ici* suffix: *mysici* [musiˈsi] Exception: *c* spellings or *c + e, i* or *y* in foreign loan words or proper names: *Caesar* [se:ˈzar], *celesta* [səˈlɛsta]	[z]	*z* spellings: *zoem* [zum] *x + e* spellings: *xenofobie* [zeᵊnufuᵊˈbi]
[ʃ]	*sj* spellings in foreign loan words: *Sjina* ['ʃina] Initial *ch* spellings: *chef* [ʃɛf] Exceptions: *ch* spellings can result in various pronunciations: [k] *chloor* [klʊᵊr], [x] *chemie* ['xeᵊmi], [tʃ] *chilli* ['tʃili]		
[ɦ]	*h* spellings: *heimwee* ['ɦəjmveᵊ] Like the English [h] but with a slight breath lift before initiating the sound. The result is a slightly less aspirated [ɦ] with decreased breath energy.		

[ç]	Initial *g* + *ie* or *ee* spellings: *gier* [çi:r] *geel* [çeᵊl]	[x]	Initial *g* + single vowel or consonant: *gister* ['xəstər], *glimlag* ['xləmlax] *ge-* prefixes: *geluk* [xə'lœk] *gg* spellings: *liggaam* ['ləxa:m] Final *g* spellings: *mag* [max]

Glides

[j]	*j* spellings: *ja* [ja:] Exception: *j* spellings in words of foreign origin: *jellie* ['dʒeli]	[kw]	Consonant + *w*: *kwaad* [kwa:t]

Consonant Clusters

[sk]	Initial *sch*: *Schoeman* ['skuman]	[sp]	*sp* spellings: *speel* [speᵊl]
[st]	*st* spellings: *stad* [stat]		
[ts]	Final *ds*: *aards* [a:rts]	[tʃ]	Initial *tj*: *tjek* [tʃɛk] Exception: *-tjie* spellings: *dogtertjie* ['dɔxtərki]

Liquid Consonants

[l]	*l* spellings: *lees* [leᵊs]	[m]	*m* spellings: *moeder* ['mudər] Exceptions: see Assimilation and Amalgamation of Consonants below.
[n]	*n* spellings: *nou* [nœu] Exceptions: see Assimilation and Amalgamation of Consonants below.	[ŋ]	*ng* spellings: *sing* [səŋ], *nk* spellings: *lank* [laŋk]

Rolled Consonant

[r]	*r* spellings: *roos* [rʊᵊs]		

Off-Glide

[ᵊ] Diphthongization between stressed [e]: *veer* [feᵊr], [u]: *boom* [bʊᵊm]
Exception: No diphthongization if e or o are followed by a nasalized consonant: *onmiddelik* [ɔ'mədələk]
[ᵃ] Spelling *e* + *l*: *geld* [xæᵃlt]
[ɦ] Spelling *î* + *e*: *wîe* ['və:ɦə] (rare)

Assimilation and Amalgamation of Consonants

[b]	Spelling *p* + *b*: *kapblok* ['kablɔk]
[d]	Spelling *t* + *d*: *totdat* ['tɔdat] When *t* and *d* occur in adjacent words in a slow tempo, the singer may either assimilate or pronounce both consonants: *Omdat die*, e.g., ['ɔmdat di] or ['ɔmda di]
[g]	Amalgamation: spelling *g* + *g*: *weg gewaai* [væ xə'va:j]
Silent [ɦ]	Spelling *g* + suffix *-heid*: *sagtheid* ['saxtəjt] Exception: *heid* in stressed position: *heiden* ['ɦəjdən]
[m]	Spelling *n* or *m* + *b*: *onbekend* [ɔmbə'kɛnt] Spelling *n* + *m*: *onmiddelik* [ɔ'mədələk]

[ŋ]	Spelling *n* + *k* or *n* + *g*: *wankel* [ˈvaŋkəl], *sing* [səŋ]
	Exceptions: Stressed prefixes ending in *n* + a word stem beginning with *g*: *ingetrek* [ˈənxəˌtræk] or Stressed prefixes ending in *n* + *k*: *inkom* [ˈənkɔm]
[ɲ]	Spelling *n* + *t* or *d*: *prentjie* [ˈprɛɲki]
[p]	Amalgamation: spelling *p* + *p*: *op pale* [ɔˈpaːlə]
[s]	Amalgamation: spelling *s* + *s*: *jy's sy* [jəj səj]

Appendix H
GLOSSARY

Aandblom: Translated as 'evening-flower' (*Geophyte*), a species of *Hesperanthus, Gladiolus, Freesia*, and *Iridacae*. It has soft hairy leaves and petals that range in color from dark purple, nearly black, to an occasional pale yellow. Found in various regions of the Western Cape Province, these flowers bloom at nighttime. Their scent resembles cinnamon.

Afrikaans: A language that evolved mainly from seventeenth-century Dutch dialects spoken by settlers and seafarers who arrived at the Cape of Good Hope from 1652 onward. Considered one of the youngest Germanic languages, it was influenced by various languages from the Indonesian archipelago, French, German, and Portuguese. While the Afrikaans language has a contentious history due to the legacy of apartheid, it became an official language in 1925 and remains one of the twelve official languages of South Africa.

Afrikaner(s): Descendants of the Dutch, German, and French-Huguenot settlers who arrived in southern Africa from the seventeenth century onward. Afrikaans is this ethnic group's first language. While many urban-based settlers at the Cape were initially referred to as Afrikaners, during the Great Trek this ethnic group later came to include the "Boers," translated as 'farmers,' who were predominantly rural settlers. Afrikaners played and continue to play a significant role in the history of South Africa.

Apartheid: A legal system imposed by the South African government from 1948 to the early 1990s institutionalizing racial segregation and discrimination that impacted all areas of daily life. Its goal was to maintain white minority rule while restricting and controlling non-white (predominantly Black) South Africans through legal and political means.

Berggans: Translated as 'mountain goose,' most likely refers to the Cape shelduck (*Tadorna cana*) which is indigenous to southern Africa. It belongs to the *Anatidae* family, a group of small- to large-sized monogamous water birds, including swans, geese, and ducks. This term could also refer to the Egyptian goose (*Alopochen aegyptiaca*), which the ancient Egyptians considered sacred. These mountain geese, commonly found along the Nile Valley and in sub-Saharan Africa, have distinctive dark chocolate-brown colored eye patches.

Big five: This phrase was initially coined by big game hunters in reference to the five most challenging and dangerous animals to hunt on foot in Africa. They include lions, leopards, rhinoceroses, elephants, and water buffalo.

Blatjang: A tangy chutney-like sauce made of dried fruit (usually apricots) and chilies cooked in vinegar, sugar, and spices. It is traditionally served as a condiment with South African meat and curry dishes.

Boer(e)/Boers: Descendants of the Dutch, German, and French settlers who arrived in southern Africa from the seventeenth century onward, translated as 'farmer(s).' They usually inhabited rural areas and later became part of the Afrikaner ethnic group during the Great Trek. Many made significant contributions to South African history, particularly during the two Anglo-Boer Wars (1880–1881 and 1899–1902). They are known for their independence and self-determination.

Boereplaas: Translated as 'farm.' This term is generally connected to various agricultural activities such as crop and livestock farming.

Boland: Translated as 'highland,' it is a wine-making region in the Western Cape Province with an elevated, highly fertile terrain.

Bosveld (Bushveld): An expansive African prairie consisting of mainly uncultivated countryside. It is situated in the Limpopo and a small portion of the North West Provinces. Its grassy plains contain clusters of tall trees and shrubs.

Great Trek: A journey of Afrikaners known as "Voortrekkers," translated as 'forerunners' or 'pioneers,' who migrated through the interior of the country from the mid-1830s onward in hopes of creating their own independent communities, due to dissatisfaction with British colonization and conflicts with Indigenous ethnic groups at the Cape. The term "Afrikaner" was originally associated with urban-based descendants of the Dutch, German, and French Huguenots who settled at the Cape, while the term "Boers," translated as 'farmers,' referred to rural settlers. The "Boers" later became part of the Afrikaner ethnic group during the Great Trek. These designations are somewhat interchangeable in modern-day South Africa.

Hantam: A mountainous, semi-desert region in the Northern Cape Province in the region of Calvinia. Known for its unusual landscape and agricultural activities including sheep farming, its name hails from a Khoi word for 'mountains where the bulbs grow.'

Heimwee: Translated as 'longing, nostalgia, or homesickness,' it refers to a profound, intense longing for one's homeland or the past.

Hoëveld: Translated as a 'high field,' it is known for its cooler climate which forms a portion of the South African inland plateau with an altitude of over 4,921 feet, but below 6,890 feet. The Highveld boasts many beautiful areas, including nature reserves and charming towns. Popular attractions include God's Window, Bourke's Luck Potholes, and the Blyde River Canyon. Lower-lying areas support both crop and livestock farming.

isiXhosa: One of the official languages of South Africa, it is the second most widespread indigenous language and is mainly spoken by the Xhosa people. It utilizes click consonants and has a rich oral tradition.

isiZulu: One of the official languages of South Africa, it is the most widely spoken Indigenous home language and is predominantly spoken by the Zulu people. Highly influential, it is of great cultural importance.

Karoo/Kro: A semi-arid desert, divided into the Great Karoo and the Little Karoo, both lacking in surface water. It encompasses the Eastern, Western, and Northern Cape provinces. Its name is derived from the Khoi word for 'land of thirst.' Covering approximately one-third of the total area of South Africa, the Karoo's biodiversity includes assorted succulents and low scrub bushes, plains, fossils, and unique geographical formations.

Khoi: The language of the Khoikhoin/Khoikhoi/Khoi people. It consists of numerous distinctive clicks.

Khoikhoin/Khoikhoi/Khoi: These terms are the current accepted terms used to refer to the First Nation/Indigenous peoples of southern Africa who were historically skilled hunter-gatherers and livestock herders, known for the distinctive clicks of the Khoi languages.

Kirstenbosch National Botanical Garden: Established in 1913, it is one of nine National Botanical Gardens in South Africa. Situated on the eastern slopes of Table Mountain in Cape Town, this world-famous garden is 528 hectares (1,300 acres) in size. It showcases over 7,000 plant species indigenous to southern Africa and plays an important role in conservation education.

Kloof(s): Canyon-like deep glens or ravines in South Africa that may be wooded.

Krokos: Staple food of the Karoo region. In Afrikaans this word can also refer to a tiny parched, seasonal creek found in infertile regions of southern Africa.

Maroela/Marula trees (*Sclerocarya birrea*): Medium-sized deciduous dioecious trees indigenous to southern Africa. They are single stemmed with a wide spreading crown. The trunk is characterized by gray mottled bark. Giraffes (*Giraffa*), rhinoceroses (*Rhinocerotidae*), and elephants (*Elephantidae*) are known for grazing on Marula fruit, which is edible, succulent, tart, and has a distinct nutty flavor. This fruit is also the key ingredient of marula beer and the world-famous Amarula Cream Liqueur.

Namaqualand: The name of a predominantly arid region in the Northern Cape Province, derived from the Khoi word for 'Khoi people's land.' It overflows with exquisite wildflowers in a myriad of colors during the rainy Spring season.

Nou-nou: A colloquial phrase relating to an unspecified time period which will elapse before the given task is completed. It is somewhat nebulous, however, as it can mean anything from right now or very soon, to next week, beyond, or never.

Onderveld: Translated as 'under field,' initially belonging to the original Cape Province. Situated east and north of the Hex River Mountains, these lower-lying grassy prairies and plains were later expanded to include portions of the former Orange Free State (Free State) and Transvaal provinces, which previously included parts of the Limpopo, Mpumalanga, Gauteng, and North-West provinces.

Poetoepap: Also spelled *putu pap*, or *phuthu*, it is the name of a popular South African traditional dish often found at *braais* (the South African term for barbeques). A staple food in many homes, it is made of maize and water, milk, or butter. Various cooking methods result in many different textures. For example, *poetoe* can resemble grits when in liquid form, or when its consistency hardens, a crumbly porridge called *krummel pap*.

Protea (*Proteaceae*): A flowering fynbos shrub with a distinctive head and center consisting of many woody spikes. Indigenous to southern Africa, it has a distinctive chalice-shaped flower head and ranges in color from cream to bright red. Proteas are the South African national flower and the nickname of the national cricket team.

Province: In the South African context, this refers to a major administrative division of the country, with each province containing its own provincial government. South Africa currently has nine provinces: Gauteng, North-West, Limpopo, Mpumalanga, Western Cape, Eastern Cape, Northern Cape, KwaZulu-Natal, and the Free State.

Quagga (*Equus Quagga Quagga*): Native to South Africa, quaggas were an unusual subspecies of zebra that became extinct in the late nineteenth century. They had stripes only on the front half of their bodies, while their rear halves were brown.

Twelve official languages of South Africa: These include Sepedi, Sesotho, Setswana, siSwati, Tshivenda, Xitsonga, Afrikaans, Englishw, isiNdebele, isiXhosa, isiZulu, and South African Sign Language (added on October 16, 2023).

Veld: An expansive African prairie, field, or pasture, comprising a wide variety of vegetation which may be used in various ways, including agriculture or uncultivated countryside.

Voortrekker(s): A group of Afrikaners, translated as 'forerunners' or 'pioneers,' who migrated through the interior of the country from the mid-1830s in hopes of creating their own independent communities, due to dissatisfaction with British colonization and conflicts with Indigenous ethnic groups at the Cape. The term "Afrikaner" was originally associated with urban-based descendants of the Dutch, German, and French Huguenots who settled at the Cape from 1652 onward.

Wag-'n-bietjie-bos: The buffalo thorn (*Ziziphus mucronata*) is a small- to medium-sized tree with an extended canopy. Found throughout southern Africa, its leaves are a favorite food of giraffes (*Giraffa*) and impala (*Aepyceros*). Its hooked thorns give the tree its Afrikaans name, *wag-'n-bietjie*, which means 'wait-a-minute.' The Zulu people have used these trees historically as grave markers for deceased Zulu chiefs and call them *umLahlankosi*, translated as 'that which buries the chief.'

INDEX OF FIRST LINES AND TITLES

For the benefit of digital users, indexed terms that span two pages (e.g., 52–53) may, on occasion, appear on only one of those pages.

Aandblom is 'n Witblom, 24
*Aan die lyn oor die groene gras (**Middagslapie**)*, 214
*Ag, had ek 'n eie ou huisie (**Die Wapad is my Woning**)*, 200
Agter Akkerskraalsekop, 20
*Al die velde's vrolik (**Lenteliedjie**)*, 122
As ek moet sterwe, liefste, 241
As ek my vreemde Liefde bloot moes lê, 59
*As iemand sterf (**Die Wolke**)*, 12
As jy by my kom kuier, 44
*Askoektrap op die traporreltjie (**Loeriesfontein**)*, 103
As my Hart nou wil sing, 66
*As saans die son stilwygend sterf (**As saans**)*, 93
*Awend vrede uit die blou (**Droomtyd**)*, 73

Bitterbessie dagbreek, 89
Blaas op die Pampoenstingel, 21
*Blou was die glans van die hemel (**Liefdeswee**)*, 71
Boggom en Voertsek, 107
Bo in die Solder, 52
Buite suis die sagte Windjie, 168

*Daar is blomme in die tuintjie waar my liefste sawens staan (**Amoreuse Liedeken**)*, 153
*Daar onder in my tuintjie (**Die Roosknoppie**)*, 142
*Daar oorkant in Transvalia (**Kalwerliefde**)*, 206
*Daar's lentevreug op berg en dal (**Kom huistoe, Liefste!**)*, 79
*Daar's nog goed met wreder name (**Ensovoorts**)*, 193
*Daar's 'n huisie in die Bosveld (**Bosveldhuisie**)*, 57
Daar's 'n Tyd, 154
*Daar was in my oë geen jonkman so flink (**Sannie**)*, 220
*Dans, wilde see! (**Die Branders**)*, 29
Die Berggansveer, 22
*Die blommetjies ná die reën (**Namakwaland se Blommetjies**)*, 103

*Die blydskap het oornag soos nuwe sneeu (**Eerste Sneeu**)*, 181
Die branders breek ('n Lied van die See), 97
*Die dag roer uit sy papie (**Ontnugtering**)*, 88
*Die droster met sy vaal karos (**Die Renoster**)*, 191
*Die goue son het ek gevra (**Vraag en Antwoord**)*, 228
Die Haaie in die See, 48
*Die harige ou harlekyn (**Die Dromedaris**)*, 191
Die Hart van die Daeraad, 61
*Die jaar word ryp in goue akkerblare (**Vroegherfs**)*, 178
*Die jare kom die bulte oor (**Die swarte Osse**)*, 198
Die Kat se Kies, 51
*Die kind in my het stil gesterf (**Puberteit**)*, 87
*Die kind is nie dood nie (**Die Kind**)*, 90
*Die ligman van die voortyd (**Die Son**)*, 9
*Die nag het duisend oë (**Duisend-en-een**)*, 203
*Die osse stap aan deur die stowwe (**Die Ossewa**)*, 31
Die ou Kameeldoringboom, 101
*Die ou langenekker op-en-af (**Die Kameelperd**)*, 193
*Die ou vetsak wat daar woedend brul (**Die Seekoei**)*, 192
Die Pêrel se Klokkies, 195
Die See is wild, 108
*Die son is vol en rond (**Die Son en die Maan**)*, 11
*Die son slaap onder 'n kombers (**Die Sterre**)*, 10
*Die spore van die hart van die dagbreek! (**Hart-van-die-dagbreek**)*, 147
*Die stad is so stil in die herfsaand (**Herfsaand**)*, 175
*Die tortel op die boomtak (**Aan Stella**)*, 164
*Die voëltjies vry en skaterlag in voorjaarsblaartjies (**Amors Konfetti**)*, 30
*Die vrou is vir die man gemaak (**Man en Vrou**)*, 212
Die werk wat sal groei soos die Meester syn ('n Doringkroon), 29
*Die Windvoël het reeds van die voortyd (**Die Wind**)*, 13

INDEX OF FIRST LINES AND TITLES

Dingaan, die Zoeloe, 110
Dis altyd jy, net altyd jy (*Die Liefde in my*), 183
Dis die blond, dis die blou (*Dis al*), 3–5, 34
Dis omdraaislaan soos Handomkeer, 17
Dit gaan goed met die mens (*U het my Skuld vergewe*), 243
Dit is die maand Oktober (*Oktobermaand*), 126
Dit is laat in die Nag, 94
Doedoe my skapie (*Slaapdeuntjie*), 173
Doer bo teen die Rant, 25

Eis van die Vonk, 111
Ek het gedink, 87
Ek het my aan jou oorgegee, 60
Ek het 'n duifie gehad (*Die Duifie*), 75
Ek hou van die Môre, 231
Ek is die lappop wat nie praat (*Lied van die Lappop*), 85
Ek is die Ster, wat uit die Ooste skyn (*Die Ster uit die Ooste*), 152
Ek ken jou nou, 238
Ek ken jou skaars, 237
Ek kom hier aan, 49
Ek kry 'n klein klein Beiteltjie (*Die Beiteltjie*), 182
Ek ry in die veld in die môre (*Salut d'Amour*), 219
Ek sing van die Wind, 112
Ek skuil by die Here, 242
Ek weet dat in die kalme Samesyn, 63
Ek wonder steeds of ons eendag (*Die Donker Stroom*), 194
Elke sproetjie op haar snoetjie (*Sproetenooi*), 100
Êrens in die Kro het ek 'n Skerm, 19

Fladder, fladder vlindertjie (*Lentelied*), 171
Fluit, Windswael, sing en fluit, 113

Gampta, my vaal Sussie (*Die Woestyn-lewerkie*), 145
Gee my Sonlig, gee my rose (*Gee my*), 169
Gee vir my 'n Trouring, 114
Gelukkig en bly was die dag (*Geboorte van die Lente*), 203
God, hierdie angs, hierdie angs (*Paniese Angs*), 188
Gomverdorie, Poetoepap, 46
Grondmannetjie, ek sal jou kry! (*Grondmannetjie my Skaduwee*), 204

Het jy gehoor by die voor (*Kokkewiet*), 3–5, 160
Hierdie gomlastiekkalant (*Die Olifant*), 190
Hoe stil kan dit word as Sedoos gaan lê, 15

Hoor die Janfiskaal van die Grootrivier (*Die Grootrivier se Voël*), 102
Hotnotsgot en Spinnekop, 45

Ik sal nou maar so saggies aan (*Klaas Vakie*), 96
Ik sien jouw beeld in elke blom (*Adoratio*), 93
In die stilte van my Tuin, 58
In 'n Gat daar onder die Sukkeldoring, 115

Jeug van my Volk, 143
Jong Pappelierbas glad en koel, 16
Jy bly klein, 45
Jy is die leeurik (*Van Verlore-vlei*), 222
Jy't gekom om my siel uit sy smart te haal (*Waarom?*), 238
Jy was my jeug (*Opdrag*), 187

Kaggen het sy skoen gegooi (*Die Maan*), 10
Keur van die Beste, 118
Klein Piedeplooi, 22
Klim op, klim op met die Slingerpad!, 119
Klossie, jul bewe en bibber, 120
Koel druppels water (*Rus en Stilte*), 69
Kom daar 'n mens te sterwe (*Wieglied*), 13
Kom dans Klaradyn, 232
Kom dans met my!, 120
Kom met my na die verre see (*Rots by die See*), 161
Kom na my skaduwee, edele vrou (*Lied van die Wonderboom*), 211
Kom saam met my na Toorberg, 42
Kom sluimer as ruimer die winde beminde (*Sluimer, Beminde*), 157
Kom vannag in my Drome, 185
Konsternasie, hoenderpiep! (*Konsternasie*), 54
Koud is die Wind, 59
Kriekie, jy wat op die Solder sanik, 122
Krulkop-klonkie, waarvandaan kom jy (*Krulkop-klonkie*), 104
Kry jy Papelellekoors, 52
Kyk hoe die aandson die bulte kleur (*Die Aandblom*), 39

Laat ons sing van ons heideweelde (*Heideweelde*), 77
Land van die eike met helder groen lower (*Land, Volk en Taal*), 209
Langsamerhand, geruisloos skuif die vlek van skadu (*Sonsverduistering*), 162
Langs stille Waters, 81

INDEX OF FIRST LINES AND TITLES   281

Liefste Tannie, ons bring rosies (**Met 'n Mandjie Rose**), 213

Met Skemering, 64
My Hart gaan terug as die skemer val (**Tot die Oggendgloor**), 83
My Hart verlang na die stilte (**Heimwee**), 170
My Koekiesveerhen jou Verkereveer, 24
My naakte siel wil sonder skrome (**Grense**), 184
My Siel is siek van Heimwee, 172

'n Druppel gal is in die soetste wyn (**Skoppensboer**), 148
'n Harp het gehang (**Toewyding**), 221
'n Knapie sag 'n rosie staan (**Die Howenier**), 165
'n Moeder dwaal onder graffies rond (**Die soekende Moeder**), 32
'n Vrou wag by die skemervuur (**Die Melkweg**), 11
Ná al die sonskyn is dit donker (**Eerste Winterdag**), 139
Nee, liewer die Dood, 64
Neem 'n stukkie Son, 44
Net soos 'n lammetjie so lief (**Klein Sonneskyn**), 208
Nou is sy oud, en afgeleef (**Moeder**), 98
Nou lê die aarde nagtelank en week (**Winter**), 180

O, Boereplaas, 233
O diep rivier, o donker stroom (**Diep Rivier**), 147
O gits en gaats, 48
O, Heer, ek dank U (**Balansstaat**), 37
O, hoor die gesang (**Die Veldwindjie**), 33
O koud is die Windjie en skraal (**Winternag**), 2–5, 146
O magtige osean (**See-Sonnet**), 235
O vra my nie my liefde (**Ek hou van blou**), 95
O vreemde Liefde, 65
O wilgerboom, wat oor die water waak (**'n Treurlied**), 132
Omdat die Dood, 216
Ons het mekaar gegroet, 68
Ons soek mekaar by Krymekaar (**Krymekaar**), 25
Oor ver, verre lande (**Aandblik**), 141
Op die hoëveld sterwe die dag (**Huistoe**), 78
Op my ou Ramkietjie, 106
Ou Damon loop sy Lammertroppie om, 16
Ou Poegenpol op Pale, 18
Ouma het 'n Weglêhoender, 47

Petronella, Kokkerot, 47
Piet Fourie het 'n kramp gekry (**Piet Fourie**), 53
Pluk die Snare, blaas die Fluit, 42

Reën op die Veld, 102
Rolbos is 'n Tolbos, 43
Rooidag, rooidag wat bring jy (**Rooidag**), 189

Sag oor die velde wyd (**Die Karoovlakte**), 159
Satanskinders laat my gril, 49
Sekretarisvoël met jou langebene (**Sekretarisvoël**), 105
Siembamba, Siembamba, mamma se kindjie (**'n Nuwe Liedjie op 'n ou Deuntjie**), 124
Sing, Vinkie, sing!, 128
Sing weer vir my, 129
Slapedoe, slapedoe, my lief klein kindjie (**Slaapliedjie**), 177
Soos 'n borrelende Vink sy Hart verlos, 130
Soos die Windjie wat suis, 76
Spit, o Tuinman, spit diep (**Die Tuinman**), 199
Staan, Poppie, staan!, 150
Susanna Viljee dra onpaar skoene (**Susanna Viljee**), 55
Swakkeling met Vrou en Kind, 62

Te kort jou skoonheids-duur (**Die Roos**), 196
Toeral, loeral, la, 131
Tortelduifie, in die vlug (**Tortelduifie**), 51
Tuinroos tussen die Tulpe, 133
Twaalf Sardientjies in 'n Blik, 50

Uit hierdie ligte en wye herfstyd straal (**Uit hierdie ligte Herfs**), 179

Van die Lotosland waar die Lelies groei - Lied van Mali, die slaaf, 134
Van Kirstenbosch tot in Namakwaland, 27
Van lae Hartstog, diep bedrog (**'n Gebed**), 67
Van Rietvleisemoorsand tot by Soetbatsfontein, 20
Vanmôre was Japie nog hier (**Japie**), 117
Vermoeide Pelgrim, 84
Verwag my in die awend liefste (**Die Balling se Boodskap**), 155
Vonkel, sterretjie, vonkel (**Die Sterretjie**), 109
Vryheid, woord van alle woorde (**Voor in die Wapad brand 'n Lig**), 224

Waar die Nag in ademlose Stilte, 35
Waar slaap my liefde (**Windliedjie**), 86
Waarom is die Duiwel vir die Slypsteen bang, 23
Wank'lende skepies op went'lende bare (**Nimmer of nou**), 215
Warrelwind kom warrel my (**Warrelwind**), 43
Was ek 'n Sanger, 229

282 INDEX OF FIRST LINES AND TITLES

Was jy 'n rosebloesem (**Prinses van verre**), 217
Wat is die verskil?, 53
Wat word van die meisie wat altyd alleen bly (**Die Towenares**), 144
Weer skyn die volkome somermaan (**Voor die Venster**), 139

Wees jy, my lied (**Die Rose van herinnering**), 196
Wieg my in sluimer (**Sluimerlied**), 240
Wies getik en wiesit kwyt, 18
Wit is die wêreld van outyd se wee (**Vaalvalk**), 138
Wit soos die pêrelskuim (**Sneeu op die Berge**), 70
Wys my die Plek, 135

INDEX OF COMPOSERS AND THEIR WORKS

For the benefit of digital users, indexed terms that span two pages (e.g., 52–53) may, on occasion, appear on only one of those pages.

Aerts, Peter (1912-1996), 95, 106, 124
  Ek hou van Blou (Dedicated to Elza De Clerq), 95
  'n Nuwe Liedjie op 'n ou Deuntjie (*Siembamba*) (Dedicated to Miss. Helena Strauss), 124
  Op my ou Ramkietjie (Dedicated to Anna Neethling-Pohl), 106

Amyot, E. (n.d.), 112
  Ek sing van die Wind, 112

Ashworth, Alexander Hargreaves (Alex) (1895-1959) published under A. H. Ashworth, 31, 34, 93, 96, 97, 146
  Adoratio, 93
  Die Ossewa, 31
  Klaas Vakie, 96
  Dis al, 34
  'n Lied van die See, 97
  Winternag, 146

Barnes, L. (n.d.), 146
  Winternag, 146

Barton, Horace Percival (1872-1951) published under Horace Barton, 5, 93, 96, 198
  As saans, 93
  Die swarte Osse, 198
  Klaas Vakie, 96

Bell, William Henry (1873-1946) published under W. H. Bell, 146
  Winternag, 146, (Seven Afrikaans Songs for Solo Voice and Orchestra, no. 1), 146

Beyers, Doris (n.d.), 30, 70, 130, 131, 141, 194, 196, 211
"Cupid's Confetti and Five Other Songs" (*Amors Konfetti en Vyf ander Liedere*), 30, 70, 141
  1. *Amors Konfetti*, 30
  2. *Aandblik*, 141
  3. *Sneeu op die Berge*, 70

Die Donker Stroom, 194, "Three Songs" (*Drie Liedere*), 194
Die Rose van Herinnering, 196
Lied van die Wonderboom, 211
Soos 'n borrelende Vink sy Hart verlos, 130, "Three Songs" (*Drie Liedere*), 130
Toeral, loeral, la, 131 "Three Songs" (*Drie Liedere*), 131

Bon Sr., Gerrit (1901-1983), 134, 148, 153, 196, 215, 217, 229
  Amoreuse Liedeken, 153
  Die Roos, 196
  Die Rose van Herinnering, 196
  Nimmer of Nou, 215, "Voortrekker/Pioneer Festival Songs" (*Voortrekker Feessange, no. 2*), 215
  Prinses van Verre, 217
  Skoppensboer, 148
  "Lied van Mali, die Slaaf" from the poem *Van die Lotosland waar die Lelies groei* (*Lied van Mali, die Slaaf*), 134
  Was ek 'n Sanger, 229

Bosman, Gysbert Hugo (1882-1967) a.k.a. Vere Bosman di Ravelli, published under Bosman di Ravelli, 3–5, 33, 146, 165
  "Three Songs" (*Drie Liederen*), 33, 146, 165
  1. *Die Howenier*, 165
  2. *Winternag*, 146
  3. *Die Veldwindjie* (Dedicated to Lady Rose-Innes), 33

Bouws, Jan (1902-1978), 34, 93, 106, 110
  "Eleven Afrikaans Songs" (*Elf Afrikaanse Liedere*), 34, 106
  1. *Op my ou Ramkietjie*, 106
  2. *Dis al*, 34

  As saans, 93
  Dingaan, die Zoeloe, 110

Brent-Wessels, Judith (1910-n.d.), 73, 104, 112, 146, 147
Droomtyd (Dedicated to Wynand), 73
Diep Rivier, 147
Ek sing van die Wind, 112
Krulkop-klonkie (Dedicated to Christine du Plessis), 104
Winternag, 146

Brinne, Dirk Jan (1909-1974), 96
Klaas Vakie, 96

Brown, Leonard (n.d.), 112
Ek sing van die Wind, 112

Clement, Daniel (1902-1980), 34, 112, 114, 117, 124, 126, 146, 200, 206, 209, 220, 228, 233
"South Africa Onwards" (*Suid-Afrika vorentoe*), 34, 112, 114, 117, 124, 126, 146, 200, 206, 209, 220, 233
  4. *Land, Volk en Taal*, 209
  5. *O, Boereplaas*, 233
  6. *Japie*, 117
  7. *"Siembaba"* from the poem *'n Nuwe Liedjie op 'n ou Deuntjie* (*Siembamba*), 124
  13. *Dis al*, 34
  14. "Loitering Ditty" (*Slampamperliedjie*) from the poem *Gee vir my 'n Trouring*, 114
  15. "Loitering Ditty" (*Slampamperliedjie*) from the poem *Ek sing van die Wind*, 112
  19. *"Die Wapad"* from the poem *Die Wapad is my Woning*, 200
  23. *Winternag*, 146
  29. *Oktobermaand*, 126
  33. *Sannie*, 220
  34. *Kalwerliefde*, 206

Vraag en Antwoord, 228

Cohen, Peter Lawrence (1937-n.d.), 138
Vaalvalk, "Three Serious Songs" (*Drie ernstige Liedere*) Song Cycle for Baritone and Piano, Op. 14, no. 2, 138

de Jong, Marinus (1891-1984), 124, 139, 146, 188
"Six South African Songs" (*Zes Zuidafrikaanse Liederen*), 124, 139, 146, 188
  1. *Paniese Angs*, 188
  2. *Winternag*, 146
  3. *Voor die Venster*, 139
  5. *'n Nuwe Liedjie op 'n ou Deuntjie* (*Siembamba*), 124

de Villiers, Dirk Izak Cattogio (Dirkie) (1920-1993) published under Dirkie de Villiers, 35, 96, 146, 148, 183, 184
Grense, 184
Klaas Vakie, 96
Skoppensboer, 148
Waar die Nag in ademlose Stilte - 'n Kerslied (Dedicated to Mrs. Jo Ross), 35
"Winterbome" from the poem *Die Liefde in my*, 183
Winternag, 146

de Villiers, Gisela (b. 1955), 95
Ek hou van blou, 95

de Villiers, Marthinus Lourens (1885-1977) published under M. L. de Villiers, 2–5, 29, 69, 219
"Six Afrikaans Art Songs" (*Ses Afrikaanse Kunsliedere*), 29
  3. *'n Doringkroon* (Dedicated to Prof. Hans Endler), 29
  4. *Die Branders*, 29
  5. *Rus en Stilte*, 69

Salut d'Amour, 219

de Villiers, Pieter Johannes (1924-2015) published under P. J. de Villiers or Pieter de Villiers, 5, 21, 37, 95, 115, 119, 130, 132, 162, 214, 235, 242, 243
"Three Leipold Songs" (*Drie Leipoldt-liedjies*), 119, 130, 132
  1. *Soos 'n borrelende Vink sy Hart verlos*, 130
  2. *'n Treurlied*, 132
  3. *Klim op, klim op met die Slingerpad!*, 119
Sewe Boerneef-liedjiesSewe lawwe Liedjies (Dedicated to (Elizabeth) Betsy de la Porte), 21
  1. *Blaas op die Pampoenstingel*, 21
  2. *Klein Piedeplooi*, 22
  3. *Die Berggansveer*, 22
  4. *Waarom is die Duiwel vir die Slypsteen bang*, 23
  5. *Aandblom is 'n Witblom*, 24
  6. *My Koekiesveerhen jou Verkereveer*, 24
  7. *Doer bo teen die Rant*, 25
"Four Songs of Doubt and Faith" (*Vier Liedere van Twyfel en Geloof*), 37, 162, 242, 243
  1. *Sonsverduistering*, 162
  2. *Ek skuil by die Here*, 242
  3. *Balansstaat*, 37
  4. *U het my Skuld vergewe*, 243

Ek hou van blou (Dedicated to Joyce Barker), 95

In 'n Gat daar onder die Sukkeldoring (Dedicated to Rina Hugo), 115
Middagslapie, 214
See-Sonnet (Dedicated to Cecilia Wessels), 235

de Villiers, Septimus Catorzia (1895-1929) published under S. C. de Villiers, 31, 109
Die Ossewa, 31
Die Sterretjie, 109

de Vos, Herre (1877-1948), 117
Japie (Dedicated to Antoinette van Dijk), 117

de Vos, Philip, 42–56
O togga! 'n Gogga - Lawwe Versies vir stout Kinders, Sangsiklus, 42
  1. *Pluk die Snare, blaas die Fluit*, 42
  2. *Kom saam met my na Toorberg*, 42
  3. *Warrelwind*, 43
  4. *Rolbos is 'n Tolbos*, 43
  5. *Neem 'n stukkie Son*, 44
  6. *As jy by my kom kuier*, 44
  7. *Jy bly klein*, 45
  8. *Hotnotsgot en Spinnekop*, 45
  9. *Gomverdorie, Poetoepap*, 46
  10. *Petronella, Kokkerot*, 47
  11. *Ouma het 'n Weglêhoender*, 47
  12. *Die Haaie in die See*, 48
  13. *O gits en gaats*, 48
  14. *Ek kom hier aan*, 49
  15. *Satanskinders laat my gril*, 49
  16. *Twaalf Sardientjies in 'n Blik*, 50
  17. *Die Kat se Kies*, 51
  18. *Tortelduifie*, 51
  19. *Bo in die Solder*, 52
  20. *Kry jy Papelellekoors*, 52
  21. *Piet Fourie*, 53
  22. *Wat is die verskil?*, 53
  23. *Konsternasie*, 54
  24. *Susanna Viljee*, 55

Dopper, Cornelius (1870-1939), 96
Klaas Vakie, 96

du Plessis, Hubert (1922-2011), 5, 22, 25, 59, 60, 61, 62, 63, 64, 65, 104, 105, 106, 107, 146
Vier Slampamperliedjies, Op. 23 (Dedicated to Mimi Coertse), 104
  1. *Krulkop-klonkie*, 104
  2. *Sekretarisvoël*, 105
  3. *Op my ou Ramkietjie*, 106
  4. *Boggom en Voertsek*, 107

Vreemde Liefde, Op. 7, 59
  1. *As ek my vreemde Liefde bloot moes lê*, 59
  2. *Ek het my aan jou oorgegee*, 60
  3. *Die Hart van die Daeraad*, 61
  4. *Swakkeling met Vrou en Kind*, 62
  5. *Ek weet dat in die kalme Samesyn*, 63
  6. *Nee, liewer die Dood*, 64
  7. *Met Skemering*, 64
  8. *Vreemde Liefde*, 65

"Ten Boerneef Songs for Tenor, Op. 38" (Dedicated to Helmut Holzapfel)
  1. *Doer bo teen die Rant*, 25
  3. "Die Berggans" from the poem *Die Berggansveer*, 22

Winternag, "Three Nocturnes, for dramatic Soprano, Op. 36, no. 3," 146

du Plessis, Mornay André (1909-1941), 71
Liefdeswee (Dedicated to Madame Cecilia Wessels), 71

Eagar, Fannie Edith Starke (1920-n.d.), 195
Die Pêrel se Klokkies, 195

Elbrecht, Berend (1883-1954), 93, 96
As saans, 93
Klaas Vakie, 96

Ellis, Arthur (b. 1931), 39, 177, 195, 196, 200, 203, 224
Die Aandblom, 39
Die Pêrel se Klokkies, 195
Die Roos, 196
Die Wapad is my Woning, 200
Duisend-en-een, 203
Slaapliedjie (Dedicated to L. de W.), *Voor in die Wapad brand 'n Lig*, 177, 224

Endler, Johann Franz (Hans) (1871-1947) published under Hans Endler, 76, 129
Sing weer vir my, 129
Soos die Windjie wat suis, 76

Engela, Dawid Sofius (1931-1967) published under Dawid S. Engela, 60, 68, 187
"Songs of a Futile Love" (*Liedere van 'n vergeefse Liefde*), 60
  1. *Ek het my aan jou oorgegee*, 60
  4. *Ons het mekaar gegroet*, 68

Opdrag, 187, "Two Songs" (*Twee Liedere, no.1*), 187

286 INDEX OF COMPOSERS AND THEIR WORKS

Fagan, Gideon (1904-1980), 3–5, 75, 111, 135, 208, 211, 216
"Loitering Ditties" (*Slampamperliedjies*), 111, 135
  1. *Wys my die Plek*, 135
  2. *Eis van die Vonk wat spartel*, 111

  Die Duifie, 75
  Klein Sonneskyn, 208
  Lied van die Wonderboom, 211
  Omdat die Dood, 216

Fagan, Johannes Jacobus (1898-1920) published under Johannes J. Fagan, 3–5, 32, 76
  Die soekende Moeder, 32
  Soos die Windjie wat suis, 76

Faul, Lourens Abram (b. 1931) published under Lourens Faul, 27, 106, 113, 128, 131, 135, 190
Noag, se Ark (Dedicated to Eva Noel Harvey), 190
  1. *Die Olifant*, 190
  2. *Die Renoster*, 191
  3. *Die Dromedaris*, 191
  4. *Die Seekoei*, 192
  5. *Die Kameelperd*, 193
  6. *Ensovoorts*, 193
"Two Loitering Dities" (*Twee Slampamperliedjies*) (Dedicated to Cato Brink), 106, 135
  1. *Op my ou Ramkietjie*, 106
  2. *Wys my die Plek*, 135

  "*Fluit, Windswael*" from the poem *Fluit, Windswael, sing en fluit*, 113
  Sing, Vinkie, sing!, 128
  Toeral, loeral, la, 131
  Van Kirstenbosch tot in Namakwaland (Dedicated to Jeanette Bezuidenhout-Harris), 27

Gertsman, Blanche (1910-1973), 29, 138, 237–39
  Sangsiklus vir Sopraan en Klavier, 237
  1. *Ek ken jou skaars*, 237
  2. *Ek ken jou nou*, 238
  3. *Waarom?*, 238

  Die Branders, 29
  Vaalvalk, 138

Grové, Stephans (1922-2014), 34, 85
Vyf Liedere op Tekste van Ingrid Jonker, Sangsiklus, 85
  1. *Lied van die Lappop*, 85
  2. *Windliedjie*, 86

  3. *Puberteit*, 87
  4. *Ek het gedink*, 87
  5. *Ontnugtering*, 88

  Dis al, 34, (*Drie Liedere, no. 1*), 34

Haasdijk, P. W. (n.d.) a.k.a. P. W. Haasdyk, 93
  As saans, 93

Hallis, Adolf (1896-1987), 147
  Diep Rivier, 147

Hartman, Anton Carlisle (1918-1982) a.k.a. Anton Hartman, 185
Kom Vannag in my Drome (Dedicated to Jossie), 185

Harvey, Eva Noel (1900-1976), 5, 104, 113, 120, 126, 128, 131, 147, 219
"Three New Songs" (*Drie nuwe Liedere*), 104, 219
  1. *Salut d'Amour*, 219
  2. *Krulkop-klonkie*, 104

  Fluit, Windswael, sing en fluit, 113
  Kom dans met my!, 120
  "*O Diep Rivier*" from the poem *Diep Rivier*, 147
  Oktobermaand, 126
  Sing, Vinkie, sing!, 128
  Toeral, loeral, la, 131

Hirschland, Heinz (1901-1960), 5, 67, 69, 128
"Fourteen Afrikaans Songs" (*Veertien Afrikaanse Liedere*), 67, 69
  7. *'n Gebed*, 67
  9. *Rus en Stilte*, 69

  Sing, Vinkie, sing!, 128

Hofmeyr, Hendrik (b. 1957), 5, 86, 89, 90, 146, 147, 178
Vier Gebede by Jaargetye in die Boland, 178
  1. *Vroegherfs*, 178
  2. *Uit hierdie ligte Herfs*, 179
  3. *Winter*, 180
  4. *Eerste Sneeu*, 181
"Two Poems by Eugène Marais" (*Twee Gedigte van Eugène Marais*), 146, 147
  1. *Winternag*, 146
  2. *Diep Rivier*, 147

  Die Kind (wat doodgeskiet is deur soldate by Nyanga) (*Woorde in die Wind, no. 4*), 90

Windliedjie (*Woorde in die Wind, no. 1*) 86
Bitterbessie Dagbreek, 89

Hullebroeck, Emiel (1878-1965), 109
Die Sterretjie, "Six Songs" (*Zes Liederen, no. 3*) (Dedicated to Miss. M. van Westrheene), 109

Hylton-Edwards, Stewart (1924-1987), 25, 147
Krymekaar, 25
Diep Rivier - Die Lied van Juanita Perreira (Dedicated to Saline Koch), 147

Idelson, Jeremiah (Jerry) (1893-n.d.) published under Jerry Idelson, 150
Staan, Poppie, staan!, 150

Joubert, Hennie (1926-1986), 95
Ek hou van blou, 95

Joubert, Aletta Margaretha Lettie (1894-1966) published under Mrs. H. C. de Kock, Lettie Joubert and L. Joubert, 214, 229
Middagslapie, 214
Was ek 'n Sanger, 229

Kennedy, Spruhan Keith (1901-n.d) published under S. Kennedy, 139
Eerste Winterdag, 139, "Five Songs for Baritone" (*Vyf Liedere vir Bariton, no. 1*), 139

Kerrebijn, Marius (1882-1930), 96
Klaas Vakie (Dedicated to the composer's parents), 96
Klatzow, Peter James Leonard (1945-2021) published under Peter Klatzow, 5, 42, 178
Kom saam met my na Toorberg, 42
Vroegherfs, 178, (*Vier Gebede by Jaargetye in die Boland, no. 1*), 178

Kratz, Anton E. (1917-1980), 95
Ek hou van blou, 95
Kromhout, Jan (1886-1969), 98, 204
Grondmannetjie (*My Skaduwee*), 204
Moeder, 98

Lamprecht, Chris (b. 1927), 5, 101–3
Aan die Noordweste, 101
  1. *Die ou Kameeldoringboom*, 101
  2. *Die Grootrivier se Voël*, 102
  3. *Reën op die Veld*, 102

4. *Namakwaland se Blommetjies*, 103
5. *Loeriesfontein*, 103

Lamprecht, Con (n.d.), 133, 229
Tuinroos tussen die Tulpe (Dedicated to (Elizabeth) Betsy de la Porte), 133
Was ek 'n Sanger, 229

Lamprechts-Vos, Anna Catharina (1876-1932) published under Anna Lambrechts and Anna Lambrechts-Vos, 67, 120, 170
'n Gebed, 67, "Great South Africa" (*Groot Suid–Afrika*)Songs in Five Volumes: Vol. I, Op. 41 no. 3, 67
Heimwee, 170, "Songs of Anna Lambrechts Vos" (*Liederen van Anna Lambrechts–Vos, Op. 51, no. 3*), 170
Kom dans met my!, 120, "Great South Africa" (*Groot Suid–Afrika*)Songs in Five Volumes: Vol. V, Op. 45 nos. 21 and 22, two settings of the same poem exist, 120

Lapin, Lily (1893-n.d.), 194
Die Donker Stroom, 194, "Two Songs for Bass Voice, no. 2,", 194

le Roux Marais, Stephanus (1896-1979) published under S. le Roux Marais, 5, 30, 34, 57, 66, 67, 69, 77, 81, 93, 94, 96, 97, 98, 126, 132, 134, 146, 152, 153, 154, 155, 157, 168, 169, 170, 171, 172, 173, 175, 189, 194, 196, 203, 211, 213, 214, 219, 232, 240, 241
"The Rose and Other Afrikaans Songs" (*Die Roos en ander Afrikaanse Liedere*) (Dedicated to Mrs. Dr. B. de Preez), 34, 93, 196, 213
  1. *Die Roos*, 196
  2. *Dis al*, 34
  3. *As saans*, 93
  5. *Met 'n Mandjie Rose*, 213
"New Songs" (*Nuwe Liedere*), 66, 67, 69, 94, 126, 154, 155, 189, 194, 203, 241
  1. *Oktobermaand*, 126
  2. *Die Donker Stroom*, 194
  3. *Duisend-en-een*, 203
  4. *Die Balling se Boodskap*, 155
  5. *Rus en Stilte*, 69
  6. *'n Gebed*, 67
  7. *Daar's 'n Tyd*, 154
  8. *As ek moet sterwe, liefste*, 241
  9. *Dit is laat in die Nag*, 94
  10. *Rooidag*, 189
  11. *As my Hart nou wil sing*, 66

288 INDEX OF COMPOSERS AND THEIR WORKS

le Roux Marais, Stephanus (1896-1979) published
under S. le Roux Marais (*cont.*)
"Six Art Songs" (*Ses Kunsliedere*), 57, 98, 132, 153,
211, 219
  1. *Moeder*, 98
  2. *Bosveldhuisie*, 57
  3. *Salut d'Amour*, 219
  4. *Lied van die Wonderboom*, 211
  5. *Amoreuse Liedeken*, 153
  6. *Treurlied*, 132
"Five Art Songs" (*Vyf Kunsliedere*) (Dedicated to
Mrs. B. du Preez), 134, 157, 203
  2. *Geboorte van die Lente*, 203
  3. "Mali, die Slaaf, se Lied" from the poem *Van
die Lotosland waar die Lelies groei - Lied van
Mali, die Slaaf*, 134
  5. *Sluimer, Beminde*, 157
"Fifteen Afrikaans Lullabies" (*Vyftien Afrikaanse
Slaapdeuntjies*), 96, 168, 173, 214
  2. *Slaapdeuntjie* from the poem "Doe-doe, my
baba," 173
  3. *Slaapdeuntjie* from the poem "Doe-doe, my
baba," 173
  4. *Buite suis die sagte Windjie*, 168
  6. *Buite suis die sagte Windjie*, 168
  13. *Middagslapie*, 214
  14. *Klaas Vakie*, 96

Amors Konfetti, 30, "Four Afrikaans Song
Snippets" (*Vier Afrikaanse Sangstukkies,
no.4*), 30
Die Ster uit die Ooste, 152, "South African
Carols,", 152
Gee my, 169, "To the Bushveld and Two Other
Songs" (*Bosveldtoe en Twee ander Liedere,
no. 2*), 169
Heideweelde, 77, "Golden Sheaf" (*Goue Gerf*), 77
Heimwee, 170
My siel is siek van Heimwee, 172
Herfsaand, 175
Kom dans Klaradyn, 232
Langs stille Waters, 81, "Two Sacred Songs"
(Twee gewyde Sangstukke, no. 1), 81
Langs stille Waters, "Hymn, Second Choral
Album" (Lofgesang, Second Choral Album,
no. 5), 81
Lentelied, 171
'n Lied van die See, 97

Sluimerlied, 240
Winternag, 146
Lea-Morgan, John (n.d.), 215
Nimmer of Nou, 215

Lemmer, Petrus Johannes (1896-1989) published
under P. J. Lemmer, 3–5, 95, 98, 100, 143, 159,
160, 161, 164, 172, 217
"Golden Sheaf" (*Goue Gerf*), 100, 143, 164
  3. *Aan Stella*, 164
  20. *Jeug van my Volk*, 143
  34. *Sproetenooi*, 100

Die Karoovlakte, 159
Ek hou van blou, 95
Kokkewiet, 160
Moeder, 98
My Siel is siek van Heimwee (Dedicated to
Pat de Wet), 172
Prinses van Verre, 217
Rots by die See, 161

Lewald, Otto Albrecht (1905-1988) published under
Otto A. Lewald and O. A. Lewald, 34, 98
Dis al, 34 "Six Songs to Words by Jan F. E.
Cilliers, no. 3,", 34
Moeder, 98

Loots, Joyce Mary Ann Dougall née (1907-n.d.)
published under Joyce Loots, 108, 169
"Three Afrikaans Songs" (*Drie Afrikaanse
Liedere*), 108, 169
  1. *Gee my*, 169
  3. *Die 108, See is wild*

Löwenherz, Ernst (1874-1958) published under
Ernst Lowenhertz, 34, 117, 120, 128, 214, 229
Dis al, *Op. 42*, 34
Japie, 117
Kom dans met my!, 120
Middagslapie, *Op. 27, no. 2*, 214
Sing, Vinkie, sing!, 128
Was ek 'n Sanger, 229

Manca, Joseph Salvatore (1908-1985) published
under J. S. Manca, 203, 221
  Geboorte van die Lente, 203
  Toewyding, 221

INDEX OF COMPOSERS AND THEIR WORKS   289

Maske, Hans Herbert (1927-1976), 135
  Wys my die Plek, 135

Matthews, Hayden Thomas (1894-1958) published
    under Johannes Joubert, 5, 34, 78, 79, 83, 84,
    112, 150, 217, 231, 233
  Dis al, 34
  Ek hou van die Môre, 231
  Ek sing van die Wind, 112
  Huistoe, 78
  Kom Huistoe, Liefste!, 79
  O, Boereplaas, 233
  Prinses van Verre, 217
  Staan, Poppie, staan!, 150
  Tot die Oggend gloor, 83
  Vermoeide Pelgrim, 84

Mengelberg, Rudolf (Kurt) (1892-1959) published
    under Rudolf Mengelberg, 34
  Dis al, 34 "Nine South African Songs, no. 6,", 34

Nel, Charles (1890-1983), 3–5, 34, 106, 132, 146
  Dis al, 34, "Three Afrikaans Songs"
    (*Drie Afrikaanse Liedere, no.2*) – Various
    settings of this poem by the
    same composer exist from 1914 etc, 34
  Op my ou Ramkietjie, 106
  'n Treurlied, 132
  Winternag, 146

Nepgen, Rosa Sophia Cornelia (1909-2001)
    published under Mrs. W.E.G. Louw and Rosa
    Nepgen, 5, 15, 22, 25, 34, 58, 95, 106, 107, 118,
    130, 131, 132, 133, 146, 147, 182, 183, 194, 196,
    199, 203, 219, 221, 222
*Op die Flottina: Nege Liedere vir Middelstem en
    Klavier*, 15
  1. *Hoe stil kan dit word as Sedoos gaan lê*, 15
  2. *Jong Pappelierbas glad en koel*, 16
  3. *Ou Damon loop sy Lammertroppie om*, 16
  4. *Dis omdraaislaan soos handomkeer*, 17
  5. *Ou Poegenpol op Pale*, 18
  6. *Wies getik en wiesit kwyt*, 18
  7. *Êrens in die Kro het ek 'n Skerm*, 19
  8. *Agter Akkerskraalsekop*, 20
  9. *Van Rietvleisemoorsand tot by
      Soetbatsfontein*, 20
Sewe Boerneef LiedjiesSewe lawwe Liedjies, 21, 22, 25

  1. *Die Berggansveer*, 22
  7. *Doer bo teen die Rant*, 25
Drie Marais-Liedere
  1. *Winternag*, 146
  2. *Hart-van-die-dagbreek*, 147
  3. *Diep-rivier*, 147

  Boggom en Voertsek, 107
  Die Beiteltjie, 182
  Die Donker Stroom, 194
  Die Liefde in my, 183
  Die Tuinman, 199
  Dis al, 34
  Duisend-en-een, 203
  Ek hou van blou, 95
  In die silte van my tuin, 58
  Keur van die Beste, 118
  'n Treurlied, 132
  Op my ou Ramkietjie, 106
  Salut d'Amour, 219
  Soos 'n borrelende Vink sy Hart verlos, 130
  Toeral, loeral, la, 131
  Toewyding, 221
  Tuinroos tussen die Tulpe, 133
  Van Verlore-vlei, 222
  "*Wees jy, my Lied, 'n goue Kelk*" from the poem
    Die Rose van Herinnering, 196

Oxtoby, Charles Francis (1912-1978), 76
  Soos die Windjie wat suis 76, Op. 36, no. 2, 76

Pescod, John Kilburn (1898-1985) published
    under John Pescod, 5, 31, 122, 126, 142, 219
  Die Ossewa, 31
  Die Roosknoppie, 142
  Lenteliedjie, 122
  Oktobermaand, 126
  Salut d'Amour, 219

Rentzke, Suzanne (b. 1982), 95
  Ek hou van blou, 95

Richfield, Sydney (1882-1967), 5, 109, 142, 146,
    194, 215
  Die Donker Stroom, 194
  Die Roosknoppie, 142
  Die Sterretjie, "Two Evening Songs" (*Twee
    Aandliedere, no. 2*), 76, 109

Richfield, Sydney (1882-1967) (*cont.*)
   Nimmer of nou, 215
   Winternag, 146

Roode, David Johannes (1900-1983) published
   under D. J. Roode, 126
   Oktobermaand, 126

Roode, Maarten Christiaan (1907-1967) published
   under M. C. Roode, 93, 194, 212
   As saans, 93
   Die Donker Stroom, 194
   Man en Vrou, 212

Söhnge, Wilhelm Ernst Heinrich (1909-n.d.), 109
   "Vonkel, Sterretjie, vonkel" from the poem
   Die Sterretjie, 109
Spiethoff, Walther (1884-1953) a.k.a.W. Spiethoff, 112
   Ek sing van die Wind, 112

Temmingh Jr., Roelof Willem (1946-2012), 146
   Winternag, 146

Temmingh Sr., Roelof Willem (1913-2001), 124
   "Choral Paraphrase: Siembaba" (Koorparafrase:
   Siembaba) from the poem *'n Nuwe Liedjie op
   'n ou Deuntjie* (**Siembaba**), 124

van den Berg, Sarel Francois (b. 1954) published
   under Sarel Francois Van den Berg and
   Francois Van den Berg, 95
   Ek hou van blou, 95 "Two Songs for Soprano"
   (*Twee liedere vir sopraan, no. 2*), 95

van der Mark née de Jongh, Huigrina (Maria)
   (1912-n.d.) published under Maria van der
   Mark, 120, 122, 130, 133, 189, 199, 221
   "Six Songs on Words by Leipoldt" (*Ses Liedere
   op Woorde van Leipoldt*), 133
   1. *Tuinroos tussen die Tulpe*, 133
   5. *Kom dans met my!*, 120

   Die Tuinman, 199
   Klossies, jul bewe en bibber (For Dina), 120
   Kriekie, jy wat op die Solder sanik, 122
   Rooidag, 189, "Eight Songs on Words by N. P.
   van Wyk Louw" (Agt Liedere op Woorde van
   N. P. van Wyk Louw, no. 4), 189

Soos 'n borrelende Vink sy Hart verlos
   (Dedicated to Anna Bender), 130
Toewyding, 221

van der Watt, Niel (b. 1962), 5, 9, 89
*Die Wind dreun soos 'n Ghoera:'n Boesman
   sangsiklus*, 9
   1. *Die Son*, 9
   2. *Die Sterre*, 10
   3. *Die Maan*, 10
   4. *Die Son en die Maan*, 11
   5. *Die Melkweg*, 11
   6. *Die Wolke*, 12
   7. *Die Wind*, 13
   8. *Wieglied*, 13

   Bitterbessie Dagbreek, 89

van Dijk, Peter Louis (b. 1953), 95
   Ek hou van blou, 95

van Eck, Henk, 189
   Rooidag, 189

van Oostrum, Omius (1862-1948), 97
   'n Lied van die See, 97

van Wyk, (Arnold)us Christian Vlock
   (1916-1983) published under
   Arnold van Wyk, 5, 58, 64, 107, 138,
   144, 147
Van Liefde en Verlatenheid, 144
   1. *Die Towenares*, 144
   2. *Die Woestyn-lewerkie*, 145
   3. *Winternag*, 146
   4. *Hart-van-die-dagbreek*, 147
   5. *Diep Rivier*, 147
Vier weemoedige Liedjies, 138
   1. *Vaalvalk*, 138
   2. *Eerste Winterdag*, 139
   3. *In die stilte van my Tuin*, 58
   4. *Koud is die Wind*, 59

   Boggom en Voertsek, 107
   Met Skemering, 64

Vischer, Harold C. (1865-1928), 96
   Klaas Vakie, 96

INDEX OF COMPOSERS AND THEIR WORKS 291

Watt, Martin (b. 1970), 146
    4. *Winternag,* 146, "Five Songs on Poems by
      Eugène Marais, no. 4,", 146

Wegelin, Arthur Willem (1908-1995) published
    under Arthur Wegelin, 119, 144
    Die Towenares, 144
    Klim op, klim op met die Slingerpad!, 119

Wierts, Johannes Petrus Jodocus
    (1866-1944) published under
    J. P. J. Wierts, 31, 96, 112
    Die Ossewa, 31
    Ek sing van die Wind, 112
    Klaas Vakie, 96, "Six Afrikaans
      Songs" (*Ses Afrikaanse Liedere,
      no. 2*), 96

INDEX OF COMPOSERS AND SONGS BY VOICE CATEGORY

For the benefit of digital users, indexed terms that span two pages (e.g., 52–53) may, on occasion, appear on only one of those pages.

High Voice

du Plessis, Hubert (1922-2011), 5, 22, 25, 59, 60, 61, 62, 63, 64, 65, 104, 105, 106, 107, 146
Vier Slampamperliedjies, Op. 23 (Dedicated to Mimi Coertse) - high voice, preferably lyric-coloratura soprano, 104
  1. *Krulkop-klonkie*, 104
  2. *Sekretarisvoël*, 105
  3. *Op my ou Ramkietjie*, 106
  4. *Boggom en Vortsek*, 107

  Doer bo teen die Rant, "Ten Boerneef Songs for Tenor, Op. 38, no. 1" (Dedicated to Helmut Holzapfel) - high voice, preferably tenor, 25
  "Die Berggans" from the poem *Die Berggansveer*, "Ten Boerneef Songs for Tenor, Op. 38, no. 3" (Dedicated to Helmut Holzapfel) - high voice, preferably tenor, 22

Ellis, Arthur (b. 1931), 39, 177, 195, 196, 200, 203, 224
  Die Aandblom - high voice, preferably soprano, 39
  Die Pêrel se Klokkies - high voice, preferably soprano, 195
Faul, Lourens Abram (b. 1931) published under Lourens Faul, 27, 106, 113, 128, 131, 135, 190
"Two Loitering Ditties" (*Twee Slampamperliedjies*) (Dedicated to Cato Brink) - high voice, preferably soprano/tenor, 106, 135
  1. *Op my ou Ramkietjie*, 106
  2. *Wys my die Plek*, 135

  Van Kirstenbosch tot in Namakwaland (Dedicated to Jeanette Bezuidenhout-Harris) – high voice, preferably soprano, 27

Gertsman, Blanche (1910-1973), 29, 138, 237–39
  Die Branders - high voice, preferably soprano, may be sung by medium-high voices with a secure top; also arranged for voice and orchestra, 29

Vaalvalk - high voice, preferably soprano, may be sung by medium-high voices with a secure top; also arranged for voice and orchestra, 138

Grové, Stephans (1922-2014), 34, 85
Vyf Liedere op Tekste van Ingrid Jonker, Sangsiklus - high voice, preferably soprano with some flexibility and a secure middle voice, may be sung by medium-high voices with flexibility and a secure top, 85
  1. *Lied van die Lappop*, 85
  2. *Windlietjie*, 86
  3. *Puberteit*, 87
  4. *Ek het gedink*, 87
  5. *Ontnugtering*, 88

Harvey, Eva Noel (1900-1976), 5, 104, 113, 120, 126, 128, 131, 147, 219
  Fluit, Windswael, sing en fluit - high voice, preferably soprano, 113

Hofmeyr, Hendrik (b. 1957), 5, 86, 89, 90, 146, 147, 178
Vier Gebede by Jaargetye in die Boland - high voice, exists in multiple keys, 178
  1. *Vroegherfs*, 178
  2. *Uit hierdie ligte Herfs*, 179
  3. *Winter*, 180
  4. *Eerste Sneeu*, 181

"Two Poems by Eugène Marais" (*Twee Gedigte van Eugène Marais*) - high voice, may be performed by medium-high voices with a secure top, 146, 147
  1. *Winternag* – also arranged for SATB chorus, 146
  2. *Diep Rivier*, 147

  Die Kind (wat doodgeskiet is deur soldate by Nyanga) - high voice, exists in multiple keys, 90

Lamprecht, Con (n.d.), 133, 229
  Was ek 'n Sanger - high voice, 229

Lemmer, Petrus Johannes (1896-1989) published
    under P. J. Lemmer, 3–5, 95, 98, 100, 143, 159,
    160, 161, 164, 172, 217
  Die Karoovlakte - high voice, preferably
    soprano, may be sung by medium-high voices
    with a secure top, 159

le Roux Marais, Stephanus (1896-1979) published
    under S. le Roux Marais, 5, 30, 34, 57, 66, 67,
    69, 77, 81, 93, 94, 96, 97, 98, 126, 132, 134, 146,
    152, 153, 154, 155, 157, 168, 169, 170, 171, 172,
    173, 175, 189, 194, 196, 203, 211, 213, 214, 219,
    232, 240, 241
  Amors Konfetti, "Four Afrikaans Song
    Snippets" (*Vier Afrikaanse Sangstukkies,
    no. 4*) - high voice, 30
  Gee my, "To the Bushveld and Two Other
    Songs" (*Bosveldtoe en Twee ander Liedere,
    no. 2*) medium low/medium/medium
    high/high voice, 169
  Heimwee – medium-high/high voices with a
    secure middle, 170
  "Heimwee na die See" from the poem *My siel is siek
    van Heimwee* - high voice, may also be sung by
    medium-high voices with a secure top, 172
  Lentelied - high voice, preferably lyric-coloratura
    soprano, has a cadenza, 171

Nel, Charles (1890-1983), 3–5, 34, 106, 132, 146
  'n Treurlied - high voice, may be sung by
    medium-high voices with a secure top, 132
  Winternag - high voice, may be sung by
    medium-high voices with a secure top, 146

Nepgen, Rosa Sophia Cornelia (1909-2001)
    published under Mrs. W.E.G. Louw and Rosa
    Nepgen, 5, 15, 22, 25, 34, 58, 95, 106, 107, 118,
    130, 131, 132, 133, 146, 147, 182, 183, 194, 196,
    199, 203, 219, 221, 222
  Die Liefde in my – high voice, may be sung by
    medium-high voices, 183

Pescod, John Kilburn (1898-1985) published
    under John Pescod, 5, 31, 122, 126, 142, 219
  Oktobermaand - high voice, preferably coloratura/
    lyric-coloratura soprano, has two optional
    cadenzas, may be sung by medium-high voices

if the second cadenza is excluded (Available in
    anthologies *So sing ook die Hart* in F major; *FAK
    Kunsliedbundel* in G major), 126

Richfield, Sydney (1882-1967), 5, 109, 142, 146,
    194, 215
  Die Roosknoppie - high voice, preferably
    soprano, may be sung by medium-high voices
    with a secure top, 142

van den Berg, Sarel Francois (b. 1954) published
    under Sarel Francois Van den Berg and
    Francois Van den Berg, 95
  Ek hou van blou, "Two Songs for Soprano"
    (*Twee liedere vir sopraan, no. 2*) - high voice,
    preferably soprano, 95

van der Mark née de Jongh, Huigrina (Maria)
    (1912-n.d.) published under Maria van der
    Mark, 120, 122, 130, 133, 189, 199, 221
  Soos 'n borrelende Vink sy Hart verlos
    (Dedicated to Anna Bender) - high voice,
    preferably coloratura soprano, 130

Wegelin, Arthur Willem (1908-1995) published
    under Arthur Wegelin, 119, 144
  Die Towenares - high voice, preferably
    soprano, 144

Wierts, Johannes Petrus Jodocus (1866-1944)
    published under J. P. J. Wierts, 31, 96, 112
  Klaas Vakie, "Six Afrikaans Songs" (*Ses
    Afrikaanse Liedere, no. 2*) - high voice, 96

Medium-High/High Voice

Beyers, Doris (n.d.), 30, 70, 130, 131, 141, 194, 196, 211
  "Cupid's Confetti and Five Other Songs" (*Amors
    Konfetti en Vyf ander Liedere*) - medium-high/
    high voice, preferably soprano, 30, 70, 141
    1. *Amors Konfetti*, 30
    2. *Aandblik*, 141
    3. *Sneeu op die Berge*, 70

Bon Sr., Gerrit (1901-1983), 134, 148, 153, 196, 215,
    217, 229
  "Lied van Mali, die Slaaf" from the poem *Van die
    Lotosland waar die Lelies groei* (*Lied van Mali,
    die Slaaf*) - medium-high/high voice, 134

INDEX OF COMPOSERS AND SONGS BY VOICE CATEGORY   295

de Villiers, Dirk Izak Cattogio (Dirkie) (1920-1993)
   published under Dirkie de Villiers, 35, 96,
   146, 148, 183, 184
   Grense - medium-high/high voice, preferably
      soprano/tenor, 184

de Villiers, Pieter Johannes (1924-2015) published
   under P. J. de Villiers or Pieter de Villiers, 5, 21,
   37, 95, 115, 119, 130, 132, 162, 214, 235, 242, 243
   Sewe Boerneef-liedjies/Sewe lawwe Liedjies
      (Dedicated to (Elizabeth) Betsy de la Porte) –
      medium-high/high voice, preferably soprano
      with a secure and warm middle, 21
      1. *Blaas op die Pampoenstingel,* 21
      2. *Klein Piedeplooi,* 22
      3. *Die Berggansveer,* 22
      4. *Waarom is die Duiwel vir die Slypsteen bang,* 23
      5. *Aandblom is 'n Witblom,* 24
      6. *My Koekiesveerhen jou Verkereveer,* 24
      7. *Doer bo teen die Rant,* 25

   Ek hou van blou (Dedicated to Joyce Barker) -
      medium-high/high voice, preferably
      dramatic soprano, 95
   See-Sonnet (Dedicated to Cecilia Wessels) -
      medium-high/high voice, preferably
      dramatic soprano, 235

du Plessis, Hubert (1922-2011), 5, 22, 25, 59, 60, 61,
   62, 63, 64, 65, 104, 105, 106, 107, 146
   Winternag, "Three Nocturnes, for dramatic
      Soprano, Op. 36, no. 3" – medium-high/high
      voice, 146

du Plessis, Mornay André (1909-1941), 71
   Liefdeswee (Dedicated to Madame Cecilia
      Wessels) - medium-high/high voice,
      preferably dramatic soprano, 71

Endler, Johann Franz (Hans) (1871-1947)
   published under Hans Endler, 76, 129
   Sing weer vir my - medium-high/high voice;
      also arranged as a duet for high and low
      voice, preferably soprano and alto, 129

Fagan, Gideon (1904-1980), 3–5, 75, 111, 135, 208,
   211, 216
   "Loitering Ditties" (*Slampamperliedjies*) -
      medium-high/high voice with secure middle
      and low registers, 111, 135

      1. *Wys my die Plek* - also arranged for voice and
         orchestra, 135
      2. *Eis van die Vonk wat spartel* - also may be
         sung by medium-low/medium voices, 111

   Klein Sonneskyn - medium high/high
      voice, 208

Fagan, Johannes Jacobus (1898-1920) published
   under Johannes J. Fagan, 3–5, 32, 76
   Die soekende Moeder - medium-high/high
      voice, 32

Faul, Lourens Abram (b. 1931) published under
   Lourens Faul, 27, 106, 113, 128, 131, 135, 190
   "Two Loitering Dities" (*Twee Slampamperliedjies*)
      (Dedicated to Cato Brink) - high voice,
      preferably soprano/tenor, may be sung by
      medium-high voices with a secure top,
      106, 135
      1. *Op my ou Ramkietjie*, 106
      2. *Wys my die Plek*, 135

   "Fluit, Windswael" from the poem *Fluit, Windswael,
      sing en fluit* - medium-high/high voice, 113

Gertsman, Blanche (1910-1973), 29, 138, 237–39
   Sangsiklus vir Sopraan en Klavier - medium-
      high/high voice, preferably soprano; also
      arranged for voice and orchestra, 237
      1. *Ek ken jou skaars*, 237
      2. *Ek ken jou nou*, 238
      3. *Waarom?*, 238

Harvey, Eva Noel (1900-1976), 5, 104, 113, 120,
   126, 128, 131, 147, 219
   Salut d'Amou,r "Three New Songs" (*Drie nuwe
      Liedere, no. 1*) - medium-high/high voice,
      preferably soprano, 104, 219
   Krulkop-klonkie, "Three New Songs" (*Drie
      nuwe Liedere, no. 2*) - medium-high/high
      voice, preferably soprano, 104, 219

   Kom dans met my! - medium-high voice, 120
   Oktobermaand - medium-high/high
      voice, 126
   Sing, Vinkie, sing! - medium-high/high
      voice, 128
   Toeral, loeral, la - medium-high/high
      voice, 131

Hofmeyr, Hendrik (b. 1957), 5, 86, 89, 90, 146, 147, 178
Vier Gebede by Jaargetye in die Boland – medium-high/high voice, exists in multiple keys, 178
1. *Vroegherfs*, 178
2. *Uit hierdie ligte Herfs*, 179
3. *Winter*, 180
4. *Eerste Sneeu*, 181

Windliedjie, "Words in the Wind" (*Woorde in die Wind, Op. 216, no. 1*) - preferably for lyric or lyric-coloratura sopranos with secure middle and low registers, exists in two keys, may also be sung successfully by lyric or lyric-coloratura sopranos or mezzo-sopranos with flexibility and a secure top, 86
Die Kind (wat doodgeskiet is deur soldate by Nyanga), "Words in the Wind" (*Woorde in die Wind, Op. 216, no. 4*) – medium-high/high voice, exists in multiple keys, 86, 90
Bitterbessie Dagbreek, 89

Hylton-Edwards, Stewart (1924-1987), 25, 147
Krymekaar - medium-high/high voice, preferably soprano with secure middle and low registers, 25
Diep Rivier - Die Lied van Juanita Perreira (Dedicated to Saline Koch) - medium-high/ high voice, preferably soprano, 147

Klatzow, Peter James Leonard (1945-2021) published under Peter Klatzow, 5, 42, 178
Vroegherfs (*Vier Gebede by Jaargetye in die Boland, no. 1*) - medium/high voice, preferably soprano; also arranged for soprano and orchestra; and arranged for baritone and string quartet, 178

Lamprecht, Chris (b. 1927), 5, 101–3
Aan die Noordweste - medium-high/high voice, preferably soprano; also arranged for SATB chorus, 101
1. *Die ou Kameeldoringboom*, 101
2. *Die Grootrivier se Voël* (alternate notes exist to accommodate medium-low/medium voices), 102
3. *Reën op die Veld*, 102
4. *Namakwaland se Blommetjies*, 103
5. *Loeriesfontein*, 103

Lamprecht, Con (n.d.), 133, 229
Tuinroos tussen die Tulpe (Dedicated to Betsy de la Porte) - medium-high voice, may be sung by medium voices with a secure top, 133

Lamprechts-Vos, Anna Catharina (1876-1932) published under Anna Lambrechts and Anna Lambrechts-Vos, 67, 120, 170
Kom dans met my!, "Great South Africa" (*Groot Suid-Afrika*) Songs in Five Volumes: Vol. V, Op. 45 nos. 21 and 22, two settings of the same poem exist - medium-high voice, may be sung by medium voices with a secure top, 120

Lemmer, Petrus Johannes (1896-1989) published under P. J. Lemmer, 3–5, 95, 98, 100, 143, 159, 160, 161, 164, 172, 217
"Golden Sheaf" (*Goue Gerf*) - medium-high voice, may be sung by medium voice, 100, 143, 164
Aan Stella, "Golden Sheaf" (*Goue Gerf, no. 1*) - medium-high voice, may be sung by medium voices 164
Jeug van my volk, "Golden Sheaf" (*Goue Gerf, no. 20*) - medium-high voice, may be sung by medium voices, 143
Sproetenooi, "Golden Sheaf" (*Goue Gerf, no. 34*) - medium-high voice, may be sung by medium voices, 100

Kokkewiet, medium-high/high voice, preferably soprano, 160
My Siel is siek van Heimwee (Dedicated to Pat de Wet) - medium-high voice; also arranged for soprano descant, SATB, violin obbligato and piano, exists in multiple keys, 172
Prinses van Verre - medium-high/high voice, preferably tenor; also arranged for two-part and three-part treble chorus, 217

le Roux Marais, Stephanus (1896-1979) published under S. le Roux Marais, 5, 30, 34, 57, 66, 67, 69, 77, 81, 93, 94, 96, 97, 98, 126, 132, 134, 146, 152, 153, 154, 155, 157, 168, 169, 170, 171, 172, 173, 175, 189, 194, 196, 203, 211, 213, 214, 219, 232, 240, 241
Dis al, "The Rose and Other Afrikaans Songs" (*Die Roos en ander Afrikaanse Liedere, no. 2*) (Dedicated to Mrs. Dr. B. de Preez) - medium-high/high voice, 34, 93, 196, 213
As saans, "The Rose and Other Afrikaans Songs" (*Die Roos en ander Afrikaanse Liedere*,

no. 3) (Dedicated to Mrs. Dr. B. de Preez) - medium-high/high voice, 34, 93, 196, 213

Met 'n Mandjie Rose, "The Rose and Other Afrikaans Songs" (*Die Roos en ander Afrikaanse Liedere, no. 5*) (Dedicated to Mrs. Dr. B. de Preez) - medium-high/high voice, 34, 93, 196, 213

"New Songs" (*Nuwe Liedere*)–medium-high/high voice, 66, 67, 69, 94, 126, 154, 155, 189, 194, 203, 241

   1. *Oktobermaand*, 126
   2. *Die Donker Stroom*, 194
   3. *Duisend-en-een*, 203
   4. *Die Balling se Boodskap*, 155
   5. *Rus en Stilte*, 69
   6. *'n Gebed*, 67
   7. *Daar's 'n Tyd*, 154
   8. *As ek moet sterwe, liefste*, 241
   9. *Dit is laat in die Nag*, 94
   10. *Rooidag*, 189
   11. *As my Hart nou wil sing*, 66

"Six Art Songs" (*Ses Kunsliedere*) - medium-high/high voice, 57, 98, 132, 153, 211, 219

   1. *Moeder*, 98
   2. *Bosveldhuisie*, 57
   3. *Salut d'Amour*, 219
   4. *Lied van die Wonderboom*, 211
   5. *Amoreuse Liedeken*, 153
   6. *Treurlied*, 132

Geboorte van die Lente, "Five Art Songs" (*Vyf Kunsliedere, no. 2*) (Dedicated to Mrs. B. du Preez) - medium-high/high voices with a secure middle, may be sung by medium voices with a secure top, 134, 157, 203

"Mali, die Slaaf, se Lied" from the poem *Van die Lotosland waar die Lelies groei - Lied van Mali, die Slaaf,* "Five Art Songs" (*Vyf Kunsliedere, no. 3*) (Dedicated to Mrs. B. du Preez) - medium-high/high voices with a secure middle, may be sung by medium voices with a secure top, 134, 157, 203

Sluimer, Beminde, "Five Art Songs" (*Vyf Kunsliedere, no. 5*) (Dedicated to Mrs. B. du Preez) - medium-high/high voices with a secure middle, may be sung by medium voices with a secure top, 134, 157, 203

Amors Konfetti, "Four Afrikaans Song Snippets" (*Vier Afrikaanse Sangstukkies, no. 4*) - high voice, may be sung by medium-high voices with a secure top, 30

Gee my, "To the Bushveld and Two Other Songs" (*Bosveldtoe en Twee ander Liedere, no. 2*) - medium-low/medium/medium-high/ high voice, 169

Heimwee – medium-high/high voices with a secure middle, 170

"Heimwee na die See" from the poem *My siel is siek van Heimwee* - high voice, may be sung by medium-high voices, 172

Kom dans Klaradyn – medium-high voice, may be sung by medium voices, alternate low notes exist, 232

Sluimerlied - medium-high voice, may be sung by medium voices, 240

Winternag - medium-high/high voice, 146

Löwenherz, Ernst (1874-1958) published under Ernst Lowenhertz, 34, 117, 120, 128, 214, 229

Sing, Vinkie, sing! - medium-high/high voice, 128

Matthews, Hayden Thomas (1894-1958) published under Johannes Joubert, 5, 34, 78, 79, 83, 84, 112, 150, 217, 231, 233

O, Boereplaas - medium-high voice; also arranged for SATB chorus, 233

Prinses van Verre - medium/medium-high voice, preferably mezzo-soprano, 217

Staan, Poppie, staan! - medium/medium-high voice, 150

Ek sing van die Wind - medium-high/high voice, 112

Nepgen, Rosa Sophia Cornelia (1909-2001) published under Mrs. W.E.G. Louw and Rosa Nepgen, 5, 15, 22, 25, 34, 58, 95, 106, 107, 118, 130, 131, 132, 133, 146, 147, 182, 183, 194, 196, 199, 203, 219, 221, 222

"Three Marais Songs" (*Drie Marais Liedere*) - medium-high/high voice

   1. *Winternag*, 146
   2. *Hart-van-die-dagbreek*, 147
   3. *Diep-rivier*, 147

Die Berggansveer (*Sewe Boerneef Liedjies/ Sewe lawwe Liedjies, no. 2*) - medium-high/ medium/medium-low voice; also arranged for *a capella* mixed chorus and *a capella* male chorus - commissioned by the King's Singers, University of Cambridge, 21, 22, 25

Die Liefde in my - medium-high/high voice, 183

Nepgen, Rosa Sophia Cornelia (1909-2001)
  published under Mrs. W.E.G. Louw and
  Rosa Nepgen (*cont.*)
  Dis al - medium-high/high voice, 34
  Duisend-en-een - medium-high/high
    voice, 203
  Keur van die Beste - medium-high voice, may
    be sung by medium voices with a secure
    top, 118
  'n Treurlied - medium-high voice, may be sung
    by medium voices with a secure top, 132
  Salut d'Amour - medium-high/high voice, 219
  Soos 'n borrelende Vink sy Hart verlos -
    medium-high voice, may be sung by medium
    voices with a secure top, 130
  Toeral, loeral, la - medium-high voice, may be
    sung by medium voices with a secure top, 131
  Toewyding - medium-high voice, may be sung
    by medium voices with a secure top, 221
  Van Verlore-vlei - medium-high/high voice, 222

Pescod, John Kilburn (1898-1985) published
  under John Pescod, 5, 31, 122, 126, 142, 219
  Die Roosknoppie - medium-high voice, may be
    sung by medium voices with a secure top, 142
  Salut d'Amour - medium-high voice, 219

Richfield, Sydney (1882-1967), 5, 109, 142, 146,
  194, 215
  Die Sterretjie, "Two Evening Songs" (*Twee
    Aandliedere, no. 2*) - medium-high /medium/
    medium-low voice, 109

Roode, David Johannes (1900-1983) published
  under D. J. Roode, 126
  Oktobermaand - medium-high/high voice,
    preferably soprano, 126

van der Mark née de Jongh, Huigrina (Maria)
  (1912-n.d.) published under Maria van der
  Mark, 120, 122, 130, 133, 189, 199, 221
  Klossies, jul bewe en bibber (For Dina) -
    medium-high/high voice, 120
  Kriekie, jy wat op die Solder sanik - medium-
    high voice, may be sung by medium voices
    with a secure top, 122

van Wyk, (Arnold)us Christian Vlock (1916-1983)
  published under Arnold van Wyk, 5, 58, 64,
  107, 138, 144, 147
  Met Skemering - medium-high voice, 64

Watt, Martin (b. 1970), 146
  Winternag, "Five Songs on Poems by Eugène
    Marais, no. 4" - medium-high voice,
    preferably soprano/tenor, 146

Wegelin, Arthur Willem (1908-1995) published
  under Arthur Wegelin, 119, 144
  Klim op, klim op met die Slingerpad! - medium-
    high/high voice, preferably soprano, 119

Medium / Medium-High Voice

Aerts, Peter (1912-1996), 95, 106, 124
  'n Nuwe Liedjie op 'n ou Deuntjie (Siembamba)
    (Dedicated to Miss. Helena Strauss) -
    medium/medium-high voice, 124
  Op my ou Ramkietjie (Dedicated to Anna
    Neethling-Pohl) - medium/medium-high
    voice, 106

Brown, Leonard (n.d.), 112
  Ek sing van die Wind - medium/medium-high
    voice, 112

de Villiers, Dirk Izak Cattogio (Dirkie) (1920-
  1993) published under Dirkie de Villiers, 35,
  96, 146, 148, 183, 184
  Waar die Nag in ademlose Stilte - *'n Kerslied*
    (Dedicated to Mrs. Jo Ross) - medium voice,
    may be sung by medium-low voices, 35

Ellis, Arthur (b. 1931), 39, 177, 195, 196, 200,
  203, 224
  Slaapliedjie (Dedicated to L. de W.) - medium/
    medium-high voice, 177

Fagan, Gideon (1904-1980), 3–5, 75, 111, 135, 208,
  211, 216
  Die Duifie - preferably mezzo-soprano, 75
  Omdat die Dood - medium/medium-high
    voice, 216

Faul, Lourens Abram (b. 1931) published under
  Lourens Faul, 27, 106, 113, 128, 131, 135, 190
Noag, se Ark (Dedicated to Eva Noel Harvey) -
    medium/medium-high voice, 190
    1. *Die Olifant*, 190
    2. *Die Renoster*, 191
    3. *Die Dromedaris*, 191
    4. *Die Seekoei*, 192

INDEX OF COMPOSERS AND SONGS BY VOICE CATEGORY

5. *Die Kameelperd*, 193
6. *Ensovoorts*, 193

Hartman, Anton Carlisle (1918-1982) a.k.a. Anton
Hartman, 185
Kom Vannag in my Drome (Dedicated to Jossie) -
medium/medium-high voice, 185

Idelson, Jeremiah (Jerry) (1893-n.d.) published
under Jerry Idelson, 150
Staan, Poppie, staan! - medium voice, may be
sung by medium-high voices with secure low
notes, 150

Klatzow, Peter James Leonard (1945-2021)
published under Peter Klatzow, 5, 42, 178
Vroegherfs (*Vier Gebede by Jaargetye in
die Boland, no. 1*) - medium/high voice,
preferably soprano; also arranged for
baritone and string quartet; also arranged for
soprano and orchestra 178

Lamprechts-Vos, Anna Catharina (1876-1932)
published under Anna Lambrechts and
Anna Lambrechts-Vos, 67, 120, 170
Kom dans met my!, "Great South Africa" (*Groot
Suid-Afrika*) Songs in Five Volumes: Vol. V,
Op. 45 nos. 21 and 22, two settings of the same
poem exist - medium/medium-high voice, 120

Lamprecht, Con (n.d.), 133, 229
Tuinroos tussen die Tulpe (Dedicated to Betsy de
la Porte) - medium/medium-high voice, 133

le Roux Marais, Stephanus (1896-1979) published
under S. le Roux Marais, 5, 30, 34, 57, 66, 67,
69, 77, 81, 93, 94, 96, 97, 98, 126, 132, 134, 146,
152, 153, 154, 155, 157, 168, 169, 170, 171, 172,
173, 175, 189, 194, 196, 203, 211, 213, 214, 219,
232, 240, 241
Geboorte van die Lente, "Five Art Songs" (*Vyf
Kunsliedere, no. 2*) (Dedicated to Mrs. B.
du Preez) - medium-high/high voices with
a secure middle, may be sung by medium
voices with a secure top, 134, 157, 203
"Mali, die Slaaf, se Lied" from the poem *Van
die Lotosland waar die Lelies groei - Lied
van Mali, die Slaaf*, "Five Art Songs" (*Vyf
Kunsliedere, no. 3*) (Dedicated to Mrs. B.
du Preez) - medium-high/high voices with

a secure middle, may be sung by medium
voices with a secure top, 134, 157, 203
Sluimer, Beminde, "Five Art Songs" (*Vyf
Kunsliedere, no. 5*) (Dedicated to Mrs. B.
du Preez) - medium-high/high voices with
a secure middle, may be sung by medium
voices with a secure top, 134, 157, 203

Sluimerlied - medium/medium-high voice, 240

Lemmer, Petrus Johannes (1896-1989) published
under P. J. Lemmer, 3–5, 95, 98, 100, 143, 159,
160, 161, 164, 172, 217
"Golden Sheaf" (*Goue Gerf*) – medium voice, may
be sung by medium-high voice, 100, 143, 164
Aan Stella, "Golden Sheaf" (*Goue Gerf, no. 1*) -
medium-high voice, may be sung by medium
voices 164
Jeug van my volk, "Golden Sheaf" (*Goue Gerf,
no. 20*) - medium-high voice, may be sung by
medium voices, 143
Sproetenooi, "Golden Sheaf" (*Goue Gerf, no. 34*) -
medium-high voice, may be sung by medium
voices, 100

Loots, Joyce Mary Ann Dougall née (1907-n.d.)
published under Joyce Loots, 108, 169
Gee my, "Three Afrikaans Songs" (*Drie
Afrikaanse Liedere, no. 1*) - medium/medium-
high voice, 108, 169
Die See is wild, "Three Afrikaans Songs" (*Drie
Afrikaanse Liedere, no. 3*) - medium/medium-
high voice, 108, 169

Löwenherz, Ernst (1874-1958) published under
Ernst Lowenhertz, 34, 117, 120, 128, 214, 229
Kom dans met my! - medium/medium-high
voice, 120

Matthews, Hayden Thomas (1894-1958) published
under Johannes Joubert, 5, 34, 78, 79, 83, 84,
112, 150, 217, 231, 233
Ek hou van die Môre - medium/medium-high
voice, 231
Kom Huistoe, Liefste! - medium/medium-high
voice, 79
Prinses van Verre - medium/medium-high
voice, preferably mezzo-soprano, 217
Staan, Poppie, staan! - medium/medium-high
voice, 150

300 INDEX OF COMPOSERS AND SONGS BY VOICE CATEGORY

Nepgen, Rosa Sophia Cornelia (1909-2001)
published under Mrs. W.E.G. Louw and Rosa
Nepgen, 5, 15, 22, 25, 34, 58, 95, 106, 107, 118,
130, 131, 132, 133, 146, 147, 182, 183, 194, 196,
199, 203, 219, 221, 222
Keur van die Beste - medium/medium-high
voice, 118
'n Treurlied - medium/medium-high voice, 132
Soos 'n borrelende Vink sy Hart verlos -
medium/medium-high voice, 130
Toeral, loeral, la - medium/medium-high voice, 131
Toewyding - medium/medium-high voice, 221

Pescod, John Kilburn (1898-1985) published
under John Pescod, 5, 31, 122, 126, 142, 219
Die Roosknoppie - medium/medium-high
voice, 142
Salut d'Amour - medium-high voice, 219

van der Mark née de Jongh, Huigrina (Maria)
(1912-n.d.) published under Maria van der
Mark, 120, 122, 130, 133, 189, 199, 221
Kriekie, jy wat op die Solder sanik - medium/
medium-high voice, 122

van der Watt, Niel (b. 1962), 5, 9, 89
*Die Wind dreun soos 'n Ghoera:'n Boesman
sangsiklus* - medium voice, 9
1. *Die Son*, 9
2. *Die Sterre*, 10
3. *Die Maan*, 10
4. *Die Son en die Maan*, 11
5. *Die Melkweg*, 11
6. *Die Wolke*, 12
7. *Die Wind*, 13
8. *Wieglied*, 13

van Wyk, (Arnold)us Christian Vlock (1916-1983)
published under Arnold van Wyk, 5, 58, 64,
107, 138, 144, 147
Van Liefde en Verlatenheid - medium/medium-
high voice, 144
1. *Die Towenares*, 144
2. *Die Woestyn-lewerkie*, 145
3. *Winternag*, 146
4. *Hart-van-die-dagbreek*, 147
5. *Diep Rivier*, 147
Vier weemoedige Liedjies - medium/medium-
high voice, 138
1. *Vaalvalk*, 138
2. *Eerste Winterdag*, 139

3. *In die stilte van my Tuin*, 58
4. *Koud is die Wind*, 59

Medium Voice

Bosman, Gysbert Hugo (1882-1967) a.k.a. Vere
Bosman di Ravelli, published under Bosman
di Ravelli, 3–5, 33, 146, 165
"Three Songs" (*Drie Liederen*) - medium voice,
33, 146, 165
1. *Die Howenier*, 165
2. *Winternag*, 146
3. *Die Veldwindjie* (Dedicated to Lady Rose-
Innes), 33

Brent-Wessels, Judith (1910-n.d.), 73, 104, 112,
146, 147
Krulkop-klonkie (Dedicated to Christine de
Plessis) - medium voice, 104

Cohen, Peter Lawrence (1937-n.d.), 138
Vaalvalk, "Three Serious Songs" (*Drie ernstige
Liedere*) Song Cycle for Baritone and Piano,
Op. 14, no. 2, 138

de Villiers, Pieter Johannes (1924-2015) published
under P. J. de Villiers or Pieter de Villiers, 5,
21, 37, 95, 115, 119, 130, 132, 162, 214, 235,
242, 243
"Four Songs of Doubt and Faith" (*Vier Liedere van
Twyfel en Geloof*) - medium voice, preferably
baritone, 37, 162, 242, 243
1. *Sonsverduistering*, 162
2. *Ek skuil by die Here*, 242
3. *Balansstaat*, 37
4. *U het my Skuld vergewe*, 243

de Villiers, Septimus Catorzia (1895-1929)
published under S. C. de Villiers, 31, 109
Die Ossewa - medium voice, preferably mezzo-
soprano, 31

du Plessis, Hubert (1922-2011), 5, 22, 25, 59, 60, 61,
62, 63, 64, 65, 104, 105, 106, 107, 146
Vreemde Liefde, Op. 7 - medium voice, 59
1. *As ek my vreemde Liefde bloot moes lê*, 59
2. *Ek het my aan jou oorgegee*, 60
3. *Die Hart van die Daeraad*, 61
4. *Swakkeling met Vrou en Kind*, 62
5. *Ek weet dat in die kalme Samesyn*, 63
6. *Nee, liewer die Dood*, 64

INDEX OF COMPOSERS AND SONGS BY VOICE CATEGORY 301

7. *Met Skemering*, 64
8. *Vreemde Liefde*, 65

du Plessis, Mornay André (1909-1941), 71
Liefdeswee (Dedicated to Madame Cecilia
Wessels) - medium/medium-high/high
voice, preferably dramatic soprano, 71

Hirschland, Heinz (1901-1960), 5, 67, 69, 128
'n Gebed, "Fourteen Afrikaans Songs" (*Veertien
Afrikaanse Liedere, no. 7*) – medium voice, 67
Rus en Stilte, "Fourteen Afrikaans Songs" (*Veertien
Afrikaanse Liedere, no. 9*) – medium voice, 69

Hofmeyr, Hendrik (b. 1957), 5, 86, 89, 90, 146,
147, 178
Vier Gebede by Jaargetye in die Boland –
medium/low/high voice, arranged for voice
and piano; also arranged for medium voice
and orchestra, 178
1. *Vroegherfs*, 178
2. *Uit hierdie ligte Herfs*, 179
3. *Winter*, 180
4. *Eerste Sneeu*, 181

Idelson, Jeremiah (Jerry) (1893-n.d.) published
under Jerry Idelson, 150
Staan, Poppie, staan! – medium/medium-high
voice, 150

Kennedy, Spruhan Keith (1901-n.d) published
under S. Kennedy, 139
Eerste Winterdag, "Five Songs for Baritone"
(*Vyf Liedere vir Bariton, no. 1*) - also arranged
for baritone and orchestra, 139

Lemmer, Petrus Johannes (1896-1989) published
under P. J. Lemmer, 3–5, 95, 98, 100, 143, 159,
160, 161, 164, 172, 217
"Golden Sheaf" (*Goue Gerf*) - medium voice, 100,
143, 164
Aan Stella, "Golden Sheaf" (*Goue Gerf, no. 1*) -
medium-high voice, may be sung by medium
voices 164
Jeug van my volk, "Golden Sheaf" (*Goue Gerf,
no. 20*) - medium-high voice, may be sung by
medium voices, 143
Sproetenooi, "Golden Sheaf" (*Goue Gerf,
no. 34*) - medium-high voice, may be sung by
medium voices, 100

le Roux Marais, Stephanus (1896-1979) published
under S. le Roux Marais, 5, 30, 34, 57, 66, 67,
69, 77, 81, 93, 94, 96, 97, 98, 126, 132, 134, 146,
152, 153, 154, 155, 157, 168, 169, 170, 171, 172,
173, 175, 189, 194, 196, 203, 211, 213, 214, 219,
232, 240, 241
Geboorte van die Lente, "Five Art Songs" (*Vyf
Kunsliedere, no. 2*) (Dedicated to Mrs. B.
du Preez) - medium-high/high voices with
a secure middle, may be sung by medium
voices with a secure top, 134, 157, 203
"Mali, die Slaaf, se Lied" from the poem *Van
die Lotosland waar die Lelies groei - Lied
van Mali, die Slaaf*, "Five Art Songs" (*Vyf
Kunsliedere, no. 3*) (Dedicated to Mrs. B.
du Preez) - medium-high/high voices with
a secure middle, may be sung by medium
voices with a secure top, 134, 157, 203
Sluimer, Beminde, "Five Art Songs" (*Vyf
Kunsliedere, no. 5*) (Dedicated to Mrs. B.
du Preez) - medium-high/high voices with
a secure middle, may be sung by medium
voices with a secure top, 134, 157, 203

Slaapdeuntjie, "Fifteen Afrikaans Lullabies"
(*Vyftien Afrikaanse Slaapdeuntjies, no. 2*)
from the poem "Doe-doe, my baba"-
arranged for medium voice; also arranged for
unison chorus, 96, 168, 173, 214
Klaas Vakie, "Fifteen Afrikaans Lullabies"
(*Vyftien Afrikaanse Slaapdeuntjies, no. 14*) -
medium voice; also arranged for unison
chorus, 96

Die Ster uit die Ooste, "South African
Carols" - medium voice, 152
Gee my, "To the Bushveld and Two Other
Songs" (*Bosveldtoe en Twee ander Liedere,
no. 2*) - medium/ medium-low/medium-
high/high voice, 169
Heideweelde, "Golden Sheaf" (*Goue Gerf*) -
medium voice, 77
Herfsaand - medium voice, 175
Kom dans Klaradyn – medium/medium-
high/high voice, alternate notes are
present, 232
Langs stille Waters, "Two Sacred Songs"
(*Twee gewyde Sangstukke, no. 1*) - medium
voice, 81
'n Lied van die See - medium voice, 97

Matthews, Hayden Thomas (1894-1958) published under Johannes Joubert, 5, 34, 78, 79, 83, 84, 112, 150, 217, 231, 233
Huistoe - medium voice, 78
Tot die Oggend gloor - medium voice, 83
Vermoeide Pelgrim - medium voice, 84

Nepgen, Rosa Sophia Cornelia (1909-2001) published under Mrs. W.E.G. Louw and Rosa Nepgen, 5, 15, 22, 25, 34, 58, 95, 106, 107, 118, 130, 131, 132, 133, 146, 147, 182, 183, 194, 196, 199, 203, 219, 221, 222
Op die Flottina: Nege Liedere vir Middelstem en Klavier - medium voice, 15
 1. *Hoe stil kan dit word as Sedoos gaan lê*, 15
 2. *Jong Pappelierbas glad en koel*, 16
 3. *Ou Damon loop sy Lammertroppie om*, 16
 4. *Dis omdraaislaan soos handomkeer*, 17
 5. *Ou Poegenpol op Pale*, 18
 6. *Wies getik en wiesit kwyt*, 18
 7. *Êrens in die Kro het ek 'n Skerm*, 19
 8. *Agter Akkerskraalsekop* - also arranged for *a capella* mixed chorus, 20
 9. *Van Rietvleisemoorsand tot by Soetbatsfontein*, 20

Die Berggansveer (*Sewe Boerneef Liedjies/ Sewe lawwe Liedjies, no. 1*) - medium/ medium-low/medium-high voice; also arranged for *a capella* mixed chorus and *a capella* male chorus - commissioned by the King's Singers, University of Cambridge, 21, 22, 25
Boggom en Voertsek - medium voice, 107
Die Donker Stroom - medium voice, 194
Die Tuinman - medium voice, 199
In die silte van my tuin - medium voice, 58
Op my ou Ramkietjie - medium voice, 106
"Wees jy, my Lied, 'n goue Kelk" from the poem *Die Rose van Herinnering* - medium voice, 196

Richfield, Sydney (1882-1967), 5, 109, 142, 146, 194, 215
Die Sterretjie, "Two Evening Songs" (*Twee Aandliedere, no. 2*) - medium/medium-low/ medium-high voice, 109

van der Watt, Niel (b. 1962), 5, 9, 89
Bitterbessie Dagbreek - medium voice, 89

Medium-Low / Medium Voice

Bouws, Jan (1902-1978), 34, 93, 106, 110
Op my ou Ramkietjie, "Eleven Afrikaans Songs" (*Elf Afrikaanse Liedere, no. 1*), 106
Dis al, "Eleven Afrikaans Songs" (*Elf Afrikaanse Liedere, no. 2*), 34

Dingaan, die Zoeloe - medium-low/medium voice, 110

Brent-Wessels, Judith (1910-n.d.), 73, 104, 112, 146, 147
Droomtyd (Dedicated to Wynand) - medium-low/medium voice, 73
Ek sing van die Wind - medium-low/medium voice, 112

Clement, Daniel (1902-1980), 34, 112, 114, 117, 124, 126, 146, 200, 206, 209, 220, 228, 233
Land, Volk en Taal, "South Africa Onwards" (*Suid-Afrika vorentoe, no. 1*) - medium-low/ medium voice, 34, 112, 114, 117, 124, 126, 146, 200, 206, 209, 220, 233
O, Boereplaas, "South Africa Onwards" (*Suid-Afrika vorentoe, no. 2*) - medium-low/medium voice, 34, 112, 114, 117, 124, 126, 146, 200, 206, 209, 220, 233
Japie, "South Africa Onwards" (*Suid-Afrika vorentoe, no. 6*) - medium-low/medium voice, 34, 112, 114, 117, 124, 126, 146, 200, 206, 209, 220, 233
"Siembaba" from the poem *'n Nuwe Liedjie op 'n ou Deuntjie* (*Siembamba,*) "South Africa Onwards" (*Suid-Afrika vorentoe, no. 7*) - medium-low/medium voice, 34, 112, 114, 117, 124, 126, 146, 200, 206, 209, 220, 233
Dis al, "South Africa Onwards" (*Suid-Afrika vorentoe, no. 13*) - medium-low/medium voice, 34, 112, 114, 117, 124, 126, 146, 200, 206, 209, 220, 233
"Loitering Ditty" (*Slampamperliedjie*) from the poem *Gee vir my 'n Trouring,* "South Africa Onwards" (*Suid-Afrika vorentoe, no. 14*) - medium-low/medium voice, 34, 112, 114, 117, 124, 126, 146, 200, 206, 209, 220, 233
"Loitering Ditty" (*Slampamperliedjie*) from the poem *Ek sing van die Wind,* "South Africa Onwards" (*Suid-Afrika vorentoe, no. 15*) - medium-low/medium voice, 34, 112, 114, 117, 124, 126, 146, 200, 206, 209, 220, 233

INDEX OF COMPOSERS AND SONGS BY VOICE CATEGORY

"Die Wapad" from the poem *Die Wapad is my Woning,* "South Africa Onwards" (*Suid-Afrika vorentoe, no. 19*) - medium-low/medium voice, 34, 112, 114, 117, 124, 126, 146, 200, 206, 209, 220, 233

Winternag, "South Africa Onwards" (*Suid-Afrika vorentoe, no. 23*) - medium-low/medium voice, 34, 112, 114, 117, 124, 126, 146, 200, 206, 209, 220, 233

Oktobermaand, "South Africa Onwards" (*Suid-Afrika vorentoe, no. 29*) - medium-low/medium voice, 34, 112, 114, 117, 124, 126, 146, 200, 206, 209, 220, 233

Sannie, "South Africa Onwards" (*Suid-Afrika vorentoe, no. 33*) - medium-low/medium voice, 34, 112, 114, 117, 124, 126, 146, 200, 206, 220, 233

Kalwerliefde, "South Africa Onwards" (*Suid-Afrika vorentoe, no. 34*) - medium-low/medium voice, 34, 112, 114, 117, 124, 126, 146, 200, 206, 209, 220, 233

Vraag en Antwoord - medium-low/medium voice, 228

Cohen, Peter Lawrence (1937-n.d.), 138
Vaalvalk, "Three Serious Songs" (*Drie ernstige Liedere*) Song Cycle for Baritone and Piano, Op. 14, no. 2, 138

de Jong, Marinus (1891-1984), 124, 139, 146, 188
Paniese Angs, "Six South African Songs" (*Zes Zuidafrikaanse Liederen, no. 1*) - medium-low/medium voice, 124, 139, 146, 188

Winternag, "Six South African Songs" (*Zes Zuidafrikaanse Liederen, no. 2*) - medium-low/medium voice, 124, 139, 146, 188

Voor die Venster, "Six South African Songs" (*Zes Zuidafrikaanse Liederen, no. 3*) - medium-low/medium voice, 124, 139, 146, 188

'n Nuwe Liedjie op 'n ou Deuntjie (Siembamba), "Six South African Songs" (*Zes Zuidafrikaanse Liederen, no. 5*) - medium-low/medium voice, 124, 139, 146, 188

de Villiers, Dirk Izak Cattogio (Dirkie) (1920-1993) published under Dirkie de Villiers, 35, 96, 146, 148, 183, 184
Waar die Nag in ademlose Stilte - 'n Kerslied (Dedicated to Mrs. Jo Ross) - medium-low/medium voice, 35

de Vos, Herre (1877-1948), 117
Japie (Dedicated to Antoinette van Dijk) - medium-low/medium voice, 117

Ellis, Arthur (b. 1931), 39, 177, 195, 196, 200, 203, 224
Die Wapad is my Woning - medium-low/medium voice, 200
Duisend-en-een - medium-low/medium voice, 203

Fagan, Gideon (1904-1980), 3–5, 75, 111, 135, 208, 211, 216
Eis van die Vonk wat spartel, "Loitering Ditties" (*Slampamperliedjies, no. 2*) - medium-low/medium voice, 111
Lied van die Wonderboom - medium-low/medium voice, 211

Hullebroeck, Emiel (1878-1965), 109
Die Sterretjie, "Six Songs" (*Zes Liederen, no. 3*) (Dedicated to Miss. M. van Westrheene) - medium-low/medium voice, 109

Lea-Morgan, John (n.d.), 215
Nimmer of Nou – medium-low/medium voice, 215

Louw, Albertus Johannes (Albie) Louw (1926-2017) published under Albie Louw, 42–56
O togga! 'n Gogga - Lawwe Versies vir stout Kinders, Sangsiklus - medium-low/medium voice, 42
1. *Pluk die Snare, blaas die Fluit*, 42
2. *Kom saam met my na Toorberg*, 42
3. *Warrelwind*, 43
4. *Rolbos is 'n Tolbos*, 43
5. *Neem 'n stukkie Son*, 44
6. *As jy by my kom kuier*, 44
7. *Jy bly klein*, 45
8. *Hotnotsgot en Spinnekop*, 45
9. *Gomverdorie, Poetoepap*, 46
10. *Petronella, Kokkerot*, 47
11. *Ouma het 'n Weglêhoender*, 47
12. *Die Haaie in die See*, 48
13. *O gits en gaats*, 48
14. *Ek kom hier aan*, 49
15. *Satanskinders laat my gril*, 49
16. *Twaalf Sardientjies in 'n Blik*, 50
17. *Die Kat se Kies*, 51
18. *Tortelduifie*, 51

Louw, Albertus Johannes (Albie) Louw (1926-2017)
published under Albie Louw (*cont.*)
  19. *Bo in die Solder*, 52
  20. *Kry jy Papelellekoors*, 52
  21. *Piet Fourie*, 53
  22. *Wat is die verskil?*, 53
  23. *Konsternasie*, 54
  24. *Susanna Viljee*, 55

Pescod, John Kilburn (1898-1985) published
  under John Pescod, 5, 31, 122, 126, 142, 219
Die Ossewa - medium-low/medium voice, 31
Lenteliedjie - medium-low/medium voice, 122

van der Mark née de Jongh, Huigrina (Maria)
  (1912-n.d.) published under Maria van der
  Mark, 120, 122, 130, 133, 189, 199, 221
Tuinroos tussen die Tulpe, "Six Songs on
  Words by Leipoldt" (*Ses Liedere op Woorde
  van Leipoldt, no. 1*) - medium-low/medium
  voice, 133
Kom dans met my!, "Six Songs on Words
  by Leipoldt" (*Ses Liedere op Woorde van
  Leipoldt, no. 5*) - medium-low/medium voice,
  120, 133

Toewyding - medium-low/medium voice, 221

van Wyk, (Arnold)us Christian Vlock (1916-1983)
  published under Arnold van Wyk, 5, 58, 64,
  107, 138, 144, 147
Boggom en Voertsek - medium-low/medium
  voice; also arranged for unison chorus with
  small ensemble), 107

Wierts, Johannes Petrus Jodocus (1866-1944)
  published under J. P. J. Wierts, 31, 96, 112
Ek sing van die Wind - medium-low/medium
  voice, 112

Medium-Low Voice

de Villiers, Pieter Johannes (1924-2015) published
  under P. J. de Villiers or Pieter de Villiers, 5, 21,
  37, 95, 115, 119, 130, 132, 162, 214, 235, 242, 243
In 'n Gat daar onder die Sukkeldoring -
  medium-low voice, 115

du Plessis, Hubert (1922-2011), 5, 22, 25, 59, 60, 61,
  62, 63, 64, 65, 104, 105, 106, 107, 146

Vreemde Liefde, Op. 7 – medium/medium-low
  voices, 59
  1. *As ek my vreemde Liefde bloot moes lê*, 59
  2. *Ek het my aan jou oorgegee*, 60
  3. *Die Hart van die Daeraad*, 61
  4. *Swakkeling met Vrou en Kind*, 62
  5. *Ek weet dat in die kalme Samesyn*, 63
  6. *Nee, liewer die Dood*, 64
  7. *Met Skemering*, 64
  8. *Vreemde Liefde*, 65

Hartman, Anton Carlisle (1918-1982) a.k.a. Anton
  Hartman, 185
Kom Vannag in my Drome (Dedicated to
  Jossie) - medium-low/medium-high voice,
  preferably baritone, 185

Lemmer, Petrus Johannes (1896-1989) published
  under P. J. Lemmer, 3–5, 95, 98, 100, 143, 159,
  160, 161, 164, 172, 217
Rots by die See - medium-low voice, preferably
  baritone, 161

le Roux Marais, Stephanus (1896-1979) published
  under S. le Roux Marais, 5, 30, 34, 57, 66, 67,
  69, 77, 81, 93, 94, 96, 97, 98, 126, 132, 134, 146,
  152, 153, 154, 155, 157, 168, 169, 170, 171, 172,
  173, 175, 189, 194, 196, 203, 211, 213, 214, 219,
  232, 240, 241
Gee my, "To the Bushveld and Two Other
  Songs" (*Bosveldtoe en Twee ander Liedere,
  no. 2*) - medium-low/medium/medium-
  high/high voice, 169

Maske, Hans Herbert (1927-1976), 135
Wys my die Plek - medium-low voice, preferably
  baritone, 135

Matthews, Hayden Thomas (1894-1958) published
  under Johannes Joubert, 5, 34, 78, 79, 83, 84,
  112, 150, 217, 231, 233
Dis al - medium-low voice, 34

Nepgen, Rosa Sophia Cornelia (1909-2001)
  published under Mrs. W.E.G. Louw and Rosa
  Nepgen, 5, 15, 22, 25, 34, 58, 95, 106, 107, 118,
  130, 131, 132, 133, 146, 147, 182, 183, 194, 196,
  199, 203, 219, 221, 222
*Die Berggansveer, (Sewe Boerneef Liedjies/
  Sewe lawwe Liedjies, no. 1*) - medium-low/

medium/medium-high voice, has many alternate notes; also arranged for *a capella* mixed chorus and *a capella* male chorus - commissioned by the King's Singers, University of Cambridge, 22

Richfield, Sydney (1882-1967), 5, 109, 142, 146, 194, 215
Die Sterretjie, "Two Evening Songs" (*Twee Aandliedere, no. 2*) - medium-low/medium/medium-high voice, has many alternate notes; 109

Low/Medium-Low Voice

Barton, Horace Percival (1872-1951) published under Horace Barton, 5, 93, 96, 198
Die swarte Osse – low/medium-low voice, 198

Bon Sr., Gerrit (1901-1983), 134, 148, 153, 196, 215, 217, 229
Die Rose van Herinnering - low/medium-low voice, 196

de Villiers, Marthinus Lourens (1885-1977) published under M. L. de Villiers, 2–5, 29, 69, 219
'n Doringkroon, "Six Afrikaans Art Songs" *Ses Afrikaanse Kunsliedere, no. 3* - low/medium-low voice (Dedicated to Prof. Hans Endler), 29
Die Branders, "Six Afrikaans Art Songs" *Ses Afrikaanse Kunsliedere, no. 4* - low/medium-low voice, 29
Rus en Stilte, "Six Afrikaans Art Songs" *Ses Afrikaanse Kunsliedere, no. 5* - low/medium-low voice, 29, 69

de Villiers, Pieter Johannes (1924-2015) published under P. J. de Villiers or Pieter de Villiers, 5, 21, 37, 95, 115, 119, 130, 132, 162, 214, 235, 242, 243
Middagslapie - low/medium-low voice, 214

Engela, Dawid Sofius (1931-1967) published under Dawid S. Engela, 60, 68, 187
Ek het my aan jou oorgegee, "Songs of a Futile Love" (*Liedere van 'n vergeefse Liefde, no. 1*) - low/medium-low voice, 60
Ons het mekaar gegroet, "Songs of a Futile Love" (*Liedere van 'n vergeefse Liefde, no. 4*) - low/medium-low voice, 68

Hofmeyr, Hendrik (b. 1957), 5, 86, 89, 90, 146, 147, 178
Vier Gebede by Jaargetye in die Boland - low voice, exists in multiple keys, 178
  1. *Vroegherfs*, 178
  2. *Uit hierdie ligte Herfs*, 179
  3. *Winter*, 180
  4. *Eerste Sneeu*, 181

Lapin, Lily (1893-n.d.), 194
Die Donker Stroom, 194, "Two Songs for Bass Voice, no. 2,", 194

Nepgen, Rosa Sophia Cornelia (1909-2001) published under Mrs. W.E.G. Louw and Rosa Nepgen, 5, 15, 22, 25, 34, 58, 95, 106, 107, 118, 130, 131, 132, 133, 146, 147, 182, 183, 194, 196, 199, 203, 219, 221, 222
Die Beiteltjie - low voice, 182

Richfield, Sydney (1882-1967), 5, 109, 142, 146, 194, 215
Die Donker Stroom - low/medium-low voice, 194

Roode, Maarten Christiaan (1907-1967) published under M. C. Roode, 93, 194, 212
As saans - low/medium-low voice, 93

van der Mark née de Jongh, Huigrina (Maria) (1912-n.d.) published under Maria van der Mark, 120, 122, 130, 133, 189, 199, 221
Die Tuinman - low/medium-low voice, 199

Ensemble

Bell, William Henry (1873-1946) published under W. H. Bell, 146
Winternag, "Seven Afrikaans Songs for Solo Voice and Orchestra, no. 1," 146

de Villiers, Pieter Johannes (1924-2015) published under P. J. de Villiers or Pieter de Villiers, 5, 21, 37, 95, 115, 119, 130, 132, 162, 214, 235, 242, 243
"Three Leipold Songs" (*Drie Leipoldt-liedjies*) – arranged for *a capella* four-part mixed chorus, 119, 130, 132
  1. *Soos 'n borrelende Vink sy Hart verlos*, 130
  2. *'n Treurlied*, 132
  3. *Klim op, klim op met die Slingerpad!*, 119

306 INDEX OF COMPOSERS AND SONGS BY VOICE CATEGORY

Dopper, Cornelius (1870-1939), 96
Klaas Vakie - canon arranged for two voices
and four violins accompaniment, and as a
choral piece for children, 96

Ellis, Arthur (b. 1931), 39, 177, 195, 196, 200,
203, 224
Voor in die Wapad brand 'n Lig - arranged for
SATB chorus, 224

Endler, Johann Franz (Hans) (1871-1947)
published under Hans Endler, 76, 129
Sing weer vir my - arranged as a duet for high
and low voice, preferably soprano and
alto, 129

Faul, Lourens Abram (b. 1931) published under
Lourens Faul, 27, 106, 113, 128, 131, 135, 190
Sing, Vinkie, sing! - arranged as a three-part
round, 128
Toeral, loeral, la - arranged as a three-part
round, 131

Fagan, Gideon (1904-1980), 3–5, 75, 111, 135, 208,
211, 216
Wys my die Plek, "Loitering Ditties"
(*Slampamperliedjies, no. 1*) - arranged for
voice and orchestra; also arranged for
medium-high/high voice, 111, 135

Gertsman, Blanche (1910-1973), 29, 138, 237–39
Sangsiklus vir Sopraan en Klavier - arranged
for voice and orchestra; also arranged
for medium-high/high voice, preferably
soprano, 237
1. *Ek ken jou skaars*, 237
2. *Ek ken jou nou*, 238
3. *Waarom?*, 238
Die Branders - arranged for voice and
orchestra, also arranged for high voice and
piano, preferably soprano, 29
Vaalvalk - arranged for voice and orchestra,
also arranged for high voice and piano,
preferably soprano, 138

Hofmeyr, Hendrik (b. 1957), 5, 86, 89, 90, 146,
147, 178
Winternag (*Twee Gedigte van Eugène Marais,
Op. 91, no. 1.*), arranged for SATB/mixed
chorus, 146

Windliedjie, Op. 215, arranged for children or
treble chorus SSAA, 86

Joubert, Aletta Margaretha Lettie (1894-1966)
published under Mrs. H. C. de Kock, Lettie
Joubert and L. Joubert, 214, 229
Middagslapie - arranged for three-part treble
chorus, 214

Kennedy, Spruhan Keith (1901-n.d) published
under S. Kennedy, 139
Eerste Winterdag, "Five Songs for Baritone"
(*Vyf Liedere vir Bariton, no. 1*) - arranged for
baritone and orchestra; also arranged for
baritone and piano, 139

Kerrebijn, Marius (1882-1930), 96
Klaas Vakie (Dedicated to the composer's
parents) - arranged for children's voices and
piano, 96

Klatzow, Peter James Leonard (1945-2021)
published under Peter Klatzow, 5, 42, 178
Kom saam met my na Toorberg - arranged for
children's chorus and orchestra, 42
Vroegherfs (*Vier Gebede by Jaargetye in die
Boland, no. 1*) - arranged for soprano and
orchestra; arranged for baritone and string
quartet; also arranged for medium/high
voice and piano, preferably soprano; 178

Kromhout, Jan (1886-1969), 98, 204
Grondmannetjie (*My Skaduwee*) - arranged for
children's chorus, 204

Lamprecht, Chris (b. 1927), 5, 101–3
Aan die Noordweste – cycle arranged for SATB
chorus; also arranged for medium-high/high
voice and piano, preferably soprano, 101
1. *Die ou Kameeldoringboom*, 101
2. *Die Grootrivier se Voël*, 102
3. *Reën op die Veld*, 102
4. *Namakwaland se Blommetjies*, 103
5. *Loeriesfontein*, 103

Lemmer, Petrus Johannes (1896-1989) published
under P. J. Lemmer, 3–5, 95, 98, 100, 143, 159,
160, 161, 164, 172, 217
Ek hou van blou - arranged for SATB
chorus, 95

My Siel is siek van Heimwee (Dedicated to Pat de Wet) - arranged for soprano descant, SATB, violin obbligato and piano; also arranged for medium-high voice and piano, 172

Prinses van Verre - arranged for two-part and three-part treble chorus, also arranged for medium-high/high voice and piano, preferably tenor, 217

le Roux Marais, Stephanus (1896-1979) published under S. le Roux Marais, 5, 30, 34, 57, 66, 67, 69, 77, 81, 93, 94, 96, 97, 98, 126, 132, 134, 146, 152, 153, 154, 155, 157, 168, 169, 170, 171, 172, 173, 175, 189, 194, 196, 203, 211, 213, 214, 219, 232, 240, 241

Slaapdeuntjie from the poem *"Doe-doe, my baba,"* "Fifteen Afrikaans Lullabies" (*Vyftien Afrikaanse Slaapdeuntjies, no. 2*) - arranged for unison chorus; also arranged for medium voice; and (*Vyftien Afrikaanse Slaapdeuntjies, no. 3*) - arranged for four-part chorus, 96, 168, 173, 214((

Buite suis die sagte Windjie, "Fifteen Afrikaans Lullabies" (*Vyftien Afrikaanse Slaapdeuntjies, no. 4*) - arranged for unison chorus; and (*Vyftien Afrikaanse Slaapdeuntjies, no. 6*) - arranged for four-part chorus, 96, 168, 173, 214((

Middagslapie, "Fifteen Afrikaans Lullabies" (*Vyftien Afrikaanse Slaapdeuntjies, no. 13*) arranged for two-part chorus, also arranged for medium-high/high voice, 96, 168, 173, 214

Klaas Vakie, "Fifteen Afrikaans Lullabies" (*Vyftien Afrikaanse Slaapdeuntjies, no. 14*) - medium voice; also arranged for unison chorus, 96, 168, 173, 214

Langs stille Waters, "Hymn, Second Choral Album" (*Lofgesang, Second Choral Album, no. 5*) - arranged for chorus, 81

Matthews, Hayden Thomas (1894-1958) published under Johannes Joubert, 5, 34, 78, 79, 83, 84, 112, 150, 217, 231, 233

O, Boereplaas - arranged for SATB chorus; also arranged for medium-high voice, 233

Nepgen, Rosa Sophia Cornelia (1909-2001) published under Mrs. W.E.G. Louw and Rosa Nepgen, 5, 15, 22, 25, 34, 58, 95, 106, 107, 118, 130, 131, 132, 133, 146, 147, 182, 183, 194, 196, 199, 203, 219, 221, 222

Agter Akkerskraalsekop, Op die Flottina: Nege Liedere vir Middelstem en Klavier, no. 8 - arranged for *a capella* mixed chorus; also arranged for medium voice and piano, 15, 20

Die Berggansveer (*Sewe Boerneef Liedjies/ Sewe lawwe Liedjies, no. 1*) - arranged for *a capella* mixed chorus and *a capella* male chorus - commissioned by the King's Singers, University of Cambridge; also arranged for medium-low/medium/medium-high voice and piano, 21, 22, 25

Doer bo teen die Rant (*Sewe Boerneef Liedjies/ Sewe lawwe Liedjies, no. 7*) - arranged for *a capella* mixed chorus; also arranged for voice and piano, 21, 22, 25

Roode, Maarten Christiaan (1907-1967) published under M. C. Roode, 93, 194, 212

Man en Vrou - arranged for two-part treble chorus (S1, S2), 212

Temmingh Jr., Roelof Willem (1946-2012), 146

Winternag - arranged for treble chorus with piano, 146

Temmingh Sr., Roelof Willem (1913-2001), 124

"Choral Paraphrase: Siembaba" (*Koorparafrase: Siembaba*) from the poem *'n Nuwe Liedjie op 'n ou Deuntjie: Siembaba* - arranged for chorus, 124

van Wyk, (Arnold)us Christian Vlock (1916-1983) published under Arnold van Wyk, 5, 58, 64, 107, 138, 144, 147

Boggom en Voertsek - arranged for unison chorus with small ensemble; also arranged for medium-low/medium voice and piano, 107

Wierts, Johannes Petrus Jodocus (1866-1944) published under J. P. J. Wierts, 31, 96, 112

Die Ossewa - arranged for unison chorus and piano, 31

Without Recommendations

Aerts, Peter (1912-1996), 95, 106, 124

Ek hou van Blou (Dedicated to Elza De Clerq), 95

INDEX OF COMPOSERS AND SONGS BY VOICE CATEGORY

Amyot, E. (n.d.), 112
    Ek sing van die Wind, 112

Ashworth, Alexander Hargreaves (Alex) (1895-1959)
    published under A. H. Ashworth, 31, 34, 93, 96,
    97, 146
    Adoratio, 93
    Die Ossewa, 31
    Klaas Vakie, 96
    Dis al, 34
    'n Lied van die See, 97
    Winternag, 146

Barnes, L. (n.d.), 146
    Winternag, 146

Barton, Horace Percival (1872-1951) published
    under Horace Barton, 5, 93, 96, 198
    As saans, 93
    Klaas Vakie, 96

Beyers, Doris (n.d.), 30, 70, 130, 131, 141, 194,
    196, 211
    Die Donker Stroom, "Three Songs" (*Drie
    Liedere*), 194
    Die Rose van Herinnering, 196
    Lied van die Wonderboom, 211
    Soos 'n borrelende Vink sy Hart verlos, "Three
    Songs" (*Drie Liedere*), 130
    Toeral, loeral, la, "Three Songs" (*Drie Liedere*), 131

Bon Sr., Gerrit (1901-1983), 134, 148, 153, 196, 215,
    217, 229
    Amoreuse Liedeken, 153
    Die Roos, 196
    Prinses van Verre, 217
    Skoppensboer, 148
    Was ek 'n Sanger, 229

Bouws, Jan (1902-1978), 34, 93, 106, 110
    As saans, 93

Brent-Wessels, Judith (1910-n.d.), 73, 104, 112, 146, 147
    Diep Rivier, 147
    Winternag, 146

Brinne, Dirk Jan (1909-1974), 96
    Klaas Vakie, 96

de Villiers, Dirk Izak Cattogio (Dirkie) (1920-1993)
    published under Dirkie de Villiers, 35, 96,
    146, 148, 183, 184
    Klaas Vakie, 96

    Skoppensboer, 148
    "Winterbome" from the poem *Die Liefde in
    my*, 183
    Winternag, 146

de Villiers, Gisela (b. 1955), 95
    Ek hou van blou, 95

de Villiers, Marthinus Lourens (1885-1977) published
    under M. L. de Villiers, 2–5, 29, 69, 219
    Salut d'Amour, 219

de Villiers, Septimus Catorzia (1895-1929)
    published under S. C. de Villiers, 31, 109
    Die Sterretjie, 109

Eagar, Fannie Edith Starke (1920-n.d.), 195
    Die Pêrel se Klokkies, 195

Elbrecht, Berend (1883-1954), 93, 96
    As saans, 93
    Klaas Vakie, 96

Ellis, Arthur (b. 1931), 39, 177, 195, 196, 200, 203, 224
    Die Roos, 196

Endler, Johann Franz (Hans) (1871-1947)
    published under Hans Endler, 76, 129
    Soos die Windjie wat suis, 76

Engela, Dawid Sofius (1931-1967) published under
    Dawid S. Engela, 60, 68, 187
    Opdrag, "Two Songs" (*Twee Liedere, no.1*), 187

Grové, Stephans (1922-2014), 34, 85
    Dis al (*Drie Liedere, no. 1*), 34

Haasdijk, P. W. (n.d.) a.k.a. P. W. Haasdyk, 93
    As saans, 93

Hallis, Adolf (1896-1987), 147
    Diep Rivier, 147

Harvey, Eva Noel (1900-1976), 5, 104, 113, 120,
    126, 128, 131, 147, 219
    "O Diep Rivier" from the poem *Diep Rivier*, 147
Hirschland, Heinz (1901-1960), 5, 67, 69, 128
    Sing, Vinkie, sing!, 128

Joubert, Aletta Margaretha Lettie (1894-1966)
    published under Mrs. H. C. de Kock, Lettie
    Joubert and L. Joubert, 214, 229
    Was ek 'n Sanger, 229

Joubert, Hennie (1926-1986), 95
Ek hou van blou, 95

Kratz, Anton E. (1917-1980), 95
Ek hou van blou, 95

Kromhout, Jan (1886-1969), 98, 204
Moeder, 98

Lamprechts-Vos, Anna Catharina (1876-1932) published under Anna Lambrechts and Anna Lambrechts-Vos, 67, 120, 170
'n Gebed, "Great South Africa" (*Groot Suid-Afrika*) Songs in Five Volumes: Vol. I, Op. 41 no. 3, 67
Heimwee, "Songs of Anna Lambrechts-Vos" (*Liederen van Anna Lambrechts-Vos, Op. 51, no. 3*), 170

Lemmer, Petrus Johannes (1896-1989) published under P. J. Lemmer, 3–5, 95, 98, 100, 143, 159, 160, 161, 164, 172, 217
Moeder, 98

Lewald, Otto Albrecht (1905-1988) published under Otto A. Lewald and O. A. Lewald, 34, 98
Dis al, "Six Songs to Words by Jan F. E. Cilliers, no. 3," 34
Moeder, 98

Löwenherz, Ernst (1874-1958) published under Ernst Lowenhertz, 34, 117, 120, 128, 214, 229
Dis al, Op. 42, 34
Japie, 117
Middagslapie, Op. 27, no. 2, 214
Was ek 'n Sanger, 229

Manca, Joseph Salvatore (1908-1985) published under J. S. Manca, 203, 221
Geboorte van die Lente, 203
Toewyding, 221

Mengelberg, Rudolf (Kurt) (1892-1959) published under Rudolf Mengelberg, 34
Dis al, "Nine South African Songs, no. 6," 34

Nel, Charles (1890-1983), 3–5, 34, 106, 132, 146
Dis al "Three Afrikaans Songs" (*Drie Afrikaanse Liedere, no. 2*) - Various settings of

this poem by the same composer exist from 1914, etc, 34
Op my ou Ramkietjie, 106

Nepgen, Rosa Sophia Cornelia (1909-2001) published under Mrs. W.E.G. Louw and Rosa Nepgen, 5, 15, 22, 25, 34, 58, 95, 106, 107, 118, 130, 131, 132, 133, 146, 147, 182, 183, 194, 196, 199, 203, 219, 221, 222
Ek hou van blou, 95
Tuinroos tussen die Tulpe, 133

Oxtoby, Charles Francis (1912-1978), 76
Soos die Windjie wat sui,s Op. 36, no. 2, 76

Rentzke, Suzanne (b. 1982), 95
Ek hou van blou, 95

Richfield, Sydney (1882-1967), 5, 109, 142, 146, 194, 215
Nimmer of nou, 215
Winternag, 146

Roode, Maarten Christiaan (1907-1967) published under M. C. Roode, 93, 194, 212
Die Donker Stroom, 194

Söhnge, Wilhelm Ernst Heinrich (1909-n.d.), 109
"Vonkel, Sterretjie, vonkel" from the poem *Die Sterretjie*, 109

Spiethoff, Walther (1884-1953) a.k.a. W. Spiethoff, 112
Ek sing van die Wind, 112

van der Mark née de Jongh, Huigrina (Maria) (1912-n.d.) published under Maria van der Mark, 120, 122, 130, 133, 189, 199, 221
Rooidag, "Eight Songs on Words by N. P. van Wyk Louw" (*Agt Liedere op Woorde van N. P. van Wyk Louw, no. 4*), 189

van Dijk, Peter Louis (b. 1953), 95
Ek hou van blou, 95

van Oostrum, Omius (1862-1948), 97
'n Lied van die See, 97

Vischer, Harold C. (1865-1928), 96
Klaas Vakie, 96

GENERAL INDEX

For the benefit of digital users, indexed terms that span two pages (e.g., 52–53) may, on occasion, appear on only one of those pages.

Aerts, Peter, 95, 106, 124
Afrikaans Kunslied/Art Song, xxi, 2, 3–6, Appendix C, Appendix D
Afrikaans Language, xxi, 1–5
Afrikaans Pronunciation Guide xxi, S2, Afrikaans Lyric Diction Summary Appendix G
Amyot, E., 112
Anonymous, 240
Ashworth, A. H, 31, 34, 93, 96, 97, 146
Aucamp, Hennie, 7–14

Barnes, L., 146
Barton, Horace, 5, 93, 96, 198
Bell, W. H., 146
Beyers, Doris, 30, 70, 130, 131, 141, 194, 196, 211
Biblical Texts, 241–45
Bon Sr., Gerrit, 134, 148, 153, 196, 215, 217, 229
Bosman, Jan Gysbert Hugo aka Bosman di Ravelli, 3–5, 33, 146, 165
Bouws, Jan, 34, 93, 106, 110
Brent-Wessels, Judith, 73, 104, 112, 146, 147
Brinne, Dirk Jan, 96
Brown, Leonard, 112

Celliers, Jan Francois Elias, aka Jan F. E. Celliers, 2–3, 29–34
Clement, Daniel, 34, 112, 114, 117, 124, 126, 146, 200, 206, 209, 220, 228, 233
Cohen, Peter Lawrence, 138

de Jong, Marinus, 124, 139, 146, 188
de Villiers, Dirkie, 35, 96, 146, 148, 183, 184
de Villiers, Doll, 35–36
de Villiers, Gisela, 95
de Villiers, Izak Louis, aka I. L. de Villiers, 37–38
de Villiers, M. L., 2–5, 29, 69, 219
de Villiers, Pieter Johannes, published under P. J. de Villiers or Pieter de Villiers, 5, 21, 37, 95, 115, 119, 130, 132, 162, 214, 235, 242, 243
de Villiers, S. C., 31, 109
de Villiers Pienaar, Pierre, aka P. de Villiers Pienaar, 39–41

de Vos, Herre, 117
de Vos, Philip 42–56
Dopper, Cornelius, 96
Dreyer, Ben, 57
du Plessis, Hubert, 5, 22, 25, 59, 104, 146
du Plessis, Izak David, aka I. D. du Plessis, 58–70
du Plessis, Mornay André, 71–72
du Toit, Jacob Daniël, pseudonym Totius, 2–3, 165–67

Eagar, Fannie Edith Starke, 195
Eitemal, Erlank, 73–74
Elbrecht, Berend, 93, 96
Ellis, Arthur, 39, 177, 195, 196, 200, 203, 224
Endler, Hans, 76, 129
Engela, Dawid S., 60, 68, 187
Eybers, Elizabeth, 3

Fagan, Gideon, 3–5, 75, 111, 135, 208, 211, 216
Fagan, Henry Allan, aka H. A. Fagan, 76
Fagan, Johannes J., 3–5, 32, 76
Faul, Lourens, 27, 106, 113, 128, 131, 135, 190

Gericke, Burger, aka B. Gerike, 77
Gerstman, Blanche, 29, 138, 237
Grové, Stephans, 34, 85

Haasdyk, P. W., 93
Hallis, Adolf, 147
Hartman, Anton, 185
Harvey, Eva Noel, 5, 104, 113, 120, 126, 128, 131, 147, 219
Hirschland, Heinz, 5, 67, 69, 128
Hofmeyr, Hendrik, 5, 86, 89, 90, 146, 147, 178
Hullebroeck, Emiel, 109
Hylton-Edwards, Stewart, 25, 147
Hyssen, Stephen, 3–5

Idelson, Jerry, 150

Jandrell, Theodore Walter, aka Theo W. Jandrell, 78–84
Jonker, Ingrid, 85–92

Joubert, Hennie, 95
Joubert, Johannes, aka Hayden Thomas Matthews, 5, 34, 78, 79, 83, 84, 112, 150, 217, 231, 233
Joubert, Lettie, 214, 229

Keet, Albertus Daniël, aka A. D. Keet, 93–99
Kennedy, S., 139
Kerrebijn, Marius, 96
Klatzow, Peter, 5, 42, 178
Kotzé (née Badenhorst), Bessie, 100
Kratz, Anton E., 95
Kromhout, Jan, 98, 204

Lamprecht, Chris, 5, 101–3
Lamprecht, Con, 133, 229
Lamprechts-Vos, Anna, 67, 120, 170
Langenhoven, C. J., 2–3
Lapin, Lily, 194
le Roux Marais, S., 5, 30, 34, 57, 66, 67, 69, 77, 81, 93, 94, 96, 97, 98, 126, 132, 133, 134, 146, 152, 153, 154, 155, 157, 168, 169, 170, 171, 172, 173, 175, 189, 194, 196, 203, 211, 213, 214, 219, 232, 240, 241
Lea-Morgan, John, 215
Leipoldt, Christian Frederick Louis, aka C. Louis Leipoldt, 2–3, 104–37
Lemmer, P. J., 3–5, 95, 98, 100, 143, 159, 160, 161, 164, 172, 217
Lewald, O. A., 34, 98
Loots, Joyce, 108, 169
Louw, Albie, 42
Louw, William Edward Gladstone, aka W. E. G. Louw, 3, 138–40
Löwenherz, Ernst, 34, 117, 120, 128, 214, 229

Malherbe, Daniël François, aka D. F. Malherbe, 2–3, 141–43
Manca, J. S., 203, 221
Marais, Eugène, 2–5, 144–51
Marais, Francois, 152
Maske, Hans Herbert, 135
Mengelberg, Rudolf, 34
Mostert, Dirk, 153–58

Nel, Charles, 3–5, 34, 106, 132, 146
Nepgen, Rosa, 5, 15, 22, 25, 34, 58, 95, 106, 107, 118, 130, 131, 132, 133, 146, 147, 182, 183, 194, 196, 199, 203, 219, 221, 222

Osborne, S. J. M., 159–61
Oxtoby, Charles Francis, 76

Pescod, John, 5, 31, 122, 126, 142, 219
Philander, Peter John, 162–63
Postma, Hilda, 164

Rentzke, Suzanne, 95
Richfield, Sydney, 5, 109, 142, 146, 194, 215
Roode, D. J., 126
Roode, M. C., 93, 194, 212

Sohnge, Wilhelm Ernst Heinrich, 109
Spiethoff, W., 112

Temmingh Jr., Roeloff Willem, 146
Temmingh Sr., Roeloff Willem, 124

van Bruggen, Jan Reinder Leonard, aka J. R. L. van Bruggen, 168–74
van den Berg, Francois, 95
van den Heever, Christian Maurits, aka C. M. van den Heever, 175–76
van der Mark, Maria, 120, 122, 130, 133, 189, 199, 221
van der Merwe, Izak Wilhelmus, pseudonym Boerneef, 3, 15–28
van der Watt, Niel, 5, 9, 89
van Dijk, Peter Louis, 95
van Eck, Henk, 189
van Oostrum, Omius, 97
van Vene, Steven, 177
van Wyk, Arnold, 5, 58, 64, 107, 138, 144, 147
van Wyk Louw, Nicolaas Petrus, aka N. P. van Wyk Louw, 3, 178–89
Vischer, Harold C., 96
Visser, Andries Gerhardus, aka A. G. Visser, 190–230
Visser, Cornelius Francois, aka C. F. Visser, 231–34

Wassenaar, Theo, 235–36
Watt, Martin, 146
Wegelin, Arthur, 119, 144
Weich, C. H., 237–39
Wierts, J. P. J., 31, 96, 112
Winternag, 2–5